T0373412

Rewired

Rewired

Cybersecurity Governance

Edited by

Ryan Ellis
Vivek Mohan

This edition first published 2019
© 2019 John Wiley & Sons, Inc.

Registered Office
John Wiley & Sons, Inc., 111 River Street, Hoboken, NJ 07030, USA

Editorial Office
111 River Street, Hoboken, NJ 07030, USA

For details of our global editorial offices, customer services, and more information about Wiley products visit us at www.wiley.com.

Wiley also publishes its books in a variety of electronic formats and by print-on-demand. Some content that appears in standard print versions of this book may not be available in other formats.

Library of Congress Cataloging-in-Publication data is applied for

Hardback ISBN: 9781118888216

Cover design: Wiley
Cover image: "U.S. Army Photo" of Two Women Operating ENIAC from the archives of the ARL Technical Library, Historic Computer Images is in the Public Domain.

Set in 10/12pt Warnock by SPi Global, Pondicherry, India

Printed in the United States of America

V10008955_032119

Contents

Notes on Contributors

Samantha A. Adams was a political scientist with additional background in gender studies and STS. She was Associate Professor of eHealth Governance and Regulation at the Tilburg Institute for Law, Technology, and Society (TILT), Tilburg University. She worked on medical informatics, medical sociology, qualitative research methods, and external cyberattacks on health systems.

Jason Blackstock is Associate Professor of Science and Global Affairs at University College London (UCL) and cofounder of UCL Department of Science, Technology, Engineering and Public Policy (STEaPP) which he led as Head of Department from 2013 to 2018. He has a unique background spanning quantum physics research, Silicon Valley technology development, international public policy, and higher education innovation and leadership.

Irina Brass is Lecturer in Regulation, Innovation and Public Policy and Deputy Lead of the MPA Programme in Digital Technologies and Public Policy at University College London (UCL) Department of Science, Technology, Engineering and Public Policy (STEaPP). Her research focuses on the regulation of disruptive technologies, especially digital technologies. She is working closely with policymakers and standards development communities.

Madeline Carr is Associate Professor of International Relations and Cyber Security at University College London (UCL) Department of Science, Technology, Engineering and Public Policy (STEaPP) and Director of its Digital Policy Lab. She has a strong interest in the international policy challenges posed by cybersecurity and is coinvestigator for Standards, Policy and Governance Stream of the PETRAS IoT Research Hub.

Jim Dempsey is Executive Director of the Berkeley Center for Law & Technology. From 1997 to 2014, he was at the Center for Democracy & Technology, including as Executive Director. He served as a Senate-confirmed Member of the Privacy and Civil Liberties Oversight Board from 2012 to

January 2017. He is coauthor (with David Cole) of Terrorism & the Constitution (New Press 2006) and coeditor (with Fred Cate) of Bulk Collection: Systematic Government Access to Private-Sector Data (Oxford 2017).

Karine e Silva LL.M. is PhD candidate at TILT, Tilburg University on the NWO-funded BotLeg project. Her research interest is in botnets since the launch of the EU Advanced Cyber Defense Centre (ACDC) in early 2013. Her research involves legal issues surrounding botnet mitigation and the role of public and private sectors.

Jacqueline Eggenschwiler is a doctoral researcher at the University of Oxford. Her research interests include cybersecurity governance and norm-construction. She holds degrees in International Affairs and Governance, International Management, and Human Rights from the University of St Gallen and the London School of Economics and Political Science.

Amit Elazari Bar On is a Doctoral Law Candidate at UC Berkeley School of Law and a Berkeley Center for Long-Term Cybersecurity Grantee, as well as a Lecturer at Berkeley's School of Information Master in Cybersecurity Program. She graduated Summa Cum Laude three prior degrees in law and business (B.A., LL.B., LL.M.). Her research in the field of technology law and policy has been published and featured in leading journals and conferences, as well as popular press.

Ryan Ellis is an Assistant Professor of Communication Studies at Northeastern University. His research and teaching focuses on topics related to communication law and policy, infrastructure politics, and cybersecurity. He is the author of the upcoming *Letters, Power Lines, and Other Dangerous Things: The Politics of Infrastructure Security* (MIT Press).

Miles Elsden spent his early academic career in Europe and the next 10 years providing advice to the UK government most recently as Chief Scientist in Transport. He now works as a consultant at the boundary between policy, technology, and strategy.

Trey Herr is a visiting fellow with the Hoover Institution at Stanford University working on international cybersecurity and risk. His research focuses on the role of nonstate actors in cybersecurity governance, the proliferation of malware, and the evolving character of risk in cyber insurance. He is also a senior security strategist with Microsoft where he handles cloud-computing security and supply-chain risk for the Global Security Strategy and Diplomacy team.

Jonah Force Hill is Senior Cyber Policy Advisor at the U.S. Secret Service, where he advises on a range of cybercrime policy and strategy matters. He is also a (non-resident) Cybersecurity Fellow at New America and a Term Member at the Council on Foreign Relations. He came to the Secret Service after several years at the U.S. Commerce Department, where he focused on global digital economy policy. He holds an MTS and MPP from Harvard University and a BA from UCLA.

Bert-Jaap Koops is Professor of Regulation & Technology at the Tilburg Institute for Law, Technology, and Society (TILT), Tilburg University. His main research interests are cybercrime, cyber-investigation, privacy, and data protection. He is also interested in DNA forensics, identity, digital constitutional rights, techno-regulation, and regulation of human enhancement, genetics, robotics, and neuroscience.

Andreas Kuehn is a Senior Program Associate within the EastWest Institute's Global Cooperation in Cyberspace program. As a Cybersecurity Fellow, Dr. Kuehn conducted research on cybersecurity policy, vulnerability markets and disclosure arrangements at Stanford University's Center for International Security and Cooperation and was an adjunct researcher at the RAND Corporation, where he worked on cyber risk and the cyber insurance industry.

Aaron Martin is a Postdoctoral Research Fellow at the Tilburg Law School in the Netherlands. He was previously a Vice President of Cyber Policy at JPMorgan Chase in New York (2015–2018). He is also an Oxford Martin Associate at the University of Oxford's Global Cyber Security Capacity Centre.

Vivek Mohan is an attorney in private practice based in Northern California. Vivek entered private practice from the Privacy, Data Security, and Information Law group at Sidley Austin LLP, where he counseled clients in the technology, telecommunications, healthcare, and financial services sectors. Vivek is the coeditor and author of the PLI treatise "Cybersecurity: A Practical Guide to the Law of Cyber Risk" (3d. 2018). Vivek has worked as attorney at Microsoft, at the Internet Bureau of the New York State Attorney General (under a special appointment), and at General Electric's corporate headquarters (on secondment). For five years, Vivek was a resident fellow and later a nonresident associate with the Cybersecurity Project at the Harvard Kennedy School. Vivek holds a JD from Columbia Law School and a BA from the University of California, Berkeley.

Matthew Noyes is the cyber policy & strategy director for the U.S. Secret Service and a Major in the U.S. Army assigned to the Office of Secretary of Defense for Cyber Policy. His work focuses on law enforcement efforts to counter transnational cyber crime and related policy topics. Matt holds a Mater in Public Policy from the Harvard Kennedy School and a BS in Computer Science and Applied Computational Mathematics from the University of Washington.

Emilian Papadopoulos is president of Good Harbor, a boutique consultancy advising Boards, CEOs, and government leaders on cyber security. He is an adjunct lecturer at Georgetown University and previously worked for the Government of Canada in Ottawa and Washington. He is a graduate of the University of Toronto and of Harvard University's Kennedy School, where he also serves as the elected chair of the global Alumni Board.

Valeria San Juan is an Analyst at Fundbox in San Francisco, CA. She was previously a Cyber Policy Analyst at JPMorgan Chase in New York (2017).

Elaine Sedenberg is a PhD Candidate at the UC Berkeley School of Information and Affiliate at the Harvard Berkman Klein Center. She previously served as the codirector of the Center for Technology, Society & Policy (CTSP). Her research examines information-sharing arrangements for public good uses including security, public health, and research activities.

James Shires is a Research Fellow with the Cybersecurity Project at the Belfer Center for Science and International Affairs, Harvard Kennedy School. His research focuses on cybersecurity issues in the Middle East.

Evan Sills is a Director with Good Harbor, where he advises corporate executives on governance, risk management, cybersecurity incident response, and legislative and regulatory activities. He was a Global Governance Futures 2027 Fellow and is a graduate of The George Washington University Law School and Elliott School of International Affairs.

Leonie Maria Tanczer is Lecturer in International Security and Emerging Technologies at UCL's Department of Science, Technology, Engineering and Public Policy (STEaPP). She is member of the Advisory Council of the Open Rights Group, affiliated with UCL's Academic Centre of Excellence in Cyber Security Research, and former Fellow at the Alexander von Humboldt Institute for Internet and Society in Berlin. She is interested in the intersection points of technology, security, and gender.

Michael Thornton is a PhD candidate in History and Philosophy of Science at the University of Cambridge. He uses the philosophy of public health to reframe how we think about digital networks and information. Before Cambridge, Michael was a Director of Product Management at Truaxis, a MasterCard company.

Bart van der Sloot specializes in questions revolving around privacy and Big Data. He works as a senior researcher at TILT, Tilburg University, is General Editor of the *European Data Protection Law Review*, coordinator of the Amsterdam Platform for Privacy Research, and scientific director of the Privacy and Identity Lab.

Acknowledgments

The idea for this book started when we sat at adjoining desks inside the same office at the Harvard Kennedy School; the book was finished many years later while we sit over three thousand miles apart. Along the way a number of individuals and institutions helped make this book possible. First and foremost, Venkatesh (Venky) Narayanamurti served as our academic mentor during our time at the Harvard Kennedy School's Belfer Center for Science and International Affairs. Venky provided unfailing support and encouragement to us when we were new fellows at the Belfer Center and has remained a generous supporter in the succeeding years. Simply put, without Venky this book would not exist. We owe him a significant debt. A number of other faculty members and colleagues at Harvard were instrumental in shaping our thinking about the topics covered in the pages that follow. Joe Nye warmly welcomed us into his cyber seminar series and offered us both the opportunity to hear from a number of policy and academic heavyweights and, perhaps most importantly, catch his sharp and probing questions. Jim Waldo provided an invaluable perspective – what a technologist thinks about policy – and offered enough wisdom to fill at least another book. Michael Sulmeyer encouraged this project and kindly kept us engaged with the Center as its interest in cyber policy continues to grow and thrive. Colleagues associated with the joint MIT and Harvard project, "Explorations in Cyber International Relations," including Nazli Choucri and Michael Siegel, provided important insight. Early-stage preparatory work on this volume was funded, in part, by the Office of Naval Research under award number N00014-09-1-0597. Any opinions, findings, and conclusions, or recommendations expressed in this publication are those of the author and do not necessarily reflect the views of the Office of Naval Research.

Emily Silk Marie provided expert editorial assistance in preparing the draft manuscript. At Wiley, Beryl Mesiadhas, Michael Leventhal, and Bob Esposito offered patience and care in assembling the volume.

Ryan would also like to thank his current colleagues at Northeastern University's Department of Communication Studies, the Global Resilience Institute, and the School for Public Policy and Urban Affairs. Northeastern has provided a creative and supportive intellectual environment. Previous colleagues at the Naval Postgraduate School and Stanford's Center for International Security and Affairs also helped lay the seeds for this project. Additionally, staff support at the Belfer Center and Northeastern's Communication Department was vital. Karin Vander Schaaf, Patricia McLaughlin, Sarah Donahue, and Angela Chin assisted with issues both big and small during the preparation of the book. Their efforts were instrumental in making this book a reality. Ryan thanks his family for their love and encouragement.

Vivek would like to thank Jack Goldsmith of Harvard Law School, whose encouragement and mentorship over the years provided needed focus; and spurred the curiosity and passion to explore both the practice and the learning of the law. Alan Raul and Ed McNicholas of Sidley Austin LLP, and through their introduction, Peter Lefkowitz and Jane Horvath, for teaching Vivek the law, and how to practice it; and to all of the above for their continued friendship. Of course, Vivek would like to thank his infinitely patient wife Ariana, who has provided loving support and has acted as a sounding board for many of editorial comments and perspectives contained herein.

Finally, we would like to dedicate this book to one of the contributing authors – Samantha Adams. Samantha tragically passed away during the production of this book. The chapter included here is one of her last pieces of finished work.

Introduction

Ryan Ellis[1] and Vivek Mohan[2]

[1] Communication Studies, Northeastern University, Boston, MA, USA
[2] Attorney in Private Practice, Northern California, USA

I.1 Making Sense of Cybersecurity Governance

On 23 September 1982, Representative Don Edwards, a longtime member of the United States House of Representatives, presided over a congressional hearing to consider a new type of crime – "computer-related crime." Edwards set the scene:

> As the use of computers expands in our society, the opportunity to use computers to engage in or assist in criminal activities also expands. In response to this perceived problem, a number of States has enacted legislation specifically aimed at computer fraud. The Federal Bureau of Investigation offers its agents specialized training in computer fraud. Private industry is attempting to enhance the security of its computer facilities.[1]

Edwards' statement would, with slight tweaking here and there, more or less be repeated like boilerplate for the better part of the next three-and-a-half decades. Repeatedly, various policymakers sitting in subcommittee meetings, policy forums, and other public venues would note that computers were increasingly ubiquitous and that their diffusion was, among other things, leading to new types of harm that call for new types of solutions. At times, the claimed harms were speculative or theoretical; equally often, the calls for solutions followed publicized incidents that increasingly resonated in the public consciousness.

A little over 15 years after Edwards introduced the hearing on computer-related crime, US Senator Fred Thompson introduced a similar hearing to examine the public risks presented by weak computer security. Thompson could have been reading from Edwards' prepared remarks. He noted that, "[c] omputers are changing our lives faster than any other invention in our history. Our society is becoming increasingly dependent on information technologies that which are changing at an amazing rate."[2] Thompson would go on to note that these trends create new vulnerabilities that we must now confront.

In time, the lexicon slid into the expansive and ill-defined catch-all of "cybersecurity," a term initially loathed by technical experts but embraced with such vigor within policy-circles that it appears to be here to stay. "Cybersecurity" issues are repeatedly framed as an eternally new problem – something that is just peaking over the horizon that must be confronted *now*. This framing is attractive: it captures the sense that new technologies create new problems and dilemmas; and it freights the problem with a sense of urgency – we must act now before it is too late. This frenetic energy – which has escalated to a fever pitch over the last decade and shows no sign of abating – imbues discussants with cause and reason to reject incrementalism. At times, this provides the necessary fora to be receptive to novel or transformative ideas.

But this presentation obscures as much as it illuminates. Presenting cybersecurity as a fundamentally new and unaddressed problem elides the long history of security interventions. It shoves to the side the lattice of institutions – laws, organizational practices, and formal and informal rules – that have been built over time to address the myriad challenges associated with the rise of networked computers. Some of these practices have been useful, others have been hopeless dead-ends. But, ignoring them and assuming that we are confronting a new problem and need to invent a new set of tools and approaches ignores the stubborn reality: we have been confronting these challenges in various forms for decades.

Cyberspace is not an ungoverned space outside of laws, institutions, and power. As Joe Nye, Laura DeNardis, Jack Goldsmith, Tim Wu, and others have usefully pointed out, there is a rich thicket of organizations and institutions that provide structure, shape, and limits in cyberspace.[3] There are vital and enduring analogs between the cyber and physical domains.[4] The world of digital devices and networks is dotted with points of control.[5] This insight is equally useful when it comes to examining the narrower question of cybersecurity governance. The security space is not a free-for-all. Far from it. It is a space defined by competing organizations and institutions that seek to impose some form of control in the name of security. What exactly is meant by security is always an open and contested question. In some settings it might mean the protection of devices, data, or networks; in others, security might be translated into control of forms of speech or expression that are seen as politically unpalatable; in still other arenas, security might mean protection from non-state actors, but say little about governmental efforts to subvert technical protections over personal data. Questions about cybersecurity – just like questions about security in a broader sense – are always open to multiple interpretations. Two questions always hang in the air either explicitly or implicitly: Security *of what?* And security *from whom?*

This collection looks to make sense of the governance of cybersecurity. It explores through various case studies some of the competing organizational efforts and institutions that are attempting to secure cyberspace. The book looks not to the future – to hypothetical new possibilities to confront a new set of previously unknown problems – but to the recent past and the present. It examines some of the in-place and unfolding institutional and organizational efforts to confront the challenges of cybersecurity. Rather than examining these efforts through a purely narrow normative lens – does it work? – it considers the broader implications of these efforts. It traces how different notions of cybersecurity are deployed and built into stable routines and practices, what can be termed the "bureaucratization of risk." In doing so, the chapters collected here share a set of common interest: how are fears over *cyber-insecurity* being distilled into organizational efforts and institutional frameworks? Importantly, what are the larger implications – for workers, firms, the public, and competing sets of values – of these organizational practices and frameworks? Security is, and has long been, a key axis upon which decisions about communications technologies and networks sit. Looking closely at these efforts as forms of governance – efforts to control and manage something seen as unruly – helps draw into clear relief what is at stake: Cybersecurity efforts are (and have been for quite some time) remaking the digital technologies that are the foundations of contemporary life. Examining more closely the various efforts documented in the chapters that follow offers a partial portrait at some of the ways that these efforts are unfolding and what we are gaining and losing in the process.

In the pages that follow, readers are encouraged to consider the deep engagement of various communities working to define and respond to cybersecurity issues. At the same time, readers may consider the impact and import of the siloed verticals that define many of the case studies. As the number of cybersecurity professionals continues to grow at exponential rates, the risk of failing to learn from not only our recent past, but what is happening right beside us, becomes ever more evident. That is not to say that these silos must in each case be broken down – while enterprising readers may be able to stitch together their own "Grand Unified Field Theorem" for cybersecurity policy, the editors are hopeful (and view it as perhaps far more likely) that these deep dives present useful lenses into different policy, legal, and technical approaches to various facets of the "cybersecurity problem." The case studies intentionally take different approaches in their commentary, but three shared thematic threads run through the book.

I.2   Connective Tissue: Common Themes

I.2.1   Cybersecurity is Contextual

Cybersecurity does not exist in a vacuum. It is always contextual. Cybersecurity efforts are rooted in the specifics of time and place. These efforts are molded by the preexisting outlines of political organizations and institutions, industrial ecosystems, and larger regional and international political rivalries and alliances. To understand how certain issues are framed as cybersecurity challenges and how certain approaches to these challenges are developed and deployed, it is important to ground these efforts within these larger contexts. Elaine Sedenberg and Jim Dempsey's "Cybersecurity Information Sharing Governance Structures: An Ecosystem of Diversity, Trust, and Trade-offs" (Chapter 1) offers a sober account of what happens when context is ignored. In their analysis of cybersecurity information sharing efforts and the Cybersecurity Information Sharing Act of 2015 (CISA), Sedenberg and Dempsey argue that policy lacking historical memory is doomed to fail. CISA was an ambitious attempt to kick-start new information sharing efforts. But, it ignored the institutional labyrinth and information-sharing mechanisms that already existed. Information sharing is much more than a technical problem. As the chapter notes, the failure to account for this broader context limits the efficacy of CISA.

In "Cybersecurity Governance in the GCC" (Chapter 2), James Shires offers a detailed account of cybersecurity in the six states of the Gulf Cooperation Council (GCC). Shires illustrates how national and regional politics shape cybersecurity governance. In drawing an overview of regional incidents, key government organizations and cybersecurity firms, and relevant strategies, laws, and standards, the chapter makes the case that cybersecurity is regionally specific. The contours of cybersecurity are influenced by larger circulating cultural notions and pressures, but national and regional politics plays a decisive role in shaping how cybersecurity is both understood and confronted. Shires work serves as a call for regional and national specialization. This call is ably answered by Leonie Maria Tanczer, Irina Brass, Miles Elsden, Madeline Carr, and Jason Blackstock in "The United Kingdom's Emerging Internet of Things (IoT) Policy Landscape" (Chapter 3). Tanczer and coauthors explore how the United Kingdom is confronting the security challenges of IoT, a sea change in the deployment of sensors and connected technologies that emerged quickly and largely with little regulatory guidance. They explore how UK IoT efforts are linked to and defined by a dense institutional landscape. They offer a tantalizing note: as the United Kingdom prepares to exit the European Union, it is unclear how this political realignment will upset existing cybersecurity efforts.

Understanding the relationship between context and cybersecurity is not only a matter of mapping existing political institutions. Emilian Papadopoulos and Evan Sills' "Birds of a Feather: Strategies for Collective Cybersecurity in the

Aviation Ecosystem" (Chapter 4) examines the interplay between industrial ecology and cybersecurity. Focusing on cybersecurity and aviation, they observe a complex industry that includes thousands of organizations, from global giants, such as Lufthansa and United Airlines, to smaller or more obscure players, such as regional airports, the manufacturers of In-Flight Entertainment systems, and luggage management organizations. This knot of organizations creates shared cybersecurity risks, collective risks that cannot be adequately addressed by a single firm or organization. Papadopoulos and Sills discover that the unique nature of the aviation industry is leading to new collective approaches to risk management. Their insights offer a useful reminder: cybersecurity cannot be stripped from a larger political, economic, and organization context. For both practitioners looking to develop workable policies and scholars examining cybersecurity critically, focusing on context is vital.

I.2.2 Cybersecurity is Dynamic

Cybersecurity joins together government and industry in a set of contingent relationships. The interplay between the public and private sector is not easy to pin down. At some moments, they are willing and engaged partners working hand in glove; at others, they are adversaries working at cross-purposes. The chapters that follow chart all manner of public and private configurations. Jacqueline Eggenschwiler's "An Incidents-Based Conceptualization of Cybersecurity Governance" (Chapter 5) describes various formal approaches to cybersecurity governance. In looking at three different cases – a 2016 cyber-espionage case involving RUAG, a key Swiss defense contractor; the collaborative containment activities of the Conficker Working Group (CWG); and Symantec's cybersecurity practices – Eggenschwiler fleshes out the contours of hierarchical, multi-stakeholder, and market-based modes of cybersecurity governance. The chapter concludes that there is no one-size-fits-all approach to cybersecurity governance.

Eggenschwiler's observation echoes across a number of chapters. Valeria San Juan and Aaron Martin's "Cyber Governance and the Financial Services Sector: The Role of Public–Private Partnerships" (Chapter 6) looks at the cooperation challenges within the financial services sector. Calling for public–private partnerships to tackle the thorny problems of cybersecurity is a familiar and evergreen recommendation: Who could possibly argue *against* cooperation? But, such efforts can also be something of an empty promise: a recommendation that shirks defining lines of responsibility and accountability and, in their place, leaves an ill-defined commitment to work together without thinking through the difficult mechanics of putting these into practice. Looking at the financial services sector, San Juan and Martin provide an up-close examination of three different public–private partnerships. They find both cause for optimism and caution in the multi-stakeholder model of public–private cooperation. In their telling, neither industry or government can confront the challenges of cybersecurity alone. They argue that public–private efforts stumble when attempting to address systemic risk.

The challenges of confronting long-term and systemic risk reappears in Samantha A. Adams, Karine e Silva, Bert-Jaap Koops, Bart van der Sloot's "The Regulation of Botnets: How Does Cybersecurity Governance Theory Work When Everyone is a Stakeholder?" (Chapter 7). Adams and coauthors examine the coordination challenges that emerge when a cross-national mix of public and private players join together to combat botnets. To work in practice, the type of polycentric governance efforts that Adams and coauthors document call for either a supranational or key nation to act as a coordinating mechanism. Transnational criminal justice efforts to date, however, have largely been reactive, focusing on immediate challenges while leaving long-term issues unaddressed (Tanczer and coauthors also see a similar challenge in the United Kingdom's IoT strategy in Chapter 3).

Trey Herr's investigation of the cybersecurity insurance market, "Governing Risk: The Emergence of Cyber Insurance" (Chapter 8), uncovers another configuration of public and private. Herr finds a useful interplay between the insurance industry's development of cybersecurity policies and the enforcement of standards. While the federal government has largely, though not exclusively, taken a voluntary approach to developing and implementing cybersecurity standards, insurers have the power to transform these standards into binding and enforceable rules. This model of governance skirts the often politically unpalatable prospect of direct regulation, with a model that is led by the market with significant space for input from both public and private standards bodies.

Michael Thornton's "Containing Conficker: A Public Health Approach" (Chapter 9) examines the limits of purely private approaches to cybersecurity governance. Thornton examines how "the cabal," an ad hoc group of experts that would be later renamed the CWG, came together to respond to the Conficker worm. Thornton finds an argument in favor of hierarchy and government. Members of the CWG referenced the informality of the group as a key strength, but, as the chapter notes, this model can significantly diverge from or even thwart larger public goals. Popular accounts framed CWG as superheroes that swooped in to save the day – the private sector rescuing the public from nasty malware. But, as Thornton wryly remarks, "[t]he problem with the X-Men is that sometimes they save the planet and sometimes they start a civil war." Thornton argues that in praising or adopting these informal and ad hoc (and nongovernmental) approaches, we sacrifice accountability and larger ethical considerations. In place of purely private efforts, Thornton argues for the adoption of a public health approach to confronting cybersecurity that carves out a key space for government participation.

The public and private sector are not only willing or even tentative allies, occasionally they are adversaries. Andreas Kuehn and Ryan Ellis examine the rise of the market for software flaws in "Bug Bounty Programs: Institutional

Variation and the Different Meanings of Security" (Chapter 10). As Google, Microsoft, Facebook, and hundreds of other companies rush to start purchasing flaws in their software and services, they are drawn into competition with intelligence agencies, militaries, and others that also seek to purchase flaws in order to exploit them for gain. Here, as Kuehn and Ellis show, the private sector is attempting to use the market to improve software security and, to some degree, keep flaws out of the hands of those that want to use them for surveillance, sabotage, or crime. The institutional model of bug bounty programs is still forming. As the authors note, multiple different bounty models are currently being tried and tested. In each case, within these efforts there is a tension between the desire to improve the broader software ecosystem and the desire of governments to use the holes in this ecosystem for law enforcement, intelligence, or military purposes. The public and private sectors are not simply allies: they are at times direct competitors.

I.2.3 Cybersecurity is Never Value-Free

Cybersecurity is a way of ordering competing values. Cybersecurity efforts explicitly and implicitly arrange different and at times oppositional goals. Security efforts always bump against other important values. Jonah Force Hill and Matthew Noyes examine the tension between state sovereignty and globalized data flows in "Rethinking Data, Geography, and Jurisdiction: A Common Framework for Harmonizing Global Data Flow Controls" (Chapter 11). Modern data storing slices data into fine-grained portions – "sharded" – and distributes it across the globe. As Hill and Noyes detail, the fragments then slosh across legal jurisdictions, moving from one geography to another, as cheaper storage become available elsewhere. Here, we see tensions that can emerge within cybersecurity. How do we reconcile globalized data with the needs of law enforcement, local or regional privacy laws, and more generally core questions of national sovereignty? Hill and Noyes argue that it is time to radically rethink the piecemeal approach to solving these sorts of questions. Developing a common framework for global data flows, as they show, requires facing head on the competing values at play.

Amit Elazari Bar On visits the world of bug bounties in "Private Ordering Shaping Cybersecurity Policy: The Case of Bug Bounties" (Chapter 12). Elazari Bar On provides the first comprehensive analysis of bug bounty legal terms. The chapters find a raw tension between software security and the security of hackers participating in these budding programs. The use of form-contracts in bounty programs can – and does – leaves security researchers in legal jeopardy. While bounty programs prioritize fixing software and improving security, they create legal precarity or *insecurity* for market participants. As Elazari Bar On argues, a legal regime that hopes to foster ethical hacking must work to offer researchers better legal safeguards.

Conflict and competition among competing values and interests sit at the heart of much of cybersecurity governance. Indeed, this core theme appears repeatedly across the pages of the book. Shires (Chapter 2) sheds light onto how cybersecurity can be reinterpreted for political purposes. Security is elastic, it can be stretched to serve all manner of ends. Even when cybersecurity is not deliberately repurposed to instrumentally serve larger political ends, it cannot but help implicate other values. Tanczer and coauthors (Chapter 3) see the United Kingdom's IoT strategy as a veiled referendum on privacy. Thornton (Chapter 9) shows how security efforts raise vital questions about how we balance security with accountability. In these and many other of the cases that follow questions about security are *always* about something larger: They are about the values we hold dear and the difficult work of mapping and acknowledging trade-offs between competing interest. It is our hope that the cases assembled in the book will help shed some light on the sorts of bargains we are making in the name of cybersecurity and allow interested readers to start sorting out the wise from the foolhardy.

Notes

1 Don Edwards. United States House of Representatives Committee on the Judiciary, United States Subcommittee on Civil and Constitutional Rights, House of Representatives. "Federal Computer Systems Protection Act of 1981." September 23, 1982, 1.
2 Fred Thompson, United States Senate Committee on Governmental Affairs. "Weak Computer Security in Government: Is the Public at Risk?" May 19, 1998, 1.
3 Joseph S. Nye, Jr., "The Regime Complex for Managing Global Cyber Activities," 2014. https://www.cigionline.org/sites/default/files/gcig_paper_no1.pdf; Laura DeNardis, The Global War for Internet Governance (New Haven: Yale University Press, 2014); Jack Goldsmith and Tim Wu, Who Controls the Internet? Illusions of a Borderless World (New York: Oxford University Press, 2006).
4 *See* e.g. Jack L. Goldsmith, "Against Cyberanarchy," *University of Chicago Law Review* 65, no. 4 (1998): 1199–1250; Joseph S. Nye, Jr. "Nuclear Lessons for Cyber Security," *Strategic Studies Quarterly* Winter (2011): 18–38.
5 David Clark, "Control Point Analysis," 2012 TRPC (September 10, 2012), https://ssrn.com/abstract=2032124 or http://dx.doi.org/10.2139/ssrn.2032124.

1

Cybersecurity Information-Sharing Governance Structures

An Ecosystem of Diversity, Trust, and Trade-offs

Elaine Sedenberg[1] and Jim Dempsey[2]

[1] *School of Information, University of California, Berkeley, CA, USA*
[2] *Berkeley Center for Law & Technology, School of Law, University of California, Berkeley, CA, USA*

1.1 Introduction

Policymakers and corporate representatives have frequently discussed cybersecurity information sharing as if it were a panacea. The phrase itself refers to many different activities and types of exchanges, but from about 2009 to the end of 2015, the cybersecurity policy debate in Washington, DC, was dominated by calls for greater information sharing. [1] Influenced in part by the post-9/11 theme of "connecting the dots," both policymakers and the private sector commonly accepted that improved cybersecurity depended on – and would flow inexorably from – expanded information sharing within the private sector and between the private sector and the federal government.[2] This view seemed to rest upon the assumption that with more information, systems may be made more secure through prevention measures or rapid remediation. Policymakers, reluctant to regulate cybersecurity standards, viewed voluntary information sharing as a tangible coordination activity that could be incentivized through policy intervention and sometimes directly facilitated by federal government roles.[3] The policy debate culminated with the 2015 passage of the Cybersecurity Information Sharing Act (CISA).[4] The law sought to encourage information sharing by the private sector by alleviating concerns about liability for sharing otherwise legally restricted information. It also sought to improve sharing within the federal government and between the government and the private sector.

CISA was debated and adopted after several decades of efforts within law enforcement and national security agencies to coordinate and increase information sharing with and within the private sector. The US Secret Service (USSS) established the New York Electronic Crimes Task Force (ECTF) in 1995

Rewired: Cybersecurity Governance, First Edition. Edited by Ryan Ellis and Vivek Mohan.
© 2019 John Wiley & Sons, Inc. Published 2019 by John Wiley & Sons, Inc.

to facilitate information exchanges among the private sector, local and national law enforcement, and academic researchers. In 2001, the USA PATRIOT Act mandated that the USSS create a nationwide network of ECTFs, which eventually consisted of over 39 regional hubs.[5] In 1998, Presidential Decision Directive 63 (PDD-63) authorized the Federal Bureau of Investigation (FBI) to create a National Infrastructure Protection Center (NIPC) as a focal point for gathering and disseminating threat information both within the government and with the private sector.[6] PDD-63 simultaneously directed the national coordinator for infrastructure protection to encourage the private sector to create an Information Sharing and Analysis Center (ISAC).[7] The role of the private sector center was to collect and analyze private-sector information to share with the government through the NIPC, but also to combine both private-sector information and federal information and relay it back out to industry.[8] Although PDD-63 anticipated that there would be one national ISAC, various sectors ultimately formed their own ISACs focused on industry-specific security needs.[9]

Over time, additional federal agencies also developed their own information-sharing systems and procedures. For instance, US Computer Emergency Readiness Team (US-CERT) – an organization that took over many of NIPC's functions after it was dissolved following a transfer to the Department of Homeland Security (DHS) – releases vulnerability information and facilitates response to particular incidents. Various other information exchanges and feeds – each with its own scope, access policies, and rules – were established across federal agencies charged with securing aspects of cyberspace. For example, in 2001 the FBI formally announced its "InfraGard" project, designed to expand direct contacts with private-sector infrastructure owners and operators, as well as to share information about cyber intrusions, exploited vulnerabilities, and infrastructure threats.[10]

In addition to these piecemeal federal efforts to expand cyber information sharing, private-sector information-sharing arrangements also proliferated. Antivirus software companies agreed to share virus signatures with each other, essentially deciding to differentiate themselves on platform usability and support instead of competing for data.[11] Additionally, security researchers and individual corporate professionals formed ad hoc arrangements around critical responses to major incidents such as the Conficker worm and the Zeus botnet – threats that required coordination of response as well as exchange of information.[12]

Consequently, even before CISA was enacted, an ecosystem of information exchanges, platforms, organizations, and ad hoc groups had arisen to respond to increasingly pervasive and complex security threats within all industries. Today, this ecosystem of information-sharing networks is characterized by a high degree of diversity – the result of years of evolving policies and cooperative models, driven by both the federal government and private sector. Information-sharing models and structures operate in different niches – working sometimes in silos, occasionally duplicating efforts, and sometimes complementing each other.[13]

CISA attempted to advance information sharing on four dimensions: within the private sector, within the federal government, from the private sector to the government, and from the government to the private sector. However, the legislation was enacted without first fully mapping the ecosystem that had developed in the preceding years. Little effort was made to identify what was working effectively and why, or to de-conflict existing federal programs. Instead, the private sector repeatedly stated – and policymakers accepted – that concerns over legal liability (mainly arising, it was asserted, from privacy laws) were inhibiting information sharing. Therefore, one of CISA's major provisions was liability protection for private sector organizations as an incentive for more information sharing.

CISA's usefulness and impact on the information-sharing ecosystem has yet to be demonstrated. On the contrary, our study suggests that the law did little to improve the state of information sharing. If anything, it only added more hurdles to federal efforts by mandating that the federal portal include unnecessary technical details (free-field text entry) and cumbersome submission methods (e-mail). The law lacked specificity on how federal efforts would work with each other and with already existing information-sharing networks in the private sector. Focusing almost solely on the private sector's liability concerns, it failed to address other key factors associated with sharing, including trust management, incentives, reciprocation, and quality control. In sum, CISA was a policy intervention divorced from existing sharing mechanisms and lacking a nuanced view of important factors that could enable agile exchanges of actionable information.

This chapter focuses on cybersecurity information within the private sector and between the private sector and federal government (leaving to others the issue of sharing within the federal government itself). It examines how governance structures, roles, and associated policies within different cybersecurity information-sharing organizations impact what information is shared (and with whom) and the usefulness of the information exchanged. This research is based on a qualitative analysis of 16 semi-structured interviews with cybersecurity practitioners and experts. Using these interviews and other available information on cybersecurity sharing, we have created a taxonomy of governance structures that maps the ecosystem of information-sharing organizations – each of which fills particular security needs and is enabled by different policy structures. This chapter discusses the implications of these policies and structures for values that directly impact sharing, particularly the trade-off between trust and scalability. This research illustrates how different governance models may result in different degrees of success within the complex and changing cybersecurity ecosystem. Our findings point to lessons – mainly cautionary ones – for policymakers seeking to encourage improvements in cybersecurity. This chapter focuses on information sharing within the United States, but given the multinational nature of many private sector companies, some findings may be relevant internationally.

The types of cybersecurity-related information that could be shared to improve cybersecurity defenses and incident response include incidents (including attack methods), best practices, tactical indicators, vulnerabilities, and defensive measures. Generally, the organizations we describe in this chapter are engaged in sharing tactical indicators, often called "indictors of compromise" (IOCs). An IOC can be defined as an artifact that relates to a particular security incident or attack. IOCs may be filenames, hashes, IP addresses, hostnames, or a wide range of other information. Cybersecurity defenders may use IOCs forensically to identify the compromise or defensively to prevent it.[14]

1.2 Taxonomy of Information-sharing Governance Structures and Policies

Over time, different cybersecurity information-sharing structures have arisen to address particular needs or challenges. Given the wide range of information types, federal roles, industry sectors, and information sensitivities at issue, it is perhaps inevitable that an array of information arrangements has formed, each serving particular perceived needs, each with its own priorities and challenges, and each with its own respective membership policies and governance structures. Our research identified at least seven information-sharing models:

1) Government-centric
2) Government-prompted, industry-centric
3) Corporate-initiated, peer-based (organizational level)
4) Small, highly vetted, individual-based groups
5) Open-source sharing platforms
6) Proprietary products
7) Commercialized services

To understand these governance models, our taxonomy articulates different policy and organizational approaches to sharing, as well as their impact on mission, participation, risk/benefit trade-offs, and efficacy (Table 1.1).

1.2.1 Government-centric Sharing Models

The cybersecurity policy of the US federal government is simultaneously oriented towards many different goals, ranging from national security, to protecting federal IT systems, to investigating and punishing cybercrime, with

Table 1.1. Taxonomy of information-sharing models.

Classification	Organizational units	Example organizations	Governance types
Government-centric	Government operated; private-sector members can be corporations, private sector associations (e.g. ISACs), nonprofits (e.g. universities), or individuals	DHS AIS; US-CERT; ECTF; FBI's e-guardian; ECS	Federal laws and policies; voluntary participation; rules range from open sharing subject to traffic light protocol or FOUO (for official use only) to classified information restrictions (ECS)
Government-prompted, industry-centric	Sector or problem specific	ISACs; ISAOs	Sector or problem specific; voluntary participation; generally organized as nonprofits, use terms of service or other contractual methods to enforce limits on re-disclosure of information
Corporate-initiated, peer-based (organizational level)	Specific private companies	Facebook ThreatExchange; Cyber Threat Alliance	Reciprocal sharing; closed membership; information controlled by contract (e.g. ThreatExchange Terms and Conditions)
Small, highly vetted, individual-based groups	Individuals join, take membership with them through different jobs	OpSec Trust; secretive, ad hoc groups	Trust based upon personal relationships and vetting of members; membership and conduct rules
Open-source sharing platforms		Spamhaus Project	Information published and open to all; no membership but may be formed around community of active contributors and information users; one organization may manage platform infrastructure
Proprietary products	Organization or individuals participate by purchasing the product	AV and firewall vendors	Information via paid interface; responsibility and security management still in-house
Commercialized services	Organizations purchase service	Managed security service providers	Outsourcing of security

the overarching goal of ensuring a healthy and productive US economy through the protection of American critical infrastructures and intellectual property. Each goal results in different information-sharing priorities.[15] Given the number of federal agencies involved in some aspect of cybersecurity, the growth of information-sharing systems is not surprising – even if it is frustrating to information consumers. Federal information-sharing programs range from the FBI's eGuardian and InfraGard, to DHS's Automated Information Sharing (AIS) program and its narrowly tailored Enhanced Cybersecurity Services (ECS) program, USSS ECTF alerts, and US-CERT alerts and tips.

The role of the federal government in improving cybersecurity may be viewed from a public good perspective, whereby federal investment in cybersecurity would adjust for underinvestment by individuals and the private sector.[16] However, for such public investment to be effective would require first an understanding of what the private sector lacks and whether the government has what is lacking or could effectively acquire it and make it available in a timely fashion. In fact, leaving aside the question of whether the private sector really suffers from a lack of cybersecurity information, there are limitations to the federal government's ability to quickly and efficiently share information. Accordingly, there are significant challenges associated with expecting the federal government to fulfill a role as central information collector and disseminator.

Given the network of national security, intelligence, and law-enforcement entities, some government-held information becomes trapped within classification restrictions, involving extensive security standards for personnel, IT networks, and physical facilities, and severely limiting recipients and methods of disbursement. The Pentagon' Defense Industrial Base (DIB) cybersecurity program and DHS's ECS program were developed to disseminate such classified data within special security agreements. These programs trade limited access for greatly improved information quality. As implemented, they appear not to be intended to support dissemination to a wide number of recipients. Instead, they disseminate information to just a handful of communications service providers (AT&T, CenturyLink, and Verizon) plus Leidos (formerly SAIC), entities that provide cybersecurity services to a multitude of customers and have the capability to ingest and act upon the information provided. In contrast, the reach of DHS's Cyber Information Sharing and Collaboration Program (CISCP) is broader (although still restricted), but it focuses on sharing analytic products with the private sector and therefore trades speed for context. (CISCP offers a range of products, including indicator bulletins intended to support faster action to thwart attacks and remediate vulnerabilities.[17])

At the other end of the spectrum, membership requirements for organizations such as the USSS ECTFs are much less strenuous, requiring a referral by someone already in the organization. The ECTFs disseminate information mainly by e-mail (and in-person meetings). Information shared on the listserv is regulated using the traffic light protocol, where each color defines how it may be used and re-disclosed.[18] Only the USSS sends information to the ECTF listservs, although the information may originate from many different sources.

Several interviewees discussed a hesitation after the Snowden revelations to share information with any US government agency, regardless of the formal governance mechanisms. They cited general cultural unease, as well as fear of negative publicity if and when the sharing came to light. One federal employee involved in information sharing commented that "post-Snowden, and almost certainly now post-WikiLeaks, [getting the private sector to share] is going to become more difficult for us. We are battling a lot of perception." Internationally, for any company subject to European regulation, these cultural and reputational concerns are heightened and augmented by the assumption that sharing information with the US government would violate the 2016 EU General Data Protection Regulation (GDPR).

The regulatory and law-enforcement powers of the federal government at times may discourage sharing from the private sector. Yet, the existence of those powers may also incentivize sharing, at least on a case-by-case basis, for they represent capabilities to act against cyberthreats in ways not available to the private sector.[19] One cybersecurity practitioner commented: "Law enforcement [are] the people who are able to take special action to identify and attribute this information to individuals, who have authority to utilize rule of law, court orders, subpoenas, everything that's required essentially to take authoritative action and prosecute these individuals. Nothing pulls them [attackers] out of the ecosystem quite as well as putting them in jail for their crimes."

Even when legal barriers and the government's negative reputation are mitigated, sharing with the government can be difficult. Interviewees complained that there is a high barrier to participation in DHS's AIS due to the technical requirements for setting up the sharing interface.

The fact that the US government's role in information sharing remains fractured among many different agencies – each with its own respective priorities to share inside or outside of the government itself – is not necessarily undesirable. It might be effective to have different agencies play different roles. However, it is not clear that there is a unified policy or strategy for the proliferation of federal information-sharing programs with broadly defined and overlapping missions. What we see is a failure in both directions: private entities share relatively little information with the government, and what information the government shares is outdated or otherwise not actionable. Outside of specialized sharing arrangements such as the ECS, there are weak incentives for the private sector to take on the reputational risks and the administrative and technical burdens of sending information to the government.

Contrasted with the publicly endorsed but not yet realized goal of large-scale, large-volume sharing arrangements, the most effective reciprocal sharing between the private sector and the federal government may occur on an ad hoc basis, founded on personal connections between security professional in and out of government and on the unique strengths of particular agencies. For example, a national security agency may have the most to offer when an attacker is a foreign government, the FBI may have the most to offer when the attack appears to be a criminal matter, and the DHS or US CERT may be particularly useful in terms of remediation. In some reaches of the cybersecurity community, as one interviewee noted, there is a high crossover of personal relationships between "feds" and the private sector – which allows for direct sharing and consultation through interpersonal connections, as opposed to automated or systematic means. Given current trends, it seems there is a long way to go before the federal government could function as a central collector and switching hub for all cybersecurity information. Federal information-sharing programs could benefit from a more realistic assessment of the federal government's strengths in partnering with, and responding to the needs of, the private sector.

1.2.2   Government-Prompted, Industry-Centric Sharing Models

As noted above, in 1998, President Bill Clinton directed his national coordinator for security and counterterrorism to consult with owners and operators of critical infrastructure in order to encourage them to create "a private sector information sharing and analysis center." Although Clinton's directive contemplated a single center for all of the private sector, multiple ISACs were established over the next two decades, mainly on an industry-specific basis, to serve as collection and analysis points for private-sector entities to share data on a peer-to-peer basis, to feed information into the federal government, and to provide a channel for federal information to flow out to the private sector. Though prompted by federal action, ISACs were intended to be led by the private sector. There are currently more than 20 ISACs. Their industry-specific focus seems to be based on the assumption that cybersecurity threats are most effectively shared among those within a single industry.[20]

In 2015, President Barack Obama encouraged the creation of Information Sharing and Analysis Organizations (ISAOs) to supplement the ISACs. This support for ISAOs was based on the belief that some companies do not fit neatly within a traditional industry classification.[21] ISAOs have sprung up around a variety of organizing principles, including industry (e.g. legal services and sports), region (e.g. Maryland, Southern California, and Northeastern Ohio), or problem (e.g. Trustworthy Accountability Group [TAG] and Cyber Resilience Group).[22]

The Financial Services ISAC (FS-ISAC) is widely cited as the canonical example of a successful information-sharing arrangement. As of October 2017, it had 7000 members, including commercial banks and credit unions of all sizes.[23] In its early days, the FS-ISAC benefitted from (among other factors) the financial sector's having a primary geographic hub, within New York City. Mutual dependencies among institutions in the financial services sector also helped supply the trust required to kick off the FS-ISAC. "The banks [although] competitors, are also counterparties. They know that even though they want to beat the other banks, they need them because they're on the other ends of the trades." Personal relationships between security professionals at the banks engendered trust. The importance of personal relations may have helped the FS-ISAC successfully navigate the hurdle of including law-enforcement participants, by slowly introducing into the exchange "feds" who had existing relationships with members.

Trust based on geographic proximity and personal relationships has its limits. For the FS-ISAC, there may be a trade-off between size and trust. It was reported in August 2016 that eight of the largest banks in the US had formed their own subgroup for cybersecurity information sharing and cooperation, one of "a couple dozen" subgroups within or associated with the FS-ISAC.[24] Other factors associated with maturity may also impact trust. In 2016, the FS-ISAC sold its sharing platform, Soltra, to the for-profit NC4 because management had become too burdensome for the organization. Some of our interviewees expressed uncertainty about the seemingly sudden acquisition of the open-source platform by a proprietary company. Others viewed this as a sign of success, indicating that the FS-ISAC had matured to a point where its core platform could be commercialized.

From a governance perspective, ISACs and ISAOs represent a unique model: federal policy prompted their creation, but governance was ceded to voluntary groups of organizations facing common cybersecurity threats and sharing common goals. The hands-off, partnership model has fostered a network of organizations that responds to the needs and challenges of particular sectors, while offering the opportunity to coordinate with the federal government (e.g. many ISACs contribute to DHS's AIS and include law-enforcement agencies within their membership). ISACs and ISAOs are typically nonprofits that manage membership and activities. For example, members of the FS-ISAC apply and pay a membership fee. Membership requirements vary by ISAC or ISAO, but the flexibility of the independent governance model allows each entity to reflect the needs of its community.[25] The National Council of ISACs (NCI) coordinates activities between ISACs and has a leadership presence at federal meetings, which helps to foster some high-level collaboration.[26] An ISAO Standards Organization has also been set up, as a voluntary standard-setting organization that works with information-sharing entities on standards, guidelines, and best practices.[27] It is hard to assess the effectiveness of the ISACs and, even more so, the newer ISAOs. However, the federal government seems to have facilitated internal dynamics that allow trust to seed itself by encouraging the process of ISAC and ISAO creation but allowing industry to self-govern along sectoral or thematic lines.

1.2.3 Corporate-initiated, Peer-based Groups

Some companies have undertaken on their own initiative and without government intervention to coordinate information sharing in order to address particular needs. For example, antivirus vendors have agreed to share virus signatures and other indicators of compromise, essentially deciding to not compete on the underlying information but on other features of their products.[28] In 2014, these vendors formed the Cyber Threat Alliance (CTA). The CTA requires that all participants contribute threat intelligence daily. It has designed a system that not only exchanges fresh indicators of compromise but also fosters discussions about the context for the shared data and produces "adversarial playbooks." Most recently, it has begun automating the delivery and configuration of endpoint controls on members' systems.[29] In 2017, the CTA became a nonprofit and hired leadership to manage its growing network of participants – the same governance model by which many ISACs are run.[30]

Facebook's ThreatExchange also follows the closed membership and required participation model. ThreatExchange grew out of Facebook's efforts to rapidly handle malware spam attacks on its site that were also hitting other large internet companies.[31] Membership has been generally restricted to large peer companies, including Pinterest, Twitter, and Tumblr. Unlike ISACs, it is run by Facebook, not by an independent entity.

There is an unknown number of other privately sponsored cybersecurity information-sharing entities. The Advanced Cyber Security Center (ACSC), for example, was created by Mass Insight, a Boston-based consulting and research firm. ACSC brings together industry participants from the health care, energy, defense, financial services, and technology sectors, as well as government officials and academics. It is governed by a board of directors and a participation agreement, whereby members agree to share sensitive information confidentially.[32]

By orienting around a shared set of problems, these information exchanges can be tailored to fit the specific needs of their members (or their creators). As these exchanges appear to cater to larger, more established organizations, they may be better able to achieve reciprocity in sharing. However, this may leave out smaller companies, which need to find other means to secure their networks. In addition, these organizations may face issues of sustainability. For example, as of 30 October 2017, the most recent update to the homepage for Facebook's ThreatExchange was over a year old.

1.2.4 Small, Highly Vetted, Individual-based Groups

Cybersecurity professionals have formed small, highly vetted online communities of peers to share sensitive, actionable information with the goal of promptly remediating attacks and other problems. Membership is held by individuals, not by organizations. These communities function largely in secret in order to protect their operations. Operations Security Trust is one example. Its skeletal website states: "Ops-T does not accept applications for membership. New candidates are nominated by their peers who are actively working with them on improving the operational robustness, integrity, and security of the Internet."[33] Though each group has its own membership vetting requirements and community standards, vetting usually involves a personal recommendation by a current member. Vetting rules may include restrictions on who can vet whom; some groups require that a newcomer have recommendations from individuals who do not work for the same employer as the newcomer. An interviewee noted: "Typically, the more vetted ones, they just don't typically vouch a lot of people that aren't under outside levels of trust already. With those, you may or may not get an invite. Then also, as far as kind of the vouching levels go, it may require zero vouches once you've been nominated ranging up to two or three different individuals who can vouch."

These groups are small by design, for their members require a high degree of trust in order to rapidly exchange information about ongoing attacks (which involves some disclosure of vulnerabilities), to solicit advice on how to respond, and to share lessons from attacks they have experienced (which again may involve some discussion of vulnerabilities) so others may take preventative actions. Interviewees stressed the importance of the small size of these organizations. For instance, one commented: "The unfortunate thing is the sliding scale, because as the groups become larger the pool of people may tend to start to evolve into a less trusting relationship because now there's more fingers in the pie, so to speak. You may not be quite aware of who your information is being disseminated to in some cases. More accidental or intentional or incidental leaks of information may occur as the constituency grows." The larger a group gets, the less likely it is to share sensitive information.

These clandestine and agile groups play an important role in the information ecosystem, allowing individuals to communicate quickly and completely with peers to actively mitigate incidents and devise preventative measures to protect their networks and systems. To the extent that members of these small, highly vetted groups participate in other sharing organizations with broader membership, they may help improve the functioning and effectiveness of those organizations (e.g. members of one of these small, highly vetted groups may share general knowledge with an ISAC or other sharing organization).

1.2.5 Open Communities and Platforms

Open-source sharing platforms and repositories for cybersecurity data offer a way to crowdsource collection, offer easy and unrestricted access to data, and allow for transparency and scrutiny of practices. Often associated with researchers (both independent and academic) or a host technology company, these platforms are most often focused on a particular type of data such as malware signatures or spam IP addresses. Policies about participation and use within these platforms and communities are generally liberal, and focused more on the structure and format of information shared.

Some of these open-source networks are run by nonprofits. The Malware Information Sharing Platform ("MISP") is a free, open-source platform for collecting, storing, and sharing cybersecurity indicators, initially developed by researchers from the Computer Incident Response Center of Luxembourg, the Belgian military, and NATO. Hail a TAXII.com is a repository of open-source cyberthreat intelligence feeds in STIX format, consisting of 817 631 indicators as of 15 May 2017.[34] The Spamhaus Project maintains the famous spam blocking list, which includes a Botnet Controller List, and also has an Exploits Block List, a real-time database of IP addresses of hijacked PCs infected by illegal third-party exploits. Spamhaus disseminates intelligence on both a free and subscription basis.[35] There are also publicly available resources provided by for-profit entities for free, with various enhancements that users can purchase. For example, Snort, owned by Cisco Systems, is an open-source Network Intrusion Prevention System (NIPS) and Network Intrusion Detection System (NIDS) that performs real-time traffic analysis and packet-logging.[36] An exhaustive description of platforms and repositories that could fit within this category of open-sourced material is beyond the scope of this paper, but it is important to recognize how the openness and reach of communities like these differentiate them from more formal structures.

The governance of open-source initiatives has been widely studied, although it does not appear in the context of cybersecurity information sharing.[37] In 2012, DHS launched a project on open-source cybersecurity solutions, but the effort was not sustained and, in any case, did not address information-sharing arrangements.[38] Hence, trust comes mainly from a belief in the value of transparency and the efficacy of the open-source model.

1.2.6 Proprietary Products and Commercialized Services

By "proprietary products," we refer to firewalls, antivirus software, and other software products that disseminate cybersecurity information through regular updates delivered to nodes or end user devices, often with little intervention by the network operator or end user. By "commercialized services," we refer to the wide range of outsourced cybersecurity services that use information they collect and analyze from existing information exchanges, from proprietary research, and from sensors embedded on customer networks to provide active monitoring and management of third-party devices and systems. Commercialized services include managed security service providers (MSSPs). Proprietary products and commercialized services represent models where information exchange has been commoditized by the market. Companies offering these products and services may participate in any of the other information exchanges, but they package and disseminate the information in a way that makes it available to small and medium organizations or individuals seeking to improve their security. Thus, cybersecurity information from other sharing ecosystems reaches consumers or companies who may not have the security infrastructure in place to ingest and act on data feeds themselves. Additionally, these products and services may collect information from their customers and contribute these data back into the information-sharing network, thus enlisting in the ecosystem entities that do not have the capability to collect or act upon information on their own.

From the end user perspective, proprietary products and commercialized services can be black boxes. Customers have no say in governance, and issues of trust are reduced to the single question of whether to purchase the product or service and to renew it when the initial contract term is up. It can be very hard for end users to make return on investment judgments, especially in the face of dynamic change in both the threat environment and the marketplace for these products and services. The CTA described above, now a nonprofit comprised of a dozen commercial entities, provides a form of governance, under which vendors commit to pool their intelligence. Ultimately, trade associations or other consortia may develop to offer other elements of governance.

1.3 Discussion and Conclusions

1.3.1 Trust and the Trade-offs

The taxonomy of cybersecurity information-sharing structures that we developed may help illustrate how different design and policy choices result in different information-sharing outcomes. Based on the governance models described, we identified a set of factors or determinants of effectiveness that appear in different cybersecurity information-sharing regimes.

The central role of trust in information-sharing arrangements has been cited by many and is fully confirmed by our research.[39] Our research has identified one important aspect of trust: within cybersecurity information sharing, trust must be bidirectional. By this, we mean that (i) the sharing entity needs to trust that the information will not be used against it for regulatory or liability purposes, obtained by adversaries and exploited against it as a vulnerability, or disclosed publicly to hurt the reputation of the sharer and (ii) the recipient of information needs to trust the integrity of the information shared. We also found that success in some models has an additional dimension, which is reciprocity: parties need to trust that other participants will contribute roughly equivalent information. Governance structures and their associated policies may help generate these prerequisites by restricting and vetting membership in some capacity, by reviewing and verifying information submitted by other members, or by committing all members to contribute.

In the case of CISA, federal policy attempted to alleviate trust burdens that accompany sharing private-sector information with the government, by limiting public disclosure through FOIA and by offering protections against liability and regulation. However, we found no evidence to indicate that CISA has succeeded in encouraging increased cybersecurity information sharing.[40] While it may be premature to conclude that CISA has been a failure, our research highlights some of the limitations of the statute's approach. By focusing on concerns over liability exposure, especially related to privacy laws, CISA failed to take into account other issues relevant to the sharing of private-sector data with the federal government in a post-Snowden reality – particularly issues of public perception. Aside from the negative implications of sharing with the government, CISA did not account – and perhaps no law could account – for companies' fears about the reputational harm they might incur should their vulnerability become publicly known, or their fears about future attacks if vulnerabilities fall into the wrong hands. If indeed CISA has failed to induce more cybersecurity information sharing, it may be because it did not take into account these foundational elements of trust.

Our research points toward a clear trade-off between membership size and the amount and sensitivity of information shared. Governance and policy structures can generate trust by limiting membership with some level of vetting and by requiring active participation. These dimensions of trust should be taken as governance design choices that can be worked into any organizational structure.

1.3.2 The Ecosystem and the Role of the Federal Government

The cybersecurity information-sharing ecosystem, when considered in its entirety, shows the strengths of different components of the system. It is myopic to evaluate all the components of the system on the comprehensiveness of the information shared (let alone on timeliness or any other single metric). While it is necessary for at least some groups to have more complete or sensitive access to information, not every sharing organization in the ecosystem needs to have the same level of comprehensiveness or sensitivity. Each of the governing structures should be evaluated for success metrics that fit the goals of each model. For instance, by hosting regional, face-to-face meetings, ECTFs provide value in the ecosystem of information sharing and should not be pressured to be a primary distributor of all possibly relevant information. Ad hoc groups of highly vetted individuals, on the other hand, are not in competition with organizational-based systems. Nevertheless, overlap between individuals across types of groups can reinforce the ecosystem.

Proposals that the federal government should be the central collector and distributor of cybersecurity information seem unrealistic, if for no other reason than the trust deficit the government bears. Even if the government could satisfy the first two tenets of trust, a federally dominated exchange would only work if there were reciprocity between the federal government and the private sector. Current platforms like DHS AIS are struggling to distribute the information, not to mention the challenges brought on by the trade-off of scalability and information comprehensiveness. Given classification concerns with most security-related data, it is unlikely that the federal government would ever achieve a fluid and agile reciprocation of information with the private sector.

Instead of suggesting the federal government as the central information hub for cybersecurity data, our research illustrates that other governing structures can fulfill necessary high-trust, high-sensitivity niches in the information exchanges. Certainly programs like CISCP and DIB allow the government to act in a way that fosters all the tenets of trust, but these programs will never be scalable without losing essential analytical resolution and reciprocity in sensitive sharing. Although still unsatisfying, the diverse economy of sharing models that we have identified may be, together and separately, the most feasible option.

Acknowledgments

This work was funded by a grant from the Hewlett Foundation through the Center for Long-Term Cybersecurity (CLTC) at the University of California, Berkeley and was further supported by the National Science Foundation (NSF) Graduate Research Fellowship Program under Grant No. DGE1106400. Any opinions, findings, conclusions or recommendations expressed herein are those of the authors only and do not necessarily reflect the views of the Hewlett Foundation, the NSF, or the CLTC. We are grateful to the security experts and practitioners who spoke to us in the course of our research, and especially to Nicholas Weaver.

Notes

1 Cybersecurity information could refer to, for instance, malware signatures, suspicious IP addresses, or vulnerability disclosures. For statements supporting improved information sharing, see: Department of Homeland Security, "Information Sharing," accessed May 25, 2017, https://www.dhs. gov/topic/cybersecurity-information-sharing; Brad S. Karp, "Federal Guidance on the Cybersecurity Information Sharing Act of 2015," *Harvard Law School Forum on Corporate Governance and Financial Regulation*, 2016, https://corpgov.law.harvard.edu/2016/03/03/federal-guidance-on-the-cybersecurity-information-sharing-act-of-2015/; Evan McDermott and

David Inserra, "Why Cybersecurity Information Sharing Is a Positive Step for Online Security," *The Daily Signal*, 2016, http://dailysignal. com/2016/01/25/why-cybersecurity-information-sharing-is-a-positive-step-for-online-security/.

2 See, for example, Department of Homeland Security, "Cyberspace Policy Review: Assuring a Trusted and Resilient Information and Communications Infrastructure," 2009, i, https://fas.org/irp/eprint/cyber-review.pdf.

3 For instance, Senator Richard Burr (R-NC) said of CISA, "This landmark bill finally better secures Americans private information from foreign hackers… American businesses and government agencies face cyber-attacks on a daily basis. We cannot sit idle while foreign agents and criminal gangs continue to steal Americans' personal information as we saw in the Office of Personnel Management, Target, and Sony hacks." See Andrea Peterson, "Senate Passes Cybersecurity Information Sharing Bill Despite Privacy Fears," *The Washington Post*, October 27, 2015, https://www.washingtonpost.com/news/the-switch/wp/2015/10/27/senate-passes-controversial-cybersecurity-information-sharing-legislation/?utm_term=.d9b199957b9c.

4 CISA, 129 Stat. 2936-2951, was enacted as part of the Cybersecurity Act of 2015, which itself was wrapped into the Consolidated Appropriations Act, 2016, Pub. L. 114-113 (December 18, 2015), https://www.congress.gov/114/plaws/publ113/PLAW-114publ113.pdf.

5 US Secret Service. "The Investigation Mission," accessed May 25, 2017, https://www.secretservice.gov/investigation/; Department of Homeland Security, "United States Secret Service Electronic Crimes Taskforce," n.d., 1–2, https://www.dhs.gov/sites/default/files/publications/USSS_Electronic-Crimes-TaskForces.pdf Electronic Crimes Task Force.pdf.

6 "Presidential Decision Directive/NSC-63," 1998, https://fas.org/irp/offdocs/pdd/pdd-63.htm.

7 Kristen Boon, Aziz Z. Huq, and Douglas Lovelace, eds., U.S. Preparedness for Catastrophic Attacks (New York, NY: Oxford University Press, 2012), 35, Google Books.

8 It is interesting to note that the directive cites the Centers for Disease Control and Prevention (CDC) as a model for this type of information sharing.

9 The ISACs focus on cybersecurity, but some have incorporated physical security into their missions.

10 FBI National Press Office, "The FBI and the National Infrastructure Protection Center Publicly Introduce the National InfraGard Program," Washington, DC, 2001, https://archives.fbi.gov/archives/news/pressrel/press-releases/the-fbi-and-the-national-infrastructure-protection-center-publically-introduce-the-national-infragard-program.

11 Based on interviews and additional sources. For example, Cyber Threat Alliance, "A New Way to Share Threat Intelligence," accessed May 25, 2017, https://web.archive.org/web/20150813022557/http://cyberconsortium.org/papers/Cyber_Threat_Alliance_White_Paper_9_5_2014.pdf.

12 Andreas Schmidt, "Hierarchies in Networks: Emerging Hybrids of Networks and Hierarchies for Producing Internet Security," in *Cyberspace and International Relations: Theory, Prospects and Challenges* (Berlin, Heidelberg: Springer, 2013), 181–202, doi:10.1007/978-3-642-37481-4_11.

13 Peter W. Singer and Allan Friedman, *Cybersecurity and Cyberwar: What Everyone Needs to Know*, Vol. 1 (Oxford: Oxford University Press, 2014), 224.

14 Jason Andress, "Working with Indicators of Compromise," ISSA Journal, May 2015, https://c.ymcdn.com/sites/www.issa.org/resource/resmgr/journalpdfs/feature0515.pdf.

15 Department of Homeland Security. "Cyberspace Policy Review: Assuring a Trusted and Resilient Information and Communications Infrastructure," 2009, 25, https://fas.org/irp/eprint/cyber-review.pdf.

16 Deirdre K. Mulligan and Fred B. Schneider, "Doctrine for Cybersecurity," *Daedalus* 140, no. 4 (2011): 1–30, doi:https://doi.org/10.1162/DAED_a_00116.

17 Department of Homeland Security, "Cyber Information Sharing and Collaboration Program (CISCP)," accessed May 25, 2017. https://www.dhs.gov/ciscp.

18 United States Computer Emergency Readiness Team, "Traffic Light Protocol (TLP) Definitions and Usage," accessed May 25, 2017. https://www.us-cert.gov/tlp.

19 CISA attempted to establish a shield for the private sector so that companies would not need to fear liability when reporting security information, but several interviewees remarked they did not feel the provision changed any perception about risks associated with sharing.

20 The number of ISACs is based upon members of the National Council of ISACs. National Council of ISACs, "Member ISACs," accessed May 25, 2017, https://www.nationalisacs.org/member-isacs.

21 Executive Office of the President. Executive Order 13691 (February 13, 2015). "Promoting Private Sector Cybersecurity Information Sharing." https://www.whitehouse.gov/the-press-office/2015/02/13/executive-order-promoting-private-sector-cybersecurity-information-shari.

22 ISAO Standards Organization, "INFORMATION SHARING GROUPS," accessed May 25, 2017, https://www.isao.org/information-sharing-groups/.

23 See the FS-ISAC LinkedIn page (https://www.linkedin.com/company/fs-isac/) and "Testimony of John W. Carlson on behalf of the Financial Services Information Sharing & Analysis Center (FS-ISAC) before the U.S. House of Representatives Committee on Financial Services (June 24, 2015)," https://www.fsisac.com/sites/default/files/news/JCarlson%20June%2024%20Testimony%20FINAL.pdf.

24 Robin Sidel, "Big Banks Team Up to Fight Cyber Crime," *Wall Street Journal*, August 9, 2016; Penny Crosman, "A Glimmer of Hope for Cyberthreat Data Sharing," *American Banker*, August 16, 2016, https://www.americanbanker.com/news/a-glimmer-of-hope-for-cyberthreat-data-sharing.

25 FSIAC, "Membership Benefits," accessed May 25, 2017, https://www.fsisac. com/join.

26 National Council of ISACs, "About NCI," accessed May 25, 2017, https://www. nationalisacs.org/about-nci.

27 ISAO Standards Organization, "Information Sharing Groups About Us," accessed May 25, 2017 https://www.isao.org/about/.

28 Eugene Kaspersky, "The Contemporary Antivirus Industry and Its Problems," *SecureList*, 2005, https://securelist.com/ the-contemporary-antivirus-industry-and-its-problems/36063/.

29 Rick Howard, "The Cyber Threat Alliance: How Far We've Come and Where We're Going," *Palo Alto Networks Blog*, 2017, https://researchcenter. paloaltonetworks.com/2017/02/cso-cyberthreat-alliance-far-weve-come-going/.

30 Cyber Threat Alliance, "Cyber Threat Alliance Expands Mission through Appointment of President, Formal Incorporation as Not-for-Profit and New Founding Members," 2017, https://web.archive.org/web/20170301141408/ http://www.cyberthreatalliance.org/pr/pr-021317.html.

31 Rex Santus, "Facebook's ThreatExchange Is a Social Platform for Sharing Cybersecurity Threats," *Mashable*, 2015, http://mashable.com/2015/02/11/ threatexchange-facebook/#jnGMpTqOlZqb.

32 Advanced Cyber Security Center (ACSC), "ACSC Membership," accessed July 1, 2017, https://www.acscenter.org/membership/.

33 "Mission Operations Security Trust (or 'Ops-T')," accessed July 1, 2017, https://portal.ops-trust.net/.

34 "Hail a TAXII," accessed July 1, 2017, http://hailataxii.com/.

35 "The SpamHaus Project," 2017, https://www.spamhaus.org/.

36 Cisco, "SNORT," *2017*, accessed July 1, 2017, https://www.snort.org; see also Gulshan Tweak, "Snort - What Is Snort (Network Intrusion Detection System)," *YouTube*, 2014, https://www.youtube.com/watch?v=S9J4SpbeJJE.

37 See, for example, Siobhan O'Mahoney, "The Governance of Open Source Initiatives: What Does It Mean to be Community Managed?" *Journal of Management and Governance* 11, no. 2 (June 2007), 139–150; Sonali K. Shah, "Motivation, Governance, and the Viability of Hybrid Forms in Open Source Software Development," *Management Science* 52, no. 7 (July 2006), 1000–1014.

38 See DHS, Homeland Open Security Technology (HOST), https://www.dhs. gov/science-and-technology/csd-host.

39 Matthew Harwood, "Lack of Trust Thwarts Cybersecurity Information Sharing," *Security Management*, 2011.

40 None of our interviewees had observed a change in information sharing post-CISA. Several cybersecurity professionals we talked to said they were not aware of CISA; those who were aware of it indicated that it had not had any effect.

2

Cybersecurity Governance in the GCC

James Shires

Belfer Center for Science and International Affairs, Harvard Kennedy School, Cambridge, Massachusetts, USA

2.1 Introduction

This chapter examines cybersecurity governance in the six states of the Gulf Cooperation Council (GCC): Bahrain, Kuwait, Oman, Qatar, Saudi Arabia, and the United Arab Emirates (UAE). It has five sections. The first highlights why the GCC is an important case study; the second gives an overview of key regional cybersecurity incidents; the third details relevant government organizations; the fourth examines strategies, laws, and standards; and the fifth analyzes the cybersecurity industry. The chapter concludes by identifying three themes: the regional *specificity* of cybersecurity governance, especially in relation to defense and telecoms; the importance of an international *image* of cybersecurity governance; and the *reinterpretation* of the scope of cybersecurity governance for political purposes.

First, a definitional note. "Governance" is a supremely agnostic term, in that it implies nothing about *who* governs, what structures or technologies are used, or the extent of their power. This is in many ways an analytical advantage, as in the following discussion I refer to governments, companies, technologies, professions, and people. Nonetheless, different academic traditions writing about governance, from those focused on "global governance"[1] to those examining it as "governmentality,"[2] agree on two things. First, governance is a power relationship which is fundamentally interactive, requiring the continual engagement of the governing, the governed, and intermediaries. Second, this relationship is flexible, in that many techniques of governance can be employed, ranging from the blunt to the fine-grained. Both characteristics appear in this chapter.

Rewired: Cybersecurity Governance, First Edition. Edited by Ryan Ellis and Vivek Mohan.
© 2019 John Wiley & Sons, Inc. Published 2019 by John Wiley & Sons, Inc.

2.2   Why the GCC?

The literature on cybersecurity in International Relations predominantly focuses on "Western," liberal, democratic countries in Europe and the United States, or on their traditional "great power" competitors, Russia and China.[3] The GCC states provide a different perspective, as they are not major threats – in fact, they are strong allies of Western states – and they do not share many of the governing characteristics that are taken for granted in the cybersecurity literature.[4] The GCC countries have patriarchal systems of government, in which male members of the ruling family control key government departments and maintain influence in many private-sector organizations. The degree of consultation in government differs across the GCC: Kuwait has a relatively independent parliament, for instance, while Oman and Saudi Arabia have only nominally representational bodies.[5] Wider neo-patrimonial ties occur across and through all organizations. The social contract has been described as "rentier state," in which citizens (a narrow definition tied to the male line of descent) receive many benefits from extractives revenue.[6] Leadership is based partly on co-option of potential threats, and partly on narratives that associate leaders with state creation, tribal authority, and Islam.[7]

Questions of cybersecurity arise within a general security environment very different from that in Europe or the United States. After ending their colonial relationship with Britain, the GCC states remained under the security umbrella of the United States for the last half century (excluding Oman, which retained British connections), with growing arms and defense cooperation since the Gulf War.[8] Domestically, the public sphere in the GCC is relatively diminished,[9] and the extensive powers of internal security agencies were magnified following the Arab Spring in 2011, with repression of protests across the GCC. The current Saudi rivalry with Iran hides extensive historic Iranian involvement in the Gulf.[10] There are several conflicts nearby: an ongoing war and humanitarian catastrophe in neighboring Yemen, where all GCC states other than Oman (and Qatar since June 2017) are in a coalition led by Saudi Arabia, and the wars in Syria and Libya, where GCC states are both actively involved and indirectly assist various parties.[11] The internal and external security situations are intertwined, with domestic concerns around Islamist extremism and Iranian interference tied to the above conflicts.

GCC states also differ from many cases used in cybersecurity analyses due to their initially ambivalent adoption of the internet. On the one hand, as GCC nations attempted to diversify from oil and gas revenues, they capitalized on high per capita income and education to attract multinational businesses, with attendant technological requirements including high-grade internet access.[12] On the other hand, internet adoption was sometimes limited outside the big cities, and has incorporated restrictions on the public sphere in keeping with a broader cautious approach to new communications technologies due to their potential political effects.[13] The ability of the internet to affect society on a massive scale was demonstrated in the Arab Spring, when the Egyptian government resorted to a complete severance of internet connections following the January 2011 revolution,[14] and protests in the Gulf states were coordinated on social media.[15] In sum, the GCC states have become "wired for business, but not politics."[16]

Cybersecurity governance, in its unique position between two wider regional characteristics – a complex security environment and ambivalent adoption of the internet – is a key aspect of politics in the GCC. This study is therefore not only an important case for those seeking to understand cybersecurity governance, rarely examined in the literature,[17] but also highlights a crucial topic for the region more broadly.

2.3 Key Cybersecurity Incidents

The emergence of governance structures around an issue is often *reactive*, following specific events, although the form such structures take depends on the existing available conceptual and political resources. Consequently, cybersecurity governance in the GCC can only be understood within the background of key cybersecurity incidents. While the events below do not all fit easily into a single definition of cybersecurity, they have all been described within this bracket; I thus treat cybersecurity as found "in the wild." Although there is a sense in which cybersecurity incidents cannot be localized due to the global reach of the internet, regional perspectives can still be identified, with the caveat that they fit into a wider global pattern.

The first key incident relevant to the GCC was the "Stuxnet" malware, discovered in July 2010 and reportedly built by US and Israeli intelligence agencies to target a nuclear enrichment facility in Iran.[18] Stuxnet not only demonstrated that malware could have physical effects but also showed the cybersecurity industry that the Middle East was a potential market. In late 2011 and early 2012, further malware attributed to the United States and Israel was discovered,[19] and a "wiping" component from these was reverse-engineered and used on the Saudi national oil company Aramco and the Qatari company RasGas in August 2012.[20] It is difficult to overstate the impact of this attack, often referred to as Shamoon. If the US government – and by extension, the global cybersecurity community – described it as a "wake-up call,"[21] it had a rather more forceful impact for these states.[22] Despite the malware's lack of sophistication, Shamoon was quickly given the industry label of "Advanced Persistent Threat" (APT).

Following Shamoon, cybersecurity incidents in the GCC broadened substantially. Notable APTs included: Chinese espionage malware repurposed by a regional actor for political purposes[23]; malware written by a Kuwaiti that became prevalent across the region, with Arabic language support for users[24];

and specific energy-sector malware.[25,26] Leaks, "defacement," and denial of service incidents were associated with the Israel–Palestine conflict,[27,28] groups claiming affiliation with the Islamic State in Syria,[29] and broader collectives such as Anonymous.[30]

The GCC financial sector received its own wake-up call after BankMuscat in Oman and RAKBank in Qatar were compromised by a transnational criminal network in 2013, with millions withdrawn in cash.[31] Leaks became more common, including from the Saudi Ministry of Foreign Affairs[32] and Qatar National Bank.[33] Cybersecurity also became a social issue with a regional cultural dimension, following the exploitation of children and adolescents with smartphones across the region.[34] Finally, Shamoon returned in late 2016 and early 2017, again attributed to Iran.[35] The remodeled Shamoon malware used the date of the original incident as part of its wiping program, and persisted for several months. This time, more organizations were affected, including many Saudi Arabian government entities, with a temporary halt to operations at the Civil Aviation Authority.[36]

This brief overview suggests that cybersecurity incidents are deeply entangled with the regional political and security situation. Although the following sections demonstrate that a range of factors shape cybersecurity governance, it is initially catalyzed by events that both stem from and are interpreted according to their regional context.[37]

2.4 Government Organizations

The development of organizations for cybersecurity governance in the GCC must first be placed in the wider context of international internet governance. Internet governance is often described as a binary choice between liberal "multistakeholder" views, in which government, civil society, and businesses all participate,[38] and authoritarian desires for larger state sovereignty and governmental control of information flows across national borders.[39] In fact, this picture is much more complex, with a variety of approaches to internet governance in both camps.[40] The GCC states are often grouped in the latter category, due to their broader conception of security and to events at the World Congress on Information Technology (WCIT) in December 2012 in Dubai, UAE.

At this conference, a motion was proposed for the International Telecommunications Union (ITU) to take responsibility for the naming and numbering functions of the internet, as well as implementing internet security measures through state-level regulation. The initial verbal proposal was made by the host and supported by Bahrain, Saudi Arabia, Russia, and Iraq, while a written version was signed by the UAE and Saudi Arabia, with Russia and China among other signatories.[41] The proposal was widely represented in Western media as a power-grab by authoritarian regimes.[42] It is likely that security concerns at least partially motivated this proposal, given the security focus of other standards discussed at the summit,[43] although the proposal was framed as a means to "correct historical imbalances" and "US dominance."[44]

The binary narrative of internet governance can be made more nuanced by examining the role of the ITU in establishing cybersecurity organizations in the region. Prior to ITU involvement in the GCC, public cybersecurity functions were ostensibly performed by national CERTs.[45] The ITU had provided telecommunications (originally telegraph) standards since 1865, and first attempted to include cybersecurity in its remit through the International Multilateral Partnership Against Cyber Threats (IMPACT), created with Malaysian funding and physical location in 2008.[46] IMPACT was named the official ITU "executing arm" for cybersecurity in 2011. Throughout 2012 it was negotiating with the Omani government,[47] which agreed to pay $2 million for the first "Regional Cybersecurity Centre" in Muscat, launched officially in March 2013.[48] Along with relatively high levels of funding for the ITU from Saudi Arabia – half that of the United States, but similar to that of Russia and China[49] – there were a range of close links between the GCC and the ITU, ensuring they would support the WCIT proposal.

There were also elements of regional competition. The first regional ITU cybersecurity drill was in Jordan in July 2012, before the Oman center was established.[50] After this, the next drill was held in October 2013 – but described by the Omani press as the first one in the region.[51] Also in late 2012 and early 2013, the UAE and Saudi Arabia created national cybersecurity entities to match the Omani one: the National Electronic Security Agency in the UAE, and the National Electronic Security Centre in Saudi Arabia. Despite the announcements, they were not operational for another two years.[52] The proliferation of cybersecurity bodies, despite their initial lack of capability, highlights the importance placed by GCC governments on an international image of cybersecurity governance rather than its domestic implementation, which is explored in the next section.

I now turn to other government organizations with cybersecurity responsibilities and capabilities in the GCC. There are few public pronouncements in local ministries of defense on cyber capabilities, despite procurement of sophisticated military technologies for electronic warfare.[53] The UAE is the exception, and announced its intention to create a cyber command in September 2014. When operational, it will run "in parallel" with NESA[54]; how much this is coordination, and how much conflict, remains to be seen. The only direct GCC-level contributions to cybersecurity are a joint GCC CERT, established in 2006, and a cyber working group with the United States, established in mid-2015,[55] although the wider 2012 GCC joint security agreement covers related matters, such as information-sharing between governments.[56] As others have noted, formal GCC-level structures are often token gestures,[57] suggesting that presenting an image of cooperative cybersecurity governance and military preparedness is also a major aim of the above initiatives.

The other government organizations involved in cybersecurity are interior ministries and intelligence services. As there is little official data available, their role must be inferred from observing them in action. The Citizen Lab, a research organization based at the University of Toronto, has detailed the use of several cyber capabilities against human rights activists in the GCC. The earliest examples come from 2012, when targeted surveillance software owned at that time by Gamma Group, a multinational company with a UK subsidiary, was identified on the devices of activists in Bahrain, and similar software by Italian company Hacking Team was identified in the UAE.[58] In 2013, the Bahraini Ministry of Interior used IP address identification for Twitter accounts to prosecute activists,[59] and in 2014, Hacking Team software was also identified in the Qatif region of Saudi Arabia,[60] a Shia region with a long history of protest and violent responses by security forces.[61] More recent attempts to install monitoring software on the devices of activists and journalists have been identified in the UAE and Qatar, the former using software made by the Israeli company NSO Group.[62]

Based on the examples above, three points should be stressed. First, the distribution of targeted surveillance capability across the region is uneven: for example, Kuwait is not the focus of Citizen Lab reports, partly due to lower levels of international attention, but maybe also due to differences in intelligence techniques or suppliers.[63] Second, these capabilities are mainly provided by private companies. This led to the amendment of the Wassenaar Arrangement arms control agreement in 2013, requiring a license regime within the exporting country for such technologies.[64] Finally, the integration of these capabilities into violent and repressive security practices means that for activists, journalists, and political opponents who are imprisoned and mistreated,[65] this aspect of cybersecurity is more of a threat than any incidents listed in the preceding section. Cybersecurity governance, from the perspective of those governed, thus forms part of the coercive state mechanisms that turn devices and systems of communication into a battleground in wider political struggles.

2.5 Strategies, Laws, and Standards

The strategies, laws, and standards that constitute the policy and regulatory environment for cybersecurity follow broader state policy. All GCC states have long-term national plans – the most well-known being Saudi Arabia's bold "Vision 2030," championed by the Crown Prince Mohammed bin Salman – and these display three broad similarities. First, they claim to refocus the economy from extractive industries towards technology and innovation, whether through smart cities, e-government, or other skilled sectors such as health and finance. Second, they aim to reduce the role of the public sector in all areas of life. Third, they aim to reduce high expatriate numbers (well over 50% in the smaller states) through extensive training and preferential treatment for citizens. National cybersecurity strategies (published, often in draft form, in 2013 and 2014 in all GCC states other than Kuwait) echo these wider goals, presenting an image of carefully planned cybersecurity governance to their audiences.

The two earliest and most dissimilar strategies, those of Qatar and Saudi Arabia,[66] have several interesting differences, especially given their political disputes at the time (which have since escalated).[67] First, they characterize cybersecurity and its object differently in both English and Arabic versions. Qatar uses *al-fidaʾ al-ʾiliktruni* (lit: electronic space) for cyberspace, and the loan word *al-ʾamn al-sibrani* for cybersecurity, appealing to an international audience. Saudi Arabia, on the other hand, does not describe cyberspace, instead talking about networks and connections, with the focus being on *ʾamn al-muʿalumat* (information security). While both recognize that their object has no borders or restraints, the Qatar strategy emphasizes the risks to people, companies, and the state, whereas the Saudi strategy emphasizes the cultural and economic threats of information to companies and the state, a point not made by senior Saudi figures writing in US journals.[68] Thus, even within the GCC, there are significant differences in the conceptualization of cybersecurity governance in national strategy documents.

The legal environment combines regulation of electronic financial transactions, unauthorized access to systems and data, and the use of communications technologies to send or receive information that has harmful effects. Laws concerning electronic financial transactions were first introduced in the early 2000s in the UAE and Bahrain to attract global investment, followed sporadically by the other GCC states.[69] The GCC has a disparate approach to data protection: while privacy is a right in all GCC states, the application of technical and organizational safeguards to personal data is covered by a patchwork of laws, including telecoms, health, and labor laws, as well as the penal codes and constitutions, with little personal protection.[70] Although there is little legislation against third-party provision of data services or moving organizational data between sites or countries,[71] there is a strong practical push against it in most corporations and governments.[72]

Cybersecurity legislation in the GCC has a broad scope. By mid-2015, all GCC countries had passed cybercrime legislation, which included defamation or libel (refusing truth as a defense) and wide definitions of public morals and "national unity."[73] Combined with local terrorism legislation, this increases the penalties on, and restricts, freedom of expression.[74] This is in keeping with wider censorship and historical practice, although it contradicts international human rights standards.[75] For this chapter, the relevant point is that this censorship and restriction is carried out *as cybersecurity governance*, by widening notions of cybersecurity and cybercrime. GCC governments have thus reinterpreted cybersecurity legislation to their advantage in political struggles against domestic and regional opposition.

Finally, I turn to cybersecurity standards, which enable organizations in both public and private sectors to manage cybersecurity risks. In the GCC, all national cybersecurity organizations are involved in maintaining standards such as PCI DSS and ISO27001. Oman has extensive cybersecurity policies and standards due to its role as the ITU Regional Cybersecurity Centre, mentioned above, and was ranked third in the ITU-run World Cybersecurity Index in 2014. The UAE has introduced national standards based on the US model of National Institute of Standards and Technology (NIST), although these standards overlap and compete even domestically; Dubai created its own standards and authority at the same time as Abu Dhabi introduced the nation-wide standards.[76] Implementation of these standards, whether global or local, remains problematic: a survey of GCC cybersecurity professionals in 2015 indicated that 80% are unaware of cybersecurity legislation,[77] and only two-thirds "believe their company has a security policy," to which half have "low-to-moderate adherence."[78]

To unpack this further, I draw on three surveys of ISO27001 implementation in Saudi Arabia. With low levels of overall implementation – in one 2010 study, no defense sector organizations had been certified[79] – standards were low on the list of security professionals' top problems, below personnel issues like training, expertise, or salary, and organizational ones such as management involvement.[80] One survey identified Saudi Arabian culture as a major obstacle, along with the different challenge of even identifying an organization's assets.[81] It is important to read these studies in context: they are "problem-solving" in an engineering and consultancy tradition. Viewing them through a more politically oriented lens suggests that rather than a simple lack of cybersecurity awareness, these survey responses demonstrate how cybersecurity governance in the form of global standards permeates through many organizational levels and relies on influencing behavior at the micro level. These structures encounter *indirect* resistance in the form of cultural and management problems, as well as direct resistance through lack of implementation.

2.6 The Cybersecurity Industry

In the previous sections, the focus has largely been on governments; here, I turn to the private sector. In general, Carr's analysis of public–private partnerships in cybersecurity must be altered for the GCC. While she argues that partnerships suffer from the different commercial and national interests at play,[82] here the relationship is more symbiotic. Not only do governments have several ways of influencing private-sector organizations (some overt, others based on personal relationships), but also businesses are embedded at the heart of government: national strategies are written with consultancies, and government organizations are set up with technical, advisory, and day-to-day services provided by private companies. Furthermore, the individuals involved have no single affiliation, and move between both sides with ease.

Gartner valued the 2014 "Middle East and North Africa" cybersecurity market at just over a billion dollars, rising to 1.3 billion in 2016.[83] Other reports, although using higher values than Gartner, put the region at around 7% of the global cybersecurity market in value.[84] Unsurprisingly, health, finance, and energy sectors feature heavily in market analyses, and the UAE and Saudi Arabia are commonly highlighted as regional targets: the UAE due to its positioning as a global business hub, and Saudi Arabia due to its relative population size and large oil reserves, despite the severe effects of the collapse in oil prices in 2014–2015. The cybersecurity industry centers on large companies with a prior presence in the region, as there are significant obstacles to setting up companies in much of the GCC, although the UAE is significantly less demanding.[85] Established resellers and conglomerates channel existing economic power into the new domain, in part due to their extensive connections, but also as obligatory partners for multinational companies.

One particularly interesting example is the defense industry. Worldwide, major defense multinationals have bought specialized cybersecurity companies, creating a "cyber–military–industrial complex."[86] Regionally, the defense industry has a massive interest in the GCC states: around 10% of GDP is spent on defense, often in long-term contracts with US and UK manufacturers.[87] Often these contracts include "offsets," where the manufacturer invests in other sectors so the money does not leave the purchasing country.[88] While cybersecurity is not necessarily part of offset arrangements – being a sales target in itself – defense companies such as BAE Systems, Raytheon, and Lockheed Martin have a long history of establishing technology companies and engineering faculties in local universities as part of offset programs.[89] Overall, this structure provides a twin advantage to defense multinationals: first, they have existing military and security relationships and a trusted national security role; second, they actively create new technological industries in the GCC.

The other key sector is telecoms. This sector was quasi-liberalized in the early 2000s, with a single national entity split into two or three privatized ones; however, most still have a substantial government share. The main form of competition in the GCC is insular, as the national carriers of each country enter one another's markets, although some, such as the UAE's Etisalat, range more widely across the region. These national companies funded the undersea internet cables connecting the Gulf, and are characterized as critical information infrastructure throughout the GCC. Some, such as Etisalat and its competitor Du, have made this a commercial advantage, developing managed cybersecurity services to sell across public and private sectors.

National telecoms companies maintain strong ties with their and other GCC governments, and have two further roles, based on the content that travels over their networks. First, they control access to encrypted communications, especially given high smartphone use. Many VOIP services are blocked, with little indication whether for profit or national security.[90] Sometimes the approach is less blunt, as in a widely reported disagreement between RIM and the UAE government over the encryption of Blackberry Messenger in 2010, which ended with RIM agreeing to certain conditions.[91] A year earlier, Etisalat had updated all Blackberry phones with a "security update," which in fact allowed third-party access to communications.[92] This not only highlights clashing interpretations of cybersecurity (a national sense of cybersecurity disguised as a users' one), but also demonstrates Etisalat's close relationship with UAE security agencies, on whose instruction this was presumably issued.

Second, national telecoms companies facilitate national monitoring and web filtering. Citizen Lab investigations in 2012 demonstrated that devices manufactured by US manufacturer Blue Coat were in all GCC countries except Oman, with McAfee's Smartfilter also in Saudi Arabia and the UAE.[93] In the UAE, technological sophistication has since increased, as a "telecommunications solutions provider" reportedly owned by an Israeli individual was contracted to install a city monitoring system in Abu Dhabi.[94] Such requirements affect foreign penetration: in Saudi Arabia, contracts for the operator Virgin Mobile were delayed to "satisfy state security concerns."[95] In Bahrain, private telecoms companies are obliged to install filtering systems, which probably led to their increased use of the commercial software Netsweeper in 2016.[96] Finally, telecoms access is useful not only for regional governments but also for strategic allies: the Snowden disclosures in 2013 indicated the existence of a Government Communications Headquarters (GCHQ) base in Oman intercepting undersea cables since 2009.[97] In sum, the telecoms sector is an essential aspect of cybersecurity governance, not only due to its advantageous industry position and gatekeeper role for new technologies but also its role in monitoring and filtering.

2.7 Conclusion

The analysis of cybersecurity governance in this chapter has been based on two premises. First, that cybersecurity should not be defined a priori, but observed "in the wild," to obtain a fuller picture of its variation in different regions. Second, that governance is fundamentally a multifaceted relation of power between those governing and those governed, which depends on many micro- and mid-level interactions involving a variety of actors. Cybersecurity governance looks different depending on perspective: for some, it is mainly technocratic and administrative, while for others it is part of political struggles and violent state actions.

Given these premises, we can identify three themes. First, *image* plays a crucial role in cybersecurity governance, in that the appearance of governance is as important as its actions. From capturing the attention of the ITU and the competitive creation of central authorities, to the bold claims of national strategies and mixed implementation of international standards, presenting an image of successful governance is a constant concern. This presentation is predominantly to an international audience, and as such may be an attempt at deterring offensive behavior as well the result of maneuvering between elites.

Second, cybersecurity itself has been reinterpreted to fit the political situation in the region; namely, low tolerance of political expression, especially after the Arab Spring, and the use of severe criminal punishments to enforce local public speech norms on social media, both of which contravene international human rights standards. Although this has led analysts to label some GCC government organizations as "enemies of the internet,"[98] the picture must be nuanced: each country has taken different strategies, and the line they draw is often not only in opposition to a supposed "Western" notion of governance but also in opposition to other paradigms within the GCC, with Qatar, the UAE, and Saudi Arabia disagreeing strongly.

Third, the fast-growing cybersecurity industry can only be understood in the context of the specific historical and economic situation it inherits. This includes dominance by the defense industry and a close relationship between government and the telecoms sector, especially given the examples of highly sophisticated surveillance provided by their close allies in the United Kingdom and United States. While there is tension created by public–private partnerships which set commercial incentives against cybersecurity goals, the more symbiotic path described in this chapter brings with it different issues, including difficulties in stimulating local innovation. Overall, the GCC thus provides not only new lessons for cybersecurity governance but also new warnings.

Acknowlegments

An earlier version of this chapter was presented at the Oxford Cyber Studies Working Group. I thank all participants and Katharin Tai for their comments, and all remaining errors are mine.

Notes

1 Anne-Marie Slaughter, "Everyday Global Governance," *Daedalus* 132, no. 1 (2003): 83–90; Elke Krahmann, "Conceptualizing Security Governance," Cooperation and Conflict 38, no. 1 (March 1, 2003): 5–26.
2 Roger Deacon, "Strategies of Governance: Michel Foucault on Power," Theoria: A Journal of Social and Political Theory, no. 92 (1998): 113–148; Michael Dillon and Andrew Neal, "Introduction," in *Foucault on Politics, Security and War*, ed. Michael Dillon and Andrew Neal (Springer, 2015), 1–20.

3 Martin C. Libicki, *Cyberdeterrence and Cyberwar* (RAND Corporation, 2009); Joseph S. Nye, "Nuclear Lessons for Cyber Security?" Strategic Studies Quarterly 5, no. 4 (2011): 18; David J. Betz and Tim Stevens, *Cyberspace and the State: Toward a Strategy for Cyber-Power* (Routledge, 2011); Lucas Kello, "The Meaning of the Cyber Revolution: Perils to Theory and Statecraft," International Security 38, no. 2 (October 1, 2013): 7–40; Jon R. Lindsay, Tai Ming Cheung, and Derek S. Reveron, *China and Cybersecurity: Espionage, Strategy, and Politics in the Digital Domain* (Oxford University Press, 2015).

4 For introductions, see F. Gregory Gause, *Oil Monarchies* (New York: Council on Foreign Relations Press, 1994); Rosemary Said Zahlan, *The Making of the Modern Gulf States: Kuwait, Bahrain, Qatar, the United Arab Emirates and Oman* (Ithaca: Ithaca Press, 1998); Sean Foley, *The Arab Gulf States: Beyond Oil and Islam* (Boulder: Lynne Rienner Publishers, 2010).

5 Shaul Yanai, *Political Transformation of Gulf Tribal States: Elitism & the Social Contract in Kuwait, Bahrain & Dubai, 1918-1970s* (Brighton: Sussex Academic Press, 2014), 229–236; Francis Owtram, *A Modern History of Oman: Formation of the State since 1920* (London: I.B.Tauris, 2004), 179–180; Miriam Joyce, *Bahrain from the Twentieth Century to the Arab Spring* (London: Palgrave Macmillan, 2012), 54, 113; Madawi Al-Rasheed, *A History of Saudi Arabia* (Cambridge: Cambridge University Press, 2010), 182–183.

6 Hazem Beblawi and Giacomo Luciani, eds., *The Rentier State* (Routledge, 2016), 27.

7 Andrea B. Rugh, *The Political Culture of Leadership in the United Arab Emirates* (Basingstoke: Palgrave Macmillan, 2010), 219; A. Souaiaia, *Anatomy of Dissent in Islamic Societies: Ibadism, Rebellion, and Legitimacy* (London: Palgrave Macmillan, 2013), 39–45; Christopher M. Davidson, *The United Arab Emirates: A Study in Survival* (Lynne Rienner Publishers, 2005), 70–87.

8 Matteo Legrenzi, *The GCC and the International Relations of the Gulf: Diplomacy, Security and Economic Coordination in a Changing Middle East* (I.B. Tauris, 2015), 74–76.

9 Emma C. Murphy, "Theorizing ICTs in the Arab World: Informational Capitalism and the Public Sphere," International Studies Quarterly 53, no. 4 (December 1, 2009): 1148.

10 Laurence Potter, ed., *The Persian Gulf in Modern Times: People, Ports, and History* (London: Palgrave Macmillan, 2014), 11–12.

11 Taimur Khan, "UAE Joins Airstrikes on ISIL Bases in Syria," *The National*, 2014, https://www.thenational.ae/world/mena/uae-joins-airstrikes-on-isil-bases-in-syria-1.238060; Roula Khalaf and Abigail Fielding Smith, "Qatar Bankrolls Syrian Revolt with Cash and Arms," *Financial Times*, May 16, 2013; C. J. Chivers and Eric Schmitt, "In Shift, Saudis Are Said to Arm Rebels in Syria," *The New York Times*, February 25, 2013, https://www.nytimes.com/2013/02/26/world/middleeast/in-shift-saudis-are-said-to-arm-rebels-in-syria.html.

12 David Held and Kristian Ulrichsen, eds., *The Transformation of the Gulf: Politics, Economics and the Global Order* (Routledge, 2011), 9.
13 Jon W. Anderson, "Is Informationalization Good for the Middle East?" Arab Media & Society Summer, no. 18 (June 12, 2013), 2–3; Ilhem Allagui, "Internet in the Middle East: An Asymmetrical Model of Development," Internet Histories 1, no. 1–2 (January 2, 2017): 97–105.
14 Matt Richtel, "Egypt Cuts Off Most Internet and Cellphone Service," *The New York Times*, January 28, 2011, https://perma.cc/RSH4-HYDR.
15 Toby Matthiesen, *Sectarian Gulf: Bahrain, Saudi Arabia and the Arab Spring That Wasn't* (Stanford: Stanford University Press, 2013), 39.
16 Philip N. Howard, *The Digital Origins of Dictatorship and Democracy: Information Technology and Political Islam* (Oxford: Oxford University Press, 2010), 80.
17 James Andrew Lewis, "Cybersecurity and Stability in the Gulf" (CSIS, January 2014), https://perma.cc/ST48-NVGX; Nir Kshetri, "Cybersecurity in the Gulf Cooperation Council Economies," in *The Quest to Cyber Superiority: Cybersecurity Regulations, Frameworks, and Strategies of Major Economies* (New York: Springer, 2016), 183–194.
18 Kim Zetter, *Countdown to Zero Day* (New York: Penguin Random House, 2014).
19 Symantec, "*W32.Duqu: The Precursor to the next Stuxnet*" (Symantec, November 23, 2011); Kaspersky Lab, "*Gauss: Abnormal Distribution*" (Kaspersky Lab, August 9, 2012).
20 Christopher Bronk and Eneken Tikk-Ringas, "The Cyber Attack on Saudi Aramco," Survival 55, no. 2 (May 1, 2013): 81–96.
21 Infosecurity, "Saudi Aramco Cyber Attacks a 'Wake-up Call,' Says Former NSA Boss," May 8, 2014, https://perma.cc/NXT5-3J57.
22 Awad Mustafa, "UAE To Double Security Budget, Focus on Cyber," February 25, 2014, https://perma.cc/8GYK-2FTL.
23 Nart Villeneuve, Thoufique Haq, and Ned Moran, "Operation Molerats: Middle East Cyber Attacks Using Poison Ivy," *FireEye*, August 23, 2013, https://perma.cc/6UJT-WKZ2.
24 Symantec, "Simple NjRAT Fuels Nascent Middle East Cybercrime Scene," *Symantec Security Response*, March 30, 2014, https://perma.cc/3CVF-QKGP.
25 Christian Tripputi, "New Reconnaissance Threat Trojan.Laziok Targets the Energy Sector," *Symantec Security Response*, March 30, 2015, https://perma.cc/Z6NW-M6U9.
26 For earlier instances of energy sector malware targeting the Middle East, see McAfee Labs, "Global Energy Cyberattacks: 'Night Dragon'" (McAfee, February 10, 2011). The high value and sensitivity of geographical research makes this industry an attractive target for commercial espionage.
27 Nick Enoch, "Hamas Hails Hack Attack against Websites of Israel's Stock Exchange, El Al Airline and Three Banks," *Mail Online*, January 16, 2012, https://perma.cc/B4UK-G9Q3.

28 This cyber conflict has a much longer history: see Sean Lawson, "Cyber-Intifada Resource Guide: A Resource for Tracking the Intifada in Cyberspace" (The Arab Information Project, Georgetown University, 2001).

29 Laith Alkhouri, Alex Kassirer, and Allison Nixon, "Hacking for ISIS: The Emergent Cyber Threat Landscape" (Flashpoint, 2016).

30 David Gilbert, "Anonymous Knocks Saudi Government Websites Offline," *International Business Times*, September 28, 2015, https://perma.cc/6Q8Y-4DVN.

31 Marc Santora, "In Hours, Thieves Took $45 Million in A.T.M. Scheme," *The New York Times*, May 9, 2013, https://perma.cc/3A8A-5RG6.

32 Waqas, "Hackers Leak Confidential Data from Saudi Ministry of Foreign Affairs! It's Crazy," *HackRead*, May 22, 2015, https://perma.cc/R923-JR9H.

33 MEE, "Qatar National Bank Allegedly Hacked, Data of 1,200 Entities Leaked," *Middle East Eye*, April 27, 2016, https://perma.cc/6TMA-VCDC.

34 BBC, "Four Jailed in Bahrain for Duping British Boys into Sex Acts," *BBC News*, April 25, 2014, https://perma.cc/V6YX-5PVN; BBC, "Sex, Honour, Shame and Blackmail in an Online World," *BBC News*, October 26, 2016, https://perma.cc/Y3JT-6FY8.

35 Kaspersky Lab, "From Shamoon to Stonedrill: Wipers Attacking Saudi Organizations and Beyond" (Kaspersky Lab, March 7, 2017).

36 Michael Riley, Glen Carey, and John Fraher, "Saudi Arabia Has Just Suffered a Series of Major Cyber Hack Attacks," *Bloomberg.Com*, December 1, 2016, https://perma.cc/FRK8-AV2P.

37 This chapter was prepared prior to the complete blockade of Qatar by Bahrain, Saudi Arabia, and the UAE in June 2017. This deep rupture in the GCC was precipitated by a cybersecurity incident: the release of a fake story on the Qatari national news channel attributed to actors associated with the UAE. There is no space to consider this incident, or its extensive implications for both cybersecurity and regional politics, in this chapter.

38 John E. Savage and Bruce W. McConnell, "Exploring Multi-Stakeholder Internet Governance" (EastWest Institute, January 2015), 4–5.

39 Paul Cornish, "Governing Cyberspace through Constructive Ambiguity," *Survival* 57, no. 3 (May 4, 2015), 161–165.

40 Milton Mueller, Andreas Schmidt, and Brenden Kuerbis, "Internet Security and Networked Governance in International Relations," *International Studies Review* 15, no. 1 (March 1, 2013): 86–104.

41 Eli Dourado, "Behind Closed Doors at the UN's Attempted 'Takeover of the Internet," *Ars Technica*, December 20, 2012, https://perma.cc/TCG3-2LST.

42 Rory Cellan-Jones, "Divisions over Internet Governance Intensify in Dubai," *BBC News*, December 10, 2012, https://perma.cc/9TUB-BS7D.

43 Elise Ackerman, "Will A Secretive Summit In Dubai Mark The End Of The Open Internet?" *Forbes*, December 10, 2012, https://perma.cc/2TY7-DLKL.

44 Sheetal Kumar, "Cybersecurity: What's the ITU Got to Do with It?," July 9, 2015, https://perma.cc/BE4P-SBQ5.

45 CERTS were established in Qatar (2005), Saudi Arabia (2006), the UAE (2008), Oman (2010), and Bahrain (2014).

46 Rita Boland, "Countries Collaborate To Counter Cybercrime," *SIGNAL Magazine*, July 28, 2008, https://perma.cc/WUY2-TCT2. The original proposal, made in Texas in 2006, was for a speculative partnership against cyber *terrorism*, joining the international attention and finance provided by the global war on terror.Carol Ko, "Fighting Cyber Terrorism," *Computerworld*, June 17, 2008, https://perma.cc/6CZF-QG2J.

47 ITU, "ITU-IMPACT Establishes First Cybersecurity Innovation Centre for Arab Region," *Global Security Mag Online*, December 2012, https://perma.cc/MF8F-GZ83.

48 ITU, "Regional Cybersecurity Centres," 2017, https://perma.cc/VB8H-6SF3.

49 Eli Dourado, "Protecting the Open Internet May Require Defunding the ITU," *Washington Post*, September 18, 2013, https://perma.cc/H2WS-2CFP.

50 eGov innovation, "ITU-IMPACT to Hold Arab Cross-Border Cyber Drill," *Enterprise Innovation*, July 3, 2012, https://perma.cc/BAY6-YHAX.

51 OCERT, "OCERT Event Details", October 23, 2013, https://perma.cc/XY4F-7ZBN.

52 Stephen McBride, "UAE Cyber-Security Authority Unveils Policies, Standards," *ITP.Net*, June 25, 2014, https://perma.cc/HF7X-VFH5.

53 Al Defaiya, "Saudi Arabia to Host Electronic Warfare Symposium," October 18, 2013, https://perma.cc/5E6S-4HEZ.

54 Thomas Bindiya, "UAE Military To Set Up Cyber Command," *Defense World*, https://perma.cc/VP7F-EEXF.

55 TRA, "TRA Heads Bahrain's Delegation to US-GCC Cyber Security Strategic Cooperation Forum," September 14, 2015, https://perma.cc/2JCT-55BA.

56 This agreement has been described as both the culmination of long-awaited security integration (Habib Toumi, "GCC Ministers Sign Major Security Agreement," *GulfNews*, November 12, 2012, https://perma.cc/5S7N-CBN5) and as a danger to human rights across the region (Human Rights Watch, "GCC: Joint Security Agreement Imperils Rights," *Human Rights Watch*, April 26, 2014, https://perma.cc/5LLC-BXEE).

57 Michael Barnett and F. Gregory Gause, "Caravans in Opposite Directions: Society, State and the Development of a Community in the GCC," in *Security Communities*, ed. Emmanuel Adler and Michael Barnett (New York: Cambridge University Press, 2008), 177.

58 Bill Marczak and Morgan Marquis-Boire, "From Bahrain with Love: Finfisher's Spy Kit Exposed?" (Citizen Lab, July 25, 2012); Morgan Marquis-Boire, "Backdoors Are Forever: Hacking Team and the Targeting of Dissent?" (Citizen Lab, October 10, 2012).

59 Bahrain Watch, "The IP Spy Files: How Bahrain's Government Silences Anonymous Online Dissent," 2013, https://bahrainwatch.org/ipspy/viewreport.php.

60 Morgan Marquis-Boire, John Scott-Railton, Claudio Guarnieri, and Katie Kleemola, "Police Story: Hacking Team's Government Surveillance Malware" (Citizen Lab, June 2014).

61 Toby Matthiesen, *The Other Saudis: Shiism, Dissent And Sectarianism* (New York: Cambridge University Press, 2014), 101–109.

62 Bill Marczak and John Scott-Railton, "The Million Dollar Dissident: NSO Group's IPhone Zero-Days Used against a UAE Human Rights Defender" (Citizen Lab, August 24, 2016); Amnesty International, "Operation Kingphish: Uncovering a Campaign of Cyber Attacks against Civil Society in Qatar and Nepal" (Amnesty International, February 14, 2017).

63 Oman also receives less attention, although it probably bought Gamma's software through another company, Dreamlab: Pratap Chatterjee, "Turkmenistan and Oman Negotiated to Buy Spy Software: Wikileaks in Spy Files, *WikiLeaks Supporters Forum*, September 4, 2013, https://perma.cc/J264-JW5U.

64 Colin Anderson, "Considerations on Wassenaar Arrangement Control List Additions for Surveillance Technologies" (Access, 2015), 10–15.

65 Mahmoud Cherif Bassiouni, "Report of the Bahrain Independent Commission of Inquiry" (BICI, December 10, 2011), 285–290; Human Rights Watch, "Saudi Arabia: 7 Convicted for Facebook Postings About Protests," Human Rights Watch, June 29, 2013, https://perma.cc/39GS-52ED; Human Rights Watch, "UAE: Concerns About Muslim Brotherhood Trial," *Human Rights Watch*, November 4, 2013, https://perma.cc/DB8R-6HH3.

66 MCIT, "National Information Security Strategy" (Saudi Arabia: Ministry of Communications and Information Technology, January 2011), 4; ictQatar, "Qatar National Cyber Security Strategy" (Government of Qatar, May 2014), i. Although the Saudi strategy is dated January 2011, it was officially released in February 2013: ENISA, "National Cyber Security Strategy of Saudi Arabia," https://perma.cc/4RW3-WUH4.

67 Madawi Al-Rasheed, "Saudi-Qatar Tensions Divide GCC," *Al-Monitor*, March 6, 2014, https://perma.cc/Y597-CYZJ.

68 Naef bin Ahmed Al-Saud, "A Saudi Outlook for Cybersecurity Strategies: Extrapolated from Western Experience," Joint Forces Quarterly, no.64 (2012): 75–81.

69 Mohammed Saleh Altayar, "A Comparative Study of Anti-Cybercrime Laws in the Gulf Cooperation Council Countries," *IEEEExplore*, 2017.

70 UN-ESCWA, "Cyberlaws and Regulations for Enhancing E-Commerce" (ESCWA Cyber Legislation Digest, March 2015), 4.

71 Chad Dowle and Corey Judson, "Data Protection in United Arab Emirates," *Thomson Reuters Practical Law*, May 10, 2016, https://perma.cc/35XY-M5QF.

72 Rouda Alamir Ali, "Cloud Computing in Arab States: Legal Aspect, Facts and Horizons" (ITU Arab Regional Office, July 2016), 5.

73 Matt Duffy, "Arab Media Regulations: Identifying Restraints on Freedom of the Press in the Laws of Six Arabian Peninsula Countries," Berkeley Journal of Middle Eastern & Islamic Law 6, no. 1 (April 1, 2014), 12.

74 Lara-Zuzan Golesorkhi, "Cases of Contention: Activism, Social Media and Law in Saudi Arabia," Arab Media & Society, no. 20 (2015), 4–5.

75 Patrick Wintour, "UN Accuses Saudi Arabia of Using Terror Laws to Suppress Free Speech," *The Guardian*, May 4, 2017, https://perma.cc/X9LP-YTCM. This tension is complicated by the growing influence of the GCC states in defining and upholding these standards:Owen Bowcott, "UK and Saudi Arabia 'in Secret Deal' over Human Rights Council Place," *The Guardian*, September 29, 2015, https://perma.cc/9CAT-J66L; Somini Sengupta, "United Nations Chief Exposes Limits to His Authority by Citing Saudi Threat," *The New York Times*, June 9, 2016, https://perma.cc/3XJ8-GNSK.

76 Andy Sambridge, "Dubai Sets up E-Security Centre to Fight Cyber Criminals," *ITP.Net*, June 13, 2014, https://perma.cc/F7LX-R2VZ.

77 CISCO, "Cisco and GBM Outline Key Steps for Digitization to Help Middle East Organizations Become IoT Ready," October 19, 2015, https://perma.cc/UZA5-5ACM.

78 BI-ME, "Cisco and GBM Unveil Latest UAE Security Research at GITEX 2014," October 14, 2014, https://perma.cc/EU3X-Z9W3.

79 Syed Irfan Nabi, Abdulrahman A. Mirza, and Khaled Alghathbar, "Information Assurance in Saudi Organizations – An Empirical Study," in *Security Technology, Disaster Recovery and Business Continuity*, ed. Wai-chi Fang, Muhammad Khurram Khan, Kirk P. Arnett, Heau-jo Kang, and Dominik Slezak, (Springer, Berlin, Heidelberg, 2010), 24.

80 Khalid I. Alshitri and Abdulmohsen N. Abanumy, "Exploring the Reasons behind the Low ISO 27001 Adoption in Public Organizations in Saudi Arabia," in *2014 International Conference on Information Science Applications* 2014, 1–4.

81 Belal AbuSaad, Fahad A. Saeed, Khaled Alghathbar, Bilal Khan, "Implementation of ISO 27001 in Saudi Arabia – Obstacles, Motivations, Outcomes, and Lessons Learned," *Australian Information Security Management Conference*, January 1, 2011, 4.

82 Madeline Carr, "Public–private Partnerships in National Cyber-Security Strategies," International Affairs 92, no. 1 (January 1, 2016), 61.

83 Gartner, "Middle East & North Africa Information Security Spending to Reach US$1.3 Billion in 2016," October 31, 2016, https://perma.cc/3LWW-GUGP.

84 Micromarketmonitor, "Middle East and Africa Cyber Security Market Research Report," 2015, https://perma.cc/3EV9-PFDE.

85 Steffen Hertog, "The Private Sector and Reform in the Gulf Cooperation Council" (Kuwait Programme on Development, Governance and Globalisation in the Gulf States, July 2013), 3.

86 Ronald J. Deibert and Rafal Rohozinski, "The New Cyber Military-Industrial Complex," *The Globe and Mail*, March 28, 2011, https://perma.cc/PJL9-AKGU.

87 Sam Perlo-Freeman, "SIPRI Background Paper: Arms Transfers to the Middle East" (SIPRI, July 2009).

88 Ron Matthews, "The UK Offset Model: From Participation to Engagement," *RUSI*, July 29, 2014.

89 Bilal Y. Saab, "The Gulf Rising: Defense Industrialization in Saudi Arabia and the UAE" (The Atlantic Council, May 2014), 32.

90 A leaked US cable suggests it is a mixture of both. Wikileaks Forum, "WikiLeaks Cable: Skype Crackdown in Oman," May 17, 2013, https://perma.cc/XFS9-2WE7.

91 Josh Halliday, "UAE to Tighten BlackBerry Restrictions," *The Guardian*, April 18, 2011, https://perma.cc/PH46-HF32.

92 Ben Thompson, "UAE Blackberry Update Was Spyware," *BBC News*, July 21, 2009, https://perma.cc/97UP-3APN.

93 Morgan Marquis-Boire, John Scott-Railton, Claudio Guarnieri, and Katie Kleemola, "Some Devices Wander by Mistake: Planet Blue Coat Redux" (Citizen Lab, July 9, 2013); Bennett Haselton, "Smartfilter: Miscategorization and Filtering in Saudi Arabia and UAE" (Citizen Lab, November 28, 2013).

94 Rori Donaghy, "Falcon Eye: The Israeli-Installed Mass Civil Surveillance System of Abu Dhabi," *Middle East Eye*, February 28, 2015, https://perma.cc/3WX8-XMM5.

95 Auri Aittokallio, "Virgin Mobile Launches in Saudi Arabia," *Text, Telecoms. Com* (September 30, 2014), https://perma.cc/N29W-QBCY.

96 Jakub Dalek Jakub Dalek, Ron Deibert, Bill Marczak, Sarah McKune, Helmi Noman, Irene Poetranto, and Adam Senft, "Tender Confirmed, Rights at Risk: Verifying Netsweeper in Bahrain" (Citizen Lab, September 21, 2016).

97 Duncan Campbell, "Revealed: GCHQ'S Beyond Top Secret Middle Eastern Internet Spy Base," *The Register* (June 3, 2014), https://perma.cc/K3YU-66XZ.

98 Reporters without Borders, "Enemies of the Internet," 2014, accessed June 1, 2017, https://rsf.org/sites/default/files/2014-rsf-rapport-enemies-of-the-internet.pdf.

3

The United Kingdom's Emerging Internet of Things (IoT) Policy Landscape

Leonie Maria Tanczer, Irina Brass, Miles Elsden, Madeline Carr, and Jason Blackstock

Department of Science, Technology, Engineering and Public Policy (STEaPP), University College London, London, UK

3.1 Introduction

Just as cybersecurity is becoming a central concern for policymakers, corporations, and civil society, discussions about its governance are further complicated by the increased adoption and dissemination of the Internet of Things (IoT). These interconnected "things" and systems are the direct and indirect extension of the internet into a range of physical objects, devices, and products. The emerging IoT ecosystem is characterized by: a proliferation of visible and hidden sensors that collect and transmit data; systems that interpret and make use of the aggregated information; and actuators that, on the basis of this information, take action without direct human intervention. Such "smart" or "digitally upgraded"[1] products can communicate with each other and/or humans, have unique identifiers such as internet protocol (IP) addresses, can be remotely controlled, and function as physical access points to networked services. Their application areas are wide, stretching from personal fitness to assisted living devices, from home appliances such as smart fridges to utilities such as smart energy meters, and from smart traffic management systems to connected and autonomous vehicles and transport infrastructures.

Within the European Union (EU), the IoT is regarded "as the next step of disruptive digital innovation,"[2] with the European Commission having pushed IoT-related initiatives since 2005.[3] In the United States (US), the Federal Trade Commission is at the heart of this new digitalization process and has recently been involved in its first major lawsuit against a global IoT manufacturer whose weak security practices endangered consumers' privacy.[4] Put simply, the IoT represents a significant amplification in the already complex global governance challenges of digital technologies.

Rewired: Cybersecurity Governance, First Edition. Edited by Ryan Ellis and Vivek Mohan.
© 2019 John Wiley & Sons, Inc. Published 2019 by John Wiley & Sons, Inc.

While the IoT offers significant benefits such as patient-centered healthcare,[5] and promises societal and economic progress through productivity gains and cost savings,[6] it also creates profound challenges and coordination problems in terms of security and privacy. The IoT adds more complexity to global supply chains and amplifies jurisdictional issues, all of which create elevated risks. In addition to these security issues, real-time collection and processing of data raises concerns about the privacy of the personal information that is being gathered and stored, and about data protection and confidentiality. A number of research programs, initiatives, and policies have emerged to try to address these issues, but they have to mediate between competing interests working to shape the nascent IoT realm and are also faced with coordination problems across the vast range of potential IoT applications.

The governance of this space is consequently becoming a major task, and a responsibility that is unlikely to be left solely to the private sector. Policymakers strive to balance maximizing the IoT's benefits against giving too much ground on its privacy and security challenges. Effective management of these conflicting demands will be essential to the fundamental integrity and resilience of the IoT ecosystem.

The IoT has evolved in the absence of IoT-specific legislation, both in the United Kingdom (UK) and elsewhere.[7] These new technologies are emerging amid a regulatory landscape that applies a variety of existing laws across telecommunications, competition, intellectual property, health and safety, data protection, security, and risk management.[8] As the IoT is still in its infancy, many of these regulations are not a perfect fit for the cyber–physical challenges that the IoT creates. Nonetheless, there is a widely shared expectation that relevant and adequate policies will be rapidly implemented in the next few years. This can be seen in the case of the proposed US "Internet of Things (IoT) Cybersecurity Improvement Act of 2017," which aims to provide minimal operational cybersecurity standards for internet-connected devices purchased by US federal agencies.[9]

With both policy approaches and academic research on the governance of the IoT still in an early stage, the current chapter sets out to provide an overview of the IoT policy landscape in the UK. As one of the world's biggest economies and as a central insurance and banking hub, the UK has an interest in actively engaging in this "fourth industrial revolution" and fostering the IoT's innovation and uptake while protecting industry and society from the IoT's potential systemic risks.[10] In 2017, the government released its Digital Strategy, which aims to make "the UK the safest place to" live, work, and do business online.[11] In many ways, the IoT both facilitates and complicates these intentions. As the cybersecurity landscape is still evolving, the IoT is adding another layer of coordination demands upon the UK government. In response, the UK government is developing a range of institutions and programs, some of which previously focused mainly on issues related to cybersecurity, but are, or will soon be, also concerned with the security of interconnected devices and services.[12]

The chapter will therefore examine the institutional landscape that underpins the IoT in the UK, and review the government strategies and policies within which the IoT is developing. The rapid evolution of technology means that this review represents a synoptic snapshot: it identifies core challenges connected to the evolving interdependent ecosystem, and provides a recommendation for more adaptive policymaking in this space.[13] Thus, the chapter extracts some general principles and lessons that can be applied more widely to the development of emerging technologies, including the use of forward-thinking and monitoring policy tools in order to respond to new conditions and potential market failures. It does so through assessment of the IoT's inherent risks and uncertainties, the fragmentation of the UK's institutional and policy landscape, and the IoT's respective governance challenges. The chapter concludes with future directions for researchers, practitioners, and policymakers, as well as an appeal to apply adaptive policymaking to the management of rapidly evolving IoT technologies.

3.2 The IoT's Risks and Uncertainties

Whereas previous IT security and privacy concerns were confined to a single device or service, the IoT increases attack vectors and adds another layer of complexity to cybersecurity. Adapting existing information-security concepts and practices to IoT systems is therefore not straightforward.[14] One has to secure not just one, but multiple connected devices, each of which has individual parts linked to diverse network components with distinct functions. This disparity requires acknowledgement of all potential weak spots in the vulnerability chain, and calls for a security understanding that is holistic and dynamic, with cybersecurity being part of a continuous process of improvement.[15] There are three distinct IoT threat vectors:

First, the IoT is a new attack vector in and of itself. The Mirai botnet was an example of such a potential IoT risk trajectory and revealed the IoT's pervasiveness and transnational character. Mirai is a malware strain that successfully turned globally dispersed IoT devices, such as video cameras or baby monitors, into remotely controlled appliances that were used in one of the most disruptive Distributed Denial of Service (DDoS) attacks in 2016.[16] Due to the botnet's unprecedented size, attackers were able to target the internet's foundational infrastructure through attacks on Domain Name Service firms such as Dyn and OVH.[17] The assault of such elementary services affected many websites and caused downtime for popular online businesses. The core reason for Mirai's striking capability and magnitude was quickly found in the IoT's inherent security vulnerabilities. On the one hand, small-scale IoT devices often have limited capacity to provide sufficient cybersecurity, with manufacturers frequently failing to enforce password resets and automatic software updates. Industry actors often engage in trade-offs between adding security features and enhancing other attributes such as battery life and storage power. On the other hand, many IoT devices were also easily compromised because users themselves relied on default factory passwords. The Mirai attack points therefore to some of the threats and failures that an insecure and unregulated IoT market may pose.

Second, IoT devices and services are themselves targets of attacks, resulting in implications for the privacy and security of data. Malicious actors can exploit security vulnerabilities at the device-, network-, and cloud-level. They may take control over IoT-enabled cameras or connected and autonomous vehicles for malicious intent, to compromise the security and privacy of users and other innocent bystanders. Real-world examples include the Wi-Fi-enabled Hello Barbie™ doll that allowed unauthorized third parties to intercept its communication, with the potential to expose users' account information and MP3 files recorded by the doll.[18] Similarly, internet-connected stuffed animal toys were affected by a large-scale data breach that resulted in criminals holding the data for ransom.[19] These privacy concerns are exacerbated by a lack of consideration for security features at the product design stage,[20] opening the way for attacks on IoT devices and services, which require proper security precautions. This is especially true for the complex, safety-critical IoT systems found in such industries as healthcare and infrastructure.

Third, the IoT creates new cyber–physical security risks and increases the attack surface of devices overall. These risks differ from "traditional" threats, as they couple software and hardware risks, resulting not only in a complex and uncertain system surface but in growing attack vectors, sometimes with potentially life-threatening consequences. For instance, the Jeep Cherokee hack in 2016 allowed attackers to remotely control a car and take command of its steering and braking system.[21] Similarly, the recall of radio-controlled implantable cardiac pacemakers in 2017 highlighted the changing vulnerability landscape, as connected health devices were open to exploits from unauthorized users.[22] These examples showcase the cyber–physical risks associated with the IoT, and raises questions about the preparedness of current regulatory approaches to vehicle safety, ownership and liability, data protection, and cybersecurity.[23]

All of these outlined attack vectors are, of course, still evolving. The scale and range of IoT-specific problems will change as IoT devices and services take off. However, these challenges are not limited to deliberately malicious attacks, but also include problems arising from poor patch management, interoperability problems, and generic technological malfunction.[24] This leads to diverse and uncertain security challenges, and a demand for policy responses that relate to an increasingly heterogeneous array of IoT products and services.

3.3 Adaptive Policymaking in the Context of IoT

The IoT is a realm where there are many plausible future scenarios. One can envision substantial societal benefits and advantages from "smart" sensors and actuators, but also see how IoT security challenges may create profound uncertainties.[25] It is clearly challenging to develop policies that will perform well in all of the potential future conditions. In addition to the uncertainty, one of the biggest problems for policymakers is the speed with which technologies evolve. This is difficult to accommodate in the relatively slow, rigid process that marks "conventional" policymaking. For reasons of both pace and unpredictability, current policy mechanisms are, in many instances, not able to deal effectively with such rapid transformations.

Adaptive policymaking[26] is a concept that explicitly accounts for such inherent uncertainties and diverts from this "classical approach" of policymaking. It emerged from the global challenges of environmental policymaking,[27] in recognition that conventional policymaking mechanisms are ill-suited to manage such complexities, organizational and structural changes, and a nonequilibrium of behaviors – the same qualities that will come into play as the extensive IoT ecosystem develops. Policies need to be prepared for all potential futures; they have to be flexible enough to take immediate, short-term actions that cannot be deferred, as well as actions that may later become necessary.[28] Under this adaptive paradigm, policymakers need to create a strategic vision of the future and establish a framework to guide future responses that are sufficiently dynamic to meet changing circumstances.[29]

Adaptive policymaking approaches such as the Dynamic Adaptive Policy Pathway[30] start by describing the current situation, objectives, constraints, and uncertainties, and analyzing possible vulnerabilities and opportunities of futuristic scenarios. On the basis of these specifications, conditions for a policy to be considered "successful" are established and possible policy actions are identified.[31] This results in diverse pathways for actions, with corresponding contingency plans that are then assessed. After a thorough inquiry, one suitable, adaptive approach is chosen and implemented. Following its implementation, the plan is monitored and, if required, adjusted. Adaptive policymaking consequently focuses on evaluating and monitoring the validity of the assumptions underlying policies as time passes, knowledge increases, and events unfold. It allows for reassessment and corrective actions,[32] and provides resilience.[33]

The method is increasingly used in policy fields confronted with significant uncertainties, including climate change, population growth, and large-scale developments such as airports or transport systems.[34] There is potential for policy failures in these realms, as well as with innovations such as novel IoT technologies, highlighting how adaptive policy mechanisms could become suitable sets of actions.[35] The following sections analyze the UK's policy landscape based on its ability to adjust to the changing circumstances of the emerging IoT environment. This analysis should provide some general principles on adaptive policymaking overall.

3.4 The UK Policy Landscape

The UK government's approach to the IoT has so far been one of minimum intervention, and there is not yet a clear regulatory model for this emerging ecosystem. Although the aspiration is for the market to self-regulate and to internalize the costs of securing the IoT, market players have not yet converged on a single set of data protection, security, and safety principles for the IoT. Thus, the current standards landscape for the IoT remains profoundly fragmented.[36] Self-regulation refers to a system of rules, standards, and best practices "in which the regulatory target—either at the individual firm level or sometimes through an industry association that represents targets—imposes commands and consequences on itself."[37,38] This self-regulatory model leads to the creation of a community of shared practices. However, incidents such as the Mirai botnet highlight the limits of industry self-regulation at the transnational level, especially in efforts to achieve a global baseline of responsible security in IoT devices. The absence of universally agreed-upon and enforced security standards raises the question about the role of governments in establishing policies, rules, and regulations to set a baseline of responsible IoT security within their jurisdictions.

Up to now, the UK government has adopted a proportionate approach to regulation.[39] For instance, the 2014 "IoT Blackett Review" by the UK government Chief Scientific Advisor recommended that "[l]egislation should be kept to the minimum required to facilitate the uptake of the Internet of Things."[40] The UK government was encouraged by the authors of this publication to develop a flexible model for regulating the IoT, which would allow policymakers to react quickly and effectively to technological change. This milestone report marks the beginning of the UK's active engagement with the IoT and was followed by the establishment of IoTUK in 2015. IoTUK is a three-year national program designed to amplify the UK's IoT capability and increase adoption of IoT technologies and services; it is part of the government's £32m (or roughly $45m) IoT investment.[41]

At the ministerial level, the UK's digital portfolio is held by the Department for Digital, Culture, Media and Sport (DCMS). As the internet is part of the UK's critical infrastructure and a core part of the communication sector,[42] DCMS has been appointed as one of the leading departments that drive current internet as well as IoT-related policies. The UK government is actively investing in the IoT, supporting the establishment of projects such as a Smart City Demonstrator in Manchester (CityVerve)[43] and the PETRAS IoT Research

Hub, a consortium of nine leading UK universities that study IoT security and privacy issues.[44]

In October 2018, DCMS published its "Secure by Design" guidance which proposed the UK government's Code of Practice for industry actors developing, operating, and selling consumer IoT services and solutions. The UK government's recommended 13 guidelines include measures such as the need for IoT systems to be updatable, communication data to be encrypted, and the attack surface to be minimized. In the course of the development of the Code of Practice, DCMS sought input from a range of actors,including industry, academia, consumer bodies as well as other departments and international governments.[45] Following an extensive development and consultation and period, the guidelines bring together what is widely considered good practice in IoT security and set out practical steps for device manufacturers, IoT service providers, mobile application developers as well as retailers.[46]

In addition to DCMS, ministerial departments such as the Home Office, the Foreign Commonwealth Office, the Department for Transport, and the Cabinet Office also focus on cyber- and IoT security, and diverse agencies and cybersecurity centers were set up. In the past, these have directed the UK's cybersecurity agenda; they are now also involved in IoT-related matters. For example, in August 2017, the Department for Transport published eight principles for achieving good cybersecurity within the automotive sector.[47] The guide directs manufacturers to consider cybersecurity at every level of the design and engineering process of vehicles, and highlights the evolving interconnectedness of physical and cybersecurity considerations.

The pervasiveness of software and communication systems in all aspects of society is challenging the previously siloed approach to managing particular policy areas. Many governmental departments are exploring the IoT in their respective sectors, including trade, agriculture, health, and transport. This constellation creates further challenges for policymakers, who are now collectively responsible for cyber–physical security issues, making it increasingly difficult to delineate responsibilities and to coordinate activities. It adds to the fragmentation and coordination problems that the UK government faces, both in regards to "traditional" internet and evolving IoT security.

A recent addition to the UK's institutional landscape has been the National Cyber Security Centre (NCSC). Opened in February 2017, the NCSC is meant to unite previous independent cybersecurity attempts driven by individual departments – which had resulted in an "alphabet soup" of agencies active in cybersecurity. The coordination problem between these institutions was noted in a November 2015 speech by then-Chancellor of the Exchequer George Osborne at the British intelligence and security organization, the Government Communications Headquarters (GCHQ).[48] The NCSC replaces an array of relevant bodies and agencies involved in protecting the online environment. Thus, the NCSC not only acts as single point of contact for companies, particularly those that form Britain's critical national infrastructure, but also provides a cybersecurity "shop front" to the wider UK economy and society – including parts of the public and private sector, with which security services have traditionally not engaged directly (e.g. small- and medium-sized businesses, charities, and educational institutions).[49] In contrast to the NCSC, organizations such as GCHQ, the Centre for the Protection of National Infrastructure (CPNI), and the National Cyber Crime Unit (NCCU), which is part of the National Crime Agency, maintain a more select engagement with specific stakeholders.

The issue of cybersecurity is increasingly captured by multiple regulatory frameworks, creating a complex regulatory environment. For instance, under the Privacy and Electronic Communications Regulations (PECR 2003), providers of public electronic communication services are required to keep communications secure. However, given IoT pervasiveness, placing the responsibility for security on the communication component alone is both disproportionate and insufficient. Luckily, the recent EU NIS Directive (2016/1148), which was transposed into UK law in May 2018, extends security obligations and notification requirements to all digital service providers as well as to operators of essential services. Under this new legislation, the definition of "network and information systems" is extended to include: (i) "electronic communications networks"; (ii) "any device or group of interconnected or related devices, one or more of which, pursuant to a program, perform automatic processing of digital data"; and (iii) "digital data stored, processed, retrieved or transmitted by elements covered under points (i) and (ii) for the purposes of their operation, use, protection and maintenance" (Art 4(1) Directive 2016/1148). Thus, the NIS Directive expands security obligations to a broader set of network and information systems, most of which are components of the IoT ecosystem (e.g. groups of interconnected devices) or underpin the provision of essential services (e.g. operators of energy distribution systems and healthcare providers).

Similarly, current data-protection laws in the UK have undergone changes that will impact the IoT. The UK is currently operating under the 1995 Data Protection Directive (95/46/EC). However, in April 2016, the European Parliament and the European Council passed the General Data Protection Regulation (GDPR; 2016/679), which repeals the previous 1995 Data Protection Directive. The regulation will apply in the UK, as in all other EU member states, beginning 25 May 2018, and the UK government has confirmed that the decision to leave the EU "will not affect the commencement of the GDPR."[50] The UK is operating under the Data Protection Act 2018, which recently replaced the Data Protection Act 1998. The latest Act achieved Royal Assent in May 2018 and implemented the EU-wide General Data Protection Regulation (GDPR; 2016/679). The regulation introduces two critical principles of "data protection by design" and "data protection by default," which call for data integrity safeguards to be built into products and services from the earliest stage of development. Data minimization and privacy-friendly default settings are also required and are becoming the norm. All of these aspects will have direct relevance for privacy and data management in the IoT ecosystem, as the GDPR will affect most elements of this ecosystem, from how IoT devices are designed to how IoT service providers collect, store, and process data.

As the above review shows, the UK government's cybersecurity policy is still interlinked with that of the EU, but might change as soon as the country officially withdraws from the Union. Until then, established policies remain intact. The form and scope of future policy implementation will largely depend on the agreement that the UK and the EU establish – meaning that Brexit may pose a substantial problem to future IoT security and privacy plans.

In addition to these legislative measures, the UK government has developed cybersecurity-specific programs and strategies. The UK's main initiative to build a resilient cybersecurity sector is driven by its National Cyber Security Strategy (NCSS). The first strategy (2011–2016) focused on economic prosperity, protection of national security, and safeguarding the public's way of life by building a more trusted and resilient digital environment.[51] It was underpinned by the UK government's £860m (roughly $1.2b) National Cyber Security Programme. In its latest version (2016–2021), the UK increased the investment to £1.9 billion ($2.6b) and now focuses on policies and initiatives across defense, deterrence, and development, and, in a change to 2011, also refers to offensive cyber capabilities and the IoT.[52] Nonetheless, the emphasis given to internet-enabled devices and services is rather limited and in many instances primarily concerned with industrial IoT, rather than its far-reaching usage across diverse application areas.

Despite the considerable expenditures on initiatives like IoTUK, the UK cybersecurity policy landscape remains fragmented and has yet to develop a clear focus on the evolving interconnected environment. Many sectors retain an emphasis on conventional cybersecurity and data protection, which are undergoing changes and will ultimately create new information-sharing and coordination challenges for the diverse government agencies and departments mentioned above. The IoT is absent from many of the UK's cybersecurity related-documents, including the Cyber Essentials Scheme, which is used in government procurement;[53] the 2016 Cyber Security Regulation and Incentives Review, which assessed the need for additional regulation or mechanisms to boost cyber risk management across the wider economy;[54] and the UK's 2017 Digital Strategy, which provides a framework to increase digital infrastructure and advance digital skills in Britain.[55] In order to address the emerging IoT risks and opportunities, the UK government will need to consider an adaptive framework to guide future actions and be wary of the distinct issues this new ecosystem poses.

3.5   The IoT and its Governance Challenges

This brief overview of the UK's policy framework for privacy and security of the emerging IoT environment points to some fundamental governance gaps. These range from the implementation of data protection principles "freely given, specific, informed and unambiguous indication" of consent (GDPR, Recital 32) which is greatly complicated by the ubiquitous and pervasive nature of the IoT ecosystem, to the distribution of responsibility and liability between different stakeholders. Relevant actors will include consumers, service providers, manufacturers, network operators, and the state.

From a security perspective, the current regulatory framework is not yet equipped to adapt to the fast pace of technological development and the widespread use of IoT and related technologies such as advanced robotics and machine learning. This issue is entangled with the lack of economic incentives for firms to incorporate adequate security provisions into IoT products.[56] In the commercial realm, there are still many expectations placed on users when purchasing, setting up, maintaining, and disposing of IoT products securely.[57] Certification schemes and the development of an associated trust label for the IoT have been proposed at the EU level, and could also influence the UK market.[58] Such measures, including the EU Cybersecurity Act proposed in 2017 (COM/2017/0477) and a 2017 European Union Agency for Network and Information Security (ENISA) study on "Baseline Security Recommendations for IoT" could provide tools for IoT stakeholders to evaluate their systems' level of preparedness. Critics also emphasize the limitations of certification schemes, such as the time and effort needed to execute an evaluation.[59]

There are further questions concerning the types of standards, guidance, and best practices that will evolve in relation to the secure development and maintenance of IoT products and services, especially when it comes to software updates. This is especially challenging when looking at complex systems and the IoT-supported supply chain, where devices interconnect and frequently rely on one another.

First, when it comes to privacy, data protection, and processing, there are still questions about the extent to which all data that originate from "networked" objects are treated as personal data. These questions were raised in an "Opinion" of the Article 29 Data Protection Working Party,[60] which is a European advisory body focused on data protection, and by the Mauritius Declaration of the International Conference of Data Protection and Privacy Commissioners.[61] According to both bodies, data that could enable discernment of the life pattern of a specific individual or family should be considered personal data. In addition, the Article 29 Data Protection Working Party recognized that "the large amount of data processed automatically in the context of IoT entails risks of re-identification."[62] This approach has been regarded as enlarging the principle of "personal data" to reflect data that relates to the environment in which an individual operates, as well as data that is specifically anonymized. It further constitutes a position that has been perceived as creating uncertainty by generalizing the principle of "personal data," demanding further clarification.[63]

Second, there is the issue of "consent" as a fundamental data protection principle that gives "data subjects" control over the information being collected and processed. However, given the complex and heterogeneous nature of the IoT ecosystem, it might be difficult to obtain individual consent for each tier of the IoT.[64] These tiers range from the data collection, to the data storage, to the data processing phase that can cut across multiple suppliers and geographies. The Article 29 Working Party and the Mauritius Declaration have again reacted to this issue by proposing that end users should be "offered simple opt-outs and/or granular consent" in this process.[65] This approach is, once more, particularly challenging if applied uniformly to every aspect of data processing and data management. It raises the question of whether individual consent is in fact needed for every instance when information is accessed, or whether there are instances in which users can be sufficiently informed through a Terms of Service Agreement when signing up for an IoT-based service.

While these factors are challenging for the EU, the UK's planned exit by March 2019 raises questions about how the UK government will respond to these problems and whether it will align with future decisions made internally at EU level. The global and ubiquitous reach of the IoT will not allow for geographically limited regulation, and there will be a call for regional and international cooperation from which the UK will not be able to exclude itself.[66] Although the UK has the capacity to engage elsewhere, including the United States or Asia, the EU's size and scope permits it to sustain an active dialogue with key states such as China,[67] which might not be the case for the UK on its own. The UK's exit from the EU may consequently affect its status within international collaboration mechanisms, requiring the UK government to make forward-thinking and adaptive policies that can account for all the different futures made possible by the IoT and Brexit.

A policy development that is particularly worrying within the UK is the increasing expansion of surveillance powers that can have far-reaching consequences when applied to the IoT. For instance, the Investigatory Powers Act (2016; ruled unlawful by the Court of Appeal in January 2018) legalized a variety of tools for intercepting and hacking by UK security services.[68] Together with calls for banning encryption technologies,[69] such disproportionate legislations lay the foundation for possible misuse of internet-connected devices for monitoring purposes. As trust in IoT devices is still relatively low,[70] such dynamics, which intersect with the protection of human rights, may stifle the uptake, impacting negatively on the potential positive outcomes of the IoT.

In addition to these security and data protection concerns, questions about liability are core IoT governance challenges and come into play at different levels of the emerging IoT ecosystem. There are liability concerns in regards to the increasing reliance on the IoT in the supply chain, the evolving automation of decisions through machine learning, and the obligations that IoT manufacturers will have when it comes to product and potentially even software liability. As the EU product liability regime currently does not account for software flaws – despite the increasing interdependence of software and hardware – policymakers will need to consider mechanisms to deal with vulnerabilities that apply to services rather than solely products. Liability is a factor that might also require changes to the concept of a product warranty. Software liability is a particularly controversial topic within the industry.[71] The contestation around liability highlights the competing interests that shape the IoT ecosystem, with regulators having to mediate between diverging viewpoints and reconcile between market and consumer interests. One potential mechanism to deal with liability issues could be a shift to incentivize risk management through insurance mechanisms that would closely match the UK's status as an international banking and insurance hub and foster its position by leading the way in cyber risk and liability insurance.[72] Nonetheless, the enforcement of security, and even less likely privacy measures, cannot be left to the insurance sector alone. Such efforts also would require enforceable guidelines and policies, and the setting of minimum standards upon which risk assessments can be made.

One final challenge is that IoT security – like cybersecurity of the past – is as much about nontechnical solutions as it is about technical ones. IoT security has to account for the interaction of technology with people, processes, and organizations. This requires an established culture of security that equals other programs that foster cultures of safety and consumer awareness. The UK government has already taken an active stance to foster digital skills through its Digital Strategy,[73] as well as through activities such as the sociotechnical security blog that is part of the NCSC and the Research Institute in Science of Cyber Security (RISCS). While this does not mean that there are no further measures to be taken, there are signs that at least within this context, the UK has already managed to adjust to the changing circumstances in society through an adaptive policymaking approach that engages with a range of uncertain challenges that lie ahead.

3.6 Conclusion

This chapter explored the UK's IoT policy landscape as well as various unique governance challenges that the IoT introduces. The chapter functions as a foundational overview and snapshot of the current landscape of connections between IoT and cybersecurity governance, both in the academic as well as the practitioner's realm. It outlined the IoT's threat vectors and discussed the relevant risks and uncertainties of these interdependent systems. The assessment of the IoT's potential attack scenarios provided the foundation for the analysis of the UK government's approach to the IoT and the institutional structures and legislative foundation within which these cyber–physical systems are evolving. In particular, the diverse governance challenges that stretch from privacy-related questions to liability concerns highlight the need for flexible policy mechanisms.

Governments across the world are only beginning to develop IoT-specific policies and adjusting existing legislation to the novel privacy and security demands of the IoT. Consequently, this chapter argues that states such as the UK would do well to implement an adaptive policymaking approach that accounts for a range of potential futures and is flexible enough to foster innovation. Adaptive policymaking frameworks will enable the UK government to be more effective in managing future trade-offs and to be responsive to the uncertainties that the IoT presents. IoT-related risks require forward-thinking approaches to policymaking and governance that not only reactively respond to challenges, but proactively prepare for successes as much as for failures.

The chapter also points out some of the potential challenges and pitfalls that policymakers are facing. In particular, the lack of IoT security specifications will need to be addressed. This calls for a critical analysis of the current situation and potential futures, which can provide a basis for the development of policy pathways that are able to account for changing circumstances, and have built-in monitoring mechanisms to respond to new conditions.[74] With the establishment of the NCSC and the support of IoT-related research projects and innovation hubs, the UK government has already taken preemptive steps to prepare for the emerging IoT ecosystem. However, international and regional coordination that reflects the interconnected, co-dependent, and global character of these devices and services will also be required.

Lastly, the UK will also have to reflect critically upon the kind of "smart" society it aims to be. Any policy measures are expected to account for the security of the UK's infrastructure and society, while also guaranteeing human rights such as privacy. To achieve this, and strike a balance between diverse trade-offs and interests, the support of actors including industry, academia, and civil society will be needed. Input from all of these stakeholders is necessary, as is harmonization along the lines of the evolving international context. Such an adaptive and holistic approach can help the UK to remain connected to state-of-the-art research and concerns, have access to the European as well as international markets, and remain a significant player in this emerging field.

Notes

1 Friedemann Mattern and Christian Flörkemeier, "Vom Internet der Computer zum Internet der Dinge," *Informatik-Spektrum* 33, no. 2 (April 1, 2010): 107, https://doi.org/10.1007/s00287-010-0417-7.

2 China Academy of Information and Communication Technology and European Commission – DG CONNECT, "EU-China Joint White Paper on the Internet of Things" (Brussels: EU-China IoT Advisory Group, January 2016), 5, https://ec.europa.eu/digital-single-market/en/news/eu-china-joint-white-paper-internet-things.

3 Daniele Miorandi et al., "Internet of Things: Vision, Applications and Research Challenges," *Ad Hoc Networks* 10, no. 7 (September 2012): 1497–1516, https://doi.org/10.1016/j.adhoc.2012.02.016.

4 Lesley Fair, "D-Link Case Alleges Inadequate Internet of Things Security Practices | Federal Trade Commission," *Federal Trade Commission*, January 5, 2017, https://www.ftc.gov/news-events/blogs/business-blog/2017/01/d-link-case-alleges-inadequate-internet-things-security.

5 S. Hiremath, G. Yang, and K. Mankodiya, "Wearable Internet of Things: Concept, Architectural Components and Promises for Person-Centered Healthcare," in 2014 4th International Conference on Wireless Mobile Communication and Healthcare – Transforming Healthcare Through Innovations in Mobile and Wireless Technologies (MOBIHEALTH), 2014, 304–307, https://ieeexplore.ieee.org/document/7015971.

6 Andrea Castillo and Adam D. Thierer, "Projecting the Growth and Economic Impact of the Internet of Things," SSRN Scholarly Paper (Rochester, NY: Social Science Research Network, June 15, 2015), https://papers.ssrn.com/abstract=2618794.

7 Jim Snell and Christian Lee, "The Internet of Things Changes Everything, or Does It ? – Your Handy Guide to Legal Issue-Spotting in a World Where Everything Is Connected," *The Computer and Internet Lawyer* 32, no. 11 (2015): 1–8.

8 Mark Webber, "The Regulatory Outlook for the Internet of Things - Privacy, Security and Information Law," *Blog, Fieldfisher*, October 22, 2014, http://privacylawblog.fieldfisher.com/2014/part-2-the-regulatory-outlook-for-the-internet-of-things/.

9 "Internet of Things (IoT) Cybersecurity Improvement Act of 2017." S. 1691, 115th Congress, 2017. https://www.congress.gov/115/bills/s1691/BILLS-115s1691is.pdf.

10 Juergen Maier, "Made Smarter. Review 2017" (London: HM Government, 2017), https://assets.publishing.service.gov.uk/government/uploads/system/uploads/attachment_data/file/655570/20171027_MadeSmarter_FINAL_DIGITAL.pdf.

11 Department for Culture, Media and Sport, "UK Digital Strategy 2017" (London: Department for Culture, Media and Sport, March 1, 2017), https://www.gov.uk/government/publications/uk-digital-strategy/uk-digital-strategy.

12 Carr, Madeline and Leonie Tanczer (2018). "UK Cybersecurity Industrial Policy: An Analysis of Drivers, Market Failures and Interventions." *Journal of Cyber Policy*, 3.3 (2018): 430–444. https://doi.org/10.1080/23738871.2018.1550523

13 W. E. Walker and VAWJ Marchau, "Dealing with Uncertainty in Policy Analysis and Policymaking," *Integrated Assessment* 4, no. 1 (2003): 1–4.

14 N. Cam-Winget, A. R. Sadeghi, and Y. Jin, "Invited: Can IoT Be Secured: Emerging Challenges in Connecting the Unconnected," in *2016 53nd ACM/ EDAC/IEEE Design Automation Conference* (DAC), 2016, 1–6, https://doi. org/10.1145/2897937.2905004.

15 EPFL IRGC, "Governing Cybersecurity Risks and Benefits of the Internet of Things: Connected Medical & Health Devices and Connected Vehicles" (Lausanne: EPFL International Risk Governance Center, 2017), https://www. irgc.org/wp-content/uploads/2017/04/IRGC.-2017.-Cybersecurity-in-the-IoT.-Workshop-report.pdf.

16 Global Semiconductor Alliance and McKinsey & Company, "Security in the Internet of Things. How Semiconductor Companies Can Address the Major Obstacle to IoT Growth, and Benefit in the Process" (Texas: Global Semiconductor Alliance & McKinsey & Company, April 2017), http://www. mckinsey.com/industries/semiconductors/our-insights/security-in-the-internet-of-things.

17 Sean Gallagher, "How One Rent-a-Botnet Army of Cameras and DVRs Caused Internet Chaos," *Ars Technica UK*, October 30, 2016, https:// arstechnica.co.uk/information-technology/2016/10/inside-the-machine-uprising-how-cameras-dvrs-took-down-parts-of-the-internet/.

18 Somerset Recon, "Hello Barbie Security: Part 2 - Analysis," *Somerset Recon*, January 25, 2016, http://www.somersetrecon.com/blog/2016/1/21/ hello-barbie-security-part-2-analysis.

19 Dan Goodin, "Creepy IoT Teddy Bear Leaks >2 Million Parents' and Kids' Voice Messages," *Ars Technica UK*, February 28, 2017, https://arstechnica. co.uk/information-technology/2017/02/creepy-iot-teddy-bear-leaks-2-million-parents-and-kids-voice-messages/.

20 Mikko Hypponen and Linus Nyman, "The Internet of (Vulnerable) Things: On Hypponen's Law, Security Engineering, and IoT Legislation," *Technology Innovation Management Review* 7, no. 4 (2017): 5–11.

21 Jordan Golson, "Jeep Hackers at It Again, This Time Taking Control of Steering and Braking Systems," *The Verge*, August 2, 2016, https://www. theverge.com/2016/8/2/12353186/car-hack-jeep-cherokee-vulnerability-miller-valasek.

22 Chris Morris, "465,000 Pacemakers Recalled on Hacking Fears," *Fortune*, August 31, 2017, http://fortune.com/2017/08/31/pacemaker-recall-fda/.

23 Irina Brass, Madeline Carr, Leonie Tanczer, Carsten Maple, Jason Blackstock, "Unbundling the Emerging Cyber-Physical Risks in Connected and Autonomous Vehicles," Connected and Autonomous Vehicles: The Emerging Legal Challenges (London: Pinsent Masons, May 2017), https://www. pinsentmasons.com/PDF/2017/Freedom-to-Succeed-AMT/Connected-autonomous-vehicles-report-2017.pdf.

24 Tanczer, Leonie, Ine Steenmans, Irina Brass, and Madeline Carr. *Networked World: Risks and Opportunities in the Internet of Things*. London: Lloyds's of London (2018). https://www.lloyds.com/news-and-risk-insight/risk-reports/library/technology/networked-world

25 Tanczer, Leonie, Ine Steenmans, Miles Elsden, Jason Blackstock, and Madeline Carr. "Emerging risks in the IoT ecosystem: Who's Afraid of the Big Bad Smart Fridge?" In *Living in the Internet of Things: Cybersecurity of the IoT – 2018*. London, UK: IET (2018). https://ieeexplore.ieee.org/document/8379720

26 Darren Swanson, Stephan Barg, Stephen Tyler, Henry Venema, Sanjay Tomar, Suruchi Bhadwal, Sreeja Nair, Dimple Roy, and John Drexhage, "Seven Tools for Creating Adaptive Policies," *Technological Forecasting and Social Change, Two Special Sections: Risk and Technology Addressing Deep Uncertainty Using Adaptive Policies*, 77, no. 6 (July 1, 2010): 924–939, https://doi.org/10.1016/j.techfore.2010.04.005.

27 Swanson et al.

28 Walker and Marchau, "Dealing with Uncertainty in Policy Analysis and Policymaking."

29 Marjolijn Haasnoot, Jan H. Kwakkel, Warren E. Walker, and Judithter Maat, "Dynamic Adaptive Policy Pathways: A Method for Crafting Robust Decisions for a Deeply Uncertain World," *Global Environmental Change* 23, no. 2 (April 2013): 485–498, https://doi.org/10.1016/j.gloenvcha.2012.12.006.

30 Haasnoot et al.

31 V. A. W. J. Marchau, W. E. Walker, and G. P. van Wee, "Dynamic Adaptive Transport Policies for Handling Deep Uncertainty," *Technological Forecasting and Social Change, Two Special Sections: Risk and Technology Addressing Deep Uncertainty Using Adaptive Policies*, 77, no. 6 (July 1, 2010): 940–950, https://doi.org/10.1016/j.techfore.2010.04.006.

32 Marchau, Walker, and van Wee.

33 Walker and Marchau, "Dealing with Uncertainty in Policy Analysis and Policymaking."

34 Haasnoot et al., "Dynamic Adaptive Policy Pathways."

35 Swanson et al., "Seven Tools for Creating Adaptive Policies."

36 Rolf H. Weber, "Internet of Things – New Security and Privacy Challenges," *Computer Law & Security Review* 26, no. 1 (January 2010): 23–30, https://doi.org/10.1016/j.clsr.2009.11.008; AIOTI WG03, "High Level Architecture (HLA; Release 3.0)" (Brussels: Alliance for Internet of Things Innovation, 2017), https://aioti.eu/wp-content/uploads/2017/06/AIOTI-HLA-R3-June-2017.pdf; GSMA, "IoT Security Guidelines Overview Document. Version 1.1" (unknown: GSM Association, 2016), https://www.gsma.com/iot/wp-content/uploads/2016/02/CLP.11-v1.1.pdf.

37 Cary Coglianese and Evan Mendelson, "Meta-Regulation and Self-Regulation," in *The Oxford Handbook of Regulation*, ed. Robert Baldwin, Martin Cave, and Martin Lodge (Oxford: Oxford University Press, 2010), 150.

38 Brass, Irina, Leonie Tanczer,Madeline Carr, Miles Elsden, and Jason Blackstock. "Standardising a Moving Target: The Development and Evolution of IoT Security Standards." In *Living in the Internet of Things: Cybersecurity of the IoT – 2018.* London, UK: IET (2018). https://ieeexplore.ieee.org/document/8379711

39 Better Regulation Task Force, "Principles of Good Regulation" (London: Cabinet Office, 2003), http://webarchive.nationalarchives.gov.uk/20100407173247/http://archive.cabinetoffice.gov.uk/brc/upload/assets/www.brc.gov.uk/principlesleaflet.pdf.

40 UK Government Chief Scientific Adviser, "The Internet of Things (Blackett Review): Making the Most of the Second Digital Revolution" (London: Government Office for Science, December 18, 2014), 9, https://www.gov.uk/government/uploads/system/uploads/attachment_data/file/409774/14-1230-internet-of-things-review.pdf.

41 IoTUK, "IoTUK Launches to Support and Advance the UK's Internet of Things Capability," *IoTUK* (blog), September 10, 2015, https://iotuk.org.uk/iotuk-launches-to-support-and-accelerate-the-uks-internet-of-things-capability/.

42 Cabinet Office, "Summary of the 2016 Sector Security and Resilience Plans" (London: Cabinet Office, November 2016), https://www.gov.uk/government/uploads/system/uploads/attachment_data/file/568546/sector_security_resilience_plans_14_11_2016.pdf.

43 CityVerve, "CityVerve Manchester: Manchester's Smart City Demonstrator," *CityVerve*, 2017, http://www.cityverve.org.uk/.

44 PETRAS, "PETRAS IoT Research Hub," June 23, 2017, https://www.petrashub.org/.

45 Tanczer, Leonie, John Blythe, Fareeha Yahya, Irina Brass, Miles Elsden, Jason Blackstock, and Madeline Carr. *Summary Literature Review of Industry Recommendations and International Developments on IoT Security.* London: Department for Digital, Culture, Media & Sport; PETRAS IoT Hub (2018). 1–18.

46 Department for Digital, Culture, Media and Sport. *Code of Practice for Consumer IoT Security.* London: Department for Digital, Culture, Media & Sport (2018). 1–24.

47 Department of Transport and Centre for the Protection of National Infrastructure, "The Key Principles of Cyber Security for Connected and Automated Vehicles" (London: HM Government, August 2017), https://www.gov.uk/government/uploads/system/uploads/attachment_data/file/624302/cyber-security-connected-automated-vehicles-key-principles.pdf.

48 George Osborne, "Chancellor's Speech to GCHQ on Cyber Security," *GOV. UK*, 17, November 17, 2015, https://www.gov.uk/government/speeches/chancellors-speech-to-gchq-on-cyber-security.

49 The Committee of Public Accounts, "Protecting Information across Government. Thirty-Eighth Report of Session 2016–17" (London: House of

Commons, February 3, 2017), https://www.publications.parliament.uk/pa/cm201617/cmselect/cmpubacc/769/769.pdf.

50 Information Commissioner's Office, "Overview of the General Data Protection Regulation (GDPR)," *ICO.org.uk*, October 20, 2017, https://ico.org.uk/for-organisations/data-protection-reform/overview-of-the-gdpr/.

51 Cabinet Office, "The UK Cyber Security Strategy. Protecting and Promoting the UK in a Digital World" (London: HM Government, November 2011), https://www.gov.uk/government/uploads/system/uploads/attachment_data/file/60961/uk-cyber-security-strategy-final.pdf.

52 Cabinet Office, "National Cyber Security Strategy 2016–2021" (London: HM Government, November 1, 2016), https://www.ncsc.gov.uk/content/files/protected_files/document_files/National%20Cyber%20Security%20Strategy%20v20.pdf.

53 HM Government, "Cyber Essentials," Cyber Aware, June 17, 2017, https://www.cyberaware.gov.uk/cyberessentials/.

54 H.M. Government, "Cyber Security Regulation and Incentives Review" (HM Government, 2016), https://www.gov.uk/government/uploads/system/uploads/attachment_data/file/579442/Cyber_Security_Regulation_and_Incentives_Review.pdf.

55 Department for Culture, Media and Sport, "UK Digital Strategy 2017."

56 M. Lelarge and J. Bolot, "Economic Incentives to Increase Security in the Internet: The Case for Insurance," in *IEEE INFOCOM 2009* (Proceedings of the Twenty-Eighth IEEE International Conference on Computer Communications, Rio de Janeiro, 2009), 1494–1502, https://doi.org/10.1109/INFCOM.2009.5062066.

57 John Blythe Susan Michie, Jeremy Watson, Carmen E. Lefevre. "Internet of Things in Healthcare: Identifying Key Malicious Threats, End-User Protective and Problematic Behaviours" (London: PETRAS IoT Research Hub, 2017).

58 Infineon et al., "Common Position on Cybersecurity" (Heraklion, Greece: European Union Agency for Network and Information Security, December 2016), https://www.enisa.europa.eu/publications/enisa-position-papers-and-opinions/infineon-nxp-st-enisa-position-on-cybersecurity; European Commission, "COM(2017) 477 Final/2: Proposal for a Regulation of the European Parliament and the Council on ENISA, the 'EU Cybersecurity Agency', and Repealing Regulation (EU) 526/2013, and on Information and Communication Technology Cybersecurity Certification ("Cybersecurity Act")" (Brussels: European Commission, April 10, 2017), 2, https://ec.europa.eu/transparency/regdoc/rep/1/2017/EN/COM-2017-477-F1-EN-MAIN-PART-1.PDF.

59 Gianmaarco Baldini, Antonio Skarmeta, Elizabeta Fourneret, Ricardo Neisse, Bruno Legeard, Franck Le Gall, "Security Certification and Labelling in Internet of Things," in *2016 IEEE 3rd World Forum on Internet of Things (WF-IoT)*, Reston, VA, USA: IEEE, 2016, 627–632, https://doi.org/10.1109/WF-IoT.2016.7845514.

60 Article 29 Data Protection Working Party, "Opinion 8/2014 on the on Recent Developments on the Internet of Things" (Brussels: Article 29 Data Protection Working Party, 2014), https://www.dataprotection.ro/servlet/ViewDocument?id=1088.

61 Jacob Kohnstamm and Drudeisha Madhub, "Mauritius Declaration on the Internet of Things" (*36th International Conference of Data Protection and Privacy Commissioners*, Balaclava, Mauritius: International Conference of Data Protection and Privacy Commissioners, 2014), https://icdppc.org/wp-content/uploads/2015/02/Mauritius-Declaration.pdf.

62 Article 29 Data Protection Working Party, "Opinion 8/2014 on the on Recent Developments on the Internet of Things," 10.

63 Antonis Patrikios, "What Does EU Regulatory Guidance on the Internet of Things Mean in Practice? Part 1," *Blog, Fieldfisher* October 31, 2014, http://privacylawblog.fieldfisher.com/2014/what-does-eu-regulatory-guidance-on-the-internet-of-things-mean-in-practice-part-1/; Antonis Patrikios, "What Does EU Regulatory Guidance on the Internet of Things Mean in Practice? Part 2," *Blog, Fieldfisher*, November 1, 2014, http://privacylawblog.fieldfisher.com/2014/what-does-eu-regulatory-guidance-on-the-internet-of-things-mean-in-practice-part-2/.

64 Tanczer, Leonie, Madeline Carr, Irina Brass, Ine Steenmans, and Jason Blackstock. *IoT and Its Implications for Informed Consent*. PETRAS IoT Hub, STEaPP: London (2017). https://papers.ssrn.com/sol3/papers.cfm?abstract_id=3117293

65 Article 29 Data Protection Working Party, "Opinion 8/2014 on the on Recent Developments on the Internet of Things," 21.

66 Weber, "Internet of Things – New Security and Privacy Challenges."

67 China Academy of Information and Communication Technology and European Commission – DG CONNECT, "EU-China Joint White Paper on the Internet of Things."

68 Leonie Tanczer, "The 'Snooper's Charter' Is a Threat to Academic Freedom," *The Guardian*, December 1, 2016, sec. Higher Education Network, https://www.theguardian.com/higher-education-network/2016/dec/01/the-snoopers-charter-is-a-threat-to-academic-freedom.

69 Andrew Sparrow, "WhatsApp Must Be Accessible to Authorities, Says Amber Rudd," *The Guardian*, March 26, 2017, sec. Technology, https://www.theguardian.com/technology/2017/mar/26/intelligence-services-access-whatsapp-amber-rudd-westminster-attack-encrypted-messaging.

70 Robin Murdoch and Paul Johnson, "Digital Trust in the IoT Era" (Dublin: Accenture, 2015), https://www.accenture.com/t20160318T035041__w__/us-en/_acnmedia/Accenture/Conversion-Assets/LandingPage/Documents/3/Accenture-3-LT-3-Digital-Trust-IoT-Era.pdf.

71 AIOTI WG04, "AIOTI Digitisation of Industry Policy Recommendations" (Brussels: The Alliance for the Internet of Things Innovation, 2016), https://

aioti.eu/wp-content/uploads/2017/03/AIOTI-Digitisation-of-Ind-policy-doc-Nov-2016.pdf; AIOTI WG04, "AIOTI Working Group 4 – Policy" (Brussels: Alliance for Internet of Things Innovation, October 15, 2015), https://aioti.eu/wp-content/uploads/2017/03/AIOTIWG04Report2015-Policy-Issues.pdf.

72 Tanczer et al., *Networked World*.

73 Department for Culture, Media and Sport, "UK Digital Strategy 2017."

74 Swanson et al., "Seven Tools for Creating Adaptive Policies."

4

Birds of a Feather

Strategies for Collective Cybersecurity in the Aviation Ecosystem

Emilian Papadopoulos and Evan Sills

Good Harbor Security Risk Management, Washington, DC, USA

4.1 Introduction: The Challenge of Ecosystem Risk

Over 100 000 commercial and cargo flights occur every day.[1] Ensuring the safety and security of the airplanes, airports, goods, passengers, and other people in and around (and below) the ecosystem requires an immense amount of domestic and international cooperation by public and private organizations. As technological innovations increase connectivity between people and devices, the aviation industry faces unique cybersecurity challenges. Hub airports and "just in time" connections mean that one airline's problems can have spillover effects on the rest of the industry.

In addition to icons such as Lufthansa, American Airlines, United Airlines, LAX, and ORD, the aviation industry depends on thousands of smaller organizations as well. These range from regional airports to luggage-management organizations to manufacturers of In-Flight Entertainment (IFE) systems. At airports, vendors give employees and contractors access to sensitive areas where a malevolent or negligent person could cause catastrophic harm to physical and communication systems. Government also has many relationships with aviation, including purchasing aircraft, regulating safe air travel, administering Air Traffic Control (ATC), and owning and supplying important information, like GPS and weather data, to the industry.

Increasingly, these organizations are not only providing luggage, meals, and engine parts to airports and Original Equipment Manufacturers (OEMs) but also electronic tickets, weather data, and flight maps. When these data feeds are interrupted, the entire industry can be brought to a halt. In 2016 and 2017, Delta,[2] Southwest,[3] and British Airways experienced major information technology (IT) outages that forced the cancellation of thousands of flights and had worldwide ripple effects. In addition to critical internal corporate IT systems,

Rewired: Cybersecurity Governance, First Edition. Edited by Ryan Ellis and Vivek Mohan.
© 2019 John Wiley & Sons, Inc. Published 2019 by John Wiley & Sons, Inc.

airports and government systems such as ATC administrators also maintain numerous IT systems important to safe air travel. Finally, the industry must survive in a quickly digitizing world with hardware that was not built for an interconnected age. A bevy of digital devices now form the core of any flying experience, from Electronic Flight Bags (EFBs: devices, like smart tablets, that have replaced the suitcases full of flight data that pilots used to carry) to IFE systems to the Internet of Things (IoT) in airports.

Balancing on top of these aging, complex, and just-in-time systems are both a global economy and consumer confidence that is easily shaken by accidents and attacks. While the global transport of food, medicines, and mail can occur with little consumer interaction, many consumers can simply choose not to travel if they do not trust that they will land safely and with minimal avoidable delays. After the tragic attacks occurred on 11 September 2001, the aviation industry lost $22 billion and took three years to recover.[4] The trust between consumers, government, and airlines can be easily damaged by cyberattacks as well as physical attacks. Ransomware or disruptive malware such as WannaCry[5] and NotPetya[6] can attack systems indiscriminately and have crippled interconnected systems at law firms, hospitals, and manufacturing facilities. Such an attack on an airline, airport, or airplane (if the malware were to end up there) could result in severe disruption.

Managing these interconnected, digital risks has required a different approach to cyber-risk governance. While individual airlines also have traditional corporate IT challenges, the collective risk shared by the ecosystem cannot be mitigated adequately on an individual basis. Aviation industry members have realized that they must coordinate. While it is necessary that each organization manage its own cyber risks, interactions and shared resources also necessitate coordination and cooperation between organizations.

This case study reviews how the aviation community is developing a collective approach to cyber-risk management. Through statements of principles, mapping of the complex aviation supply chain, and a focus on table-top exercises, the aviation industry has approached cyber risk differently from many other industries. Due to the symbolic importance of the aviation industry and its many public and private partners, industry leaders have focused on understanding how collective, just-in-time incident response can be shaped to meet the needs of the aviation industry membership.

4.1.1 Aviation Is a National and Global Target

Due to the inherent dangers of flying and the complex equipment required to make flight possible, federal oversight has existed for almost as long as regular air travel. In its earliest days, aviators wanted federal oversight to ensure that pilots were properly trained and planes were adequately maintained.[7] This culminated in the Air Commerce Act (ACA), which created the Aeronautics Branch, responsible for safety oversight, within the Department of Commerce. Ultimately, this gave way to the Civil Aeronautics Act and the Federal Aviation Agency.[8]

Despite this oversight, aviation has faced serious risks from a variety of accidents and natural hazards. Increases in air travel after World War II led to a strain on oversight capabilities, contributing to a peak of 2373 deaths from 72 airliner accidents in 1972.[9] While air travel has become markedly safer since then (there were only 17 accidents, causing 258 deaths, in 2016), new threat vectors have been added as aircraft become increasingly dependent on IT and Internet-connected devices.

Alongside concerns related to equipment failures, weather, and bad information, terrorists have also played a role in the evolution of flight safety. While the first recorded aircraft hijacking took place in 1931, terrorist hijacking of airplanes peaked in the 1970s, until regulations made boarding aircraft with weapons increasingly difficult. Near-universal physical screening of passengers and baggage began in 1973, when the public was so weary of these attacks that people welcomed the inconvenience of delays in the name of safety.[10] While occasional, significant incidents continued to occur, such as the bombing of Pan Am flight 103 in 1988, aviation security largely became a secondary or "solved" issue until 11 September 2001.

The 9/11 terrorist attacks prompted a fundamental restructuring of American aviation oversight. The use of an airplane as a weapon allowed manufacturers, regulators, and passengers to reevaluate every moment from ticketing to boarding. The Transportation Security Administration (TSA), part of the Department of Homeland Security, was created after the attacks to ensure security in US airports and air travel, using classified intelligence, canine units, air marshals, screening, and any other tool that might be effective at reducing the risk.[11] As the number of federal employees focused on protecting the aviation ecosystem has increased, coordinating roles and responsibilities, sharing information, and responding to private-sector requests has become more complicated.

In recent years, the aviation system has remained both a target for malicious actors[12] and a vulnerability that demands prioritization from the US government. In his 2013 State of the Union Address, President Barack Obama identified air traffic control systems, alongside the power grid and financial institutions, as critical infrastructure targeted by enemies.[13] While the physical terrorist threat is clear in society's mind, it is important to distill the potential harms relevant to the aviation industry.

4.1.1.1 The Cyber Harm

Discussions of the cyber threat to aviation typically start and end with the risk of attackers "hacking airplanes" and causing loss of life. While this is of course an important concern, there are other disruptive and destructive possibilities that could harm components of the aviation ecosystem as well as individual liberty and privacy. Many of these attacks or incidents would be just as painful to the industry: reducing trust, impeding global trade, and harming the employees, shareholders, and customers of the aviation industry.

4.1.1.2   *Economic Harm*[14]

In June 2017, the British Airways IT outage provided some insight into how expensive a relatively limited outage can be for an airline. It took approximately three days to resolve the outage and rebook all the stranded passengers, costing British Airways over $100 million.[15] A one-day loss for any North American airline would have cost almost $50 million in 2016.[16] The International Air Transport Association expects net profits of almost $30 billion in 2017 for the global industry as a whole (down from a historic peak of $35.6 billion in 2016).[17]

Aviation has become integral to the global economy, and therefore a target to anyone who wishes to interrupt or harm international movement. As a former head of Boeing's commercial airplanes division once stated, "[T]he global aviation system is a very complex and integrated system. As dependence on this system increases, it also becomes a target for those seeking to disrupt the industry and the global economy. The impacts of an attack on our national air transportation system would be felt far beyond the aerospace industry, and solutions must take those interests into account."[18] These substantial losses would affect the aviation and aerospace industry in addition to many others in the global economy.

Traditional financial cybercrime is also a challenge for the aviation industry. Criminals typically target airline credit cards, frequent flyer miles,[19] and personal information. Airlines and the third-party vendors that support this industry must protect their corporate networks in addition to meeting the operational challenges of flight safety.[20] Direct financial theft and vendor delays can be compounded in shareholder losses when investors lose confidence in the aviation ecosystem.

4.1.1.3   Political/Governmental Harm

The events of 9/11 were a direct hit not only to the aviation industry but to the US government as well. Citizens generally believe that the Federal Aviation Administration oversees and assures safe civilian air travel, with the National Transportation Safety Board thoroughly investigating occasional problems when they arise. A successful cyberattack reduces the trust of citizens in these institutions and inhibits the government's ability to execute its missions.

4.1.1.4   Reputational Harm

Being a passenger on an airplane is a display of trust in the airline. Generally, customers have options: they can choose from a variety of airlines (or other modes of transportation) for any given departure and arrival combination. Most passengers choose a flight based on a combination of convenience, timing, and cost, because all US airlines are considered safe.

A single cyberattack – or worse, a repeated attack – affecting one airline or a subset of aircraft used by certain airlines would have major negative consequences. Reputational harm is frequently hard to measure, due to the many factors involved for a given customer. However, single events, like the Exxon Valdez oil spill,[21] can leave scars on a corporation for decades. While society seems to have an increasingly short memory, the list of companies known for major cyberattacks committed against them is lengthy and growing: Target,[22] Sony Pictures,[23] Yahoo,[24] and Equifax.[25]

4.1.1.5 Physical Harm

Using cyber means to inflict physical harm to an aircraft or component of the aviation ecosystem remains theoretical for now, thankfully. While the aircraft is understandably the focus for aviation safety, there are additional systems that could be attacked by cyber means to cause physical harm. This could happen at airports (e.g. on automated systems such as baggage movers, or with building management systems) as well as in the supply chain, where industrial cyberattacks could be devastating and delay the production of aircraft for months.

4.1.1.6 Psychological and Emotional Harm

Governments, corporations, and citizens trust airlines today to move people and cargo quickly around the world. In the months after 9/11, many people refused to fly out of fear that another terrorist attack would target their plane. A cyberattack against an airliner or cargo jet, particularly an attack without an easily identified and executed remedy, could cause many to resort to alternative forms of transportation. While this might be a boon to trains and ports, it would slow down global trade and tourism.

4.1.2 Domestic and International Challenges of Aviation Governance

To understand the governance challenges of the aviation industry, it is necessary to identify the public and private actors in this ecosystem. The complex array of regulators, vendors, and producers has grown as the major airlines have consolidated, leaving the system vulnerable to one major attack impacting a disproportionate number of key players. In order to govern cyber risks, this ecosystem needs the ability to identify threats, regulate or enforce security requirements, and respond to cyberattacks across organizations.

Within the United States, the aviation ecosystem has three main components. One is the government. Numerous government agencies have some responsibility for aviation, from the FAA and TSA to NASA and the Department of Defense. These agencies have a range of missions and responsibilities for identifying, protecting, and responding to cyber threats and attacks. In some areas, it is clear who is in charge: for example, the FAA operates the Air Traffic Management system around the country. In other areas, like responsibility for cyber threats at airports, several agencies could be in charge, and many regulations could be read to include or not include cyber threats.

The FAA's airworthiness standards require special mention because they create a difficult challenge for the industry as a whole. In order to receive certification to fly in the United States, software must work only as intended.[26] Typically (and not specific to aviation), 1 vulnerability is found in every 1000 lines of code (and this is a conservative estimate).[27] A Boeing 787 Dreamliner requires seven million lines of code to fly.[28] Even assuming an extraordinary level of caution, it is hard for many to fathom the idea that an aircraft as complex as a Dreamliner has no software vulnerabilities. Yet, to fly, the aircraft must be certified that there is no "non-intended function" in the software. This is one example of the challenge of using a static regulation in an area as complex as the software on an aircraft.

In the private sector, it is useful to distinguish the OEMs producing the aircraft (a second component in the aviation ecosystem) from the airlines, the airports, and the supply chain that supports them in their day-to-day operations (collectively, a third component). Building an aircraft requires thousands of components, many of which come with their own code, brought together by the OEM, most commonly Boeing or Airbus. This takes years from design through production and is regulated by a combination of FAA requirements and OEM contractual demands. The supply chain that enables airports and airlines to operate includes everything from maintenance teams to food services to airline reservation systems. There are hundreds of companies that could be targeted for sensitive information or disrupted in a way that could affect the entire industry.

Add to this the fact that thousands of flights leave from and arrive in the United States every day. Other countries have their own airlines, supply chains, and airports with their own risks, some physical and some related to software and hardware systems. Organizations such as IATA and CANSO provide international regulation of some components of international aviation. There are also international conventions, such as the Chicago Convention,[29] which established ICAO, and the Tokyo Convention,[30] which governs crimes committed onboard aircraft. Cyber threats have added a new layer of concerns to these structures and do not fit neatly into any existing governance model.

International organizations and foreign regulatory authorities have authority and do provide tremendous oversight and resources to ensure that aircraft operated today meet all applicable safety standards. Still, challenges remain: sharing information with international partners in a global industry; addressing security risks and staying efficient while maintaining rigorous safety standards;

ensuring security while enabling innovation for new entrants, such as unmanned aerial systems (UAS, i.e. drones); accommodating large and small companies that have vastly different resources for cybersecurity; and, being transparent about security efforts without sharing so much information that it creates vulnerabilities or causes undue panic for the traveling public. Balancing these challenges has become paramount for an industry that knows another attack could cause the same multiyear losses and dramatic reduction in confidence (not to mention the potential loss of life) that happened after 9/11.

Finally, the aviation industry has one additional wrinkle that makes it unlike most other industries: an aircraft is expected to operate for 30 or 40 years. Technology changes much faster, and intended functions can change drastically. Adding connectivity to systems that were not designed to provide secure connections between particular components can lead to additional vulnerabilities. As careful as aircraft manufacturers are, ensuring product security for aircraft is more complex than for many consumer goods, and the consequences are significantly greater.

An airplane takes years to build. Changing one line of code on an aircraft computer can require a year of testing. In that time span, an aircraft in operations may be touched by thousands of maintenance workers, pilots, flight attendants, and passengers, any of whom may attempt to alter or insert malicious code. This ecosystem is not conducive to adapting to the rapid pace of cybersecurity. The government and the private sector know they must work together and are attempting a shared responsibility approach that recognizes the interconnected nature of the aviation industry.

4.2 Progress So Far

In the face of these challenges, participants in the aviation sector have made significant efforts to improve cybersecurity and the collective governance of cybersecurity challenges. Before reviewing these efforts, it is worth observing some long-established cultural attributes and experiences of the aviation sector that form the foundation and background for many of today's efforts in cybersecurity. The aviation sector has, for a long time, been a global industry; cooperation across national lines is an established practice. The aviation industry understands the critical importance of safety and has achieved a remarkable "five 9s" record of reliability and safety, even as it operates tens of thousands of just-in-time flights daily in different systems and environments around the world. The aviation industry, especially airplane manufacturers and airlines, recognizes that rigorous design, engineering, training, and culture are all critical to achieving this safety record; changes are generally methodical and slow, and are tested and certified before being put into service. Finally, evolution in the aviation industry – as in other industries – has often been driven by a relatively small number of leading nations and companies (especially airlines and manufacturers), which set the tone and often catalyze the development of guidelines and standards. Yet, industry standards and guidelines must work for airports, nations, airlines, and suppliers both large and small. These attributes form the backdrop of the aviation industry's efforts in recent years to improve cybersecurity and the collective governance of cybersecurity challenges.

This section provides a timeline and analysis of key improvements in aviation cybersecurity. It is impossible to pinpoint "the beginning" of these efforts or a single, most important effort. However, there is one event, and even one document, that marks an appropriate starting point. This is purposely an incomplete history of aviation cybersecurity, instead looking back to a key moment and then considering what, in the past several years, has driven the conversation forward towards a model of collective governance.

4.2.1 The AIAA's Decision Paper, "The Connectivity Challenge: Protecting Critical Assets in a Networked World" (August 2013)

In the summer of 2013, the American Institute of Aeronautics and Astronautics (AIAA) gathered thousands of aviation professionals in Los Angeles for its inaugural AVIATION 2013 conference. If attendees needed a reminder of the enormity and global nature of their industry, the city where they were meeting offered it: its intercontinental hub airport, Los Angeles World Airports (LAX), was in 2013 the sixth largest airport in the world, with 66.66 million passengers that year, and growing fast.[31]

The AIAA is a global, technical society of aerospace professionals, companies, and students with more than 35 000 members worldwide. The AIAA's new conference sought, in the words of AIAA president Mike Griffin, to "go beyond the discussion of the purely technical issues that AIAA conferences often explore. We will discuss the policy, technological, and environmental challenges facing the future of flight." Cybersecurity was on the agenda. In the lead-up to the event, Michael P. Delaney – the conference executive chair and then-vice president of engineering at Boeing Commercial Airplanes – highlighted that "connectivity has provided the aviation industry with multiple opportunities to improve efficiency to create new products and services. While this influential technology holds great promise, it may also empower those who would disrupt the aviation industry."[32]

On 13 August, the AIAA published a decision paper entitled "The Connectivity Challenge: Protecting Critical Assets in a Networked World: A Framework for Aviation Cybersecurity."[33] From a cybersecurity governance perspective, the paper was notable for several reasons. First, it framed the problem around aviation's role in the global economy and the fact that "disruption to this flow can result in significant economic and social disruption that would ripple across the globe."[34] Second, while recognizing past efforts in aviation security and cybersecurity, the paper did not shy away from stating the depth of the problem bluntly: "Currently, there is no common vision, or common strategy, goals, standards, implementation models, or international policies defining cybersecurity for commercial aviation."[35]

Third, the paper presented a framework for action that did not focus exclusively on technical or policy solutions, nor on short-term or long-term fixes. Rather, it took an expansive view and identified 11 elements that should be part of a roadmap for global aviation cybersecurity:

a) Establish common cyber standards for aviation systems
b) Establish a cybersecurity culture
c) Understand the threat
d) Understand the risk
e) Communicate the threats and assure situational awareness
f) Provide incident response
g) Strengthen the defensive system
h) Define design principles
i) Define operational principles
j) Conduct necessary research and development
k) Ensure that government and industry work together[36]

Fourth, the paper enshrined the idea that securing aviation from cyber threats must be "a shared responsibility, involving governments, airlines, airports, and manufacturers." Elsewhere, the paper also highlighted the importance of the supply chain: "The interconnected global aviation system represents one of the most complex and fluid networks of systems. The nodes in this network include everything from production of aviation products to the many services required to operate airlines, airports, and air traffic services."

Fifth, the decision paper included an explicit call for action in the form of six recommendations:

The aviation community must pursue the following course of action in light of the evolving nature of cyber threats:

- implement common cybersecurity vision, strategy, goals, and framework to address evolving threats;
- increase the cooperation and focus within the aviation community, with the active participation of all major industry players;
- leverage, extend, and apply the existing industry best practices, the response team, and the research and education efforts under,way[sic];
- bring the appropriate government agencies into the discussion;
- begin building a roadmap by identifying near-, mid-, and long-term actions; and
- establish a governmental and industry framework to coordinate national aviation cybersecurity strategies, policies, and plans.[37]

By providing an encompassing definition of the problem and the path to solving it, the AIAA paper became a reference text that influenced many of the efforts that came after it.

4.2.2 The Aviation Information Sharing and Analysis Center (A-ISAC) (September 2014)

A year later, in September 2014, industry leaders established the A-ISAC.[38] The A-ISAC offers a range of services[39] to help member companies share information with each other and, increasingly, with government. It does so by providing a legal framework for communicating, providing technical means to facilitate more secure information sharing, and convening calls and meetings that build relationships and thereby encourage cooperation. The founding membership was concentrated in the airline and airplane manufacturer segments of the industry. Now in its third year, the A-ISAC is actively seeking to add more airports and companies from the supply chain.

4.2.3 The Civil Aviation Cybersecurity Action Plan (December 2014)

On 5 December 2014, five multinational organizations committed to a Civil Aviation Cybersecurity Action Plan to coordinate their efforts for aviation cybersecurity. The leaders of the Airport Council International (ACI), the Civil Air Navigation Services Organisation (CANSO), the International Air Transport Association (IATA), the International Civil Aviation Organization (ICAO), and the Aerospace and Defense Industries Association of Europe (ASD) signed the document. In it, they commit to principles and an action plan that closely resemble the AIAA framework of 2013. They recognized "the need to work together, guided by a shared vision, strategy and roadmap to strengthen the aviation system's protection and resilience against cyber-attacks." Further, they identified the following 11 commitments, which align with many of the elements of the AIAA Framework:

- Develop a common understanding of cyber threats and risks;
- Share assessments of risks;
- Agree [sic] common language and terminology;
- Develop joint positions and recommendations;
- Present a coherent approach to the public;
- Promote cooperation among State-level appropriate authorities and industry to establish a coordinated aviation cybersecurity strategies, policies, and plans;
- Promote a robust cybersecurity culture in all organizations in civil aviation;
- Promote the use of existing information security and cyber protection best practices, standards and design principles, and establish new ones, where necessary;

- Establish the mechanisms and means to share and communicate information including identification of threats, reporting of incidents and developments in defenses;
- Communicate threat-related information and assure situational awareness;
- Refine best practices, operational principles and defensive systems, as appropriate.[40]

4.2.4   Connecting the Dots on Connectivity (2015)

In 2015, the pace of activity around cybersecurity for connected aviation systems quickened, and various actors – including government agencies, aviation companies, and hackers – started to interact more, sometimes at odds with each other and sometimes cooperatively. While leaders in the aviation industry motivated colleagues to address cybersecurity issues, outside forces also pushed the industry to tackle cybersecurity – and to work with a broad community to do so – by shining a light on key risks.

In January, the Government Accountability Office (GAO) issued a report that identified a lack of security governance and "significant security control weaknesses ... in controls intended to prevent, limit, and detect unauthorized access to computer resources, such as controls for protecting system boundaries, identifying and authenticating users, and authorizing users to access systems, encrypting sensitive data, and auditing and monitoring activity on FAA's systems." The end result, the GAO said, was "placing the safe and uninterrupted operation of the nation's air traffic control system at increased and unnecessary risk."[41]

In April, the GAO issued another report, this time also addressing emerging risks for modern, connected aircraft. "As part of the aircraft certification process," the report stated, "FAA's Office of Safety (AVS) currently certifies new interconnected systems through rules for specific aircraft and has started reviewing rules for certifying the cybersecurity of all new aircraft systems."[42] Both Boeing and Airbus immediately released statements acknowledging the risks but simultaneously asserting that the systems were secure and that "such discussion might be counterproductive to security."[43] The report also identified threats to federal systems, noting that the pressure was on the government to upgrade legacy systems, conduct monitoring, and prevent cyberattacks.[44]

4.2.5   Hackers Allege Aircraft Vulnerabilities (2015)

On 17 April 2015, a search warrant was issued against Chris Roberts, a hacker who had claimed discovery of aircraft vulnerabilities while on a United Airlines flight.[45] While dialogue between hackers asserting vulnerabilities and corporations acknowledging and fixing them has existed for a long time, this was the first claim against an aircraft, and rattled the industry. The allegations were not just about the plane that he was on, but about past planes, both Boeing and

Airbus models, equipped with particular IFE systems produced by Panasonic and Thales.[46] Most disturbingly, Roberts claimed that he wrote code that gave a "climb" instruction to an engine, "caus[ing] one of the airplane engines to climb and resulting in a lateral or sideways movement of the plane during one of these flights."[47]

The response from industry was swift: what Roberts told the FBI was technically impossible.[48] In the wake of this response, Roberts, Hugo Teso, and others argued with industry and experts over whether software on an aircraft differs from any other type of software.[49] However, airlines and OEMs had no way to respond to and engage in a conversation about cyber threats to aircraft without compromising their airworthiness certification. This did not prevent some from establishing other programs intended to demonstrate that airlines were concerned with cyber threats.

4.2.6 United Airlines Opens Bug Bounty Program (2015)

In May 2015, United Airlines became the first airline to open a bug bounty program, paying hackers to search for and disclose vulnerabilities found in their proprietary systems privately.[50] Notably, not all bugs were eligible for submission. As of early 2018, bugs on customer-facing applications, cross-site scripting issues, and the United app, as well as bugs that reveal "reservations, MileagePlus numbers, PINs or passwords," are all eligible. Ineligible bugs, which hackers should not spend time finding because there is no reward for them, are those on legacy or unsupported operating systems, internal United sites, and *"bugs on onboard WiFi, entertainment systems [such as IFEs], or avionics"* (emphasis added).[51] While Chris Roberts and others focused on the ability to attack software on board an aircraft, United's bug bounty program attempted to refocus hackers away from these threats and towards more traditional attacks targeting their mobile app and website bugs. This should not be viewed as criticism: even opening a bug bounty program for avionics would suggest that software on board an aircraft might be capable of "non-intended functions."

4.2.7 Aviation Security World Conference (2015)

At this conference, the organizations and companies that make up the global aviation ecosystem had a more systemic and organized response to the major story of the year: that hackers were targeting aircraft, even if only to prove that vulnerabilities existed.[52] First, multiple aviation industry associations announced that a team had been assembled to work on a declaration on cyber-security for the United Nations' aviation safety arm in 2016.[53] IATA Director General Tony Tyler called on aircraft manufacturers to do more, asserting that they have more experience dealing with cyber threats because they also produce military aircraft.[54] And finally, James Vasatka, Boeing's then-director for aviation security, stated that Boeing hires hackers to attack their systems. According to Vasatka, "They (the hackers) are absolutely stunned at the quality we put in our software and products. It would be very difficult in today's environment to disrupt that for the flight-critical systems."[55]

Additionally, CANSO Director General Jeff Poole advocated a "twin-track" approach, combining an overall approach devised by industry partners with an individual approach from stakeholders based on their location in the aviation ecosystem.[56] He highlighted threats to technologies currently being deployed, such as Automatic Dependent Surveillance-Broadcast (ADS-B), which is intended to help aircraft identify each other and provide better information than existing technologies.[57] "Protecting our industry from cyber-threats is hard, probably one of the hardest things we have to tackle as an industry… [W] e need to find new ways to overcome the very real challenges that exist to sharing information…"

4.2.8 Conferences and Organizations Mature (2015 and Beyond)

In November 2015 and May 2016, the Aviation ISAC held its first two summits in coordination with the National Health ISAC. This coordination enabled the Aviation ISAC to reduce costs and foster information sharing with another industry (one with an ISAC that had already hosted several summits), while also bringing its own members and potential members together. The summits included briefings from cybersecurity vendors and panels specific to the aviation industry, focusing on topics such as product and supply chain cybersecurity, incident response, and public–private sector collaboration.[58]

Later in 2016, the 39th Assembly of ICAO unveiled the Dubai Declaration, the culmination of last year's promise to deliver a global declaration on the importance of cybersecurity preparedness in the aviation industry.[59] The Declaration noted the importance of sector-wide coordination, particularly among disparate entities including "air navigation service providers, aircraft and airport operators, and others…"[60] Importantly, in what is becoming a frequent refrain to cybersecurity and automation threats, the president of the ICAO council, Dr. Olumuyiwa Benard Aliu, noted the "inherent mitigation capabilities" of pilots and air traffic controllers, colloquially known as "humans in the loop."[61] In November 2017, ICAO released its Global Aviation Security Plan, which lays out objectives, priorities, and a roadmap until the 40th Session of the ICAO Assembly in 2019.[62]

Finally, in December 2016, the Aviation ISAC held its own summit at Boeing's facilities outside Washington, DC. At the event, members participated in a table-top exercise designed to test the response capabilities of participants. They also heard from experts in the public and private sector on supply chain challenges, information sharing, and the importance of collective governance.

4.2.9   Industry Takes the Lead (2017)

In 2017, private companies began organizing cybersecurity events in their own names in order to combat threats to their systems, vendors, and customers. One of the major non-US aerospace product providers, SITA, organized a conference in Dubai "to share and understand cybersecurity challenges and how we can tackle these as a community with solutions that are tailored to the needs of the air transport industry."[63] Leadership from such a company, which is a provider of products and services to organizations throughout the aviation ecosystem, will be crucial in implementing the advice of CANSO Director General Jeff Poole.[64] In addition to being a member of the Aviation ISAC, SITA has rolled out its own Community Cyber Threat Center, enabling members of its community and those who use SITA products to share and collaborate, alert other members, and receive weekly news and threat updates.[65] This is one example of how an industry member can independently tackle cyber threats on its own systems and in its ecosystem.

4.3   Aviation's Tools for Cyber Risk Governance

A review of the aviation industry's approach to cyber risks reveals some important tools that helped public and private members. While these are not the only effective methods, they were especially suited for an interconnected industry that is tackling a variety of challenges.

First, table-top exercises have been effective in bringing members together and identifying some of the key challenges within the industry. Most recently, the Aviation ISAC coordinated a table-top exercise in 2016 and 2017 that brought members together to focus on threats to the community. In addition, the US government has also coordinated a series of exercises (such as Cyber Guard[66]) that have pushed the ability of agencies to respond to cyberattacks in coordination with the private-sector owners of critical infrastructure. In addition, organizational components of the aviation ecosystem including Air Traffic Control Association (ATCA),[67] and other countries such as Singapore,[68] have organized cybersecurity exercises focused on threats to aviation.

As in other industries, information sharing has also been a focus. ISACs by nature are intended to be information-sharing centers.[69] The aviation industry is in a unique position because some of its members, like Boeing, are part of the Defense Industrial Base,[70] where they and receive classified information. Others, including most airlines, do not have or need access to vulnerabilities in military systems (except when the same as civilian systems). The Aviation ISAC has focused on integration with the Department of Homeland Security, occupying a seat on the watch floor at the National Cybersecurity and Communications Integration Center (NCCIC). The challenge continues to be how to integrate a disparate set of enterprises with vastly different resources and capabilities. Small airports do not have the funding to be part of a private information-sharing organization or invest in technology to automatically receive and resolve threat data. Through many of the key moments in the aviation cybersecurity timeline, formal and informal relationships have developed to build information-sharing connections.

The role of the Aviation ISAC in bringing key stakeholders together was necessary to the continued development of collective governance. While led initially by individual stakeholders such as aircraft manufacturers and lone voices demanding focus on a key issue, the ISAC has developed into a central node in aviation cybersecurity. Perhaps most importantly for its longevity, it has expanded from OEMs and airlines to include many parts of the supply chain and enhanced its relationship with the federal government. The Aviation ISAC has continued to play an important role in the domestic and international drive to improve cybersecurity throughout the aviation ecosystem.

In sum, key members in the aviation sector have led an industry-wide approach to cybersecurity governance. This has provided a platform for airlines, aircraft manufacturers, airports, and the government to develop a concerted effort to address cybersecurity. Their challenge, and opportunity, has been to take an extremely rigorous and successful safety culture and apply it to security, where absolute statements regarding intended use of systems may not account for purposeful manipulation by hackers, and threats change rapidly.

4.4 The Path Forward

The aviation industry has made significant strides to improve collective risk management, and there is much that can still be done. This section identifies four areas with room for enhancing collective risk management, and one key enabler that is critical to success in all four areas.

4.4.1 Collective Third-Party Risk Management

The aviation sector depends on countless third parties that provide services, products, and data that are often critical or time-sensitive. In most cases, these third parties are smaller companies than the airlines and airplane manufacturers they support, and many of them do not apply the same level of resources to assuring information security. This creates risks, including the possibility that a critical third party is disrupted and off-line for a period of time due to a cyber incident, or that a third party becomes the "weak link" through which an attacker gains a foothold in another company. Because a single third party, like a company that makes software for check-in kiosks, might provide its products and services to multiple airlines or airports, third-party disruptions can have disproportionately large effects.

As in other industries, larger companies can increasingly impose cybersecurity requirements on their suppliers, but doing so one company at a time, without coordinating, has two downsides. First, it is an inefficient use of resources for multiple companies to evaluate the same risks and programs with the same third parties. Second, responding to dozens of similar, but not quite identical, questionnaires and reviews imposes a significant compliance burden on the suppliers. For vendors with scarce resources, there is a very real risk that they will take resources away from achieving cybersecurity because they have to focus these resources on showcasing their cybersecurity program in response to many disparate, burdensome requests from customers; collective third-party risk management could solve this problem.

Participants in the aviation sector should come together to define and implement a program of collective risk assessments for third parties. In doing so, the aviation sector can build on lessons learned from other sectors, most importantly the financial sector and its Shared Assessments program, which pioneered this approach. The aviation sector can even improve on the original Shared Assessments program, thanks to advances in technology and cybersecurity practices, as well as the benefit of hindsight. The aviation sector's program should include a focus on technology-enabled continuous monitoring (rather than periodic questionnaires). It should include metrics that can indicate the organization's competency at patching, reviewing potential cybersecurity incidents, and dialogue with executive leadership.

The aviation sector could also distinguish the requirements it places on third parties based on the risks they pose. For example, a company that provides time-sensitive data but has no access or pathway to critical systems presents different risks and should be viewed differently than a company that does not provide time-sensitive services but whose products or services could offer hackers a pathway to critical systems.

Properly designed, a collective third-party risk management program would save resources and improve cybersecurity across the sector.

4.4.2 Secure Design

One of the fundamental reasons that cybersecurity is so challenging is that hardware and software are rarely designed with security in mind. Developers and manufacturers often prioritize making IT solutions that work efficiently, that are interoperable, that are flexible so they have staying power in the face of a changing IT landscape, and that can be priced competitively. Unfortunately, some of these priorities can be at odds with security. As a result, underlying IT systems are often inherently insecure and open to exploitation or misuse. People who try to secure them with bolt-on technologies and monitoring start at a disadvantage, compared to a hacker who is trying to compromise the systems. Software developers also incorporate open-source software into their products without adequate vetting, which can create additional exposure to risk.

The aviation sector should promote secure design, especially with regard to software, and across critical (not just airborne) systems. Aviation sector participants could use an industry consortium as a vehicle to fund early-stage research and development (R&D) into secure design that could deliver value via a broad range of products and across the industry. Aviation sector participants could also come together around a set of secure design principles that all companies (or companies with high risk or critical products) should implement, both internally and as part of their third-party risk management programs. Aircraft and airborne systems are already subject to certification requirements, but with the advent of increasingly connected aircraft and UAS, industry and governments should consider, via a collaborative approach, regulating secure design.

The aviation sector offers valuable lessons in designing physical and software systems to achieve high degrees of reliability and security, as the "five 9s" safety record of air travel proves. Aircraft must meet "intended use" requirements, and software in airborne systems must be designed, tested, and certified with security in mind. If the aviation industry applied this rigorous certification approach to secure design for IT systems throughout the sector, it could achieve significant gains in reducing cybersecurity risk.

4.4.3 Information Sharing, "Plus"

The aviation sector already has made strides in information sharing, as outlined in this chapter. It should aim to build on these efforts in several ways.

First, information sharing has existed primarily among larger companies (i.e. airlines, airplane manufacturers, and select others). Smaller companies should be encouraged to join information-sharing organizations, for two reasons: protecting small companies, especially critical suppliers, can be important to reducing systemic risk; and collecting information from small companies may paint an even more complete picture of the threats facing the sector than looking at information from large companies alone. Of course, this presents challenges, particularly with smaller companies that may not have the resources to contribute to, or draw value from, information-sharing organizations. The larger sector participants and industry organizations could coach smaller organizations on how to collect, deliver, and use cybersecurity information efficiently.

Second, information sharing has generally been a manual and labor-intensive process, particularly because companies need to screen data for sensitive or regulated information before sharing it. Increasingly, technology platforms may help companies do this in an automated way.

Third, information sharing has focused on threat and vulnerability information. However, organizations could expand this focus to include incident information and other forms of collaboration ("information sharing" loosely interpreted), for example, with collaboration around best practices and emerging technologies, that would reduce risk across the sector.

Fourth, the aviation sector should work to make information sharing multinational (within reason) and to break down barriers that limit the ability of governments to share information with the private sector. In the US case, the aviation industry has improved public–private information by having an A-ISAC member stationed in the operations center of the Department of Homeland Security's NCCIC. The objectives of public–private sharing and sharing across borders are linked and may be in tension, since governments typically share more information if it stays within national boundaries and among their citizenry. Nonetheless, governments and organizations could do more sharing across boundaries if the mission, trusting relationships, and legal apparatus were put in place.

4.4.4 International Norms and Standards

The aviation sector is inherently global, and, in some respect, it is already a model of collective, global governance: ICAO and other organizations have successfully promoted global standards for achieving reliable communications, interoperability, and safety. These achievements came from decades of effort and collaboration that combined senior leadership and diligent, detailed work.

Aviation sector participants should build on this global tradition when pursuing improvements in aviation cybersecurity, including those mentioned above: collective third-party risk management, secure design, and enhanced information sharing. All of these initiatives will deliver greater risk reduction if implemented somewhat uniformly across national boundaries and enabled by government-supported international norms and agreements.

Additionally, the aviation sector should seek to expand protections for aircraft and airborne systems to include protections explicitly against cyber threats. One specific improvement would be to make explicit that the Tokyo Convention applies to cyber threats against aircraft and to wrestle with the legal and jurisdictional implications if a cyberattack were directed against a connected aircraft from a remote location.

All four of these proposed areas for enhancement, and others, depend on one critical enabler: executive engagement and leadership. Many of the improvements achieved to date have been led by information security professionals within aviation sector organizations. As these organizations wrestle with assessing third parties, promoting secure design, enhancing information sharing, setting global standards, and managing collective risks, the active

participation of leaders, especially CEOs, will be critical. CEOs must understand the issues, make them a priority within their own enterprises and across the management team (especially for legal teams and teams that manage the supply chain and procurement), and engage actively with senior government leaders when necessary to shape international agreements and pave the way for information sharing and collaboration. Finally, CEOs and other executive leaders would certainly be involved in shaping the sector's response to a sector-wide cybersecurity crisis affecting dozens of companies and organizations. The time to start preparing for that eventuality, by developing the right relationships and "muscle memory" to respond quickly, is now.

4.5 Conclusion

The aviation sector's unique set of attributes complicate its cybersecurity risk profile: it is just-in-time and globally interconnected; it is increasingly digitally connected, with technological innovation happening rapidly in a sector that makes many changes slowly and methodically; it is characterized by shared passengers and vendors; and, it is a high-profile target.

For all these reasons, aviation sector participants have had to pursue a somewhat collective approach to managing cybersecurity risks. They have done so, over many years, through a broad array of tools: building informal relationships; developing institutions; preparing for worst-case scenarios through simulations and table-top exercises; sharing information; and, setting multinational standards, to name a few examples. While much has been accomplished, much remains to be done, and the cyber threat is constantly evolving. The aviation sector presents interesting lessons on how to pursue collective cybersecurity risk management and, no doubt, will continue to innovate and deliver new lessons in this area for years to come.

Notes

1 Air Traffic Transport Group, "Aviation Benefits Beyond Borders," April 2014, https://aviationbenefits.org/media/26786/ATAG__AviationBenefits2014_FULL_LowRes.pdf; Federal Aviation Administration, "Air Traffic By The Numbers," https://www.faa.gov/air_traffic/by_the_numbers/.
2 Bart Jansen, "Delta Outage A Reminder of Fragility of Airline Computers," *USA Today*, January 30, 2017, https://www.usatoday.com/story/news/2017/01/30/delta-outage-airline-technology-problems/97250834/; "British Airways says computer outage causing global delays, cancels all London flights," *CNBC*, May 27, 2017, http://www.cnbc.com/2017/05/27/british-airways-says-computer-outage-causing-global-delays.html.

3 Chris Preimesberger. Router Crashes Trigger Major Southwest IT System Failure. *eWeek,* July 21, 2016. http://www.eweek.com/enterprise-apps/router-crashes-trigger-major-southwest-it-system-failure

4 International Air Transport Association, "The Impact of September 11 2001 on Aviation," http://www.iata.org/pressroom/Documents/impact-9-11-aviation.pdf.

5 Brandon Vigliarolo, "WannaCry: The Smart Person's Guide," *TechRepublic,* June 20, 2017, http://www.techrepublic.com/article/wannacry-the-smart-persons-guide/.

6 Thomas Fox-Brewster, "Petya or NotPetya: Why The Latest Ransomware Is Deadlier Than WannaCry," *Forbes,* June 27, 2017, https://www.forbes.com/sites/thomasbrewster/2017/06/27/petya-notpetya-ransomware-is-more-powerful-than-wannacry/.

7 Mark Hansen, Carolyn McAndrews, and Emily Berkeley, "History of Aviation Safety Oversight in the United States," U.S. Department of Transportation, Federal Aviation Administration, July 2008, http://www.tc.faa.gov/its/worldpac/techrpt/ar0839.pdf.

8 Ibid.

9 Aviation Safety Network, "Fatal airliner (14+ passengers) hull-loss accidents, https://aviation-safety.net/statistics/period/stats.php?cat=A1.

10 Libby Nelson, "The US Once Had More than 130 Hijackings in 4 Years. Here's Why They Finally Stopped," *Vox,* March 29, 2016, https://www.vox.com/2016/3/29/11326472/hijacking-airplanes-egyptair.

11 Transport Security Administration, "Mission," https://www.tsa.gov/about/tsa-mission.

12 Tom Winter and Andrew Blankstein, "Feds Remind U.S. Airports, Airlines They Are Terror Targets," *NBC News,* March 22, 2017, https://www.nbcnews.com/news/us-news/feds-remind-u-s-airports-airlines-they-are-terror-targets-n737416.

13 Barack Obama, "Address Before a Joint Session of Congress on the State of the Union," February 12, 2013, online by Gerhard Peters and John T. Woolley, *The American Presidency Project,* http://www.presidency.ucsb.edu/ws/index.php?pid=102826.

14 Ioannis Agrafiotis, Maria Bada, Paul Cornish, Sadie Creese, Michael Goldsmith, Eva Ignatuschtschenko, Taylor Roberts, and David M. Upton, "Cyber Harm: Concepts, Taxonomy and Measurement," Saïd Business School WP 2016-23, August 1, 2016, SSRN, https://ssrn.com/abstract=2828646 or http://dx.doi.org/10.2139/ssrn.2828646.

15 Maria Tadeo and Christopher Jasper, "British Airways Owner Says Power Outag Cost 80 Million Pounds," *Bloomberg Markets,* June 15, 2017, https://www.bloomberg.com/news/articles/2017-06-15/british-airways-owner-says-power-outage-cost-80-million-pounds.

16 International Air Transport Association, "Another Strong Year for Airline Profits in 2017," Press Release No. 76, December 8, 2016, http://www.iata.org/pressroom/pr/Pages/2016-12-08-01.aspx.

17 Ibid.

18 American Institute of Aeronautics and Astronautics, "AIAA's Framework on Cyber Security Now Available," August 13, 2013, https://www.aiaa.org/ SecondaryTwoColumn.aspx?id=19262.

19 Jerin Mathew, "British Airways Suffers Cyber-attack Affecting Thousands of Frequent Flyer Accounts," *International Business Times*, March 30, 2015, http://www.ibtimes.co.uk/british-airways-suffers-hacking-attack-thousands-frequent-flyer-accounts-affected-1494076.

20 Lee Mathews, "Travel Giant Sabre Confirms Its Reservation System Was Hacked," *Forbes*, July 6, 2017, https://www.forbes.com/sites/leemathews/ 2017/07/06/travel-giant-sabre-confirms-its-reservation-system-was-hacked/#23755cb74b20.

21 Alan Taylor, "The Exxon Valdez Oil Spill: 25 Years Ago Today," *The Atlantic*, March 24, 2014, https://www.theatlantic.com/photo/2014/03/the-exxon-valdez-oil-spill-25-years-ago-today/100703/.

22 Jim Finkle and Dhanya Skariachan, "Target Cyber Breach Hits 40 Million Payment Cards at Holiday Peak," *Reuters*, December 18, 2013, https://www. reuters.com/article/us-target-breach/target-cyber-breach-hits-40-million-payment-cards-at-holiday-peak-idUSBRE9BH1GX20131219.

23 Andrea Peterson, "The Sony Pictures Hack, Explained," *The Washington Post*, December 18, 2014, https://www.washingtonpost.com/news/the-switch/ wp/2014/12/18/the-sony-pictures-hack-explained/?utm_term=.c6b95c35a27b.

24 Kuchler, Hannah. "Yahoo Says 2013 Cyber Breach Affected All 3bn Accounts." *Financial Times*, October 3, 2017. https://www.ft.com/content/9412c2b0-a87c-11e7-93c5-648314d2c72c.

25 Lily Hay Newman, "Equifax Officially Has No Excuse," *Wired*, September 14, 2017, https://www.wired.com/story/equifax-breach-no-excuse/.

26 Federal Aviation Administration, "Regulations and Policies," https://www.faa. gov/aircraft/air_cert/design_approvals/air_software/software_regs/.

27 Chad Perrin, "The Danger of Complexity: More Code, More Bugs," *TechRepublic*, February 1, 2010, http://www.techrepublic.com/blog/it-security/the-danger-of-complexity-more-code-more-bugs/.

28 Robert Saracco, "Guess What Requires 150 Million Lines of Code…" *IEEE Future Directions*, January 13, 2016, http://sites.ieee.org/futuredirections/2016/01/13/ guess-what-requires-150-million-lines-of-code/.

29 International Civil Aviation Organization, "Convention on International Civil Aviation – Doc 7300," https://www.icao.int/publications/pages/ doc7300.aspx

30 *Convention on offences and certain other acts committed on board aircraft.* Tokyo, September 14, 1963. *United Nations Treaty Series*, https://treaties. un.org/doc/db/terrorism/conv1-english.pdf.

31 "Top 10 Airports: Passenger Traffic in 2013," *Airport World*, February 14, 2014,http://www.airport-world.com/news/general-news/3674-top-10-airports-passenger-traffic-in-2013.

32 American Institute of Aeronautics and Astronautics, Cybersecurity of Global Aviation a Major Focus of AIAA AVIATION 2013," July 9, 2013, https://www.aiaa.org/SecondaryTwoColumn.aspx?id=18754.

33 American Institute of Aeronautics and Astronautics, "The Connectivity Challenge: Protecting Critical Assets in a Networked World; A Framework for Aviation Cybersecurity," August 2013, https://www.aiaa.org/uploadedFiles/Issues_and_Advocacy/AIAA-Cyber-Framework-Final.pdf.

34 Ibid.

35 Ibid.

36 American Institute of Aeronautics and Astronautics, "The Connectivity Challenge: Protecting Critical Assets in a Networked World."

37 Ibid.

38 Aviation Information Sharing and Analysis Center, "FAQs," https://www.a-isac.com/faqs.

39 Ibid.

40 "Civil Aviation Cybersecurity Action Plan," December 5, 2014, https://www.icao.int/cybersecurity/SiteAssets/ICAO/Civil%20Aviation%20Cybersecurity%20Action%20Plan%20-%20SIGNED.pdf.

41 United States Government Accountability Office, "FAA Needs to Address Weaknesses in Air Traffic Control Systems," January 2015, http://www.gao.gov/assets/670/668169.pdf.

42 United States Government Accountability Office, "FAA Needs a More Comprehensive Approach to Address Cybersecurity As Agency Transitions to NextGen," April 2015, http://www.gao.gov/assets/670/669627.pdf.

43 "Boeing airplanes have more than one navigational system available to pilots," the company said in a statement. "No changes to the flight plans loaded into the airplane systems can take place without pilot review and approval. In addition, other systems, multiple security measures, and flight deck operating procedures help ensure safe and secure airplane operations." Airbus released a statement, which read: "Airbus, in partnership with our suppliers, constantly assesses and revisits the system architecture of our products, with an eye to establishing and maintaining the highest standards of safety and security. Beyond that, we don't discuss design details or safeguards publicly, as such discussion might be counterproductive to security." See Kim Zetter, "Hackers Could Commandeer New Planes Through Passenger Wi-Fi," *Wired*, April 15, 2015, https://www.wired.com/2015/04/hackers-commandeer-new-planes-passenger-wi-fi/.

44 According to *CNN*, "In a letter to the GAO, Keith Washington, acting assistant secretary for administration with the FAA 'recognizes that cyberbased threats to federal information systems are becoming a more significant risk and are rapidly evolving and increasingly difficult to detect and defend against. We take this risk very seriously.'" See Matthew Hoye and Rene Marsh, "GAO: Newer

Aircraft Vulnerable to Hacking," *CNN*, April 14, 2015, http://www.cnn.
com/2015/04/14/politics/gao-newer-aircraft-vulnerable-to-hacking/index.html.

45 *Chris Roberts Application for Search Warrant*. April 17, 2015. Case No:
5:15-MJ-00154 (ATB). https://www.wired.com/wp-content/uploads/2015/05/
Chris-Roberts-Application-for-Search-Warrant.pdf

46 Kim Zetter, "Is It Possible For Passengers to Hack Commercial Aircraft?"
Wired, May 26, 2015, https://www.wired.com/2015/05/possible-passengers-
hack-commercial-aircraft/.

47 Ibid.

48 Ibid.

49 n.runs Professionals, "Aircraft Hacking Practical Aero Series," April 2013,
https://conference.hitb.org/hitbsecconf2013ams/materials/D1T1%20-%20Hugo
%20Teso%20-%20Aircraft%20Hacking%20-%20Practical%20Aero%20Series.pdf.

50 United Airlines, "United Airlines bug bounty program," https://www.united.
com/web/en-US/content/Contact/bugbounty.aspx.

51 Ibid.

52 Victoria Bryan, "Airlines Step Up Efforts to Tackle Cyber Security Risks,"
Reuters, October 26, 2015, http://www.reuters.com/article/us-airlines-
cybersecurity/airlines-step-up-efforts-to-tackle-cyber-security-risks-
idUSKCN0SK24020151026.

53 Ibid.

54 Ibid.

55 Ibid.

56 Woodrow Bellamy III, "CANSO Chief Outlines Plan to Address Aviation
Cyber Security," *Aviation Today*, October 27, 2015, http://www.aviationtoday.
com/2015/10/27/canso-chief-outlines-plan-to-address-aviation-
cyber-security/.

57 Federal Aviation Administration, "ADS-B Frequently Asked Questions
(FAQs)," https://www.faa.gov/nextgen/programs/adsb/faq/.

58 National Health ISAC & Aviation ISAC, "2016 Spring Agenda," National
Health ISAC & Aviation ISAC Spring Summit 2016, Lake Buena Vista, FL,
May 11–13, 2016, https://www.eiseverywhere.com/ehome/150989/343519/.

59 International Civil Aviation Organization, "ICAO Summit formalizes new
Dubai Declaration to ensure global aviation remains united, proactive on
cybersecurity preparedness," April 6, 2017, https://www.icao.int/Newsroom/
Pages/ICAO-Summit-formalizes-new-Dubai-Declaration-ensures-global-
aviation-remains-united-proactive-on-cybersecurity-preparedness.aspx.

60 Ibid.

61 Ibid.

62 https://www.icao.int/Security/Documents/GASEP2017_EN.pdf

63 SITA, "Aviation Cybersecurity Symposium 2017," 2017, https://www.sita.aero/
events/events-listing/2017-aviation-cybersecurity-symposium.

64 SITA, "Solutions & Services," https://www.sita.aero/solutions-and-services.
65 SITA, "Community Cyber Threat Center," https://www.sita.aero/about-us/ working-for-the-community/industry-initiatives/cyber-threat-center.
66 U.S. Cyber Command. "Cyber Guard 15 Fact Sheet." https://dod.defense.gov/ Portals/1/features/2015/0415_cyber-strategy/Cyber_Guard_15_Fact_ Sheet_010715_f.pdf
67 Air Traffic Control Association, https://www.atca.org/cyber-home.
68 Tan Weizhen, "Public, Private Sectors Take Part in Annual Cyber Security Exercise," *Today Online*, July 18, 2017, http://www.todayonline.com/ singapore/national-cyber-security-exercise-involves-all-11-critical-sectors-first-time.
69 National Council of ISACs, https://www.nationalisacs.org/.
70 Defense Industrial Base Information Sharing and Analysis Center, http://www. dibisac.net/.

5

An Incident-Based Conceptualization of Cybersecurity Governance*

Jacqueline Eggenschwiler

University of Oxford, Oxford, UK

5.1   Introduction

Many of the economic, political, and social activities of the twenty-first-century rely on computer systems and networks.[1] Given their significance to the functioning of global markets, political institutions, and wider society, their safekeeping has become an important subject for public and private actors alike. Questions regarding the security and development of cyberspace have attained considerable policy relevance. According to a report issued by the World Economic Forum in 2017, cybersecurity has become top of the agenda for the world's decision-makers.[2]

Network interruptions and defaults caused by Distributed Denial of Service (DDoS) attacks or malware strikes of other kinds (e.g. worms, viruses, ransomware, spyware) carry considerable costs and underscore the need for effective governance mechanisms.[3] Despite growing appreciation of the threats emerging from the virtual realm, there is room to refine scientific understandings of cybersecurity governance. To that end, this chapter seeks to answer the following research questions: What does cybersecurity governance entail and what types of governance mechanisms does it rely upon? The chapter proposes a tripartite conceptualization of cybersecurity governance. It contends that cybersecurity governance includes hierarchical, multistakeholder-based, and market-based modes. The chapter draws on three different examples of cybersecurity governance to support its claim: the 2016 RUAG cyberespionage case, the collaborative containment activities of the Conficker Working Group, and Symantec's cybersecurity practices.

---

* *Parts of this article were published in St Antony's International Review 13.2, pp. 64–78.* Permission for republication was obtained from the editors of the relevant issue.

Rewired: Cybersecurity Governance, First Edition. Edited by Ryan Ellis and Vivek Mohan.

The tripartite conceptualization advanced by this chapter has important implications for scholarship and practice. For one thing, it underscores the conceptual modularity of cybersecurity governance. For another thing, it draws attention to the fallacy of one-size-fits-all approaches.

With regard to methodology, the chapter uses qualitative means of data collection and analysis. It draws on a variety of sources, including academic literature and policy documents on cybersecurity governance, as well as three empirical case studies. Data were collected by means of online desk research, and analyzed based on an interpretative design.

In terms of analytical validity, it is worth noting several limitations. Cybersecurity incidents are characterized by a high degree of uncertainty, with regard to both the probability of occurrence and the scale of devastation, and generally remain difficult to quantify.[4] Rich and reliable incident data are scarce, which renders empirically driven, governance-oriented investigations difficult.[5] The paucity of empirical data mainly stems from the reluctance of governmental and nongovernmental bodies to share relevant incident records in a distributed, transparent, openly accessible, and standardized manner. Furthermore, cybersecurity governance is a highly transient topic of analysis and research. It is a concept under continuous construction.[6] Thus, the findings of this chapter are contextually and temporally specific and need to be interpreted as such.

5.2 Conceptualizing Cybersecurity Governance

Cybersecurity governance is a difficult concept to grasp. Those involved lack a common understanding, a formal definition, and even an agreement on the mere spelling of the term.[7] According to Kurbalija, cybersecurity governance constitutes one of seven baskets of internet governance policy issues,[8] and includes the regulation of cyber conflicts, critical information infrastructure protection, cybercrime, and cyberterrorism.[9] In a similar fashion, DeNardis and Raymond understand cybersecurity governance to be one of six distinct functional areas of internet governance, encompassing "the challenge of securing the essential shared infrastructures of internet governance."[10] Specifically, they consider the following tasks to fall into the remit of cybersecurity governance: securing network infrastructure; designing encryption standards; endorsing regulation; correcting software security vulnerabilities; managing patching cycles; securing routing, addressing, and DNS; responding to security problems; and certifying authentication intermediaries.[11]

The subsummation of cybersecurity governance under the broader umbrella of internet governance has not been conducive to a thorough conceptualization of the subject, especially with regards to the forms of steering involved. On the contrary, it has contributed to theoretical indoctrination: "The current approach to cybersecurity governance has been profoundly shaped, if not defined, by the idea of multistakeholder initiatives, rather than by [other approaches]."[12] This denotes a type of steering centered on bringing together, in a collaborative effort, key actors to participate in deliberation, decision-making, and implementation of solutions to problems related to the operation and development of the internet.[13] Multistakeholder governance has become the dominant mode of regulation associated with cybersecurity governance.

Opposing one-dimensional conceptualizations of cybersecurity governance, this chapter argues that such approaches fail to comprehensively capture the concept and its practices. Cybersecurity governance is a multidimensional construct with far-reaching social, political, and economic implications. Once the full spectrum of technical, sociopolitical, and economic implications is taken into account, the idea of a single governance structure for cybersecurity becomes untenable. No single model of governance is able to effectively address all of the different facets of cybersecurity. As Dutton convincingly explains, "who governs the various parts of this mosaic [varies] dramatically. Some areas [are] dominated by technical experts, others by government agencies, others by regulatory officials, others by users, and so on."[14] Hence, to speak of cybersecurity governance as a single practice is misleading. Cybersecurity governance resembles a collection of different cooperation problems, implying a multiplicity of actors and steering mechanisms.[15]

This chapter maintains that cybersecurity governance entails multiple modes of governance, including hierarchical, multistakeholder-based, and market-based modes. While not hermetically sealed, each of the three modes exhibits different operating structures and moral and political rationales.[16] To clarify, hierarchical governance describes a top-down style of regulation, guided by black-letter law, rules, and policies.[17] Emergent in contexts of crises and considerable uncertainty, hierarchical governance is characterized by authoritative systems of centralized command and control, as well as strict internal and external accountability procedures. Actor constellations are dominated by governmental and state-affiliated players.[18]

In contrast to hierarchical governance, market governance denotes a bottom-up type of regulation, organized along doctrines of competition and efficiency. Service thinking and output legitimization are at the center of this type of governance. In its ideal-typical form, market governance accounts for decentralization and the creation of independent, autonomous units (private actors).[19]

Multistakeholder governance represents something of a halfway house between hierarchical governance and market governance. Multistakeholder governance depends on exchange relationships between a wide range of governmental and/or nongovernmental stakeholders as a way of pursuing common goals.[20] Interactions are guided by trust, reciprocity, and consensus-based decision-making.

Table 5.1 Examples of cybersecurity governance efforts.

Mode of governance	Examples of cybersecurity governance efforts
Hierarchical governance	State-led inquiries following cybersecurity incidents, International legal instruments (e.g. the Convention on Cybercrime of the Council of Europe)
Multistakeholder governance	Public–private botnet takedowns (e.g. the Conficker Working Group or Dridex Partnership), Cybersecurity-related policy development in forums like ICANN or the IETF, Cybersecurity Information Sharing Partnerships (e.g. UK CiSP), Computer Emergency Response Teams (CERTs)
Market governance	Private sector responses to system and network breaches (e.g. patching practices and endpoint protection), commercial threat detection and security products providers

Source: Author.

The current cybersecurity governance arena is comprised of aspects of all three forms of steering. Cybersecurity governance involves private-sector administrative decisions and contracts among private entities as much as it does hierarchical ordering efforts and multistakeholder-based approaches. At times, these different forms of interaction and cybersecurity provision overlap; at other times, they appear in their ideal-typical form.

Table 5.1 lists examples of cybersecurity governance efforts for each of the three types of governance introduced.

To support the claim that cybersecurity governance involves multiple forms of steering, the next section dissects a selection of empirical case studies, namely, the 2016 RUAG cyberespionage case, the collaborative containment activities of the Conficker Working Group, and Symantec's cybersecurity practices.

5.3 Case Studies

5.3.1 RUAG

5.3.1.1 Background

The 2016 RUAG cyberespionage case refers to an advanced persistent threat incident against Swiss defense contractor RUAG. RUAG is the Swiss military's key supplier of munitions, and holds close ties with the Federal Department of Defense, Civil Protection, and Sport (DDPS). It develops, manufactures, assembles, services, and upgrades structural components of terrestrial and aerial defense systems.[21] By its own account, it also has "expertise in detecting and eliminating IT attacks and securing systems against them."[22] Ironically, the corporation's self-attested cybersecurity proficiency did not shield it from being the subject of an extensive cyberattack.

5.3.1.2 Events

Malicious activity on the system and network infrastructures of the state-owned technology company was first detected by the Swiss Federal Intelligence Service (FIS) in January 2016. The FIS informed the Attorney General's Office, which, on 25 January 2016, opened criminal investigations against persons unknown under Article 273 of the Swiss Criminal Code.[23]

Upon discovery of the network intrusion in January 2016, Guy Parmelin, then head of the DDPS, informed the Federal Council and relevant ministries about the attack. In an attempt to limit the repercussions of the assault, the Federal Council called upon a security taskforce to devise and implement remediation measures. Two months after the discovery of the intrusion, on 23 March 2016, the Swiss government approved a total of 14 short- and medium-term security measures identified by the security taskforce. Detailed information about the content of these measures was deliberately kept under wraps.[24] For purposes of better forensic analysis and improved reconnaissance, the government initially decided to withhold information about the attack from the public. Information concerning the incident only started to surface in May 2016, following unsanctioned disclosures. The government-induced secrecy surrounding the incident was heavily criticized by members of the public as well as parliamentary control functions.

After the attack became known to the public, the Swiss government issued a technical report concerning the cybersecurity incident in conjunction with the national Reporting and Analysis Centre for Information Assurance (MELANI). The main objective of the report was to share relevant information with potentially vulnerable parties (both state and non-state). In contrast to the earlier secrecy surrounding the event, the publication of an official cybersecurity incident report received far-reaching approval. Information security experts were particularly enthusiastic about the compilation of indicators of compromise and security recommendations, which allowed other potentially vulnerable entities to detect and block related attacks.[25] Professor of Security Studies, Thomas Rid, for example, mentioned in a tweet: "[The] new RUAG report is a very big step on the part of the Swiss. Kudos to @ GovCERT_CH for raising the bar on governmental attribution reports."[26]

The report suggested that intrusion started as early as September 2014. Forensic analysis revealed that intruders relied on a type of malware belonging to the Turla family, a Trojan artifact believed to be of Russian origin. However, the report deliberately abstained from attributing the attack to a specific threat actor.[27] Attackers were said to have demonstrated great perseverance during stages of infiltration and lateral movement, as well as enormous focus on high-value targets, including the Active Directory.[28] Retrieval and infiltration of the latter allowed intruders to command other hosts, and access (supposedly) proprietary data by escalating privileges and using appropriate permissions. In total, the malware writers were said to have exfiltrated 23 GB of data.[29] According to RUAG, this represented less than 0.01% of the volume of data managed by the defense contractor.[30]

Figure 5.1 provides a summary of the attack timeline and report findings in a flowchart.

5.3.1.3 Learnings

The cybersecurity incident response strategy adopted in the RUAG case exhibited clear features of hierarchical governance. Government bodies and institutions with strong ties to the government were at the helm of counter-action and crisis management. Responses were coordinated in close consultation with relevant federal authorities, in particular the Attorney General's Office, the Reporting and Analysis Centre for Information Assurance, as well as the DDPS. Furthermore, the means and methods of remediation employed included black letter criminal law investigations, and traditional parliamentary procedures. The RUAG case suggest that when critical (national) infrastructures are at play (even when provided by a private entity), incident response measures involve traditional, hierarchical means of command and control. The initial secrecy surrounding the attack also supports this argument.

5.3.2 The Conficker Working Group

5.3.2.1 Background

The Conficker Working Group emerged in response to a highly prevalent computer worm named Conficker (sometimes also referred to as Downadup or Kido), the first variant of which surfaced in late 2008. In total, five variants of the Conficker worm have been recorded.[31] Released with the intention of creating a large botnet (i.e. a network of compromised systems susceptible to external control), the Conficker malware infected many unpatched personal, business, and government computers across the globe. It exploited a buffer overflow vulnerability in the server service on Windows machines, which allowed remote code execution on the basis of a specially crafted remote procedure call (RPC) request.[32]

5.3.2.2 Events

The Conficker worm used a variety of techniques for propagation and exploitation, including the Domain Name System, encrypted peer-to-peer communications, and auto-run capabilities for pushing and pulling

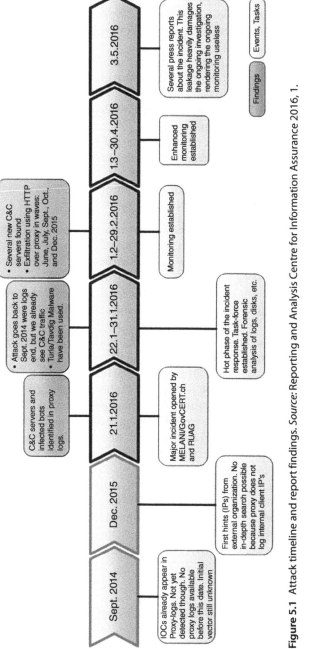

Figure 5.1 Attack timeline and report findings. *Source:* Reporting and Analysis Centre for Information Assurance 2016, 1.

executable payloads over the internet.[33] Post-installation, the malicious software executed the following steps:

1) Conficker copied itself into the system directory %systemroot%\system32 using a random name, and registered itself as a service. It also added itself into the registry.
2) Next, it checked for the infected host's internet protocol (IP) address using websites, including: www.getmyip.org, http://getmyip.co.uk, and http://checkip.dyndns.org.
3) With the IP address identified, the worm then downloaded and set up a small HTTP server on the infected machine.
4) Once the HTTP server was set up, the worm started scanning for other vulnerable systems and began sending the infected machine URL to the targets identified.
5) The targeted machines then downloaded the worm from the URL sent and started completing the same steps as outlined above.[34]

Following the emergence and speedy propagation of the worm in late 2008, a group of diverse stakeholders came together in early 2009 to contain the malicious software. Without an official sponsor or set structure, the Conficker Working Group represented an ad-hoc organization of like-minded entities.[35] Containment efforts were supported by software providers, academic researchers, antivirus vendors, law-enforcement units, and domain name registrars and registries.[36]

One of the first mitigation strategies launched by the working group was the sink-holing and preemptive registration of domain names on which the worm relied for command and control. The contribution of the Internet Corporation for Assigned Names and Numbers (ICANN), a member of the Conficker Working Group, was essential in this regard. Concerned about the pervasiveness and impact of the malicious software, ICANN agreed to waive domain name registration fees for domains used by the worm, thereby effectively supporting the group's efforts to curtail communication between the malware writers and Conficker-infected systems.

According to a 2011 "Lessons Learned" report, commissioned by the Department of Homeland Security, the Conficker Working Group considered its biggest success to be the disruption of botnet communications. Although successful in that regard, the working group did not manage to "remediate infected computers and eliminate the threat of the botnet,"[37] which tainted its achievements to some extent.

5.3.2.3 Learnings

In the case of the Conficker worm, mitigation activities exhibited strong traits of multistakeholder-based governance. Response strategies followed a collaborative logic, with trust-based cooperation between public and private entities.

Unstructured, complex problem-settings and heterogeneous stakeholder interests were bridged by means of skills-based coordination and communication.[38] The example of the Conficker Working Group suggests that when a threat is pervasive enough, diverging stakeholder interests can be aligned and containment strategies executed jointly.

5.3.3 Symantec's Cybersecurity Practices

5.3.3.1 Background

Founded in 1982 and publicly listed since 1989, Symantec Corporation is an American software company headquartered in Mountain View, California. With annual revenues of $4.834 billion for fiscal year 2018, it ranks among the largest cybersecurity companies in the world.[39] Offering a broad range of products, Symantec supports both public and private sector entities in their endeavor to secure their infrastructure and data against assault, compromise, and theft. Among the most well-known security products offered by Symantec are Norton antivirus and device protection consumer products.[40]

5.3.3.2 Events

Based on intelligence gathered from its products as well as third-party data sources, Symantec has established one of the world's largest civilian threat-collection networks. Monitoring threat activities in over 157 countries and territories, it "tracks over 700,000 global adversaries and records events from 98 million attack sensors."[41] In addition to its pervasive threat-collection network, the company has also set up an extensive vulnerability database, comprising more than 88 900 recorded vulnerabilities from 24 560 vendors representing over 78 900 products.[42]

Symantec's threat intelligence and vulnerability resources allow it to identify, analyze, and provide informed commentary on, as well as protection against, enduring and emerging assaults. When, in May 2017, the WannaCry ransomware[43] crippled parts of the United Kingdom's National Health Service (NHS), as well as businesses and home users worldwide, Symantec was able not only to protect the systems and data of its customers but also to uncover two possible links between the malicious software and the Lazarus group, a cybercriminal organization with supposed ties to the North Korean government.[44] Symantec Endpoint Protection and Norton products proactively blocked any attempts by the malware to exploit the Windows Server Message Block (SMB) vulnerability named "Eternal Blue," which served as the primary vector of attack. As a result, Symantec customers remained largely unharmed by the perils of the WannaCry ransomware.[45]

5.3.3.3 Learnings

Symantec's risk mitigation efforts showed distinct characteristics of market-based governance. During the WannaCry ransomware incident, Symantec's cybersecurity provision efforts followed a transactional logic. They were structured around licensing agreements and private contracts. The Symantec case study suggests that as long as cybersecurity incidents do not cross a certain, nonroutine event threshold, market-driven cybersecurity measures are an effective means of governance.

5.4 Utility and Limitations

The three case studies outlined above support the claim, advanced earlier in this chapter, that cybersecurity governance involves multiple modes of steering. This section briefly examines the utility of each of the three modes identified and highlights some limitations.

Hierarchical modes of governance appear to carry particular value in matters directly tied to national interests (e.g. national critical infrastructure or security) and to crisis situations. Such situations tend to require controlled action, which public actors can enforce by means of direct interventions. Furthermore, in urgent circumstances, hierarchical modes of governance are likely to occasion the smallest coordination costs, as interventions generally follow a unidirectional, top-down logic. On the other hand, however, hierarchical modes of steering are inclined to suffer from rules-based rigidity and ineffectiveness. Corrective actions propagated by public entities do not always effect the degree of change or remediation expected, and often are not transparent.

Multistakeholder-based governance setups seem to be relevant in complex, multi-actor settings. Informal collaborative efforts among stakeholders can help reduce transaction and agency costs in pervasive, unstructured circumstances. The combination of knowledge and expertise, along with skill-based specialization, has an efficiency-increasing quality. Multistakeholder-based modes of governance appear to be particularly useful for finding solutions to cybersecurity problems of a global nature. However, ad-hoc collaborative responses, such as the Conficker Working Group, may battle with issues of scalability and sustainability. In the absence of formal structures and commitments, cooperation can only go as far as members are willing to contribute resources. Also, there is a risk of mitigation efforts resulting in endless discussions and debates due to missing guidelines or unclear goals. Furthermore, as outlined by Piscitello, "informal communications may not be sufficient for all global incident response efforts, especially in situations where there is zero tolerance for error or omission."[46]

Market-based forms of steering appear to be suitable for routine security transactions, such as endpoint or information protection. Contrary to

Table 5.2 Summary of modes of governance.

	Hierarchical governance	Market governance	Multistakeholder governance
Affinity with problem types	Crises, disasters, and problems that can be solved by executing force	Routine issues, nonsensitive issues	Complex, unstructured, multi-actor issues
Types of output and outcomes	Laws, regulations, control, procedures, compliance	Services, products, contracts, voluntary agreements	Consensus, agreements, social exchange, alliances
Typical failures/ limitations	Ineffectiveness, red tape	Inefficiency, market failures	Never-ending talks, no decisions, scalability
Main actors	State actors	Non-state actors, private actors	State and non-state actors

Source: Meuleman 2008, 50–51.

multistakeholder-based modes of governance, market-oriented means of steering offer scalability. Security provision follows a competitive, contract-based logic. However, in situations of high uncertainty and considerable risk, this logic is hard to sustain, and markets tend to fail (e.g. by raising the price for security to socially unstable levels).

Table 5.2 summarizes some of the key features of the three modes of governance introduced above.

The three-pronged conceptualization of cybersecurity governance has policy implications: against a background of ever-increasing technical complexity, heterogeneity of actors, and blurring borders between external and internal, as well as public and private, matters, policymakers face the challenge of selecting the most appropriate type of governance (or combination of types) for a given cybersecurity issue area.[47] Scholars and practitioners need to take stock of the different modes of cybersecurity governance presented in this chapter, and develop adequate policy prescriptions and processes that allow for satisfactory program outcomes and effective security delivery.[48] They need to recognize that no one mode of governance can effectively regulate all the issues associated with cybersecurity. Depending on the problem type (e.g. widespread security crises, critical infrastructure attacks, or routine issues), different forms of steering may yield more effective results than others.

The next section summarizes the findings and highlights the broader theoretical and practical implications of this chapter.

5.5 Conclusion

While cybersecurity was initially regarded as a space free from intervention and control, the growing number of security incidents emerging from cyberspace has spurred calls for more regulation. Although a topic of great relevance, scholarship has struggled to offer thorough, empirically grounded conceptualizations of cybersecurity governance. In an attempt to address this deficiency, this chapter has proposed a tripartite conceptualization. It has argued that cybersecurity governance includes hierarchical, multistakeholder-based, and market-based modes. Such conceptualization offers a useful corrective to monistic theories of cybersecurity governance. On the one hand, it highlights the wide range of actors and activities involved in governance enterprises. On the other hand, it encourages academics and practitioners "to think of layers and domains of [cybersecurity] governance."[49] Cybersecurity governance has technical, socio-economic, and political aspects. Recognizing cybersecurity governance as a multidimensional concept allows for more comprehensive and rigorous theoretical examination of cyber events. It provides policymakers and researchers with a more nuanced framework for addressing the broad spectrum of security challenges and repercussions emanating from cyberspace.

Cybersecurity governance involves a complex web of distinct tasks, of "which some are appropriately relegated to the private sector, some the purview of traditional sovereign nation state governance or international treaty negotiations, and some more appropriately multistakeholder."[50] Empirical evidence appears to support this claim.

Effective regulation of cybersecurity challenges, created as cyberspace transitions into a global infrastructure at the center of trade and security, requires a multiplicity of ordering arrangements, with different degrees of organization and authority.[51] The stipulation of one-sided governance models does not appear useful. Cybersecurity as a topic of regulation is simply too complex. A modular approach, centered on the different modes of governance presented above, seems more appropriate and empirically relevant.

Notes

1 Richard A. Clarke and Robert K. Knake, *Cyber War: The Next Threat to National Security and What To Do About It. Terrorism and Political Violence* (New York: HarperCollins, 2012), https://doi.org/10.1080/09546553.2011.533082.

2 World Economic Forum, "Why Cybersecurity Is Now Top of the Agenda for the World's Decision-Makers," 2017, https://medium.com/world-economic-forum/why-cybersecurity-is-now-top-of-the-agenda-for-the-worlds-decision-makers-fb74e17b09b5.

3 Andreas Schmidt, Secrecy versus Openness, Uitgeverij BOXPress, 2014; Robert K. Knake, "Internet Governance in an Age of Cyber Insecurity," Council on Foreign Relations, 2010, 1–55;Mark Raymond and Laura DeNardis, "Multistakeholderism: Anatomy of an Inchoate Global Institution," *International Theory* 7, no. 3 (November 2015): 572–616, https://doi. org/10.1017/S1752971915000081.

4 Marshall A. Kuypers, Thomas Maillart, and Elisabeth Paté-Cornell, "An Empirical Analysis of Cyber Security Incidents at a Large Organization," 2016, 1–22.

5 Council on Foreign Relations, "Cyber Security & the Governance Gap: Complexity, Contention, Cooperation," 2014, https://ecir.mit.edu/sites/ default/files/documents/2014%20ECIR%20Conference%20Agenda.pdf.

6 William H. Dutton and Malcolm Peltu, "The Emerging Internet Governance Mosaic: Connecting the Pieces," *Information Polity* 12, no. 1–2 (2007): 63–81.

7 Nazli Choucri, Gihan Daw Elbait, and Stuart E. Madnick, "What Is Cybersecurity? Explorations in Automated Knowledge Generation," *SSRN Electronic Journal* (2012): 1–27, https://doi.org/10.2139/ssrn.2178616.

8 According to Jovan Kurbalija ("Politorbis," no. 57, 2014), the seven baskets of internet governance policy issues are: infrastructure and standardization, cybersecurity, legal, economic, development, human rights, and sociocultural.

9 Ibid.

10 Raymond and DeNardis, "Multistakeholderism," 588.

11 Raymond and DeNardis, "Multistakeholderism."

12 Karsten Friis and Jens Ringsmose, *Conflict in Cyber Space: Theoretical, Strategic and Legal Pespectives*, Routledge Studies in Conflict, Security and Technology (New York: Taylor & Francis, 2016), 125.

13 ICANNWiki, "Multistakeholder Model," 2017, https://icannwiki.org/index. php/Multistakeholder_Model. More generally, Raymond and DeNardis consider multistakeholder governance to "[entail] two or more classes of actors engaged in a common governance enterprise concerning issues they regard as public in nature, and characterized by polyarchic authority relations constituted by procedural rules." (Raymond and DeNardis "Multistakeholderism," 574).

14 Dutton and Peltu, 26.

15 Robert O. Keohane and David G. Victor, "The Regime Complex for Climate Change," *Perspectives on Politics* 9, no. 1 (2011): 7–23, https://doi.org/10.1017/ S1537592710004068.

16 Robyn Keast, Myrna P. Mandell, and Kerry Brown, "Mixing State, Market and Network Governance Modes: The Role of Government in 'Crowded' Policy Domains," *International Journal of Organization Theory and Behavior* 9, no. 1 (2006): 27–50.

17 Stephen P. Osborne, *The New Public Governance? Emerging Perspectives on the Theory and Practice of Public Governance* (New York: Routledge, 2010).

18 Jan van Dijk and Anneleen Winters-van Beek, "The Perspective of Network Government: The Struggle between Hierarchies, Markets and Networks as Modes of Governance in Contemporary Government," in *ICTs, Citizens and Governance: After the Hype!* ed. Albert Meijer, Kees Boersma, Pieter Wagenaar, 235–255 (Lancaster: Gavelle Books, 2009).

19 Louis Meuleman, *Public Management and the Metagovernance of Hierarchies, Networks and Markets*, Contributions to Management Science (Heidelberg: Physica-Verlag HD, 2008).

20 Keast, Mandell, and Brown, "Mixing State, Market and Network Governance Modes," 28.

21 RUAG, "About RUAG," 2017, https://www.ruag.com/en/ruag-home.

22 RUAG, "Cyber Attack on RUAG: Major Damage Averted," 2016, 1.

23 Federal Assembly of the Swiss Confederation, *Swiss Criminal Code*, 1937, para. 273.

24 Federal Department of Defense, Civil Protection and Sport, "Cyber-Spionage-Angriff Auf RUAG," 2016, http://www.vbs.admin.ch/de/aktuell/medienmitteilungen.detail.nsb.html/61618.html.

25 Mathew J. Schwartz, "Swiss Defense Firm Hack Tied to 'Turla' Malware," BankInfoSecurity, May 23, 2016, http://www.bankinfosecurity.com/swiss-government-ruag-hack-ties-to-turla-malware-a-91282016.

26 Thomas Rid, "Highly Significant: Swiss Gov't Publishes Detailed APT Report, Links Ruag Cyber Attack to Turla, Ancestor: Agent.BTZ," May 23, 2016, https://twitter.com/ridt/status/734662844843741184.

27 Reporting and Analysis Centre for Information Assurance, "Technical Report about the Espionage Case at RUAG," 2016.

28 "Active Directory is a Windows [operating system] directory service that facilitates working with interconnected, complex and different network resources in a unified manner. [It] provides a common interface for organizing and maintaining information related to resources connected to a variety of network directories. [It] serves as a single data store for quick data access to all users and controls access for users based on the directory's security policy" (Techopedia, "What Is Active Directory (AD)?" 2017, https://www.techopedia.com/definition/25/active-directory).

29 Analysts were not able make clear statements in regards to data propriety and sensitivity, as no wiretaps were in place prior to the attack.

30 swissinfo.ch, S. W. I., "Hackers Target Swiss Defence Ministry," May 4, 2016, https://www.swissinfo.ch/eng/politics/industrial-espionage_hackers-target-swiss-defence-ministry/42131890.

31 The Rendon Group, "Conficker Working Group: Lessons Learned," 2010.

32 Wikipedia, "Conficker," 2017, https://en.wikipedia.org/wiki/Conficker.

33 Bobby Johnson, "Conficker Worm Explained: What Is a Botnet?" *The Guardian*, March 31, 2009, https://www.theguardian.com/technology/2009/mar/31/botnets-explainer.

34 Kelly Burton, "The Conficker Worm," 2009, https://www.sans.org/security-resources/malwarefaq/conficker-worm.

35 The Rendon Group, "Conficker Working Group: Lessons Learned."

36 Entities involved in the collaborative mitigation undertaking included Microsoft, Afilias, ICANN, Neustar, Verisign, CNNIC, Public Internet Registry, Global Domains International, Inc., M1D Global, AOL, Symantec, F-Secure, ISC, researchers from Georgia Tech, the Shadowserver Foundation, Arbor Networks, and Support Intelligence (ICANN, "Microsoft Collaborates With Industry to Disrupt Conficker Worm," February 2009, https://www.icann.org/news/announcement-2-2009-02-12-en).

37 The Rendon Group, "Conficker Working Group: Lessons Learned," iii.

38 According to ICANN's Senior Security Technologist, Dave Piscitello, the collaborating parties "performed roles that were appropriate to their organisations' core competencies [that is,] malware researchers reverse engineered the dropper/installer, traffic analysis engineers identified the loci of infestations, ICANN facilitated communications between registries and parties who compiled the C&C domain lists, and registry operators blocked registrations of Conficker domains." (Dave Piscitello, "Conficker Summary and Review," 2010, 10).

39 Symantec, "2018 Annual Report," 2019. https://s1.q4cdn.com/585930769/files/doc_financials/2018annual-report/532571_015_BMK_WEB1.pd[4].pdf.

40 Symantec, "Corporate Fact Sheet," 2016, https://www.symantec.com/content/dam/symantec/docs/other-resources/symantec-corporate-fact-sheet-060517-en.pdf.

41 Symantec, "Internet Security Threat Report," April 2017, https://www.symantec.com/content/dam/symantec/docs/reports/istr-22-2017-en.pdf, 1.

42 Symantec, "Internet Security Threat Report."

43 The WannaCry malware released mid-May 2017 had two components, a self-propagating worm module and a ransomware module. Once successfully executed, the malware appended encrypted data files with the .WCRY extension, released and ran a decryptor tool, and demanded a ransom payment of $300 or $600 (via Bitcoin) for data encryption (Berry, Homan, and Eitzman 2017). For a more technical analysis of the WannaCry ransomware, readers are advised to consult the following resource: (Symantec 2017b).

44 Johnson, "Conficker Worm Explained: What Is a Botnet?"

45 Symantec 2017c.

46 Piscitello, "Conficker Summary and Review," 12.

47 Tatiana Tropina and Cormac Callanan, *Self- and Co-Regulation in Cybercrime, Cybersecurity and National Security*, SpringerBriefs in Cybersecurity

(Cham: Springer International Publishing, 2015), https://doi.org/10.1007/978-3-319-16447-2.

48 Keast, Mandell, and Brown, "Mixing State, Market and Network Governance Modes."

49 Joseph S. Nye, "The Regime Complex for Managing Global Cyber Activities," 2014, https://www.cigionline.org/sites/default/files/gcig_paper_no1.pdf, 7.

50 Raymond and DeNardis "Multistakeholderism," 610.

51 James A. Lewis, "Internet Governance: Inevitable Transitions," *Internet Governance Papers*, 2013.

6

Cyber Governance and the Financial Services Sector

The Role of Public–Private Partnerships

Valeria San Juan[1] and Aaron Martin[2]

[1] *Fundbox, San Francisco, CA, USA*
[2] *Tilburg Institute for Law, Technology, and Society, Tilburg Law School, Tilburg University, Tilburg, Netherlands*

6.1 Introduction

In 2016, the Society for Worldwide Interbank Financial Telecommunication (SWIFT), the network used by financial institutions to send and receive transaction information,[1] experienced a series of attacks resulting in the theft of millions of dollars. The first reported attack, which occurred in February 2016, resulted in an $81 million theft from the Central Bank of Bangladesh.[2] Hackers were able to exploit a vulnerability in the SWIFT network: they used the credentials of Bangladesh Central Bank employees to send fraudulent money transfer requests to the Federal Reserve Bank of New York, asking the bank to transfer money from the Central Bank of Bangladesh into accounts throughout Asia.[3] While the $81 million heist received most of the media exposure, there were several other theft attempts in June of the same year, some of which were also successful in sending fraudulent payment instructions.

In a private letter to clients, SWIFT stressed that "the threat is persistent, adaptive and sophisticated – and it is here to stay."[4] This suggests an increase in threats and attacks targeting financial institutions, not just directly but also through third-party networks and external systems like SWIFT. The SWIFT attacks demonstrate both the varied points of vulnerability within financial institutions and the interconnectedness of the global financial system. Meanwhile, the incident has prompted regulators around the world to refocus on cybersecurity requirements.

Regulatory scrutiny of cybersecurity in the financial industry is by no means new – particularly in the United States, where banks have seen more than 40

Rewired: Cybersecurity Governance, First Edition. Edited by Ryan Ellis and Vivek Mohan.
© 2019 John Wiley & Sons, Inc. Published 2019 by John Wiley & Sons, Inc.

new cybersecurity-related standards, guidelines, examination expectations, regulations, and other requirements since 2014.[5] The Clearing House, an association that advocates on behalf of large banks, points to research showing that large multinational banks spend about 40% of their cybersecurity efforts on regulatory compliance.[6]

While this flurry of regulatory activity seeks to address the wide-ranging cybersecurity challenges facing the financial services sector (FSS) by prescribing various guidelines and rules, such an approach is not the only way of governing cybersecurity. The use of public–private partnerships (PPPs) provides an alternative vehicle for achieving cybersecurity outcomes. Therefore, in this chapter we aim to explore governance through the lens of the PPPs devised by the sector to address cybersecurity challenges. In particular, we focus on sector-led bodies and their role in organizing, coordinating, and governing cybersecurity efforts.

This contribution is the first to explore in depth the various FSS organizations focused on cybersecurity and critical infrastructure (CI) protection.[7] We first discuss how governance over security and the protection of CI has increased the focus on the role of PPPs in addressing issues of cybersecurity. We continue by highlighting three sector-led bodies – the Financial Services Information Sharing and Analysis Center (FS-ISAC), the Financial Services Sector Coordinating Council (FSSCC), and the Financial Systemic Analysis and Resilience Center (FSARC) – and how each facilitates PPPs to address challenges primarily in the areas of information sharing, policy coordination, and threat analytics, respectively. The chapter concludes with a discussion of lessons learned and remarks on future cyber governance research avenues. These lessons include: (i) validation of the PPP model, with some important caveats; (ii) the need to extend PPPs beyond information sharing to address systemic risks; and (iii) the limitations of PPPs in regulated industries like finance.

6.2 Governance, Security, and Critical Infrastructure Protection

While "government" refers to an entity – most often the state – with the recognized ability to make and enforce policy decisions, the concept of "governance" is generally defined in broader terms.[8] Governance concerns the exercise of authority by both formal institutions like the government and less formal organizations like markets or civil society.[9] Governance structures can therefore exist outside of government. In fact, governance often refers to the development of governing structures and mechanisms within and across the public and private sectors that do not explicitly relate to a formal government. Another defining characteristic of governance is that it does not rely on the legislative or authoritative power of the state to drive or command action.

It is widely understood and accepted that the state is responsible for the provision of national security, the protection of the nation-state and its citizens. Since it developed after World War II, the concept of national security initially had a strong military connotation.[10] While national security is still associated with the military, the use of the term has broadened to include nonmilitary security, such as the economic security of a nation. With the broadened understanding of national security, there has been increased focus on CI and the role it plays in maintaining national security. CI refers to services, assets, systems, and networks, whether physical or digital, considered vital to society.[11] Countries define their CI based on the criticality of services or sectors to the security and safety of the government, economy, and society.[12]

CI protection has been the focus of many national laws, guidelines, and frameworks. In the United States, there have been executive orders and presidential policy directives focused on CI protection since the Clinton administration. Executive Order 13010 ("Critical Infrastructure Protection"), in effect since 1996, was key to demonstrating the government's focus on CI.[13] It established a steering committee composed of representatives from different federal agencies. This committee was responsible for identifying and consulting with the public and private sectors deemed to be CI or that support and conduct elements related to the nation's CI. This executive order paved the way for public and private entities to collaborate on issues of national security, and laid a foundation for the development of PPPs between CI and the government. Issued in 2001, Executive Order 13231 ("Critical Infrastructure Protection in the Information Age") focused more on protecting the operation of information systems important to CI.[14] Aside from highlighting the importance of CI information, the executive order also discussed the use of PPPs to enhance the security and protection of CI. Significantly, this executive order proclaimed the importance of the information systems that underpin CI and catalyzed the focus on the security of these systems.

The CI systems underpinning the economy and society are complex and diverse. They include widely distributed networks, embody a variety of operating models and ownership structures, and many times function both in a physical and cyberspace capacity.[15] Additionally, CI has complex governance structures that include varied regulations, responsibilities, and authorities.[16] Since much of the CI (e.g. finance, utilities, and transport) is owned and/or operated by the private sector, the state cannot be the sole actor responsible for ensuring its protection and security. In the United States, maintaining CI security is considered a "shared responsibility between the federal, state, local, tribal, and territorial entities, and public and private operators of critical infrastructure."[17] Due to the extensive and profound risks associated with a potential breach of CI, government and private industry have recognized and accepted the shared responsibility to assure its protection against security threats, including cyber threats.

Table 6.1 Comparison of FS-ISAC, FSSCC, and FSARC.

Industry group	Founded	Purpose	Membership
Financial Services Information Sharing and Analysis Center	1999	Information sharing	Organizations across the financial services sector (e.g. insurance, banking, and asset management)
Financial Services Sector Coordinating Council	2003	Policy coordination and critical infrastructure protection	Organizations that provide critical financial services including utilities, plus trade associations
Financial Systemic Analysis and Resilience Center	2016	Resilience and systemic risk	Limited to organizations within the financial services sector designated as critical infrastructure

The cybersecurity of CI has thus become a priority for both the public and private sectors. The shared responsibility of the state and private industry – with the state responsible for providing national security and private industry responsible for ensuring protection of the provision and operation of critical services – has resulted in the widespread use of PPPs to drive cybersecurity efforts. The FSS, in particular, has witnessed numerous PPPs in the area of cybersecurity. The next sections explore three of these partnerships in depth: the FS-ISAC, a well-established operational group; the FSSCC, a policy coordination body; and the FSARC, a newly established industry group. We discuss each organization's origins, purpose, membership/constituency, relationship to government, and (when they exist) notable accomplishments (Table 6.1).

6.3 Financial Services Information Sharing and Analysis Center

The FS-ISAC was created in 1999 in response to Presidential Decision Directive 63 (PDD-63), released in 1998.[18] The directive strongly encouraged CI industries to create private sector information sharing and analysis centers (ISACs) to gather, analyze, and share private sector information with other industry members and with the National Infrastructure Protection Center (NIPC), the unit of the government that – until its elimination in 2003 – was responsible for protecting computer and information systems of CI.[19] FS-ISAC's purpose, operations, and organizational structure were highly influenced by the operational concepts and high-level institutional framework outlined in PDD-63.

The directive outlined two main concepts that would shape the purpose and structure of FS-ISAC. In regards to the purpose, the directive called for a clear and mutual communication channel between the NIPC and the ISAC created by each CI industry. As a reciprocal communication mechanism, FS-ISAC was designed by the FSS to be both a receiver and contributor of information about physical and cybersecurity vulnerabilities, intrusions, threats, and anomalies between government and industry. As a result, the FSS uses FS-ISAC to create and disseminate information to members, as much as to collect and ingest information. Importantly, the directive mandates that an analysis and information sharing center cannot interfere with the exchange of information between private sector companies and government agencies. Considering that the FSS is in constant contact with federal and state regulatory agencies, it was important to design FS-ISAC such that its analysis and information-sharing operations did not infringe upon or emulate regulatory communications.[20]

As for structure, PDD-63 suggested that industry-specific ISACs model themselves on institutions deemed effective at information exchange with private and nonfederal sectors. The directive gave the Center for Disease Control and Prevention (CDC) as a model primarily because of its efficacy at communicating, analyzing, and reporting on different initiatives. In response to this suggestion, FS-ISAC adopted a technical focus with objectives outside regulatory and law-enforcement requirements. The directive also noted that the effectiveness of an industry-specific ISAC would depend on its capability to develop statistics and patterns across its objectives as well as on its ability to become an instrument for collecting data and sharing information within and among industry and government stakeholders.[21]

With PDD-63 largely informing its purpose and structure, FS-ISAC has evolved as the financial industry's main resource for sharing and analyzing physical and cyber "threat intelligence."[22] It operates as a member-owned nonprofit entity with a membership base of over 7000 financial services institutions as of 2016.[23] FS-ISAC's Community Institution and Associations (CIA) membership, which includes credit unions, has increased from 231 members to more than 3800 community institutions between 2014 and 2017.[24] FS-ISAC membership extends across different areas of the FSS, including financial institutions, insurance companies, utilities, payment processors, pension funds, and more. These members and partners also extend across regions including North and South America, Europe, the Middle East, and Asia Pacific. Though FS-ISAC has always had members with global operations, it was not until 2013 that board members approved sharing information with financial services firms worldwide.

FS-ISAC membership is recommended by several US federal agencies including the Department of Homeland Security (DHS), the Treasury Department, and the Office of the Comptroller of the Currency (OCC). This recommendation from multiple federal agencies demonstrates the buy-in from the government and delineates the collaborative nature of the relationship between these entities. In particular, the Treasury Department and the DHS heavily rely on FS-ISAC to quickly disseminate critical information to the sector during crises. US state and local government agencies and law enforcement also use FS-ISAC to communicate physical and cyber threat information and alerts. In addition to closely collaborating with US government and law-enforcement organizations, FS-ISAC also increasingly works with international government entities, regional computer emergency response teams (CERTs), and computer security incident response teams (CSIRTs) to meet international member requirements.[25]

FS-ISAC is particularly focused on providing anonymous information-sharing capabilities across the entire sector. Its main purpose is to disseminate information about current physical and cyber threats in a timely and organized manner to industry members and government. It constantly works to gather reliable information from its members, as well as from other financial service providers, security firms, law enforcement, and government agencies.[26] FS-ISAC fulfills its information-sharing purpose by maintaining a database where members voluntarily report information about vulnerabilities, threats, incidents, and solutions.[27] This data is only accessible to members and is used to develop trend and benchmark information for members. Though FS-ISAC operations primarily focus on communicating current and existing threats, FS-ISAC also conducts research on these threats and breaches. The research and communication operations are organized into different focus areas such as consumer payments, wholesale payments, or destructive malware.[28] In addition to research, FS-ISAC runs simulated cybersecurity exercises related to different FSS operations. For example, in 2013, FS-ISAC conducted a two-day simulated exercise related to payment, Automated Clearing House (ACH), and online banking processes deployed by banks and credit unions. This exercise enabled participating member institutions to experience realistic breach and threat scenarios, in order to train and test critical incident response practices. These exercises are often conducted in coordination with the Treasury Department and are designed to improve the attack responses of participating members.

FS-ISAC's accomplishments have centered on improving the collection, distillation, and communication of threat intelligence to member organizations and partners. Most of these accomplishments have resulted from increasing partnerships with national and international government agencies, developing ventures with FSS vendors and software providers, and establishing separate but connected organizations to improve specific aspects of communicating and assessing threat intelligence.

One such accomplishment is Soltra, the joint venture between FS-ISAC and the Depository Trust & Clearing Corporation (DTCC), a provider of post-trade market infrastructure. Created in 2014 with the support of the DHS, Soltra was built to improve the speed and security of threat intelligence information sharing between companies.[29] The name Soltra refers to a beacon fire network used to warn communities of invaders in medieval Europe.[30] As the name implies, the joint venture was designed to transfer information to a vast number of organizations for their own use. Soltra Edge was the "first industry-driven threat intelligence sharing platform designed to enable community-driven cyber defense."[31] After operating from 2014 to 2016, Soltra was sold to NC4 in November 2016.[32]

One of FS-ISAC's most notable accomplishments, Sheltered Harbor, resulted from internal efforts to create a different entity to address a specific component of cyber threat within the sector. A limited liability company (LLC) within FS-ISAC, Sheltered Harbor exclusively focuses on strengthening the sector's resilience to a major cyberattack.[33] Created in 2016, Sheltered Harbor allows financial institutions to safely store and quickly reconstitute customer data following an attack. It also allows a customer to access their own data through other financial institutions, in case the customer's bank suffers an attack and is unable to recover quickly.[34] The idea for Sheltered Harbor arose from the "Hamilton Series" of cybersecurity simulations between the private and public sectors (named after Alexander Hamilton, the first Treasurer of the United States).

The Sheltered Harbor operational model of mutual assistance in case of a damaging attack exemplifies the partnerships present within the FSS. While the financial industry competes on nearly every front, from customers to service, it organizes and collaborates on issues of cybersecurity. Similarly, the relationship between the FSS and government in matters of business operations and regulatory requirements is rigid and wary. However, in the case of cybersecurity, close collaboration and partnership is favored. This collaboration is clear through the many partnerships FS-ISAC has formed with different government agencies, both national and international. In 2015, FS-ISAC came to an arrangement with the Federal Reserve Banks to provide over 10 000 of their financial institution members with direct access to security threat information.[35] The partnership is meant to strengthen the communications between this part of the government and the sector by allowing the Federal Reserve Banks to provide FS-ISAC members with access to their Weekly Risk Summary Report, which outlines significant security threats.

As for efforts to strengthen collaboration between the FSS and international government bodies, FS-ISAC has signed memoranda of understanding and agreed to more deeply engage in threat information sharing. In 2016 alone, FS-ISAC signed a memorandum with the European Banking Federation (EBF) to intensify threat information sharing between financial institutions based in Europe and those in the Americas, Asia Pacific, and other regions.[36] The main goal of the cooperation is to increase the resilience of the FSS at a global level through "regional threat advisories, working groups, and sharing mechanisms."[37] FS-ISAC's focus on partnerships with international organizations and governments demonstrates the need to improve collaboration in order to better analyze, mitigate, and recover from cyber threats. Similar to the memorandum with EBF, FS-ISAC and the Monetary Authority of Singapore (MAS) agreed to establish an Asia Pacific Regional Intelligence Center to improve information sharing and analysis for the FSS within the region.[38] The center, launched in late 2017, is run by FS-ISAC but will primarily focus on building robust intelligence gathering, sharing, and analysis for regional financial institutions.

Members of FS-ISAC realized the need for an organization specifically focused on longer-term threat analysis, to complement FS-ISAC's focus on enhancing real-time threat information sharing, response to cyberattacks, and international cooperation. Since FS-ISAC primarily occupies itself with real-time information sharing and analysis, successful resilience-building across the FSS also requires an organization that is more strategic and deliberately focused on long-term analysis, strategy, and response. To fill this gap, FS-ISAC members formed the FSARC, the mission of which is to "proactively identify, analyze, assess and coordinate activities to mitigate systemic risk to the United States financial system."[39] This new organization is explored in depth below, following a discussion of the FSSCC.

6.4 Financial Services Sector Coordinating Council

The FSSCC was established in 2002. It is the main policy coordination and planning entity through which the sector collaborates with the Treasury Department and other government agencies to address security and resilience.[40] The FSSCC is a self-organized, self-run, and self-governed entity that uses its collaborative relationship with the federal government to provide members with a channel to promote and shape government efforts and policies on security and resilience – areas increasingly dominated by cybersecurity issues. A year after the FSSCC was formed, the Homeland Security Presidential Directive 7 (HSPD-7) established a national policy for federal agencies to "identify and prioritize critical infrastructure" to better protect these industries.[41] HSPD-7 more clearly defined the role of the Treasury Department as the sector-specific federal agency responsible for facilitating vulnerability assessments and encouraging risk-management strategies for the FSS.

In addition to addressing the need for improved security and resilience outlined in HSPD-7, the FSSCC also seeks to fulfill the national efforts indicated in Presidential Policy Directive 21 (PPD-21), released in 2013. PPD-21 called for the clarification of government and industry relationships in regards to physical and cyber threats by enhancing PPPs.[42] It outlined a PPP framework in which the private sector would work with sector-specific agencies (such as the Treasury Department in the case of the FSS) to address and mitigate risks, threats, and vulnerabilities. In turn, these agencies would coordinate and support DHS analysis and reporting requirements around CI security and resilience. HSPD-7 provided a basic outline of the federal government's responsibilities in developing a collaborative relationship with the private sector, while PPD-21 clarified the role of the DHS in coordinating efforts and providing strategic guidance for CI security and resilience. As a result, the FSSCC maintains a strong partnership with the Treasury Department and the DHS, with the goal of "identifying, prioritizing, and coordinating the protection of critical infrastructure and key resources" and of "facilitating the sharing of information about physical and cyber threats, vulnerabilities, incidents, potential protective measures, and best practices."[43]

Membership in the FSSCC is open to nongovernmental organizations within the sector. However, membership is limited to financial institutions considered CI – institutions that are systemically significant, with operations that broadly affect financial services operations and infrastructure.[44] Given the CI restriction, FSSCC membership is much smaller than that of FS-ISAC. The 70 members include financial utilities, trade associations, insurance providers, banks, and other financial institutions. Membership is predominantly composed of US organizations and those subject to US regulatory oversight and requirements.[45] International organizations that have a significant effect on United States and global operations, and that provide services widely used across the FSS, are also eligible to apply for membership. Aside from these core members, as of 2017 the FSSCC has an additional 64 volunteer member associations and financial institutions, including clearinghouses, credit rating agencies, financial advisory services, insurance companies, government-sponsored enterprises, information-sharing organizations, and electronic payment firms.[46]

The FSSCC's mission is to strengthen the resilience of the sector against physical and cyber threats by serving as the sector's main tool to communicate and collaborate with US federal government agencies. The FSSCC drives collaboration with the US federal government to proactively identify threats and to promote preparedness and protective measures for the sector. Arguably, the most important role of the FSSCC is to advocate for the interests of the sector as it relates to cybersecurity policy. As the main method of communicating and collaborating with the government, the FSSCC provides a unique mechanism for financial firms considered CI to provide their perspectives on the cyber policies and frameworks developed by the federal government. In practice, the organization seeks to inform the federal government of the sector's specific needs and pain points in regards to physical, and more importantly, cyber threats so that policy is developed with industry perspective and input.

Much of what the FSSCC does is "improve the content and process of bi-directional threat information sharing."[47] As a major enhancement to bi-directional threat information sharing, the FSSCC created an Intelligence Community (IC) Coordinator meant to facilitate the coordination of classified interactions with the federal IC. The IC Coordinator position was created to maintain and expand the FSS's influence on government agencies in cyber policy matters. The sector already has a well-established partnership with the Treasury Department and the DHS through FS-ISAC, so the FSSCC IC Coordinator is largely focused on increasing and improving information sharing with other partners, such as the FBI Cyber Crime Division.

Along with improving threat information sharing through stronger government partnerships, the FSSCC seeks to increase government research, development, and policy efforts that support the improvement of security and resilience in the sector. The FSSCC uses lobbying, letter writing, and press releases to voice the sector's opinions and to influence government actions as they relate to cybersecurity and resilience. For example, in January 2017, the FSSCC released a letter containing cybersecurity priorities and recommendations in response to the new presidential administration and Congress.[48] The campaign focused on several areas of improvement, including risk-based research and development, cybersecurity regulation, global deterrence, and cyber event response.[49]

Many of FSSCC's public letters and press releases mention the need for more government investment in risk-based research and development related specifically to the FSS. The FSSCC has advocated for stronger federal resourcing within the IC for programs that detect and analyze cyber threats as well as contingency planning and cyber event exercises. An additional FSSCC advocacy priority is a clearer and more holistic approach to federal and state cybersecurity regulation. In their January 2017 letter to the new presidential administration and Congress, FSSCC members called for more coordinated cybersecurity regulation – based on the National Institute of Standards and Technology (NIST) Cybersecurity Framework – that would reduce the number of divergent proposals, mandatory guidelines, and frameworks that federal and state governments release.[50] The FSSCC is also encouraging the government to develop a consistent data protection and breach notification law across national and state platforms, in order to reduce the burden of translating and mapping legal requirements to the current frameworks they have in place.[51] The FSSCC's call for more consistent and holistic cyber regulation was endorsed by a report on "Securing and Growing the Digital Economy," released by the Commission on Enhancing National Security (established by President Obama's Executive Order 13718). The report, completed in December 2016, outlined short- and long-term recommendations for strengthening cybersecurity in the public and private sectors.

Aside from collaborating with the Treasury Department and the DHS, the FSSCC also works with the Financial and Banking Information Infrastructure Committee (FBIIC). The FBIIC was created in 2001 by federal financial regulators in order to address the resilience of the financial sector, promote PPPs, and improve the communication and coordination of financial regulators.[52] The FBIIC consists of 18 federal and state financial regulatory organizations, including the OCC, the Securities and Exchange Commission (SEC), the Federal

Reserve Board (FRB), and others.[53] Members of the FBIIC meet monthly to work on operational and strategic issues related to CI, including cybersecurity. These monthly meetings inform the strategic and policy-level direction of the FBIIC, especially with regards to removing information-sharing obstacles, identifying best practices for cybersecurity controls, and improving incident-response planning. The FBIIC and FSSCC often hold joint meetings to promote discussion of regulatory harmonization and public–private collaboration on addressing legal barriers to information sharing, as well as to collectively discuss cyber threat, risk, and communication initiatives in the sector.

In addition to partnering with the FBIIC, the FSSCC collaborates with the Federal Financial Institutions Examination Council (FFIEC), the interagency body that prescribes standards and principles for federal examination of the FSS.[54] Through the FFIEC, regulators are able to make recommendations to promote uniformity in the regulation and supervision of financial institutions in various areas including cybersecurity.[55] In 2015, the FFIEC released the Cybersecurity Assessment Tool (CAT) to support financial institutions in their identification and analysis of cyber risk, preparedness, and response capabilities.[56] While use of the CAT is not mandatory, it is highly recommended by FFIEC regulators, resulting in its wide adoption and incorporation throughout the sector. In response, the FSSCC created an automated tool to facilitate the collection and scoring of firms' responses to the CAT (Table 6.2).

Table 6.2 FBBIC membership.

Financial and Banking Information Infrastructure Committee	
American Council of State Savings Supervisors	Federal Reserve Bank of New York
Commodity Futures Trading Commission	Federal Reserve Board[a]
Conference of State Bank Supervisors	National Association of Insurance Commissioners
Consumer Financial Protection Bureau[a]	National Association of State Credit Union Supervisors
Department of the Treasury	National Credit Union Administration[a]
Farm Credit Administration	North American Securities Administrators Association
Federal Deposit Insurance Corporation[a]	Office of the Comptroller of the Currency[a]
Federal Housing Finance Agency	Securities and Exchange Commission
Federal Reserve Bank of Chicago	Securities Investor Protection Corporation

[a] Also member of FFIEC.

6.5   Financial Systemic Analysis and Resilience Center

The FSARC was created in June 2016 after eight CEOs of the largest US banks[57] decided to improve the cyber capabilities of CI within the FSS.[58] The FSARC was established under FS-ISAC so as to better partner and collaborate with FS-ISAC members and the US government, including the Treasury Department, the DHS, the FBI, and others.[59] The FSARC's mission is "to proactively identify, analyze, assess and coordinate activities to mitigate *systemic risk* to the US financial system" (emphasis added).[60] While FS-ISAC focuses on real-time analysis and information sharing of cybersecurity threats, the FSARC takes a long-term strategic approach to improving cybersecurity capabilities at the sector and firm level. FSARC operations are not meant to replace FS-ISAC initiatives, but are intended to fill a perceived gap in the analysis of threats that affect the sector. Prior to the FSARC, there was no organization that carried out analysis specifically focused on assessing current and future cybersecurity threats with the purpose of improving sector-wide defense capabilities. Part of the FSARC's mission is to "identify ways to enhance the resilience of the critical infrastructure that underpins the US financial system," which entails identifying and analyzing systemic sector risks.[61]

Since the FSARC operates under FS-ISAC, it is able to collaborate with FS-ISAC members and government partners. The FSARC is also able to use the cybersecurity threat intelligence identified through FS-ISAC operations and its government partners for a deeper analysis of identified threats. Ultimately, the eight bank CEOs envisioned the FSARC as a mechanism to reduce the systemic risk of the FSS and as a way for CI to collaborate to understand the sector's evolving threats and develop better defenses.[62] Because the FSARC is focused on systemic risk to CI, it is led by FSS companies that the federal government has designated as "most crucial to national safety, security, and economic integrity."[63]

The FSARC was created around the time federal regulators released cybersecurity draft rules that required the FSS to recover critical business functions within two hours of a cyberattack.[64] Though the FSARC was not a response to these draft rules, its creation clearly accompanies the increased focus of the public and private sectors on cyber defense capabilities. The FSARC was designed to provide "contextualized and in-depth analyses of long and short term cyber threats," with more of a "hands-on perspective" than government or information-sharing organizations.[65] The creation of the FSARC also demonstrates the FSS's increased focus on the systemic risk facing the US financial system.[66]

The FSARC's prevention, detection, and mitigation tactics are meant to complement already established partnerships across the private and public sectors, such as FS-ISAC and FSSCC, creating a stronger connection and coalition between the different FSS PPPs. Similar to the FSARC is the National Cyber-Forensics & Training Alliance (NCFTA), a nonprofit focused on real-time information sharing and analysis of cyber threats. Founded in 2002, the NCFTA is focused on identifying, mitigating, and neutralizing cyber threats at a global level.[67] The NCFTA collaborates with subject-matter experts in the private, public, and academic sectors to proactively identify cyber threats and determine the best preventive measures to mitigate such threats.[68] While the NCFTA is not primarily focused on systemic threats facing the US financial system, it shares the FSARC's focus on best practices to mitigate threats through response planning efforts and threat analytics.

As of 2018, the FSARC has three main focus areas: intelligence collection, advanced analytics capabilities, and sharing of workforce resources with government. In collecting actionable intelligence, the FSARC seeks to identify the most critical elements and operations of the US financial system so that the gathering of intelligence can be focused on cyber threats that pose the greatest systemic risk.[69] Leaders of the FSARC argue that while government agencies are good at collecting threat intelligence, they do not necessarily have the sector-specific expertise required to contextualize and determine the motivation of attacks, assess the importance of threats to the systemic operations of the sector, or identify trends in the sector's vulnerabilities. Members of the FSARC also want to engage with government to prioritize the collection of threat intelligence in order to develop a more organized approach to sourcing.[70]

While most of the industry-led organizations work to improve PPPs in the areas of policy making and information sharing, the FSARC is also meant to enhance the sharing of advanced analytics between the private sector and government.[71] More specifically, it wants to include machine learning, artificial intelligence, and the coordination of operations in its partnership with federal government agencies.[72] Additionally, FSARC members would like the government to use the organization to coordinate public–private cyber defense operations and measures to drive broader cyber deterrence.[73] The FSARC is also advocating for the government to assign a dedicated and shared workforce of government employees to the FSARC mission of improving FSS CI security.

6.6 Lessons for Cybersecurity Governance

Having reviewed the varied roles and functions of FS-ISAC, FSSCC, and the FSARC, what are some of the lessons for cyber governance emanating from the financial sector's experiences in creating and cultivating PPPs? While the lessons are potentially innumerable, we will focus on three key observations here:

6.6.1 Lesson One: Affirmation of PPP Model, but Focus and Clarity Needed

The FSS's experience with cyber partnerships demonstrates their effectiveness in addressing complex challenges, including operational (FS-ISAC), policy

(FSSCC), and increasingly strategic (FSARC) challenges. It is clear that neither government nor industry is capable of achieving cybersecurity on its own. Industry leaders must work together through mechanisms like FS-ISAC to identify and respond to ongoing threats. Industry must also be able to rely on government partners when necessary, as in moments of crisis (e.g. sector-wide Distributed Denial of Service [DDoS] or catastrophic destructive malware attacks). Industry and government must collaborate in order to develop and implement cyber policy that is fit for its purpose and does not unintentionally harm firms' cyber defenses. Likewise, industry must increasingly rely on government partnerships to provide insights into the strategic cyber threats facing the sector, particularly with respect to systemic risk.

Though cooperation among PPPs highlights the shared purpose and interest of government and private industry in pursuing common goals like cybersecurity, at times the roles and responsibilities assigned to each set of actors in these partnerships may appear ambiguous. PPPs within cybersecurity typically avoid directly assigning strict responsibility and accountability. Instead, the governance practices resulting from these partnerships can be unclear and often revert back to legacy governance and relationship structures between government and industry (e.g. what can government do for industry?). This is particularly clear in the FSS, where government has often taken the role of a regulator.

Moreover, with the expansion of PPPs and the formation of new initiatives like FSARC, there is a risk that the respective roles and responsibilities of each organization may become confused. Tight coordination among organizations tasked with facilitating partnerships will become increasingly necessary to maintain focused objectives and eliminate duplicative or wasteful effort.

6.6.2 Lesson Two: Addressing Systemic Risk Requires more than Just Information Sharing

FS-ISAC is considered a highly successful venture and an Information Sharing and Analysis Organization (ISAO) *par excellence*. It is widely viewed as one of the premiere industry cybersecurity organizations and a leading example of an effective ISAC. However, the increasing cyber threat demands more focused analysis of longer-term strategic trends, as well as tighter industry–government coordination, particularly for highly interconnected CI sectors.

It is one thing for each CI organization within a sector to strengthen its own cyber defenses and to share information about day-to-day incidents, but underlying systemic risks may persist. Critical third parties and essential utilities must be a part of the cyber risk calculus when identifying and addressing these systemic risks. This is where constructs like the FSARC enter the fray to fill an important gap.

One challenge in this respect is how to scale constructs like the FSARC internationally, particularly where engagement with national intelligence organizations may be required. Financial systemic risks are more often than not international in scope, but the international sharing of sensitive intelligence and analytics about these risks is not yet commonplace.

6.6.3   Lesson Three: Limitations of PPPs in Regulated Industries

As noted in the introduction, the FSS has experienced a tidal wave of new regulation and policy focused on cybersecurity risk. While well intended, this has created an unfortunate situation in which financial institutions are left to reconcile differing regulatory approaches, both domestically and internationally. Industry groups, including the FSSCC in the United States, have sought to engage regulators to harmonize and align their efforts, but this has proven challenging so far.

Looking beyond the world of finance, other highly regulated industries may soon experience similar challenges. This demonstrates a potential limitation of the PPP model, in cases where government partners are regulators with different incentives than nonregulatory government agencies, and with a perceived disinterest in collaboration.

6.7   Conclusion

In this chapter, we provided a deep dive into three key FSS-led organizations that facilitate PPPs for cybersecurity across different specialty areas. We also drew out broader lessons for cyber governance, with attention to the value and limitations of the PPP model, the need to advance beyond information sharing to address the cyber threat, and the complexities of relying on PPPs for security governance in regulated sectors. We hope that these insights aid both scholars and policymakers in better understanding the benefits and challenges associated with organizing the public and private sectors around shared goals like cybersecurity.

This chapter also raises interesting questions that merit further research, particularly around the effectiveness of sector-led international partnership on security matters. It also exposes the need for a better understanding of how regulatory environments shape PPPs, particularly in the domain of cybersecurity.

Acknowledgments

The authors would like to thank Deanna Girani for her support during the drafting of this chapter. As a member of the Global Data Justice project at Tilburg University, Aaron Martin has received funding from the European Research Council under the European Unions Horizon 2020 research and innovation programme (Grant Agreement n° 757247).

Notes

1 Susan V. Scott and Markos Zachariadis, *The Society for Worldwide Interbank Financial Telecommunication (SWIFT): Cooperative Governance for Network Innovation, Standards, and Community*, Routledge Global Institutions Series (London: Routledge, 2013).
2 Kim Zetter, "That Insane, $81M Bangladesh Bank Heist? Here is What We Know," *Wired*, May 17, 2018, https://www.wired.com/2016/05/insane-81m-bangladesh-bank-heist-heres-know.
3 Ibid.
4 Jim Finkle, "Exclusive: SWIFT Discloses More Cyber Thefts Pressures Banks on Security," *Reuters*, August 31, 2018, http://www.reuters.com/article/us-cyber-heist-swift-idUSKCN11600C.
5 Ibid.
6 Greg Baer and Rob Hunter, "A Tower of Babel: Cyber Regulation for Financial Services," *The Clearing House*, June 9, 2017, https://www.theclearinghouse.org/banking-perspectives/2017/2017-q2-banking-perspectives/articles/cyber-regulation-for-financial-services.
7 But for case studies of ChicagoFIRST and FSSCC, see: Brian S. Tishuk, "Effectively Managing Partnership Evolution: A Case Study from Chicago," *Journal of Business Continuity & Emergency Planning* 6, no. 2 (2013): 111–121.
8 OECD, "Governance," last modified July 23, 2007, https://stats.oecd.org/glossary/detail.asp?ID=7236.
9 Gerry Stoker, "Governance as Theory: Five Propositions," *International Social Science Journal* 155 (1998): 17–28.
10 Joseph J. Romm, *Defining National Security: The Nonmilitary Aspects* (New York: Council on Foreign Relations Press, 1993).
11 OECD, "The Development of Policies for the Protection of Critical Information Infrastructure," *OECD Ministerial Background Report*, 2007.
12 Ibid.
13 Executive Office of the President. Executive Order 13010 (July 15, 1996). "Critical Infrastructure Protection." https://www.gpo.gov/fdsys/pkg/FR-1996-07-17/pdf/96-18351.pdf.
14 Executive Office of the President. Executive Order 13231 (October 16, 2001). "Critical Infrastructure Protection in the Information Age." https://www.gpo.gov/fdsys/pkg/FR-2001-10-18/pdf/01-26509.pdf.
15 Presidential Policy Directive/PPD-21 (February 12, 2013), "Critical Infrastructure Security and Resilience," https://obamawhitehouse.archives.gov/the-press-office/2013/02/12/presidential-policy-directive-critical-infrastructure-security-and-resil.
16 Ibid.
17 Ibid.

18 FS-ISAC, "Mission," https://www.fsisac.com/about/mission.

19 Presidential Decision Directive/PDD-63 (May 22, 1998), "Critical Infrastructure Protection," https://fas.org/irp/offdocs/pdd/pdd-63.htm.

20 Ibid.

21 Ibid.

22 Threat intelligence is a term of art, which Gartner defines as: "evidence-based knowledge, including context, mechanisms, indicators, implications and actionable advice, about an existing or emerging threat to an organization or its assets." Gartner, "Definition: Threat Intelligence." May 16, 2013, https://www.gartner.com/doc/2487216/definition-threat-intelligence.

23 FS-ISAC, "FS-ISAC Community Institution and Association Membership Grows 3,800 Members. Heather McCalman Joins as Credit Union Council Manager," March 22, 2017, https://www.fsisac.com/sites/default/files/news/FS-ISAC_Press_Release_Community_Inst_3-22-2017_Final.pdf.

24 Ibid.

25 FS-ISAC, "Membership Benefits," https://www.fsisac.com/join.

26 FS-ISAC, "About FS-ISAC," https://www.fsisac.com/about.

27 Sue Eckert, "Protecting Critical Infrastructure: The Role of the Private Sector," University of Pittsburgh Center for International Securities Studies 2005, http://www.ridgway.pitt.edu/Portals/1/pdfs/Publications/Eckert.pdf.

28 FS-ISAC, "Best Practices for Financial Institutions Reducing Risks Associated with Destructive Malware," November 23, 2015.

29 FS-ISAC, "New Soltra Network Offering to Connect and Coordinate Cyber Threat Intelligence Sharing," October 12, 2014, https://www.fsisac.com/sites/default/files/news/Soltra%20Network%20Press%20Release%20101215%20%28final%29.pdf.

30 Soltra, "The Soltra Story," https://www.soltra.com/en/about.

31 FS-ISAC, "New Soltra Network."

32 NC4, "NC4 to buy cyber threat intelligence company, Soltra, from FS-ISAC, DTCC," November 23, 2016, https://www.fsisac.com/sites/default/files/news/PR-NC4_and_Soltra_Press_Release.pdf.

33 Jeff Stone and Kate Fazzini, "U.S. Financial Sector Begins 'Sheltered Harbor' Rollout," *Wall Street Journal*, March 9, 2017, https://www.linkedin.com/pulse/us-financial-sector-begins-sheltered-harbor-rollout-jeff-stone.

34 FS-ISAC, "Sheltered Harbor," November 23, 2016, https://www.fsisac.com/sites/default/files/news/SH_FACT_SHEET_2016_11_22_FINAL3.pdf.

35 FS-ISAC, "FS-ISAC to Offer Security Threat Information to Over 10,000 Federal Reserve Bank Financial Institution Customers," September 16, 2015, https://www.fsisac.com/sites/default/files/news/FRB-FS-ISAC-Press_Release_Sept_2015FINAL.pdf.

36 FS-ISAC, "European Banking Federation and the Financial Services Information Sharing and Analysis Center (FS-ISAC) Partner on Trans-Atlantic Initiative to Fight Cyber Crime," September 30, 2016, https://

www.fsisac.com/sites/default/files/news/EBF%20and%20FS%20ISAC%20
agree%20Trans-Atlantic%20cybercrime%20cooperation.pdf.
37 Ibid.
38 Monetary Authority of Singapore, "FS-ISAC and MAS Establish Asia Pacific
(APAC) Intelligence Centre for sharing and analysing cyber threat information,"
December 1, 2016, www.mas.gov.sg/News-and-Publications/Media-
Releases/2016/FS-ISAC-and-MAS-Establish-APAC-Intelligence-Centre.aspx.
39 FS-ISAC, "Preliminary Findings from Latest DDoS Attacks," November 2016,
http://iiac.ca/wp-content/uploads/FS-ISAC-SIRG-Cybersecurity-Brief-for-
North-America-November-2016.pdf.
40 FSSCC, "About FSSCC," https://www.fsscc.org/About-FSSCC.
41 Homeland Security Presidential Directive 7/HSPD-7 (December 17, 2003),
"Critical Infrastructure Identification, Prioritization, and Protection," https://
www.dhs.gov/homeland-security-presidential-directive-7.
42 PPD-21, "Critical Infrastructure Security and Resilience."
43 Ibid.
44 FSSCC, "Financial Services Sector Coordinating Council for Critical
Infrastructure Protection and Homeland Security Charter," March 20, 2015,
https://www.dhs.gov/sites/default/files/publications/FSSCC-
Charter-03-15-508.pdf.
45 FSSCC, "About FSSCC," https://www.fsscc.org/About-FSSCC.
46 FSSCC, "Letter to Senator Warren and Representative Cummings," December
9, 2014, https://www.fsscc.org/files/galleries/FSSCC_12-09-14_Letter_to_
Sen_Warren-Rep_Cummings.pdf.
47 FSSCC, "Financial Services Sector Coordinating Council for Critical
Infrastructure Protection and Homeland Security Annual Report 2013-2014,"
https://www.aba.com/Tools/Function/Cyber/Documents/
FSSCCAnnualReport2013-2014.pdf.
48 FSSCC, "Financial Services Sector Cybersecurity Recommendations," January
18, 2017, https://www.fsscc.org/files/galleries/FSSCC_Cybersecurity_
Recommendations_for_Administration_and_Congress_2017.pdf.
49 Ibid.
50 Ibid.
51 Ibid.
52 FBIIC, "Mission and History," https://www.fbiic.gov/mission-history.html.
53 FBIIC, "FBIIC Members," https://www.fbiic.gov/fbiic-members.html.
54 The FFIEC is composed of: the Board of Governors of the Federal Reserve
System, the Federal Deposit Insurance Corporation, the National Credit
Union Administration, the Office of the Comptroller of the Currency, the
Consumer Financial Protection Bureau, and the State Liaison Committee.
55 FFIEC, "Federal Financial Institutions Examination Council (FFIEC) About,"
https://www.ffiec.gov/about.htm.

56 FFIEC, "Cybersecurity Assessment Tool," https://www.ffiec.gov/cyberassessmenttool.htm.

57 Specifically, the CEOs of Bank of America, BNY Mellon, Citigroup, Goldman Sachs, JPMorgan Chase, Morgan Stanley, State Street, and Wells Fargo.

58 JPMorgan Chase & Co., "Annual Report 2016," 2017, https://www.jpmorganchase.com/corporate/investor-relations/document/2016-annualreport.pdf.

59 Ibid.

60 FS-ISAC, "FS-ISAC announces the formation of the Financial Systemic Analysis & Resilience Center (FSARC)," October 24, 2016, https://www.fsisac.com/sites/default/files/news/FS-ISAC%20Announces%20the%20Formation%20of%20the%20Financial%20Systemic%20Analysis%20%28FSARC%29.pdf.

61 Ibid.

62 Michael Chertoff and Frank Cilluffo, "Trump Administration Can Help Finance Sector Shift Cybersecurity Paradigm," *Forbes*, January 18, 2017, https://www.forbes.com/sites/realspin/2017/01/18/trump-administration-can-help-finance-sector-shift-cybersecurity-paradigm/#3b7561db645d.

63 Ibid.

64 "New Financial System Analysis & Resilience Center Formed," *Dark Reading*, October 24, 2016, http://www.darkreading.com/threat-intelligence/new-financial-system-analysis-and-resilience-center-formed-/d/d-id/1327276.

65 Chertoff and Cilluffo, "Trump Administration."

66 JPMorgan Chase & Co., "Cybersecurity: Maintaining Strong Defenses," Vol. 2 (Spring 2017).

67 NCFTA, "Who We Are," https://www.ncfta.net.

68 Ibid.

69 JPMorgan Chase & Co., "Cybersecurity: Maintaining Strong Defenses."

70 Chertoff and Cilluffo, "Trump Administration."

71 Ibid.

72 Ibid.

73 Ibid.

7

The Regulation of Botnets

How Does Cybersecurity Governance Theory Work When
Everyone Is a Stakeholder?

Samantha A. Adams, Karine e Silva, Bert-Jaap Koops,
and Bart van der Sloot*

Tilburg Institute for Law, Technology, and Society, Tilburg University, Tilburg, Netherlands

7.1 Introduction

Because of a general impression that cyberattacks are becoming more frequent, better organized, costlier, and altogether more dangerous, countries increasingly consider cybersecurity as one of their top security issues.[1] However, organizing responses to cybersecurity threats is no easy task. This chapter explores the role of polycentric cybersecurity governance in addressing cybersecurity threats, illustrated by efforts to mitigate the threats posed by botnet infrastructures. Botnets are collections of compromised machines remotely controlled by botmasters (or botherders). They are created through the dissemination of "bots," pieces of advanced malicious software that exploit vulnerabilities and install system backdoors in various devices such as personal computers, mobile phones, tablets, and wearables. Once a bot backdoor is installed, a communication channel is established between the victim device and the network under the control of the botherders, thereby rendering the victim device's processing power and functionalities at the disposal of perpetrators.

Botnets often remain under the radar of security tools such as firewalls and antiviruses, leaving users unaware that their devices are infected. Botmasters' power is reflected in their botnet's size, complexity, and resilience, which can

---

* Samantha Adams was the lead author in the writing of this chapter. In late 2017, while the submission for this volume was under review, Samantha passed away after a brief period of illness. This chapter is one of the last pieces she wrote. The remaining authors dedicate this chapter to her memory, in gratitude for the privilege of having been able to collaborate with her.

Rewired: Cybersecurity Governance, First Edition. Edited by Ryan Ellis and Vivek Mohan.
© 2019 John Wiley & Sons, Inc. Published 2019 by John Wiley & Sons, Inc.

be used to perform further criminal acts. Because they can be updated and rewired, botnets are a "living" cybercrime infrastructure.

Recent industry reports revealed botnet infections affect 500 million computers every year, with 18 victims per second.[2] While statistics vary and industry reports should be read cautiously, a consensus exists that botnets are among the most serious threats to information security. They are also lucrative, generating income via a multitude of cybercrimes, such as system interference, spam, search engine poisoning, extortion demands through Distributed Denial of Service (DDoS) attacks and ransomware, and click fraud.[3] For example, GameOver Zeus (GOZ), a widely spread botnet that affected the international banking system until its takedown in 2014, caused an estimated loss of more than 100 million dollars worldwide.[4]

Newer types of botnets, such as the highly publicized Mirai,[5] exacerbate these issues because they move beyond just computers to attack other networked devices such as routers, CCTV cameras, thermostats, and various other Internet of Things (IoT) devices. These types of botnets form a highly decentralized threat not only to national security but also to other public interests because they compromise private devices previously off the radar of botherders, thereby increasing the number and types of players impacted by their effects. Moreover, because any device connected to the internet can potentially be attacked, and many of these devices hold critical information about individuals' location and behaviors, there are new opportunities for highly customized attacks. By targeting the IoT, perpetrators enter a new realm of action, where attacks can be socially engineered and are more likely to succeed, since IoT devices are reportedly more poorly secured than other types of machines.

The dynamic nature of botnets presents a continued challenge to developing effective security tools for detecting and disrupting botnets. Several European and non-European countries ratified the Council of Europe Cybercrime Convention[6] and maintain significant levels of international cooperation in botnet mitigation.[7] Yet, there is a shared understanding, especially regarding newer botnets forms, that current mitigation approaches are insufficient. These approaches must be coupled with the strategic power of the IT industry (e.g. device manufacturers, internet service providers [ISPs], content providers, registrars, search engines, and security developers), which has a significant capacity to deter and respond to botnet attacks. Attacks against various IoT devices potentially further expand the scope of actors responsible for mitigating botnet attacks to include individual device users.

However, effective incorporation of additional stakeholders is currently one weakness of cybersecurity in practice. We know from governance theory that coordinating between multiple stakeholders presents numerous challenges. The large number of agents makes the regulation of botnets notoriously complex; moreover, the potential stakeholders have different responsibilities to many different parties, some of which may conflict with one another. Effective coordination mechanisms are crucial for ensuring that these parties work together with confidence and trust. The case of botnets is useful for exploring whether, and to what extent, such response coordination works in practice. How does a multiple-stakeholder (polycentric) approach to governance work in complicated practical situations such as botnet mitigation?

To answer this question, we first set the stage by conceptualizing "cybersecurity," then use the case of botnets to show the intricacies of cybersecurity in practice. After these descriptive sections, we introduce ideas from governance theory that are relevant to cybersecurity. In the discussion, we examine how the theory of "cybersecurity governance" applies to the regulation and practice of botnet mitigation.

7.2 Cybersecurity

We begin with a brief outline of primary concepts and related terms, because the way in which cybersecurity is conceptualized dictates the governance approaches that may be taken. "Cyberspace" refers to the "geographically unlimited, nonphysical space, in which – independent of time, distance and location – transactions take place between people, between computers and between people and computers. Characteristic of cyberspace is the impossibility to point to the precise place and time where an activity occurs or where information traffic happens to be."[8] Cyberspace is not one homogenous space; rather, it is a myriad of virtual spaces, each providing a different form of digital interaction and communication. Cyberspace comprises both the technological components that constitute this space and the social aspects of activities taking place within it, making protection of the social and the technical equally important in approaches to cybersecurity governance.[9]

The term "security" refers to both the result and the process of taking measures to protect things, people, organizations, society, and the state.[10] Security implies an emphasis on authority, confronting threats and enemies, an ability to make decisions, and the adoption of emergency measures.[11] However, it actually demands coordinated actions on a broad range of issues and constitutes a particular type of politics applicable not only to military and political contexts but also to economic, environmental, and societal contexts.[12]

According to the Copenhagen School's theory of securitization, security is a discursive and political practice rather than a material condition or verifiable fact. The "threat-danger-fear-uncertainty discourse" is not universal, but "contextually and historically linked to shifting ontologies of uncertainty."[13] The result and the process of security practices are equally important. In this sense, security can be described as the measures taken to safeguard the interests of a state or organization against threat. Hence, more generally, security as a process can be viewed as any checks and procedures intended to keep a person, place, or thing secure.

Three more related terms are important to understanding cybersecurity:

1) *Computer security* refers to developing good programs with a limited number of (serious) bugs and systems that are difficult to penetrate by outside attackers. Cyber risk management is an evolution of classical computer security, with an increasing incorporation of business-oriented concerns such as business continuity management.[14] In that sense, cyber risk management is a synonym for cybersecurity.

2) *Information security* is "concerned with the protection of confidentiality, integrity, and availability of information in general, to serve the needs of the applicable information user."[15] Information security also includes information assurance, which deals with the underlying principles of assessing what information can or should be protected. Network security, in turn, is concerned with the design, implementation, and operation of networks – with the ultimate goal of achieving information security on networks within organizations, between organizations, and between organizations and users.[16]

3) *Critical Information Infrastructure Protection (CIIP)* refers to protecting the systems that are provided or operated by critical infrastructure providers (CIP). Critical infrastructures (or vital infrastructures) are the basal layer for socioeconomic welfare and include energy, telecommunication, banking, health, and water infrastructures. CIIP ensures that systems and networks through which critical infrastructure services operate are protected and resilient against information security and network security risks.

Conceptually, the focus of cybersecurity has evolved from computer security to information security to CIIP; practically, this evolution has also trended toward an increasing number of competing interests. When computer scientists started using the term "cybersecurity" in the early 1990s, they highlighted not only the technical aspects of protecting hardware and software but also society's general vulnerabilities.[17] Including social aspects, such as consequences for national security and the country's economic and social welfare, in the definition of cybersecurity also shifted attention from technical experts to public policy. Events such as the discovery of the nuclear-industry sabotaging *Stuxnet* computer worm, numerous tales of cyberespionage by foreign states, growing dependence on the "digital infrastructure," and increasing media attention to high-profile cyberattacks and cyberleaks, all generated more awareness of possible future cyberattacks.

Based on its components and the discussed related terms and concepts, we define "cybersecurity" as denoting both the process and the result of making cyberspace secure, where cyberspace refers not only to the space constituted by information, ICT, networks, and (ICT-based) infrastructures but also to the abstract space of digital, interconnected human and organizational activities. The security of cyberspace should consist of freedom from threats to the confidentiality, integrity, or availability of the computers, networks, and information that together constitute this space. Cybersecurity is the collection of proactive and reactive processes working toward this ideal.

7.3 Botnets

Botnets are an ideal case for examining the relationship between theory and practice, due to their complex, dynamic, resilient infrastructures and the seriousness of the threats they pose to cybersecurity. A typical botnet is developed through a lifecycle of multiple, connected stages: conception, recruitment, interaction, marketing, execution, and success.[18] Botnets start with the conception and dissemination of pieces of malware designed to install system backdoors and connect back to remote-controlling machines or other infected machines and servers. These "bots" are released in the wild internet or in a targeted network and exploit known vulnerabilities. Botnets are constructed such that, once a machine has been infected, it can serve as a new vector for spreading the same bot, creating an exponential effect of contamination. The aggregated infrastructure of compromised machines and channels form the so-called botnets, which further act as enablers for other cybercrime activity by offering perpetrators an army of devices (and their processing power) that can be triggered to launch new, powerful attacks.

Botnets present in multiple forms are traditionally categorized by their communication channels. They may be centralized, hybrid, or peer-to-peer, depending on how the infected machines communicate with one another.[19] In centralized structures, all devices connect back to compromised servers controlled by botherders (command-and-control or C&C botnets). Aware of the vulnerability of the single point of control (once the command-and-control server is hit, the entire botnet goes down), botherders create peer-to-peer communications between bot machines, thereby programming the bot software to share pre-coded instructions with other infected machines and even launch an attack without further commands. In a P2P botnet, the botherder is replaced by an autonomous and self-managed malicious network, allowing botherders to hide and only occasionally intervene. Hybrid forms combine the control feature afforded by C&C botnets and the spider web nature of P2P botnets, offering a resilient botnet.

Clearly, different types of botnets present different challenges to law enforcement and cybersecurity experts. Understanding the modus operandi of a botnet is crucial to cybersecurity efforts. Observing the communication structure is key to paralyzing a botnet before botherders have time to recode its operations. Because botherders also diversify the environment where bots operate and benefit from weaker elements of various information systems, mitigation efforts must also consider how infected devices have been compromised and the complexity of the layers in which information about the botnet can be found. For example, some known botnets exploit the darknet, a collection of non-indexed domains that are protected by multilayered structures, including The Onion Router (TOR).[20] These botnets require an incredible amount of effort to break into the anonymized features of the TOR, while newer types of botnets, such Mirai or Brickerbot,[21] move beyond computers to attack IoT networked devices.

Botnet mitigation – the collection of efforts and measures taken to prevent, share information about, disrupt, and disinfect machines from botnets – requires more than just technical measures: it must also include measures targeting public policy, social awareness and training, legislation, and cyber-crime economics. The European Union Agency for Network and Information Security (ENISA) identifies three specific approaches to fighting botnets: (i) preventing new infections, (ii) mitigating existing botnets, and (iii) minimizing criminal profit.[22]

7.3.1 Preventing New Infections

Important steps in preventing new infections include patching existing vulner-abilities and fostering a culture of security by design. Patching infections shields exposed vulnerabilities from contamination and immunizes them against new exploitation. Fixing nonzero-day exploits is paramount in thwart-ing many botnets whose modus operandi is already known to developers. A culture of security-by-design involves investment in awareness, capacity building, and training. Fostering a cybersecurity mindset among stakeholders requires the provision of incentives encouraging developers and manufactur-ers to be attentive to all security matters, even before the product/service is on the market, and the empowerment of users to protect themselves against botnet infections.

A crucial element of prevention involves sharing information about victims and botherders, and sharing data about how botnets function. Given the widespread nature of botnets, establishing a functional network of information sharing is paramount. By distributing and compiling information about suspicious and detected botnet activity, the cybersecurity community can better prevent and respond to the menace. Information sharing is useful to smaller players that do not have the resources to invest in larger cybersecurity capabilities and can benefit from expert knowledge gathered worldwide.

7.3.2 Mitigating Existing Botnets

Although security specialists have developed powerful technical solutions to tackle botnets (e.g. P2P polluting, PeerShark, Sinkholing, Sybil attacks, and Crawling), the preparation, resources, and costs associated with large operations are often prohibitive when not supported by law enforcement and state authorities. Effective botnet mitigation tools can be highly invasive, cause collateral damages, and raise ethical and legal issues. For instance, interactive honeypots (intentionally weakened systems created to attract attackers) may breach privacy and data protection when communications established with servers and victimized machines are exposed. There is also a risk of entrapment, given that the honeypot is designed to attract malware. Mitigating existing botnets also includes disinfecting machines, which can be achieved either remotely or through awareness-raising campaigns aimed at diagnosis and disinfection by end users. The importance of raising awareness about botnet disinfection should not be underestimated. As demonstrated by Asghari et al., vulnerabilities can persist years after a patch becomes available and the botnet is taken down.[23] By enabling an efficient regulatory framework and supporting private sector participation and innovation in this area, public authorities can fine-tune international cooperation models and law-enforcement powers to deliver important results – with the ultimate goals of preventing market failures from dictating security standards, and safeguarding individuals' fundamental rights.

7.3.3 Minimizing Criminal Profit

If botnets remain profitable, criminals will invest in circumventing security measures. Increasing the costs of botnets means enhancing prevention to the point that the effort to create and operate a botnet infrastructure is no longer financially interesting, and ensuring that, even when machines are infected, disruption is quick and effective. This requires raising the costs of committing botnet infection (by heightening prevention measures), raising the costs of sanctions (primarily by heightening detection and investigation capacities), and diminishing the profitability of botnets (by disrupting business models). However, these measures could merely generate replacement effects, encouraging criminal organizations to shift to targets in other sectors. If a given jurisdiction makes it more difficult to generate income through cybercrime, botnets may also migrate to countries where cybercrime is still profitable.[24]

Botnets constitute a special threat to cybersecurity because of the multiple agents involved. Any attempt to mitigate botnets must target and stop at least one phase of the aforementioned botnet lifecycle; hindering the completion of any of these stages frustrates botnet success.[25] Ideally, botnet mitigation starts in the recruitment or contamination phase, preventing bot malware from effectively infecting targeted machines. In practice, however, most botnet countermeasures only occur after recruitment and execution, when the botnet has often already caused significant costs to business and society. The large number of agents involved in such countermeasures makes the regulation of botnets notoriously complex, and a chain of responsibility among stakeholders is currently lacking. However, successful botnet disruptions – including the

GOZ, Dridex, and Ramnit takedowns coordinated by Europol's European Cybercrime Centre (EC3) and the FBI – involved action from a number of actors and relied on the expertise and extensive resources of public and private actors.

Because cybersecurity issues often involve a substantial number of players acting in a complex and international environment, many scholars have suggested that such threats cannot solely be handled by regulatory measures and should not be the exclusive domain of the state.[26] Rather, multiple states, businesses, and civil society organizations should play a role in a more hybrid and shared form of governance. The shift to this more hybrid conception of governance, and its relevance to botnet disruption, is explained in the subsequent sections.

7.4 Governance Theory

The governing authority at the centralized (nation–state) level has traditionally had a monopoly on power. Governments determine not only how a state is run but also which issues constitute the public interest. In modern societies, however, nongovernmental actors play an increasing role in influencing policy outcomes, thereby changing the role of centralized government. Most especially, changing dynamics in public–private relationships and influences at the systemic (international) level put the effectiveness and legitimacy of classical policy strategies and instruments up for discussion. To expand scholarly perspectives on these changes in politics and policymaking, the term "governance" was (re-)introduced in the academic vernacular of political science and public policy. Van Asselt and Renn describe governance as "the multitude of actors and processes that lead to collective binding decisions."[27] This definition acknowledges that (state) governments are not the only (and possibly not even the most important) actors in managing and organizing society and social processes.[28] In modern societies, the state operates in a mutually dependent triangle with the community and the market, each with its own (self-)regulatory processes. The complex interactions and dependencies within the triangle imply that all parties are affected by the unresolved problems of one.[29]

The interdependent state–community–market relationship moves public policy away from the traditional hierarchical, state-centric power structure to a decentralized, network structure. To reflect this difference, in the policy arena, a distinction is often made between horizontal and vertical relations. Horizontal relations show the network of relevant public and private actors that, within a defined geographical or functional segment, play a role in steering society around a common aim; vertical relations show the hierarchical links between them, highlighting institutional relations and balances of power.[30] It is important to note that at the nation–state level, the governance structure is never purely horizontal or vertical: it is a mix of central and local, hierarchical and networked, vertical and horizontal – a structure also referred to as polycentric governance.[31] Public–private relations are crucial in the cyber domain, and emergent governance structures for cybersecurity are both horizontal and vertical.[32]

According to Tuohy, the new governance paradigm "is meant to connote the processes and instruments of governing in the context of complex organizational networks in which no one set of actors has authority to 'command and control'."[33] This decentralization of authority is often thought to hinder effective governance, leading to questions regarding the difference between governance and regulation. The best explanation of this distinction is offered by Helderman et al.: "Whereas 'governance' can be used for several different institutional orders (including 'spontaneous coordinated action') with multiple centers or networks, regulation is more restrictedly confined to the 'sustained and focused control exercised by a public—independent—agency, over private activities that are socially valued.'"[34] The inclusion of socially valued activities in the definition distinguishes regulatory regimes from, for example, criminal justice systems, and the reference to sustained, focused control implies that regulation is not just about law-making. It extends to include gathering information, monitoring performance, and ensuring enforcement of established rules and standards. In other words, regulation is one way that modern states steer society, among several other possible processes that may be employed to steer behaviors. Governance scholarship shows how expanding the arena of possible actors and actions simultaneously restricts the capacity of nation–state governments to act. The interdependent state–community–market relationship is thus underpinned by tensions between public and private (state and market), as well as between center and nodes (of different corners of government).[35]

While governance theory has encouraged scholars to think differently about the relationship between states and societies, governance itself remains a dynamic concept. Empirical studies of governance structures and processes, with a focus on effectively addressing new challenges (including cybersecurity), point to the need for more refined and specific concepts of governance in practice. Some authors have even suggested moving away from the typology of community–market–state, public–private distinctions, and notions such as hierarchy, as all these concepts are in a state of continuous flux.[36] Moreover, changing relationships between actors indicate an increased need for actors to adapt to roles in public and private environments,[37] which may lead to new types of social actors or ad hoc coalitions.[38] This possibility raises three practical challenges.

First, the incorporation of multiple players interacting on different levels implies multiple loci of responsibility and, as such, problems with ensuring accountability for enforcement.[39] There are limits to the technical capacity of government actors to define problems and understand what needs to be done in response, as well as to their institutional capacity to act once the problem has been defined. The multicentric nature of cybersecurity, as well as the multiple agendas involved in identifying problems and creating common solutions, raises the issue of command and control. Sabel and Zeitlin argue that the combination of transnational connections and increased technological innovations has undermined the effectiveness of command and control. They offer the notion of "experimentalist" governance, defined as a recursive process of provisional goal-setting and revision based on learning from the comparison of alternative approaches to advancing control in different contexts.[40] The term "experimentalist" also points to the trial-and-error nature of dealing with new challenges – and to the possibility of finding creative solutions in the process.

The iterative, learning-focused approach required by current governance structures and processes is related to a second practical challenge. Issues confronting society are often ambiguous and complex, demanding a flexible response given strategic uncertainty about the exact nature of the problem and how best to approach it. This challenge has been especially highlighted in the context of "risk governance," which tries to anticipate and respond to uncertainty regarding what *might* happen and what the consequences will be if it does. Whereas many theories implicitly seem to assume that governance is reactive, theories of risk governance and uncertainty-induced anticipation show that governance structures and strategies must also often be proactive; it is here that the lack of a single command-and-control authority, one who can or will coordinate such proactive governance, becomes problematic. The nature of many risks requires cooperation, coordination, trust, and mutual understanding among a range of stakeholders. Because these stakeholders often have both diverging interests and contrasting perceptions of potential risks involved, the various actors (including governments) tend to have difficulty making decisions with confidence and legitimacy.[41] Moreover, these actors must not only minimize risk but also establish resilient systems that decrease general vulnerability to unanticipated events over a longer term. Like experimentalist governance, dealing with perceived risks often requires trial-and-error learning and seeking creative solutions. Translated to the case of cybersecurity, minimizing risks to systems and establishing longer-term systemic resilience are a challenge. Inherent to risk governance is the difficulty in pinpointing the source of (and, thus, the concrete solution to) a problem. Responses to threats are often demanded in situations where a clear analysis of the actual problem is lacking, which can lead to alarmism and overinflated threats.[42]

Finally, the legitimacy issues that accompany the introduction of new actors, action under uncertainty, and creative solutions (or nonsolutions) have also led to an increased demand for reflection on adopted and enacted policies and strategies. Corbridge et al. highlight the importance of attending not just to notions of governance, but to *good* governance[43] (in accordance with social understandings of what constitutes "right and wrong"), and to how these policies and strategies can be assessed. Although agendas of good governance – and the very idea of good governance itself – may be open to critique, the primary concern from a practical perspective is ensuring the balance between individual representation and the various actors involved in governing specific cybersecurity challenges.

7.5 Discussion: Governance Theory Applied to Botnet Mitigation

Although much of the effort to fortify cybersecurity seems to be premised on increasing the criminalization of threats to – or occurring through – networked technologies,[44] governance is not only about command-and-control regulation to reduce "bad" behavior. Rather, it is about the coordination of various parties in anticipation of (and in response to) potential threats – as well as the simultaneous development and implementation of longer-term structures and processes that reduce ambiguity, uncertainty, and threats from unanticipated events. Governance therefore refers to both proactive and reactive approaches to social steering, which strike a balance between stakeholder interests and the overall steering of social processes in a politically legitimate manner (i.e. in a manner that has legitimacy in the eyes of individual citizens).

Initiatives led by the ITU (IMPACT),[45] EU (ENISA CSIRT Network),[46] and private-sector organizations in the United States (M3AAWG)[47] exemplify the expansion of coordinating efforts targeted at streamlining cybersecurity practices across countries and industries. By running drills, sharing information feeds, and promoting professional training, cybersecurity initiatives have disseminated and fostered cybersecurity expertise with significant results. Yet, the world of cybersecurity information is still polarized; cybersecurity cooperation is negatively affected by the digital divide, specific industry interests, and uneven levels of political commitment. Bridging the expertise gap among consolidated and developing digital societies remains a challenge. As a deeper look into ITU-IMPACT reveals, UN assistance is much needed by countries in developing digital societies. The UN has played a strong diplomatic role in bringing together countries with conflicting political views and social systems, whereas consolidated Western digital societies have been more involved in collaborating with one another. The Joint Cybercrime Action Taskforce (J-CAT), led by the FBI and EUROPOL, symbolizes the fragmented landscape of cybersecurity cooperation among advanced economies, which arguably resembles the geopolitical alliances observed off-line.

Due to the increasing dependence of most Western societies on all sorts of digital applications, such as software-based control systems, current discussions about cybersecurity focus on the vulnerabilities of critical infrastructures, transnational interdependence, and system preparedness to deal with concrete threats.[48] Additionally, many Western states are paying more attention to other states as potential cyber-"enemies," resulting in the notion of cyberespionage (high-level penetrations of government and business computer systems), as well as to the "cross-fertilization" between cyberthreats and terrorism, where cyberthreats reinforce the danger posed by terrorists, and the terrorist nature of the cyberattacks makes them more attention-worthy.[49]

Botnets exemplify the distributed, international nature of cybersecurity threats. Deterring botnets worldwide and preventing the creation of cybercrime havens requires international cooperation and coordination. A 2015 comparative "quick scan" of cybersecurity governance in five countries – Canada, Estonia, Germany, the Netherlands, and the United Kingdom – found that botnet mitigation is largely undiscussed in national cybersecurity strategy documents, and that private actors, whose cooperation is essential, have only limited legitimate grounds for countermeasures against botnets.[50] Nonetheless, the absence of a broader regulatory debate on botnet mitigation has not impeded collaboration between Europe and North America in combatting ubiquitous botnet infections, as the case of GOZ shows.

GOZ was a widely spread botnet affecting financial transactions operated by the so-called "Business Club," a criminal ring allegedly headed by Evgeniy Mikhailovich Bogachev. Aside from capturing victims' bank data and credentials, GOZ operated as the main channel for disseminating Cryptolocker, a form of ransomware (a variety of malware that blackmails users while requesting a ransom). In the complaint directed to the US District Court of Western Pennsylvania, as part of the legal procedure that led to the takedown of GOZ in mid-2014, the US government claimed the combined losses caused by GOZ and Cryptolocker exceeded 100 million dollars and infected thousands of machines worldwide.[51]

On 3 June 2014, the District Court granted the US government request to a takedown of the infrastructure of both GOZ and Cryptolocker, takeover of the Cryptolocker DGA domains, and takeover of the peer-to-peer network of GOZ.[52] However, the efforts leading to the worldwide and almost simultaneous GOZ takedown were part of a broader international law-enforcement collaboration not limited to the US Operation Tovar, steered by the FBI and Europol (EC3), pooled the resources of public and private sector organizations across jurisdictions. It was built upon the findings of law-enforcement agents from Canada, Japan, Ukraine, and New Zealand, as well as EU Member States (including Germany and the Netherlands) and the United States, but also counted on support from private-sector partners, including Dell SecureWorks, Microsoft Corporation, McAfee, Symantec, Abuse.ch, Afilias, Crowdstrike, Delloite, F-Secure, Georgia Tech, Heimdal

Security, Level 3 Communications, Neustar, Sophos, Trend Micro, and nonprofit organizations such as Shadowserver and Carnegie Mellon.[53]

Further details on how law enforcement, industry partners, and academic and civil society organizations from various countries collaborated to take down GOZ were not made available to the public – presumably, these files have been sealed by national authorities, as disclosure about the means and methods of investigation may compromise future endeavors. Yet, it is possible to infer that the actions undertaken during the operation and the resulting outcomes necessitated the exchange of substantial amounts of evidence concerning victims and perpetrators, including information about the mitigation techniques applied to gather data and disrupt GOZ.

The secrecy applied to such high-level anti-botnet efforts has the drawback of paralyzing public scrutiny and oversight of the ways in which privacy of communications and individuals – including both information privacy and data protection – was respected throughout the investigation. While confidentiality of otherwise public procedures may be granted by the circumstances of the case, the degree and nature of participation by private-sector agents was overshadowed by reports focused on highlighting the promising results of PPPs and the social contribution of the private sector to the greater public interest. Public access to information was similarly restricted in the case of Dridex, a variation of GOZ. Dridex emerged shortly after the GOZ takedown, which clearly had not stopped its commanders from launching another devastating botnet. Although Dridex was the most prevalent Trojan online in 2013,[54] its activity period was much shorter. It was taken down in late 2015 through a collective effort, claimed to be led by the FBI[55] and involving the US-CERT, the UK National Crime Agency, Europol (EC3), German Bundeskriminalamt (BKA), Dell SecureWorks, Fox-IT, S21 sec, Abuse.ch, the Shadowserver Foundation, Spamhaus, and a Moldovan cybercrime police agency. However, access to information about the workings within the consortium remains restricted.

Although the mechanics of such supranational, public–private efforts remain somewhat obscure, they clearly are – to some extent – successful. This success is partly owed to two important elements, shared by the countries studied in the comparative quick scan: supranational legislation and national-level Computer Emergency Response Teams (CERTs). In a prime example of supranational legislation, all five countries had ratified the Cybercrime Convention, the first international treaty to address internet- and computer-related crimes. The Convention sought to approximate national laws and increase cooperation between countries, but it actually acts as a minimum catalog of offenses and investigation powers, leaving room for countries to implement its principles within their own legal cultures. Even among the five countries, there were significant differences in both criminal law and investigatory powers that made this arrangement ideal. These differences usually related to differences between civil law and common law traditions. Civil law countries, for example, more strongly emphasized the statutory limits to invasive investigative measures. Nevertheless, the Convention also enhances possibilities for international cooperation, through harmonized minimum levels of criminalization (ensuring the legal requirement of double criminality does not hamper mutual legal assistance), its investigation powers (increasing the likelihood of evidence acquisition), and its provisions for mutual assistance and a 24/7 contact-point network. Therefore, despite national variations in legal approaches to botnet mitigation, supranational law is an important facilitator in fighting botnets: ratification of the Cybercrime Convention provided a shared basis for international cooperative efforts against botnets. When coordinated action was necessary to take down a botnet, the command-and-control function of the government and police became evident.

Each of the five countries also has its own national-level CERT. These CERTs have the mandate to oversee threats on their national territory, and the procedures they follow are largely harmonized. CERTs distribute relevant information within circles of trust. Since such information is often undisclosed to a larger audience, it is not possible to evaluate the impact and the influence of national CERTs countering botnets, beyond what is made publicly available online. However, all five countries have participated in international cooperative efforts against botnets. Many of these international cooperation activities revealed a connection with Europol's (EC3) and the US FBI's efforts in fighting botnets, demonstrating the important role played by both institutions in coordinating international cooperation. To some extent, then, this disproves the theoretical view that polycentric governance lacks coordination capacity: supranational and important national state-based actors clearly can take up coordination responsibility in cybersecurity governance practice.

Botnets, especially those that target IoT devices, exemplify the convergence between three levels of cybersecurity: the macro-level, focused on protecting critical infrastructures at the nation–state level; the meso-level, focused on protecting manufacturers, service providers, and the like; and the micro-level, focused on protecting every day, ubiquitous networked personal devices. In the age of IoT and ubiquitous connectivity, the number and types of players involved with or possibly instrumental in fighting botnets has significantly increased. Because millions of infected IoT devices collectively can be used to attack various types of infrastructures, responsibility for mitigation of botnet attacks rests not only with formal authorities but also with manufacturers, service providers, and even individual citizens.

But these different players have different responsibilities to many different parties, which may come into conflict with one another. For example, ISPs have an opportunity to take preventive measures; in addition, they can be instrumental in blocking and/or tracing the sources of botnet attacks. They are also often in a good position to collect information about attackers and infected machines from a pragmatic point of view. However, it is not always clear how far ISPs can go, both legally and morally, in cooperating with public authorities – especially law enforcement – in the context of mitigation. Arguments in favor of greater ISP participation in botnet mitigation frequently emphasize their technical expertise and strategic role in managing the exchange of information among targets, compromised machines, malicious servers, and botherders. The speed with which ISPs can identify, halt, and divert attacks clearly far surpasses that of law-enforcement remedies. In addition, ISPs arguably do share a responsibility to keep the internet safe, as they are interested in both securing their reputation before customers and protecting their networks from malicious interference. Yet, advocates of ISP involvement often overlook the fact that ISPs – although they are ideally positioned to preempt, respond, and thwart botnet attacks – may lack the legitimacy to make pivotal decisions about cybercrime offenses. First, there is a prominent and ongoing debate about the legitimate role ISPs can play in delivering cybersecurity. Traditionally, matters of public security – such as guaranteeing the security and integrity of information systems and their users – are solely the task of the state; it is for public institutions and delegated agencies to define cybersecurity and crime-fighting policies. Shifting social expectations of cybersecurity, at least partly, to the hands of ISPs, does create a risk of democratic deficit: ISPs are not bound by the high standards of transparency and accountability to which public agents are subject. Ultimately, transferring the task of cybersecurity from the public to the private sector, without the safeguard of public accountability, may compromise the state's role as the primary guarantor of the rule of law. Second, increasing ISP involvement in cybersecurity may result in higher risks to information privacy. Without a proper system of accountability recalibrated to respond to the significance of ISP intervention in cybersecurity, there is a risk that information that would otherwise be collected through law-enforcement procedures – which, in general, are subject to judicial oversight and other checks and balances to minimize the impact of privacy interferences – would be amassed under lower thresholds. The absence of societal and institutional control over the collection, analysis, and distribution of information relevant to botnet mitigation – which often involves examining large sets of data pertaining to the personal identity, online behavior, and location of users – could culminate in serious privacy violations. Altogether, intensifying the participation of ISPs in botnet mitigation would necessitate revisiting the rules applicable to service providers online. This option would have to lead to higher thresholds of accountability and transparency regarding how ISPs process information, and clear liability rules implicating ISPs for potential misuse of this newly invested power.

As a result of the unresolved regulatory debate concerning the responsibilities of ISPs in cybersecurity, the types of action that ISPs can legally take are still limited. Attempts to formalize an increased role for ISPs remain limited to changing their Terms of Use to broaden the scope of the actions they can take. Such considerations are also applicable to other players involved in the spread or prevention of botnets, including cloud computing providers, software developers, hardware manufacturers, and search engines.

States can resume an authoritative position in cybersecurity by taking and stimulating both preventive and reactive measures. Preventive measures include providing more incentives for organizations to patch known vulnerabilities, ensuring greater control over the use of zero-day vulnerabilities (hotly debated in Dutch public policy in the context of police hacking)[56] and stimulating information sharing concerning intelligence data on botnets. Reactive measures include, for instance, redirecting compromised devices to safe servers and patching vulnerabilities. It is now understood that the spread of Mirai was largely due to precarious security choices made at the manufacturing level, including the use of default usernames and passwords to protect the stream of devices placed on the market.[57] Once the credential vulnerabilities were discovered by cybercriminals, brute-forcing the predictable range of hardcoded keys was an easy way to acquire control over a massive number of IoT devices. Although fixing the exploit should have been as simple as alerting users about the need to reset the default passwords and usernames, the fact that the system credentials were hardcoded into the devices made it possible for criminals to access the system panels through additional communication channels even after the reset.[58] The Mirai case exemplifies the need to internalize security from inception to manufacturing (security-by-design), but also the failure of states to ensure that basic cybersecurity standards are respected throughout the industry. Because citizens are generally unaware of the fact that they (or more precisely, their devices) are instrumental to such attacks, states can also increase awareness through public information and education programs on the importance of personal device security.

7.6 Conclusion

Cybersecurity governance refers to various approaches used by stakeholders to identify, frame, and coordinate both proactive and reactive responses to threats to the technical and social layers of information infrastructures. Over the past few years, political actors at the national level – including federal agencies, police authorities, and key interest groups – have produced policy documents that highlight the need to protect information infrastructures; increasingly, these documents also specify what constitutes a given infrastructure, the nature of possible threats to that infrastructure, and the social sectors that will feel the effects of those threats. At the same time, such documents reveal the high degree of polycentric governance within and between countries, which can lead to confusion regarding who is responsible in the case of a major incident. Increasingly, states seem to recognize that the nature of the problem is so large that it is insufficient to designate one lead agency to manage it. In many countries, various parties are even being encouraged to develop their own CERTs (in addition to those already established at the national level).

Given the increasing multitude of players interacting in the cybersecurity landscape, cooperation and coordination are necessary to prevent threats to this infrastructure and its component parts, as well as to deal with incidents when they occur. The cross-border efforts to take down large-scale botnets, led by the FBI and Europol, exemplify the ways in which law enforcement and private-sector parties are engaged in combatting ubiquitous cybercrime. In the field of cybercrime, the actions of J-CAT have become the new rule – and the model through which transnational criminal justice is pursued against cybercrime. Cybersecurity governance includes not only short-term and concrete approaches to address known threats but also the development and implementation of structures and processes to reduce uncertainty and enable responses to threats from unanticipated events over the longer term. Botnet mitigation efforts show the contours of such cybersecurity governance in practice, demonstrating that polycentric governance can work effectively if some (typically supranational or based around a key nation) actors take up responsibility for coordinating efforts, and if basic legislative frameworks are in place to facilitate international cooperation. Nevertheless, botnet mitigation efforts until now have often been more reactive than proactive, and focused on the short term rather than the long term, suggesting that risk governance is a daunting task far easier conceptualized than enacted.

Acknowledgment

This chapter was written in the context of the BotLeg project, funded by the Netherlands Organization for Scientific Research (NWO), project number 628.001.015. It is partly based on earlier research for the Research and Documentation Centre of the Netherlands Ministry of Security and Justice.

Notes

1 Myriam Dunn Cavelty, "The Militarisation of Cyber Security as a Source of Global Tension," in *Strategic Trends and Analysis: Key Developments in Global Affairs*, ed. Daniel Möckli (Zurich: Center for Security Studies, 2012), accessed November 9, 2017, http://www.css.ethz.ch/publications/pdfs/Strategic-Trends-2012-Cyber.pdf.
2 Joseph Demarest, "Taking Down Botnets," Testimony Before the United States Senate Judiciary Committee, Subcommittee on Crime and Terrorism, July 15, 2014, accessed November 9, 2017, http://www.fbi.gov/news/testimony/taking-down-botnets.
3 Alvaro A. Cardenes et al., "An Economic Map of Cybercrime," Working Paper 2009, accessed November 9, 2017, http://chess.eecs.berkeley.edu/pubs/772/cardenas_2009.pdf.

4 United States Federal Bureau of Investigation (FBI), "GameOver Zeus Botnet Disrupted Collaborative Effort Among International Partners," June 2, 2014, accessed November 9, 2017, https://www.fbi.gov/news/stories/gameover-zeus-botnet-disrupted.

5 Brian Krebs, "Who Makes the IoT Things Under Attack?" *Krebs on Security Blog*, October 3, 2016, accessed November 9, 2017, https://krebsonsecurity.com/2016/10/who-makes-the-iot-things-under-attack.

6 Convention on Cybercrime, Budapest, 2001, CETS 185.

7 Samantha Adams et al., *The Governance of Cybersecurity. A Comparative Quick Scan of Approaches in Canada, Estonia, Germany, The Netherlands and the UK* (Tilburg/The Hague: TILT/WODC, 2015), accessed November 9, 2017, https://www.wodc.nl/binaries/2484-volledige-tekst_tcm28-73672.pdf.

8 Cees J. Hamelink, *The Ethics of Cyberspace* (Thousand Oaks, CA: Sage, 2001), 9.

9 Jan van den Berg et al., "On (the Emergence of) Cyber Security Science and its Challenges for Cyber Security Education," paper presented at the NATO STO/IST-122 Symposium, Tallinn, October 13–14, 2014, 12-2.

10 "Security," *Oxford English Dictionary*, accessed November 9, 2017, www.oed.com.

11 Lene Hansen and Helen Nissenbaum, "Digital Disaster, Cyber Security and the Copenhagen School," *International Studies Quarterly* 53 (2009), 1155–1175.

12 Barry Buzan et al., *Security: A New Framework for Analysis* (London: Lynne Riener, 1998), vii, 1.

13 Niels Bubandt, "Vernacular Security: The Politics of Feeling Safe in Global, National and Local Worlds," *Security Dialog* 36 (2005): 291, as cited in Hansen and Nissenbaum "Digital Disaster," 1172.

14 Van den Berg et al., "On (the Emergence of) Cyber Security Science," 12-2–12-3.

15 Alexander Klimburg, *National Cybersecurity Framework Manual* (Tallinn, Estonia: NATO, 2012).

16 Ibid.

17 Hansen and Nissenbaum, "Digital Disaster"; Dunn Cavelty, "Militarisation of Cyber Security."

18 Rafael A. Rodriguez-Gomez et al., "Survey and Taxonomy of Botnet Research Through Life-Cycle," *ACM Computing Surveys* 45 (2013).

19 Ahmad Karim et al., "Botnet Detection Techniques: Review, Future Trends, and Issues," *Journal Zhejiang University-SCIENCE C (Computers & Electronics)* 15 (2014): 948.

20 Marie-Helen Maras, "Inside Darknet: The Takedown of Silk Road," *Criminal Justice Matters* 98 (2014): 22.

21 Trendmicro, "BrickerBot Malware Emerges, Permanently Bricks IoT Devices," April 19, 2017, accessed November 9, 2017, https://www.trendmicro.com/vinfo/us/security/news/internet-of-things/brickerbot-malware-permanently-bricks-iot-devices.

22 Jan Gassen et al., "Botnets: How to Fight the Ever-Growing Threat on a Technical Level," in *Botnets*, ed. Heli Tiirmaa-Klaar et al. (London: Springer, 2013).

23 Hadi Asghari et al., "Post-Mortem of a Zombie: Conficker Cleanup After Six Years," Proceedings of the 24th USENIX Security Symposium, 2015, accessed November 9, 2017, https://www.usenix.org/system/files/conference/usenixsecurity15/sec15-paper-asghari.pdf.

24 Nir Kshetri, *The Global Cybercrime Industry* (London: Springer, 2010), 48.

25 Rodriguez-Gomez et al., "Survey and Taxonomy."

26 Myriam Dunn Cavelty and Manuel Suter, "Public-Private Partnerships are no Silver Bullet: An Expanded Governance Model for Critical Infrastructure Protection," *International Journal of Critical Infrastructure Protection* 2 (2009): 179–187; Judith H. Germano, *Cybersecurity Partnerships* (New York: Center on Law and Security, New York University, 2014).

27 Marjolein van Asselt and Ortwin Renn, "Risk Governance," *Journal of Risk Research* 14 (2011): 431.

28 Ibid.

29 Wolfgang Streeck and Philippe Schmitter, "Community, Market, State-and Associations? The Prospective Contribution of Interest Governance to Social Order," *European Sociological Review* 1 (1985): 119.

30 See Van Asselt and Renn, "Risk Governance," 434; Broeders, *Investigating the Place and Role*, 12.

31 Eelco Van Hout et al., "Governance of Local Care and Public Service Provision," paper presented at the EGPA Conference, Madrid, September 19–22, 2007.

32 Broeders, *Investigating the Place and Role*, 16, 44.

33 Carolyn H. Tuohy, "Agency, Contract and Governance: Shifting Shapes of Accountability in the Health Care Arena," *Journal of Health Politics, Policy and Law* 28 (2003): 202.

34 Jan-Kees Helderman et al., "The Rise of the Regulatory State in Healthcare: A Comparative Analysis of the Netherlands, England and Italy," *Health Economics, Policy and Law* 7 (2012): 105. The authors quote Majone 1994 in the second half of the definition.

35 Robert H. Blank and Viola Burau, *Comparative Health Policy*, 3rd ed. (Houndmills: Palgrave Macmillan, 2010), 69.

36 See, for example,Taco Brandsen et al., "Griffins or Chameleons? Hybridity as a Permanent and Inevitable Characteristic of the Third Sector," *International Journal of Public Administration* 28 (2005), 749–765; Tim Tenbensel, "Multiple Modes of Governance," *Public Management Review* 7 (2005).

37 Van Hout et al., "Governance of Local Care."

38 Van Asselt and Renn, "Risk Governance."

39 Tuohy, "Agency, Contract and Governance."

40 Charles F. Sabel and Jonathan Zeitlin, "Experimentalist Governance," in *The Oxford Handbook of Governance*, ed. David Levi-Faur (Oxford: Oxford University Press, 2012).

41 Van Asselt and Renn, "Risk Governance."

42 Broeders, *Investigating the Place and Role*, 7–11.

43 Corbridge, S. et al., *Seeing the State* (Cambridge: Cambridge University Press, 2005), 152.

44 Cf.Bert-Jaap Koops, "Technology and the Crime Society: Rethinking Legal Protection," *Law, Innovation and Technology* 1 (2009): 93–124.

45 See Impact Alliance, "Mission & Vision," accessed November 9, 2017, http://www.impact-alliance.org/aboutus/mission-&-vision.html.

46 See CSIRTs in Europe, "Capacity Building," accessed November 9, 2017, https://www.enisa.europa.eu/topics/csirts-in-europe/capacity-building.

47 See M3AAWG, "About M3AAWG," accessed November 9, 2017, http://www.m3aawg.org/about-m3aawg.

48 Ted Koppel, *Lights Out* (New York: Penguin, 2015).

49 Dunn Cavelty, "Militarisation of Cyber Security."

50 Adams et al., *Governance of Cybersecurity*.

51 *United States of America vs. Evgeniy Mikhailovich Bogachev* [2014] Civil Action No. 14-0685 (United States District Court for the Western District of Pennsylvania).

52 Ibid.

53 Europol, "International Action Against 'GameOver Zeus' Botnet and 'Cryptolocker' Ransomware," June 4, 2014, accessed November 9, 2017, https://www.europol.europa.eu/newsroom/news/international-action-against-gameover-zeus-botnet-and-cryptolocker-ransomware.

54 Dick O'Brien, "Dridex: Tidal Waves of Spam Pushing Dangerous Financial Trojan" (Mountain View: Symantec, 2016), accessed November 9, 2017, http://www.symantec.com/content/en/us/enterprise/media/security_response/whitepapers/dridex-financial-trojan.pdf.

55 United States Federal Bureau of Investigation (FBI), "Bugat Botnet Administrator Arrested and Malware Disabled," October 13, 2015, accessed November 9 2017, https://www.fbi.gov/contact-us/field-offices/pittsburgh/news/press-releases/bugat-botnet-administrator-arrested-and-malware-disabled.

56 *Kamerstukken I* [Dutch Parliamentary Proceedings First Chamber] 2016/17, 34372, no. E, 39-45 and no. F, 2-4.

57 Brian Krebs, "Who Makes the IoT Things Under Attack?"

58 Ibid.

8

Governing Risk

The Emergence of Cyber Insurance*

Trey Herr[1,2]

[1] Hoover Institution, Stanford University, Stanford, CA, USA
[2] Microsoft, Redmond, WA, USA

8.1 Introduction

Cybersecurity is difficult. Adversaries are constantly evolving as technology enables attacks in ways never considered by the earliest pioneers in computing and internet security. The horizontal spread of connectivity creates unanticipated challenges for security professionals. In attempting to mitigate these fundamental insecurities and overcome adaptive adversaries, practitioners have spent several decades building and refining best practices for the configuration and maintenance of networked information systems. Codifying these architectural and behavioral practices as standards can help manage the risk of an attacker's success and ensure individuals and firms are taking minimum steps to protect themselves. However, enforcing these standards remains a critical challenge in public policy.

From a practical standpoint, cyber insurance has largely been limited to covering the cost of responding to a breach and the financial liability of corporate officers. This means that, while there has not yet been a billion-dollar event, or anything of comparable financial consequence to a company, the current array of cyber insurance offerings will do little to cover the principal harm when one does inevitably take place.

While true, this is a narrow perspective on what cyber insurance is doing (and might be capable of doing) to set and enforce security standards in the private sector without the need for direct regulation. When a network of companies begin to demand their partners and vendors obtain cyber

---

* Portions of this chapter are adapted from a forthcoming article, "Cyber Insurance and Private Governance: The Enforcement Power of Markets."

Rewired: Cybersecurity Governance, First Edition. Edited by Ryan Ellis and Vivek Mohan.
© 2019 John Wiley & Sons, Inc. Published 2019 by John Wiley & Sons, Inc.

insurance, insurers end up occupying a powerful market position as they can influence the security standards their customers select and implement. This chapter examines the recent growth of the cyber insurance marketplace and argues that this market, primarily in the United States, has developed features of a governance process with enforcement power over security standards.

In 2013, the retail giant Target experienced a substantial loss of customer data. Malicious software, infecting registers in stores around the country, had spent the holiday shopping season silently vacuuming up credit card information from millions of customers. Attackers gained access to Target's network through a weakness discovered in a third-party vendor: a company that helped regulate the temperature and environmental controls at outlets in the Midwest had been hacked. The breach was a national event, with banks replacing tens of millions of credit cards to contain ever-worsening incidence of fraud and theft.[1] Target's senior leadership was hauled before Congress and major retailers were put under the public microscope. In the years since the breach was first made public, Target has accounted for nearly $300 million in losses related to the theft of this customer data.[2]

However, more than $90 million of Target's losses were offset by insurance payouts to cover the costs of notifying consumers and ongoing litigation. Insurers have also been central in driving new risk-management practices at the company. Since the late 1990s, when cyber insurance policies were first offered to cover the regulatory costs of data breaches, insurers have offered companies a means to protect themselves from the financial liability associated with cybersecurity incidents.

Insurance describes an industry of firms that assume the risk of harmful events and their associated financial liability from customers for a fee.[3] Cyber insurance is a collection of firms that provide coverage against some of the consequences from cyber incidents, mostly data breaches. Growth in the cyber insurance industry spiked dramatically in 2012; alongside new and increasingly clever coverage offerings, insurers began to set and enforce security standards on their clients as a means of reducing the risk of an incident and resulting claims. The growth in this standard-setting role is still ongoing, as demonstrated by new research in 2017.[4] The design and implementation of these standards is a form of private governance, with an unusual market-based enforcement mechanism. Enforcing effective security standards requires insurers to design controls and policies that offer insight of sufficient depth and breadth across different clients to identify best practices and mitigate risk. Insurance firms also need to distinguish the risk profiles of different firms to manage their assumed liability and maintain financial solvency. Insurers can play "a key role in creating standardized cyber risk-management processes."[5] Grappling with this governance role first requires an understanding of the origins of cyber insurance.

8.2   Where Did Cyber Insurance Come From?

Cyber insurance has been touted for its ability to help identify and enforce effective security standards while simultaneously allowing firms to offload liability for major attacks.[6] As the sophistication of threat groups has increased along with the quickening drumbeat of security incidents, the security community has looked to improve and innovate in risk management.[7] As a result, insurance has become a prolific target of investment and, especially after 2012, has begun to exercise a governance role in enforcing security controls on clients.[8]

Insurers offering cybersecurity products provide a means to help firms select effective security controls, improve risk-assessment practices, and limit the potential financial liability of an attack by transferring some risk.[9] A 2013 study found that after purchasing an insurance product, firm's security posture improved, with companies relying on insurers to select controls and risk-management policies in more than 75% of situations.[10] In some cases, insurance firms may be equipped to actively monitor their clients and warn of breaches if the standards and enforcement process they have put in place allow for it. In 2014, Liberty Mutual detected attackers on a client's network and was able to notify the client in advance of a breach.[11]

Initial consideration for losses related to information technology (IT) and related organizational failure emerged in the mid to late 1980s,[12] but the first coherent insurance policy for cybersecurity was not offered until American Insurance Group (AIG) released its policy in 1997.[13] Early products focused on failures in computer security. Policies for third-party liability served to compensate victims if, for example, a hacker breached a healthcare company's customer records. Business interruption coverage would pay out to cover losses related to attacks that caused system downtime, such as those in an e-commerce site's ordering system.[14] As the market evolved, demand for data loss coverage, protection for physical (in addition to digital) information loss, and protection for privacy liability drove innovation in new products and brought more insurers into the market.[15]

The insurance market for cybersecurity products grew slowly and sporadically from 1997 to 2003, but as companies began to integrate information systems more fully into their business, new incidents resulted in further insurance innovation. Denial of service attacks, which are used to knock firms' systems off-line or off the internet, were combined with ransom demands to extort hefty fees before companies could get back online. Insurers moved to cover the losses from these attacks as well as costs associated with remediating the damage.[16] The next inflection point in industry size occurred with increasing demand for data-breach coverage, which resulted from a spate of state legislatures passing data-breach notification laws. Starting with California's enactment of SB1386 in 2003, companies that stored digital information were required to notify customers if they detected or suspected a breach.[17] Coverage for these breaches became more popular, with firms looking to cover the expenses of required investigations and notification programs as well as fines related to failure to secure systems through regulatory programs like the Health Insurance Portability and Accountability Act (HIPAA).[18] This period of market change was more substantial than early years but remained unspectacular, with less than $900 million in total premiums written.

8.2.1 Understanding Insurance

What goes into an insurance policy can help shed light on how these contracts can be used to govern the behavior of the insured. Insurance works by transferring risks posed to a company's assets and business operations over to a third party.[19] Cybersecurity risk is not a new field; indeed, natural disasters and business failure have threatened IT since the first mainframe came online more than a half century ago. The new element is the pace of evolution in the capability of threat groups and in the potential consequences of their attacks.

Transferring risk shifts the financial liability of a data breach, loss of data integrity, or other incident away from the victim firm to an insurer. This transfer can relieve companies of the burden of a costly event, leveraging the financial resources of a pool of other potential victims, mediated by the insurer, to cover the consequences. For the insurer, revenue from premiums charged to clients serves as investment capital until it must be paid out to satisfy a claim, providing a short-term material benefit.

8.2.2 Risk Pool

Selecting insurance clients and determining the scope of their coverage requires understanding the nature of risk for each applying firm. The goal is to construct a pool of clients whose collective contribution is equal to or greater than the probable cost of payouts for claims. The members of this pool should all be conscious of their risk and interested, if not actively working, to control it. The risk pool functions, in part, because although no one party can be sure if they will need to submit a claim, most will not – thereby providing both financially viable coverage to the few claimants and an incentivizing profit to the insurer. The fees associated with insurance, paid by each member of the pool according to their assessed risk, are premiums.

8.2.3 Premiums

For an insurer, the risk of any one client experiencing an incident resulting in a claim is spread among this pool of customers, each contributing financial resources in the form of a premium. This can be a flat fee common to all or a rate calculated on the assessed likely cost of all potential claims (based on the frequency and severity) in a given year. This latter approach allows firms to adjust premiums based on the risk profile and potential loss exposure associated with each individual customer – a more computationally intensive but financially efficient approach.

8.2.4 Insurer

Central to this process is the insurance firm, which is responsible for controlling membership in the risk pool, calculating equitable premiums, and ensuring the financial solvency necessary to respond to claims. Managing the total risk of the pool becomes an ongoing challenge, as the insurer can choose to set standards for members to mitigate their risk, add or drop clients to shift the firm's overall risk, or further transfer the risk through reinsurance and other financial vehicles. Underlying this decision-making process is an assessment of the risk of individual clients as well as the risk associated with the insurer's total portfolio.

8.2.5 Insurable Risk

Insurable risks, i.e. risks that can be efficiently transferred, generally impact only an individual or small set of firms. These particular risks are distinct from fundamental risks, in which all or a large portion of a population may be affected. Fundamental risks are problematic for insurers because they are likely to reduce the member-to-claimant ratio of a risk pool past the point of financial solvency. Insurance firms may prefer to select customers with varying sources of particular risk to help diversify their portfolio, or they may prefer customers with relatively common sources in order to minimize the computational overhead associated with assessing and managing a substantially heterogeneous risk pool. Regardless of pool composition, however, customers should represent a tolerably low probability of loss; otherwise, they undermine the financial viability of any insurance product.

Cybersecurity represents a mix of particular and fundamental risk. Certain technologies for credit card and contactless payment systems, as well as software like Adobe Reader, are found in a wide swath of companies that could be targeted; thus, they represent fundamental risk.[20] However, the peripheral systems that employ these technologies, the pattern of their business operations, and the security focus of the responsible companies will differ, thus translating the consequences of these widely adopted technologies into particular risk. The particular risk posed by a mutual fund's default, for example, depends on the vulnerability of different investors; some may have investments diversified among sufficiently different areas as to be protected from major loss. Fundamental risk poses the same hazard to a large segment of an insurance firm's customer base, such that the variation in their individual vulnerability is less important than the nature of the catastrophe itself. Hurricanes and other substantially destructive natural events such as floods generally fall into this category. Cybersecurity is thus a mix of particular and fundamental risk, with much of the latter stemming from nonnetworked events such as power failures or physical attacks.[21]

Another challenge is the role of systemic risk that approximates to a series of linked particular risks.[22] A company that depends on the computerized logistics system of a port facility is thus linked in some fashion to this system's security. Taken at scale, with dependencies reaching across continents and industry verticals, this systemic risk may be uninsurable. Critical to the analysis of such a scenario, however, is assessing the realistic interdependency of systems that may be linked but are otherwise independent. There are many internet-connected or internet-enabled services which could potentially communicate with each other – thus allowing the spread of contagion – but do not explicitly rely on each other's functions.

Returning to the port example, there is a difference between our notional company's dependence on the port's logistics system and its use of area Wi-Fi networks and automated cargo handlers. The logistics system may be critical, but wireless networks can be supplemented and cargo handled by human-operated equipment. A key mistake in considering systemic risk is assuming that all interconnected systems are equally vulnerable or similarly interdependent. Accurately assessing a potential chain of consequences is key to understanding where systemic risk threatens to be uninsurable.

Looking at harms generally, the cyber insurance industry has thus far demonstrated little confidence in valuing direct losses from a breach like stolen proprietary information, consumer confidence, or reputation with business partners. These first-party harms continue to evolve in form: consider, for example, the difference between the reputational harms of the Home Depot breach and Sony's loss of thousands of computers from a data wiping attack. Adding to this uncertainty over harms, recent research suggests that the typical cost of a cyber incident is much lower than conventionally assumed, less than $200 000.[23] Without a clear expectation of when and how events will generate cost to the insurer, firms are left to either engage a financially untenable amount of uncertainty or choose to offer only limited products. The result is risk management through carefully specified coverage provisions.

8.2.6 Comparisons to Terrorism

Insurance products that cover loss related to terrorist activity face a somewhat similar problem to those that cover cybersecurity events. There is limited useful historical data, and threat actors select targets based in part on their vulnerability to attack. Actions to mitigate risk in one part of a portfolio thus may increase risk elsewhere. There is also an information advantage for the state, whose intelligence or law-enforcement arms may be cognizant of a threat but unable or unwilling to pass the information on to insurers and potential victims. Insurance for terrorism has grappled with these challenges repeatedly after major incidents, but the attacks in New York, Pennsylvania, and Washington, DC in 2001 are particularly instructive.[24]

Initially after the attacks, coverage terms shrank and limits were imposed on catastrophic loss to deal with the uncertainty around the potential for new and even more destructive incidents. By 2003, however, the insurance market began to adapt and expand products again to meet the demands of customers.[25] Much of this improvement can be traced to better catastrophe modeling techniques and the beginning of analysis of adversary groups' intentions and capabilities. Insurers understood that the range of potential consequences was determined, in part, by the types of attacks being launched and the capabilities of threat groups.[26] Existing methodologies offered a chance to forecast the behavior of threat organizations and suggest high and low probability targets, allowing more careful management of risk pools.

This resurgence in the market was likely also due to state intervention, which helped put a safety net under the market for primary and secondary insurance (also called reinsurance). The Terrorism Risk Insurance Act (TRIA) made the US government a reinsurer of last resort for firms, creating a financial entity that could help bear the burden of consequences from a catastrophic attack like those in 2001.[27]

While some have compared TRIA to cybersecurity, its applicability is limited.[28] A similar law could provide a liability backstop for firms in order to encourage new policies, but it may also reinforce the belief that cybersecurity incidents are low-probability, high-consequence (LPHC), and encourage the expectation that failure can be prevented, rather than made less frequent and more recoverable. A TRIA-like law for cybersecurity would also do nothing to impact the standards selection or risk-assessment process. Identifying and enforcing these standards is critical to governance.

8.3 Security Standards in the Governance Process

The role of risk is central to explaining the emergence of cyber insurance as a form of private governance. Organizations designing a security posture take into account the likely threats to their assets, vulnerabilities to particular tactics and modes of failure, and the potential consequences of a successful attack. Weighing each of these elements against an established tolerance for risk helps drive choices about security controls and investment – what tools to buy and where to focus efforts. Among the outputs of these risk-mitigation decisions are security controls: behaviors, practices, and technology used to improve an organization's security.

The explosion in cyber insurance after 2012, which more than doubled annual measures of total coverage to more than $2 billion by 2014, has occurred alongside growth in the capabilities of attackers as well as the resulting uncertainty over their likely targets and potential to wreak havoc.[29] As a result, firms have taken advantage of insurance as a means to (i) set and enforce effective security controls and also to (ii) transfer their risk and reduce the potential financial liability for attacks. A key question for governance of these standards is their source.

8.3.1 Government-Developed Standards

The content of standards in use by insurers varies, as there are multiple public and private schemes available. US efforts to set standards can be broken into three clusters: critical infrastructure protection (CIP), private industry regulation, and federal IT. CIP efforts have focused on a largely private-owned array of industrial functions and facilities, the loss of which would be acutely felt by the country. These compromise the early history of standard setting, with the initial push beginning in 1996, and have long existed in a state of heightened importance (owing to their "criticality").

Regulation of private cybersecurity behavior in the United States is generally focused on specific industries with enforcement mechanisms focused on things like healthcare or financial information. These industries have a history of receiving exceptional treatment by regulatory authorities and lawmakers. The focus on these industries is also a byproduct of a continuing stream of breaches, which have concentrated in these industries and in retail.

The third cluster of state standard setting in cybersecurity came through executive and legislative behavior targeting the federal government's own IT infrastructure. Some of these approaches have impacted the private sector, especially the National Institute of Standards and Technology (NIST) special publications. Across the board, however, few of these standards come paired with risk assessment and management programs of comparable quality. Each of these categories encapsulates a different common theme in the history of US public sector governance behavior: the absence of strong enforcement mechanisms and risk assessment and management programs without highly specific detail. This history of federal cybersecurity standard-setting stretches back 20 years, to midway through the Clinton administration, when the protection of critical infrastructure first rose into the national policy spotlight. Until the NIST controls emerged in the mid-2000s, and in some instances afterwards, state approaches focused on functional requirements. They shied away from specifying the exact nature of the security tool or procedure, in favor of a rule that organizations do something to achieve a particular end such as secure internet communications.

Few of the standards programs came with compliance mechanisms attached in their original form, and even where they did apply to the private sector, as with security provisions of the HIPAA, the regulatory body responsible was often reluctant to strictly audit and penalize nonperforming firms. Predominantly, where state standards are applied to private organizations, they have been limited to specific industries and enforced narrowly. This trend away from direct enforcement by government has begun to change with passage of the HITECH Act, modifying HIPAA, and specifying the application of the Security Rule to business entities beyond hospitals.

Private sector standards do not come with the weight of the law, but have been developed along multistakeholder and for-profit lines. These present a more limited range of coverage, without any attempt at enforcement, but more comprehensive detail.

8.3.2 Private Sector Standards

Private-sector security standards tend to focus on business IT and the larger risk-management process. In discussions with industry executives, two schemes take particular precedence: the International Organization for Standardization (ISO) 27000 series[30] and ISACA's Control Objectives for Information and Related Technology (COBiT).[31] ISO 27000 are a set of guiding documents developed for business organizations to manage the acquisition and management of IT systems, focusing on their security. The series includes lists of detailed controls and a bevy of material on how to develop and implement both risk assessment and management programs without specifying particular procedures. The ISO series leaves much of the substantive content up to organizations and their unique requirements and risk tolerance. For more on this, look to a comparative analysis of the ISO 27000 series with several government developed approaches.[32]

COBiT was developed by an industry consortium beginning in 1996 to identify reliability and security standards for IT systems and networks in prototypical business organizations.[33] Complimenting specific controls are documentation guides to both risk assessment and the process of selecting controls. There is tremendous emphasis on stakeholder identification and engagement within business organizations. For this schema, security is important but tied to larger IT goals rather than a detailed assessment of the threat environment or potential consequences.

The advantage of these frameworks tended to be inclusion of both detailed standards and more developed risk assessment and management programs. One of the principal drivers for their development was growing need for effective risk mitigation technique within the private sector and the associated controls. Missing from these approaches, however, was a strong enforcement mechanism. Indeed, neither public nor private standard setting efforts involved broad compliance measures until the insurance industry began to see growth associated with cyber policies – and opportunity to profit from leading governance.

8.4   The Key Role of Risk

The shift toward risk transfer as a more common feature in risk-management programs is a result of both the upward trends in consequence and threat group sophistication. Risk transfer can be accomplished a variety of ways, including catastrophe bonds and liability protections, but the most common form is insurance. The push for risk transfer by firms is also the result of efforts to make cybersecurity a prominent part of company managements' decision-making process, including the 2011 Securities and Exchange Commission (SEC) guidance outlining changes to voluntary disclosure of security controls and reporting of cybersecurity risks and incidents for public firms.[34] For example, the emergence of the Chief Information Security Officer (CISO) has brought these topics into the boardroom and helped drive awareness of both the practical and the financial impact of cybersecurity incidents.[35]

Risk transfer does not directly alter the security posture of a firm, but can help it target security investments more efficiently and improve financial health. These trends did not give birth to the cybersecurity industry. Rather, they accelerated its growth tremendously and helped provide the basis for insurers' emergence as agents of private governance.

The potential for serious financial consequences from a data breach or other incident has increased markedly in the past half-decade, along with continued growth in the capability of threat groups.[36] Both trends have been major reasons for the substantial increase in coverage and attendant growth in the cybersecurity industry in recent years. A survey conducted in 2013 by the Insurance Information Institute found that 71% of respondents in US firms indicated that "their perception of the risks of cybercrime increased over the past 24 months."[37] The costs associated with attacks continued to rise, with one analysis finding a 22% increase for the average incident's related expenses between 2014 and 2015.[38] This growth in the industry tracked increases in the number of cybersecurity incidents as well, jumping from 421 in 2011[39] to 783 in 2014 across all private industry verticals.[40] These trends together drove a major spike in growth of the cyber insurance market.

Two of the principal reasons found for companies' purchase of insurance in the past several years are board-mandated reputation protection and "mitigating potential revenue loss from cyber-induced interruption of operations."[41] A 2015 report from Moody's, a credit rating agency and example coordination service firm, found that due to the evolving nature of cybersecurity risk and potential loss, "boards have become particularly focused on making sure corporations have adequate systems and controls in place to safeguard their own data and that of their customers."[42] Insurers are aware of the material benefits associated with offering coverage; firms generally receive $25 000 for every $1 million in coverage written but can charge a premium of two to three times more than normal for hard-hit areas like retail and healthcare.[43] This expanding marketplace of underwriters also drives increased competition, so new offerings by long-time participants in this market – such as AIG, Zurich, and the Lloyds consortium – provide a means to lock in benefits against newcomers.

However, the critical policy nudge for insurers came with a voluntary 2011 guidance from the Division of Corporation Finance at the U.S. Securities and Exchange Commission (SEC). Guidance from the SEC, which has a reputation post-Sarbanes Oxley as a regulator to which senior executives and boards must pay attention, spurred action by firms. The guidance outlined how companies should assess and disclose cybersecurity risks in public filings (such as quarterly and annual statements), and to disclose cybersecurity incidents (that would rise to the level of "materiality").[44] One of the specific elements of disclosing this cyber risk was describing any relevant cyber insurance coverage. The guidance, together with evolving security standards of vendors, drove investors and other companies' expectation that firms should control cybersecurity risk as a component of overall risk management and normal fiduciary obligation, reporting the impact of cybersecurity incidents as a factor in the company's material well-being.

The 2011 SEC guidance offered specific recommendations to corporate management on what could be used to describe their cyber risk profile and history to other firms. The result was to help translate cyber risk into financial terms and demonstrate the impact of preemptive (as well as post-event) behavior on a company's financial health. Connecting cybersecurity risk and firm's financial health addressed, but did not solve, the problem of how to price security measures, making costs like cyber insurance more attractive and accessible.

8.5 Enforcing Standards: Insurance Becomes Governance

Governance involves setting and enforcing standards. Cyber insurance emerged as a governance process in 2012 when insurers began to set security standards for clients. This emergence is not an accident, but rather a product of newly aligned interest between firms demanding security governance and the insurers charged to provide it. The lynchpin of the cyber insurance market is that it enables insurers to enforce security standards as well as obtain financial benefit from these activities. Enforcement and profit are tied together: insurers benefit financially when customers continue to pay premiums without experiencing an incident they can claim under their policy. As the market for these insurance products expands, so too does the potential customer base. With this broadening customer pool comes a higher likelihood of some covered event (like a data breach), so insurers must also increase their ability to assess and manage risk. A chief means of lowering the risk of an incident is enforcing good security standards on customers, so enforcement becomes critical to insurer's attempts to limit the potential for attacks and their resulting cost.

The structure of this enforcement mechanism for cybersecurity standards is the larger marketplace, as other companies help insurers drive compliance with security standards by insurance customers. Understanding this market is crucial to understanding both the process of enforcement as well as the key argument underpinning private advance; firms will participate in governance where they can derive direct material benefit from doing so.

8.5.1 Model of Modern Market Governance

Insurers are a type of coordination service firm. The role of coordination service firms is to act as part of a larger market to solve information problems and reinforce best practices within an industry. Insurance underwriters evaluate the risk profile of clients using a set of criteria; the criteria are also communicated to firms and can serve as parameters for behavior. While the interests of these firms are material benefit, the premiums that insurers derive from offering coverage, another result is the provision of standards and a market-based enforcement mechanism.

Credit rating agencies are a prominent example of the coordination service firms. Seeing themselves as "quasi-regulatory institutions," credit rating agencies provide a good explanation for the emergence of private authority as a result of the potential for material benefit and capacity to develop effective technical standards.[45] Rising to prominence out of the financial disintermediation of the 1970s and 1980s – when capital began to flow around, rather than primarily through, commercial banks – credit rating agencies enable market participants to judge the risk of new financial issues and their offering firms.[46]

The rating firms receive funding from a combination of fees paid by assessed companies and, more recently, from the sale of new financial products like bonds.[47] Their financial incentives to provide ratings are driven in part by the size and scope of the market, paid by banks as they issue new financial products, and through fees for the use of their information. This coordination role, structuring some uncertainty and quantifying risk, increases efficiency by reducing the information-gathering and -processing load by market participants as well as counteracting the natural asymmetry between sources of capital and those clamoring for it.

Credit rating agencies serve to "narrow the expectations of creditor and debtors to a certain well-understood or transparent set that is shared among themselves."[48] This coordination generally falls across two areas: information, standardizing behavior for disclosure of information and management practices; and risk, creating a means to evaluate and judge the mechanisms that firms have in place to avoid or cope with loss. The agencies' judgments and associated information impact the behavior of market actors even though the agencies are private authorities. Risk assessors play a standard-setting and, through the behavior of their subscribers, enforcement role. This structural power has "both material and normative aspects, creating 'patterns of incentives and constraints' which condition the behavior" of those being evaluated and investors who depend on the judgments of risk.[49] The complexity of credit, or cyber, risk is where these coordination service firms provide value; they usefully provide firms with abstracted or simplified information about the content and value of risk.

Rating agencies provide this private governance even though they are not backed by public institutions, and claim not to persuade but only to offer judgment on the risk of new financial instruments and the underlying creditworthiness of the offering firms. Moody's, one of the two largest such agencies alongside Standard & Poor's, offers a boilerplate disclaimer that their ratings "are, and must be construed solely as, statements of opinion and not statements of fact or recommendations to purchase, sell, or hold any securities."[50] While not constituted by state action, agencies do benefit from the shadow of the state's hierarchy. The SEC lists national recognized statistical rating agencies (NRSROs); although there are no clear standards for selecting these organizations, and no formal requirement for use of their information, firms both soliciting and investing capital are hard pressed to operate effectively outside of their scope.[51]

Through these analyses and judgments of risk, the agencies create standards of behavior, enforced by the larger market of investors who respond to ratings by their allocation of capital. This, in turn, creates a private governance mechanism that increases the efficiency of capital markets by translating uncertainty into more structured risk assessments. Critically, the evaluation of these financial issues and the offering parties does not remove risk; rather, it provides information to which investors (who have a range of risk tolerances and capital resource levels) can then respond.

The rating agencies' behavior shapes the market for investment capital, in turn influencing not only the actions but also the internal organization of recipient firms. Like insurance firms, credit rating agencies are part of a larger governance structure and derive a great deal of legitimacy from both historical precedent and perceptions of their expertise (rather than being solely determined by market position or function). They act to reduce uncertainty between parties transacting with one another. To be fair to history, neither these transacting parties nor the rating agencies themselves, assess risk perfectly (or even well) at times.[52] The rating agencies are demonstrative of a centralized risk-management function and the role of an information intermediary, much like insurance agencies.

8.5.2 Cyber Insurance: Governing Risk Through Standard Setting and Enforcement

Managing risk requires identifying and enforcing security standards. These standards are the codified lists of potential tools, best practices, and protocols that organizations use to standardize behavior. Their immediate role is to provide a structured language to evaluate the development of plans and acquisition of tools to provide security, but more significantly, they represent a means to control risk by identifying sources of insecurity and minimizing them. The development of security controls and their integration into a risk assessment and management process is a story of governance, where standards are designed and enforced to shape organizational behavior.

Finding and standardizing best practices allows insurance firms to play a central role in encouraging adoption of new security standards and behaviors.[53] In cybersecurity, rapid technological change has been accompanied by a slower expansion of organizational best practices. Selecting terms and limits of coverage involves the insurers' assessment of the likely frequency and severity of potential costly events to their customers. This ensures that insurers retain a profitable mix of risk types and can price their products accordingly.

The key to the cyber insurance market is that it both enables enforcement and drives profit for the insurers. These issues, enforcement and deriving material benefit from standards, are closely linked. Insurers profit from premiums charged on coverage, and so the wider the market for their products, the broader the pool of paying customers. This also expands the potential set of targets to whom attacks would require the insurer to pay out on its coverage. So, enforcement is also critical to an insurer's attempts to limit the potential for these incidents and their cost. Where enforcement is weak or narrow, the utility for insurance is reduced compared to a broader market where vendors and investors might demand it as part of cybersecurity risk-management plans.

Cybersecurity insurance blossomed into a private governance mechanism after a major spike in growth starting in 2012. This was due in part to a change in the landscape of business risk, and also to the evolving capabilities of attackers.[54] Figure 8.1 shows the spike after 2012 in gross premiums written, essentially total revenue to insurers. The period between 2012 and 2015 saw an increase of nearly 300%. In 2011, the SEC issued a guidance document outlining the manner in which companies should communicate cybersecurity risk to investors and outside parties: "cybersecurity risk disclosure ... must adequately describe the nature of the material risks and specify how each risk affects the registrant."[55] While not a binding regulatory output, the guidance frames the reporting requirements for risk and cybersecurity events as they relate to the financial health or structure of a firm. Since 2012, total premiums from coverage jumped from $835 million to $2 billion in 2014 and an estimated $4 billion in 2017.[56] More than 90% of underwriters saw growth in demand between 2012 and 2014, especially from the retail sector.[57]

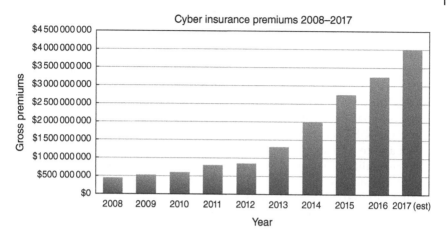

Figure 8.1 Gross premiums in cyber insurance industry. All values (except 2012) derived from the "Betterley Report – Cyber/Privacy Insurance Market Study" series. 2012 sourced from https://www.irmi.com/products/betterley-report-cyber-privacy-insurance

This expansion provided the basis for a market with participants willing to encourage standards adoption and sufficient material benefit for insurers to invest the time and expertise necessary to provide best practices and security controls to their clients. Critically, the expansion of the market also made risk transfer a legitimate option for small- and medium-sized firms. This moved insurance from the category of potential to a standard investment even for firms without massive valuation or global scope. Lastly, this rapid growth in the insurance market helped drive the consensus of legitimacy around insurers' standards, as the policies became standard fixtures in corporate cybersecurity planning. These factors established the basis for a now multi-billion-dollar market to drive adoption of the standards by targeted firms, legitimation of the standard providers, and continuing material incentives for the demand, provision, and enforcement of standards.

8.6 Conclusion and Implications

There was a time when cybersecurity standards were more akin to environmental regulations: self-governance enabled companies to keep costs low and maintain a delightful ignorance of IT mechanics or the types of threats that might be arrayed against them. Attacks, especially when they affected customers, could be treated as an externality. Cybersecurity is a prominent issue now, not just because of newfound awareness of the sorts of consequences that can be imposed by an incident but also because of increasing sensitivity to the connection between events affecting customer's data, firm's proprietary information, and the material value of these companies. The cyber insurance industry has developed into a form of private governance over the security standards used to control risk. This emergence is best explained as private advance, the activity of insurance firms looking to reap benefits from new markets and lock in their dominant market position. The ability to recognize these benefits was critically enabled by state action in the form of the NIST security controls and 2011 SEC guidance, undermining the logic of a state retreat.

The centrality of risk to the emergence of cyber insurance as a mechanism of private governance rests on an extended history of fundamentally insecure computing architectures and the adaptability of threat groups. Security standards establish practices and policies to help control this risk. Growing uncertainty around the consequences of attacks provides an incentive for the private sector to find new means to manage risk and has motivated substantial growth in the use of insurance. Like credit rating agencies, insurers provide risk assessments to structure uncertainty and identify controls to reduce it. Leaning on participants in this market to legitimate and enforce these standards, insurers occupy an unusual position within the panoply of public- and private-sector groups dealing with cybersecurity.

The policy implications for governments center on the state's willingness to craft neutral standards. Government standards bodies retain a high degree of legitimacy in the private sector, as their codification efforts have provided robust starting points for the design and implementation of security controls. This codification effort have continued with discussions at the FDA around cybersecurity-responsive development, production, and operating practices for medical device manufacturers. Continuing engagement with companies and nonprofit groups, as well as additional work to improve risk assessment practices, would be a boon to this effort and help reinforce best practices in both private- and public-sector organizations.

Cyber insurance is a rapidly expanding market; insurer's ability to recognize trends across customers and spread best practices could serve to not only enforce but also identify new security standards. At present, the market acts as a form of private governance over existing security standards, a novel form of this governance in cybersecurity. This governance, which works to break down information asymmetries in the private sector and helps enforce security standards, could well serve as model for policymakers. The keys appear to be emphasizing lateral pressure from companies against their business partners and vendors (rather than direct regulation), and emphasizing the role of certain specialized companies, like insurance firms, to monetize standards enforcement. Policymakers may find cyber insurance a helpful model for private sector-led security governance as they seek to rewire cybersecurity.

Notes

1 Saabira Chaudhuri, "Cost of Replacing Credit Cards After Target Breach Estimated at $200 Million," *The Wall Street Journal*, February 18, 2014, https://www.wsj.com/articles/cost-of-replacing-credit-cards-after-target-breach-estimated-at-200-million-1392746456?mg=prod/accounts-wsj.

2 Craig Newman, "Target's Cyber Insurance: A $100 Million Policy vs. $300 Million (So Far) In Costs," *Data Security Law Blog*, April 7, 2016, https://datasecuritylaw.com/targets-cyber-insurance-a-100-million-policy-vs-300-million-so-far-in-costs.

3 Rob Thoyts, *Insurance Theory and Practice* (New York: Routledge, 2010), Google Books.

4 Sasha Romanosky et al., "Content Analysis of Cyber Insurance Policies: How Do Carriers Write Policies and Price Cyber Risk?" in *Proceedings of the 16th Annual Workshop on the Economics of Information Security* (Workshop on the Economics of Information Security, La Jolla, CA, 2017), https://papers.ssrn.com/sol3/papers.cfm? abstract_id=2929137.

5 Laura A. Odell, J. Corbin Fauntleroy, and Ryan R. Wagner, "Cyber Insurance – Managing Cyber Risk" (Institute for Defense Analyses, April 2015), https://www.ida.org/~/media/Corporate/Files/Publications/IDA_Documents/ITSD/2015/D-5481.ashx.

6 Ranjan Pal, *Improving Network Security Through Cyber-Insurance* (University of Southern California, 2014), http://digitallibrary.usc.edu/cdm/ref/collection/p15799coll3/id/514919.

7 Susan Kelly, "Data Breaches Spur Demand for Cyber Liability Coverage," *Treasury & Risk*, accessed December 31, 2015, https://www.treasuryandrisk.com/sites/treasuryandrisk/2015/01/15/data-breaches-spur-demand-for-cyber-liability-coverage

8 Marsh Company, "Benchmarking Trends: As Cyber Concerns Broaden, Insurance Purchases Rise," *Marsh & McLennan Companies*, https://www.marsh.com/us/insights/benchmarking-trends-cyber-concerns-broaden-insurance-purchases-rise.html.

9 "Benchmarking Trends: As Cyber Concerns Broaden, Insurance Purchases Rise" (Marsh Management Research, March 2015), 3, http://usa.marsh.com/Portals/9/Documents/BenchmarkingTrendsCyber8094.pdf.

10 "Managing Cyber Security as a Business Risk: Cyber Insurance in the Digital Age" (Ponemon Institute, August 2013), 10, fig. 10, http://www.ponemon.org/local/upload/file/Cyber%20Insurance%20white%20paper%20FINAL%207.pdf.

11 Michael Hickens, "Insurer Warns Client of Possible Breach," *Wall Street Journal – CIO Journal*, March 11, 2014, http://blogs.wsj.com/cio/2014/03/11/insurer-warns-client-of-possible-breach.

12 Jay P. Kesan, Ruperto P. Majuca, and William J. Yurcik, "The Economic Case for Cyberinsurance," 2005, http://papers.ssrn.com/sol3/papers.cfm?abstract_id=577862.

13 Brian D. Brown, "The Ever-Evolving Nature of Cyber Coverage," *The Insurance Journal*, September 22, 2014, http://www.insurancejournal.com/magazines/features/2014/09/22/340633.htm.

14 Nicholas Economidis, Richard Betterley, Leigh McMullan, David Navetta, Robert A. Parisi, "Cyber Liability on Main Street: What Coverages Do You Need?" November 9, 2012, http://plusweb.org/Portals/0/Conference%20 Material%202012/Cyber%20Liability%20on%20Main%20Street.pdf.

15 Odell, Fauntleroy, and Wagner, "Cyber Insurance – Managing Cyber Risk."

16 Rainer Böhme, "Cyber-Insurance Revisited," in *Workshop on the Economics of Cybersecurity (WEIS)*, 2005, http://infosecon.net/workshop/slides/weis_5_1.pdf.

17 Brown, "The Ever-Evolving Nature of Cyber Coverage."

18 "Cyber Liability on Main Street: What Coverages Do You Need?"

19 Shaun Crawford and David Piesse, "Mitigating Cyber Risk for Insurers" (Ernst and Young, 2014), https://www.ey.com/Publication/vwLUAssets/EY_-_Insights_into_cybersecurity_and_risk_(Part_2)/$FILE/ey-mitigating-cyber-risk-for-insurers.pdf.

20 ISO/ISEC 7816. 2011, "Identification Cards – Integrated Circuit Cards," http://www.iso.org/iso/iso_catalogue/catalogue_tc/catalogue_detail.htm?csnumber=29257; and ISO/ISEC 14443. 2008, "Identification Cards – Contactless Integrated Circuit Cards," http://www.iso.org/iso/iso_catalogue/catalogue_ics/catalogue_detail_ics.htm?csnumber=39693.

21 Trevor Maynard and Nick Beecroft, "Business Blackout – The Insurance Implications of a Cyber Attack on the US Power Grid" (Lloyds of London, May 2015), https://www.lloyds.com/~/media/files/news-and-insight/risk-insight/2015/business-blackout/business-blackout20150708.pdf

22 Rainer Böhme and Galina Schwartz, "Modeling Cyber-Insurance: Towards a Unifying Framework," in *Proceedings of the 9th Annual Workshop on the Economics of Information Security*, 2010, http://www.icsi.berkeley.edu/pubs/networking/modelingcyber10.pdf.

23 Sasha Romanosky, "Examining the Costs and Causes of Cyber Incidents," *Journal of Cybersecurity* 2, no. 2 (2016): 121–135.

24 Thomas Kean, ed., *The 9/11 Commission Report: Final Report of the National Commission on Terrorist Attacks upon the United States* (Government Printing Office, 2011), Google Books.

25 Howard Kunreuther and Erwann Micheal-Kerjan, "Terrorism Insurance," *Regulation* 28 (2005): 44; Darius Lakdawalla and George Zanjani, "Insurance, Self-Protection, and the Economics of Terrorism," *Journal of Public Economics* 89, no. 9 (2005): 1891–1905.

26 Gordon Woo, "Quantifying Insurance Terrorism Risk," *Manuscript, Risk Management Solutions, Newark, CA*, 2002, http://www.rit.edu/cos/math/cmmc/conferences/2007/literature/Woo_2002b.pdf.

27 Baird Webel, "Terrorism Risk Insurance: Issue Analysis and Overview of Current Program" (Congressional Research Service, July 23, 2014), https://www.fas.org/sgp/crs/terror/R42716.pdf.

28 Elana Broitman, "Smart Cyber Legislation" (New America Cybersecurity Initiative, October 15, 2015), https://www.newamerica.org/cybersecurity-initiative/smart-cyber-legislation.

29 Trudy Knockless, "Demand for Cyber Risk Insurance Market on the Rise," *Property Casualty 360*, October 1, 2015, http://www.propertycasualty360.com/2015/10/01/demand-for-cyber-risk-insurance-market-on-the-rise.

30 International Organization for Standardization, "ISO/IEC 27001 – Information Security Management," 2013, http://www.iso.org/iso/home/standards/management-standards/iso27001.htm.

31 Brad Tuttle and Scott D. Vandervelde, "An Empirical Examination of CobiT as an Internal Control Framework for Information Technology," *International Journal of Accounting Information Systems* 8, no. 4 (2007): 240–263.

32 "Comparing the CSF, ISO/IEC 27001 and NIST SP 800-53" (HITRUST Alliance, 2014), https://hitrustalliance.net/documents/csf_rmf_related/CSFComparisonWhitpaper.pdf.

33 "COBiT 4.1 Framework" (IT Governance Institute, 2007), https://www.isaca.org/Knowledge-Center/cobit/Documents/COBIT4.pdf.

34 Division of Corporation Finance, "CF Disclosure Guidance: Topic No. 2" (Securities and Exchange Commission, October 13, 2011), https://www.sec.gov/divisions/corpfin/guidance/cfguidance-topic2.htm.

35 Nate Sheidlower, "The Rise in the Demand for CISOs," *Security Current*, July 30, 2015, https://web.archive.org/web/20170606074326/http://www.securitycurrent.com/en/analysis/ac_analysis/the-rise-in-the-demand-for-cisos.

36 "Managing Cyber Security as a Business Risk: Cyber Insurance in the Digital Age."

37 Robert P. Hartwig and Claire Wilkinson, "Cyber Risks: The Growing Threat" (Insurance Information Institute, June 2014), 7, http://www.iii.org/sites/default/files/docs/pdf/paper_cyberrisk_2014.pdf.

38 Alex Wright, "Cyber Market Dramatically Increases," *Risk & Insurance*, December 1, 2015, http://www.riskandinsurance.com/cyber-market-dramatically-increases.

39 "2011 ITRC Breach Report Key Findings," *Identity Theft Resource Center*, 2015, http://www.idtheftcenter.org/ITRC-Surveys-Studies/2011-data-breaches.html.

40 Roy Urrico, "Data Breaches on Record Pace for 2015," *Credit Union Times*, July 5, 2015, https://web.archive.org/web/20170606074326/http://www.securitycurrent.com/en/analysis/ac_analysis/the-rise-in-the-demand-for-cisos.

41 "Benchmarking Trends: As Cyber Concerns Broaden, Insurance Purchases Rise," 2.

42 Moody's, "Threat of Cyber Risk is Growing" (November, 2015) via Wright, "Cyber Market Dramatically Increases," http://riskandinsurance.com/ cyber-market-dramatically-increases

43 Deloitte, "Cyber Insurance: One Element of Risk Management – Deloitte Risk & Compliance – WSJ," *Risk and Compliance – Wall Street Journal*, March 18, 2015, http://deloitte.wsj.com/riskandcompliance/2015/03/18/cyber-insurance-one-element-of-a-cyber-risk-management-strategy.

44 Hartwig and Wilkinson, "Cyber Risks: The Growing Threat."

45 Timothy J. Sinclair, "Bond Rating Agencies and Coordination in the Global Political Economy," in *Private Authority and International Affairs*, ed. A. Claire Cutler, Virginia Haufler, and Tony Porter (Albany, NY: SUNY Press, 1999), 159, Google Books.

46 Ibid., 158–159.

47 Günter Strobl and Han Xia, *The Issuer-Pays Rating Model and Ratings Inflation: Evidence from Corporate Credit Ratings* (Mimeo, University of North Carolina, 2011), https://papers.ssrn.com/sol3/papers. cfm?abstract_id=2002186.

48 Sinclair, "Bond Rating Agencies and Coordination in the Global Political Economy," 161.

49 Timothy J. Sinclair, "Guarding the Gates of Capital: Credit Rating Processes and The Global Political Economy" (PhD Dissertation, York University, 1995), 24.

50 Sinclair, "Bond Rating Agencies and Coordination in the Global Political Economy," 120.

51 Lawrence J. White, "Credit-Rating Agencies and the Financial Crisis: Less Regulation of CRAs Is a Better Response," *Journal of International Banking Law* 25, no. 4 (2010): 170.

52 Paramount Pictures International, *The Big Short | Clip: "Jenga" | Paramount Pictures International*, accessed February 4, 2016, https://www.youtube.com/ watch?v=r7H6Go_shP8.

53 Pal, "Improving Network Security through Cyber-Insurance."

54 Dan Schutzer, "CTO Corner: An Assessment of Cyber Insurance," *Financial Services Roundtable*, February 2015.

55 Division of Corporation Finance, "CF Disclosure Guidance: Topic No. 2."

56 Knockless, "Demand for Cyber Risk Insurance Market on the Rise."

57 "Cyber Liability Insurance Market Trends: Survey" (Advisen, October 2014), 4–5, http://www.partnerre.com/assets/uploads/docs/cyber-survey-results.pdf.

9

Containing Conficker

A Public Health Approach

Michael Thornton

History and Philosophy of Science, University of Cambridge, Cambridge, UK

9.1 Introduction

In late 2008, Microsoft discovered a vulnerability in Windows which could be exploited by computer worms, a highly contagious type of self-replicating malware. While Microsoft promptly released an emergency patch, within months a sophisticated worm called Conficker spread rapidly around the world, drafting between 5 and 13 million machines into the "holy grail" of botnets.[1] While estimates of the danger vary, a botnet of that size could have credibly threatened critical infrastructure[2] (water treatment plants, emergency response systems, power plants, etc.) and possibly even the backbone of the internet itself. Despite this danger, world governments essentially did nothing to contain the worm. Luckily, a small group of security experts calling themselves The Cabal[3] (later renamed the less sinister Conficker Working Group, CWG) understood the risk. They were largely able to prevent the creators of the worm from gaining control of the botnet, by working with the companies and organizations which manage over 100 Top Level Domains (TLDs) to preregister domains that Conficker's creators might use for command and control communications.

In this chapter, I will briefly describe the spread of Conficker and assess whether the CWG is a good model for future large-scale malware mitigation efforts. Finding that model insufficient, I will explore an alternative framework for containing malware based on the philosophy and policy of public health. In this section, I will explore fundamental philosophical questions about what constitutes a matter of public concern and the proper role of government. While others have compared public health efforts to cybersecurity, this work has often focused on specific low-level applications (e.g. nomenclature[4] and network effects[5]). I will argue, however, that the philosophy and policy of

Rewired: Cybersecurity Governance, First Edition. Edited by Ryan Ellis and Vivek Mohan.
© 2019 John Wiley & Sons, Inc. Published 2019 by John Wiley & Sons, Inc.

public health is most useful as a way of thinking about the normative justification for – and the ethical limits on – governmental interventions in cybersecurity. Finally, I will apply this framework to Conficker and imagine what a public health-inspired government response might have looked like.

9.2 The Conficker Infection

On 23 October 2008, during the eighth annual meeting of the International Botnet Task Force, Microsoft released an out-of-band emergency security patch. The patch fixed a Windows vulnerability that could allow malware to spread between unprotected machines without any user interaction.[6] While releasing an emergency patch cast a spotlight on the vulnerability, Microsoft had already seen the flaw exploited in the wild. On 22 November a month after the patch's release, a new piece of highly contagious malware – the Conficker worm – was first detected. In response, Microsoft issued a security alert recommending that people immediately patch their systems.

For the most part, Conficker A (as it would come to be called) simply hid in a computer's background activity. When it was time to call home for instructions, however, the worm would contact 250 pseudorandomly generated domains spread out across 5 TLDs. Behind any of those domains, the creators of the worm could be waiting to issue commands. A few weeks later, a more sophisticated variant called Conficker B appeared; this variant could propagate via thumb drives, disable Windows Automatic Update, block certain DNS look-ups, and call domains from eight TLDs.[7] While these strategies were not new, it was unusual for so many features to be packed into a single piece of malware. More than one researcher described it as "elegant."[8] By the end of 2008, SRI International estimated that between 1 and 1.5 million computers were infected.[9] Over the next five months, three additional versions of the worm would be introduced. At its peak in 2009, the Conficker botnet grew to between 5 and 13 million machines.[10]

While Microsoft's release of an emergency patch signaled that the vulnerability was particularly dangerous, in general, the cybersecurity community was slow to recognize the scope of the problem. While the worm was discussed with increased frequency on a number of cybersecurity e-mail lists in late 2008,[11] there was little organized activity within the private sector to control the spread of the worm until early 2009. Governments, meanwhile, were entirely absent from the discussion. The security firm Qualys estimated that two months after the emergency patch was released, 30% of computers running Windows remained unpatched.[12]

A small number of security experts, who would later call themselves the CWG, did notice that Conficker threatened the internet at large. Shortly after the worm's appearance, they began to study the worm and devise ways to control it. Early members of the all-volunteer CWG, many of who knew each other from conferences and social media, included representatives of Microsoft, SRI International, and several companies that managed TLDs, as well as a number of independent security researchers and academics. Relatively quickly, they discovered that the domain names which could be used for command and control communications were not random. By running the domain name generation algorithm for a future date, the group could identify the domains that would be called and register the names themselves (often with personal credit cards) before the worm's creators could use them for passing the botnet instructions. When infected computers called these domains, the CWG redirected the traffic to designated sinkhole servers, which were then used to map the spread of the infection.

This strategy worked reasonably well until the introduction of the Conficker C variant in late February 2009. In reaction to the CWG's sinkholing project, the creators of Conficker C designed the new version to generate a list of 50 000 domains every day from among a list of 116 TLDs. Unlike in the past, this list included not only generic TLDs (e.g. .org and .biz) but over 100 country-code TLDs (e.g. .cn and .fr). Each day an infected machine would attempt to contact 500 domains from this list of 50 000. In order for the sinkholing strategy to continue to work, the organizations and companies managing these TLDs would need to block 50 000 domain names a day, forever. In some countries this approach was of questionable legality, and in some cases domains were already owned and operated for legitimate purposes. Additionally, the strategy relied on the International Corporation for Assigned Names and Numbers (ICANN) agreeing to waive its fees for registering the domains – something that had never before been asked. Despite these difficulties, the CWG – now numbering hundreds of individuals – ultimately convinced the relevant stakeholders to cooperate by leveraging personal connections. This work went on with essentially no government involvement. One member of the working group would later sum up the US government's role as "zero involvement, zero activity, zero knowledge."[13]

How much credit the CWG deserves for averting catastrophe is unclear. While the sinkholing effort generally succeeded at keeping the creators of the worm from taking control of the botnet (a few domains did slip through), later variants of the worm possessed the ability to transmit instructions via peer-to-peer connections. Even if the sinkholing project was perfect, the creators of Conficker could have circumvented the CWG's efforts by using this slower payload delivery system. Additionally, there was nothing to stop the creators from simply increasing the number of domains that needed to be blocked. Would the world community block 100 000 domains a day? What about 500 000? It may be that the pressure became too much, or the effort too costly, but whatever the reason, the creators of the Conficker botnet never implemented their master plan (if there was one to begin with).

Given this anticlimax, it is hard to gauge the success of the CWG's efforts. While most members of the group felt that the effort had been a success, they nonetheless recognized the flaws in their approach.[14] It is worth taking a close look at what worked and what did not work to determine whether the CWG is a useful model for future control and remediation efforts.

The CWG's greatest successes were rallying an unprecedented degree of private-sector collaboration, gaining cooperation from ICANN, and convincing the companies and organizations which managed 116 TLDs to block tens of thousands of domains a day. Despite at times conflicting incentives, the 20 private companies and roughly half dozen nonprofits which comprised the CWG were mostly able to work together effectively. CWG generally made decisions on information sharing and strategy by consensus, and typically decided as a group when to talk to the press. While some key members were accused of sharing information with other stakeholders or the press for selfish reasons,[15] these instances were relatively rare and ultimately not fatal to the overall project. CWG members cited the informal organization and lack of hierarchy as major factors in keeping the group together. Additionally, the fact that many members knew each other via social media helped facilitate trust.[16]

In their "Lessons Learned" report, the leaders of the CWG listed the following as failures or downsides to their model: remediation efforts, communication with internet service providers (ISPs), collaboration and information sharing with the US government, public relations, lack of accountability, lack of a tasking authority, and balancing inclusion of stakeholders with efficiency.[17] The last three entries on the list are perhaps the required cost of informal organization and reliance on social networks. In regards to government collaboration, members specifically mentioned US government representatives being willing to take information (including plagiarizing CWG slides) without providing any information or resources in return.

When thinking about the CWG as a model for future malware control efforts, the most important questions are: (i) how repeatable are the successes? and (ii) how fixable are the failures? First, I will consider the successes.

While the private-sector collaboration was impressive, the fact that companies often have conflicting incentives means there is always the risk that a collaboration effort like the CWG will break down as underlying incentives shift. Additionally, the incentives that brought private companies together for Conficker may be slightly different and less persuasive in the case of other large-scale malware threats, which nonetheless need attention (e.g. Mirai and WannaCry). One fundamental conflict is between security companies, which sell remediation tools, and Microsoft, which seeks to patch vulnerable machines before they become infected. Companies will also always have strong incentives to talk up their own efforts in the media. This caused tensions within the CWG, and surely would in future efforts as well.[18] Additionally, there is no guarantee that TLDs would voluntarily and universally support future large-scale domain registration.[19] While the sinkholing strategy was mostly successful in the case of Conficker, several TLDs dragged their feet and balked at the initial ask.[20] There remains no enforcement mechanism to ensure compliance. On the whole, while the CWG's successes were impressive and admirable within the context of this specific threat, it is unlikely that the same level of cooperation and collaboration can be counted on to control future threats. More dangerous threats may not be able to be contained by voluntary efforts, and less dangerous (or more highly targeted) threats may not sufficiently inspire broad collaboration.[21]

I am equally pessimistic that the failures of the CWG model can be easily fixed. Without a leadership structure, it is almost impossible to effectively and repeatedly assign tasks and hold people accountable. Likewise, without organizational permanence it is difficult to build better working relationships with ISPs and governments. While loose networks of technical experts may be great at solving complex engineering problems and will surely be needed to address future threats, they are ill-suited to coordinating an ongoing international crisis response effort.

In the "Lessons Learned" report, several participants suggested that many of the CWG's structural flaws could be fixed with the addition of two to three full-time administrative resources. Yet, this solution ignores the basic issue that states cannot leave the protection of critical infrastructure in the hands of volunteers. The ICANN postmortem specifically mentioned that a similar caliber of volunteer might not be available the next time around, and questioned the group's ability to potentially deal with two threats simultaneously.[22] One member reinforced this concern, saying the only reason the Zeus malware spread so widely was that everyone was focused on Conficker.[23] In *Worm*, Mark Bowden characterizes the members of the CWG as the X-Men – outsiders who possess almost supernatural skills and swoop in to save the day. The problem with the X-Men is that sometimes they save the planet and sometimes they start a civil war.

The alternative to relying on private sector and nonprofit volunteers is for governments and international institutions to take on a larger role in both ongoing malware mitigation efforts and crisis response. Rightly so, technologists have been skeptical of (or downright hostile to) government interference in the internet.[24] Historically, government forays into cybersecurity matters have been heavy handed, poorly informed, and ethically dubious (e.g. Clipper Chip in the 1990s, cryptographic backdoors, and PRISM[25]). Even in cases where the goal seems sensible, such as government agencies improving information sharing, Elaine Sedenberg and Deirdre Mulligan have identified that cybersecurity policies often lack the technological details needed to be effective and the explicit ethical safeguards needed to protect individual rights.[26]

Despite these historical failures, governments have a political obligation to ensure that critical infrastructure is secure – which, due to the interconnected nature of the internet, likely also requires promoting cybersecurity more generally. One of the biggest impediments to greater government involvement in cybersecurity, however, is the lack of an overarching framework for justifying interventions and protecting individual rights. Today, the dominant framework is a security paradigm that emerged from the domains of military intelligence and criminal justice. This paradigm is adversarial rather than collaborative, has led to an international cyber arms race through the promotion of offensive cyber capabilities, and generally limits government involvement in civilian cybersecurity to the investigation of cybercrime. Preventative cybersecurity investments, meanwhile, are left to those who own the network and individual nodes. Private companies are responsible for private networks (including 90% of critical infrastructure[27] and much of the internet), government agencies protect government networks, and individuals are responsible for their home networks. I am proposing public health as an alternative and more benevolent framework for promoting network security and robustness. While past research has explored specific, low-level applications of a public health model,[28] the real strength of the approach is as a problem-framing tool to understand the normative justification for – and the ethical limits on – governmental interventions in cybersecurity.

9.3   A Public Health Alternative

A high-level public health model is based on three principles: (i) public health focuses on populations, not individuals[29]; (ii) public health problems are shared, not merely overlapping[30]; and (iii) public health interventions are thoughtful about balancing efficacy with ethical concerns.[31] Used together in the pursuit of promoting human wellbeing, these three principles help provide normative justification for government interventions, while ensuring that individual rights are protected. I will now look at each principle in more depth.

9.3.1   Populations, Not Individuals

The first aspect of the public health model is a focus on problems and interventions that affect populations (as opposed to individuals). If a castaway contracted Tuberculosis (TB), it would not be considered a public health issue because there would be no other people to infect. Generally speaking, public health problems are those that affect a large number of people, and public health interventions – vaccination drives, public education, sanitation systems, and quarantine – are those aimed at benefitting a large number of people. In contrast, "private health" problems overwhelmingly affect individuals without affecting the broader population (e.g. broken bones); and "private health" interventions overwhelmingly benefit the individual, with relatively minor benefits for the broader population (e.g. surgery).

In some cases, individual treatments may be an important part of a public health initiative. For example, it has been estimated that an untreated individual with TB will infect 25–50% of his or her household contacts.[32] This individual treatment falls within the purview of public health because curing the individual potentially will have a meaningful impact on the overall health of the population.

By applying the distinction between public and private health to digital networks, one can start to identify what one might call "public cyberhealth" and "private cyberhealth." I am defining cyberhealth as:

> A state which encompasses the robustness, resiliency, and security of a network, be it a home network or the entire internet.

This concept is similar to cybersecurity. However, cybersecurity typically only addresses problems caused by adversaries.[33] Cyberhealth, meanwhile, also takes into account a network's ability to manage buggy code, natural disasters, bad product design, or human error. A spotty home Wi-Fi signal would be a matter of private cyberhealth, as it affects very few people and can be fixed by a single person. Meanwhile, Conficker would certainly be a matter of public cyberhealth: it affected a large number of people, mitigation efforts required the collaboration of a large number of people and organizations around the world, and it could have been averted entirely with effective population-level interventions, such as mandatory patching.

In public health, the population-level view is useful for identifying broad health trends and guiding policy. The beginnings of many health crises are undetectable when one only focuses on individual patients, due to the myriad factors that contribute to an individual's health. By taking a population-level view, public health experts can identify risk factors and calculate individual and population-level risks. These risk assessments in turn help policymakers determine how to allocate public resources for vaccines, public education, health systems, or even basic research. Frequently, this population-level view allows public health experts to identify early warning signs of a potential crisis, which in turn can encourage preventative steps. This predictive ability is particularly valuable when the necessary intervention has a long lead-time, such as the development of new vaccines. In contrast, the current state of cybersecurity is partly defined by a lack of effective population-level information sharing, a dearth of analytical tools for assessing the value of various interventions, and narrowly deployed reactive responses rather than population-level preventative measures.

9.3.2 Shared and Overlapping Problems

The second principle of the public health model defines public health problems as "shared problems" and situates the population-level approach within the political limitations of Millian liberalism – the dominant ideology underpinning liberal democracies. This principle is essential because public health policies are typically enacted by governments and exist within legal systems – which means that they must be justifiable within the context of a "defensible political theory."[34]

Within the context of Millian liberalism, public health problems are generally those in which one person's health status can adversely affect the health of another. These problems are "shared," not merely "overlapping," to use Bruce Jennings' terminology.[35] As John Coggon puts it, public health issues are those which are "all citizens' business."[36] Communicable disease is a prime example of a shared problem, whereas weight management would be an overlapping problem. In cases where one individual poses direct and substantial harm to others (e.g. Ebola), a narrow application of Mill's harm principle can justify intrusive governmental action like quarantine. In cases where the threat is less extreme (e.g. chicken pox), there is less justification for an intrusive government response.

While the default in liberal democracies is to leave overlapping problems to individuals and private markets, a softer version of Millian liberalism is often used to justify governmental interventions in cases where overlapping problems become widespread enough to generate substantial negative externalities. For example, while weight management is a paradigmatic overlapping problem, the obesity "epidemic" can strain health systems, hurt the economy, and normalize unhealthy behaviors like eating fast food or drinking soda.[37] It is important to note, however, that while some government action may be warranted to mitigate these effects, only relatively unobtrusive interventions are justifiable – as the risk posed to the general population by obese individuals is indirect, nonurgent, and relatively minor.

This notion of shared and overlapping problems further helps define spheres of public and private concern required for cohesive cyberhealth policy. Conficker is one of the clearest examples of a shared concern. Conficker spread from computer to computer and could pass commands (in its later iterations) via peer-to-peer connections. As such, it is a good candidate to be framed as a public problem; indeed, governmental intervention would be justified even within a stronger version of Millian liberalism. Not only would an uninfected device be at a greater risk of infection if it was closely connected to infected devices, but infected devices could have been wielded in a botnet that could have crippled critical infrastructure. Thus, individuals who were not even connected to the internet could have been significantly harmed. Meanwhile, the short lifespan of laptop batteries looks more like an overlapping concern. While everyone with a laptop might have the concern, my battery's lifespan will not affect yours. Like obesity, however, if there was an "epidemic" of dying batteries with broad economic consequences, then perhaps a government intervention of a relatively unobtrusive sort could be justifiable under a more expansive, softer version of Millian liberalism.

Another reason shared problems justify government intervention is that solutions to shared problems often generate substantial positive externalities – side effects which are not baked into the cost of a good. When a good produces substantial positive externalities, private markets will generally produce the good at a level below what is socially optimal. For example, when an individual is vaccinated against the flu, everyone, including the unvaccinated, have a slightly lower risk of infection. The company that produces the vaccine, however, cannot charge the person getting vaccinated for the benefit the rest of society receives. A similar phenomenon happens with cybersecurity. By securing one's own devices, one confers a free benefit to others on the network.

Public goods represent an extreme case of externalities where the marginal cost of extending the benefit to another person is essentially zero.[38] Paradigmatic examples of public goods include lighthouses, clean air, and national defense. Since private markets only work when one can charge for a good, public goods always lead to private market failure.[39] Public goods are defined as goods that are non-rivalrous and non-excludable.[40,41] When a good is non-rivalrous, my consumption of the good does not diminish your ability to benefit from the good. For example, the benefit I receive from the containment of communicable diseases or malware in no way diminishes your benefit. When a good is non-excludable, an individual who does not participate in creating the good cannot easily be prevented from gaining the benefit. For example, if a water treatment facility's network is secure, it is hard to prevent someone from gaining the benefit of clean water, even if they do not pay their taxes. These two characteristics often lead to free-riding problems where individuals or companies will gain a benefit without participating in its production. As governments are the only legitimate source of coercion in liberal democracies, it is only through government's ability to tax, fine, and enforce laws that public goods can be produced at a socially optimal level. Individuals and private markets do not possess the tools or incentives to adequately address most shared problems.

While public goods are not specific to public health, the specific public goods relevant to building healthy human networks are similar to the public goods relevant to building and maintaining robust digital networks. A few of these overlapping public goods include the containment of communicable diseases/ malware, global monitoring regimes, herd immunity, technological standards, information-sharing regimes, and the knowledge produced from basic research. As such, public goods for public health are a more useful example than lighthouses or national defense for thinking about how governments may adequately provision public goods for cyberhealth. For instance, the containment of communicable diseases/malware, unlike many other public goods, are both "Global Public Goods" (GPGs) – public goods whose benefits are "quasi universal" in terms of countries, people, and generations[42] – and "participatory public goods" – public goods which can only be produced through the active participation of individuals beyond the mere payment of taxes (i.e. get vaccinated/patch your system). The GPG distinction is particularly important because, unlike most public goods such as national defense, GPGs can only be produced via voluntary international collaboration and international institutions. For this reason, the history of international disease control efforts and the work of the World Health Organization (WHO) can serve as a particularly useful example of how states may come together to contain malware like Conficker, Mirai, and WannaCry.

9.3.3 Balancing Efficacy and Individual Rights

Beyond helping to determine which problems justify government intervention, the public health model also provides an approach for considering the ethical limits of interventions. Within public health, these ethical conflicts are common because interventions that benefit a population often infringe upon individuals' rights (e.g. personal freedom and privacy). Quarantine restricts freedom of movement and association, mandatory vaccinations may violate a person's bodily integrity or restrict their freedom of choice, and monitoring regimes may share sensitive information about a person's health history, including sexual partners or drug use. As a result, some balance must be found that takes into account the effectiveness of a specific intervention, the severity of the problem, and the impact on individuals' rights. One way to stop the spread of a disease would be to lock everyone in their homes, but such a solution is – in all but the most extreme scenarios – ethically unacceptable.

Because today's digital network interventions do not act directly on individuals, the ethical conflicts in cyberhealth are not exactly the same as those in public health. One can immunize and quarantine devices, but these interventions are not as burdensome as in the public health context. If a person's PC becomes infected with a piece of malware sufficiently dangerous for an ISP to restrict that device's internet access, the owner can simply fix the problem, buy a new device, or borrow a friend's. If a PC is automatically patched (akin to immunization), most people would not even notice. Contrast this relatively light cost with the quarantining of whole villages during the 2014–2015 Ebola outbreak, which led to rioting.[43]

While there is not a perfect equivalence, public cyberhealth interventions may still infringe on personal rights. Digital quarantining does restrict one's freedom of association and potentially one's freedom of movement – especially as virtual reality becomes more prevalent. For those with relatively few avenues to connect to the internet, this restriction can cause significant social and economic harm. Meanwhile, in the case of robotic prosthetics, forced patching may be perceived as a violation of bodily integrity quite similar to the experience of forced immunization. One example is Stephen Hawking's refusal to upgrade his robotic voice to a more natural-sounding voice, as he had come to accept the former as part of his identity.[44]

One public health tool that can inform thinking about the balance between efficacy and ethical costs is the Nuffield Council on Bioethics' Intervention Ladder. The Intervention Ladder provides a spectrum of interventions from least to most intrusive, which helps one find the right level of intervention for each problem. From the Nuffield Council on Bioethics' report on public health, the steps on the Intervention Ladder are:

1) Do nothing or simply monitor the current situation.
2) Provide information ... for example, as part of campaigns to encourage people to walk more or eat five portions of fruit and vegetables per day.
3) Enable choice ... for example, by ... providing free fruit in schools.
4) Guide choices through changing the default policy. For example ... menus could be changed to provide a more healthy option as standard....
5) Guide choices through incentives ... for example, offering tax-breaks for the purchase of bicycles that are used as a means of traveling to work.
6) Guide choice through disincentives ... for example, through taxes on cigarettes...
7) Restrict choice ... for example, removing unhealthy ingredients from foods, or unhealthy foods from shops or restaurants.
8) Eliminate choice ... for example, through compulsory isolation of patients with infectious diseases.[45]

The Intervention Ladder does not suggest any specific solutions for a particular problem, but rather lays out a set of options to facilitate thinking about what constitutes a proportional response to a specific risk. By assessing a suite of options rather than simply accepting the first that addresses the problem, one is more likely to find a politically and ethically acceptable balance between personal rights and population health.

This public health approach, which assesses a wide variety of public interventions and seeks to find the right balance between efficacy and ethical costs, is fundamentally different from the approach employed in the private technology sector. Since cybersecurity is generally treated as a private problem, companies are limited to interventions that are in their self-interest, area of expertise, and legal authority. While an ISP can shut off someone's internet, it cannot auto-enable application security updates, and it might have little direct interest in doing so even if it could. With limited capabilities and incentives that frequently conflict with the public interest, private companies are ill-suited to identify and implement the cybersecurity solution that best balances effectiveness and personal rights. It is worth acknowledging, however, that private companies are well suited to balancing effectiveness and cost, which suggests that private companies would be a critical component of any cost-effective public intervention; in many cases, specific cyberhealth measures – such as patching proprietary code – will only be able to be implemented by private companies.

The Intervention Ladder is a formal articulation of the type of thinking in which public health experts engage as part of their day-to-day work within public health institutions. The WHO's Ethics Review Committee, for instance, formally reviews all WHO-funded research involving human subjects and provides guidance to member nations on internal ethical issues pertaining to public health.[46] Similarly, the Centers for Disease Control and Prevention's (CDC) Public Health Ethics Unit seeks to raise intraorganizational awareness of ethical problems that public health interventions can cause, and to integrate this way of thinking into everyday work.[47] It may seem trite to say that the way to balance ethics and efficacy is to think about how one balances ethics and efficacy, but this basic level of ethical review used by public health institutions is almost entirely absent from the technology sector and technology policy. While some companies, such as Deep Mind, have begun to think about the ethical issues that arise specifically in the field of artificial intelligence, this type of analysis is reserved for special cases. While runaway, superintelligent artificial agents get quite a bit of attention, everyday ethical concerns are often ignored.

Lastly, because of the direct impact public health interventions often have on individuals, within public health there is a culture of involving a broad number of stakeholders in discussions surrounding specific interventions. This can take place at the individual level (e.g. with informed consent), at the local level (e.g. with public health workers engaging communities around the treatment of HIV), and at the national level (e.g. in a forum like the WHO). In contrast, the technology industry relies on impenetrable terms and conditions that leave users in the dark about their rights and industry prefers to make decisions under a veil of secrecy rather than with meaningful public discussion. These everyday capitalistic practices may have been acceptable and even appropriate when most technology problems looked more like overlapping problems, but as the internet has grown into the essential connective tissue of modern life these overlapping problems have become an increasingly shared concern.

One historical parallel is the private control of water sources and the 1854 cholera outbreak in London. At the time of the cholera outbreak, many water sources were provided by private companies with minimal oversight. While the dominant theory of the time attributed cholera to miasma (bad air), the physician John Snow identified that a specific water pump on Broad Street was the likely source by mapping incidents of the disease. He also identified that the water company was using water from sewage-polluted sections of the Thames.[48] As people increasingly came to understand the importance of clean water, governments took on a larger role in the oversight of water quality. Similarly, railroads were once run by private companies with little government involvement; but as railroads became an increasingly essential part of economies and national defense capabilities, they became a matter of public concern and responsibility.

As the internet becomes an ever more essential component of modern life – underpinning critical infrastructure, commerce, and social interactions – our notions of corporations' private rights and public responsibilities must be continually reevaluated. The alternative is to accept that the digital landscapes in which we live and the security of the critical infrastructure on which we rely will be designed to maximize profits rather than human flourishing.

9.4 A Public Health Approach to Conficker

In order to make this framework feel more concrete, I would like to explore a thought experiment: What would a Conficker response built on public health principles look like? While this question is impossible to answer definitively, a public health-inspired approach would likely involve: (i) a robust government response, (ii) institutional coordination, and (iii) a more substantial ongoing investment in public goods for cyberhealth, which would encourage early detection and prevention.

The first and most significant difference between the public health-inspired approach and the work of the CWG would be that within a public health framework, Conficker would be understood as a problem deserving government attention. Conficker and computer worms more generally are clearly shared problems with many similarities to communicable diseases. As such, governments would not only be justified in taking action, but would have had an obligation to do so once the threat grew to the point at which it might pose a danger to critical infrastructure. While one would be right to doubt the efficacy of (and maybe even fear) a robust governmental response, one cannot consider what that response might look like within the existing security paradigm. Rather, one must consider it within the broader systematic changes that a public health approach would recommend.

One of the fundamental changes that would follow from an expanded government role in cyberhealth would be greater levels of government investment in civilian-focused cybersecurity agencies. In the field of public health, organizations like the CDC and the WHO serve as world-class centers for research, crisis coordination, ongoing monitoring programs, and information sharing. Currently, there is no digital equivalent. Organizations like US Computer Emergency Readiness Team (US-CERT) are relatively limited in their mandates and do not possess the funds to attract the world's leading cybersecurity experts. A "Cyber CDC" with more substantial funding than US-CERT and a wider mandate would presumably not only be better equipped than existing agencies for dealing with the technical side of threats like Conficker, but would be better suited to coordinating a vast collective effort like the global sinkholing project. Such an organization would have ongoing relationships with the organizations and companies that manage TLDs and possess coercive tools not available to an ad-hoc volunteer group like the CWG. A "Cyber CDC" would also address many of the organizational problems of the CWG, as it would have the authority to delegate tasks and hold people and organizations accountable. This accountability would also extend to the organization itself, as governmental organizations ultimately fall under the purview of elected leaders. If the CWG had failed in its mission, there would have been no justifiable reason or mechanism to hold the members accountable for their failure. Meanwhile, a "Cyber CDC" could still preserve many of the CWG's strengths. If an issue exceeded the technical capabilities of the organization, specialized working groups of independent and private-sector security experts could still be convened – but those groups would have institutional resources and legitimate authority to implement their solutions.

The strategy of such an institution would also be substantially different from the work of the CWG, likely allowing for a more preventative approach. The CWG adopted the sinkholing strategy because it was one of the few approaches they had the power to enact. The CWG had no power to arrest the perpetrators, conduct public education campaigns, or compel/incentivize individuals and companies to update their systems. In the case of Conficker, a preventative approach would have been vastly preferable to a reactive approach. While forcing people to patch their systems may have been overly burdensome, 100% compliance would not have been necessary to mitigate the risk. A botnet of a million machines poses far less of a risk to critical infrastructure than a botnet of 10 million machines. While private companies like Microsoft can make (and have made) unilateral decisions to enable automatic updates, in many cases private incentives may not align with public interest. Recent examples include the shortcuts taken by Chinese webcam manufacturers, which contributed to the growth of the Mirai botnet responsible for the attack on the DNS provider Dyn, Inc. in October 2016: the attack disrupted access to some of the internet's most popular sites, including Twitter, Reddit, Amazon.com, Netflix, and Spotify.[49] If Conficker and other large-scale threats are seen as partly the responsibility of governments to control and clean up, governments will be incentivized to identify threats early, invest in cybersecurity research, improve standards, and hold laggards accountable.

While many of the strategies above are not unique to public health, the public health model limits the potential downsides of increased government involvement by placing a specific emphasis on balancing efficacy with individual rights, and by deploying interventions with an overall goal of promoting human wellbeing. While a security paradigm might allow highly invasive network monitoring as long as it disrupts criminal activity, the public health model would likely not as the negative effects of the loss of privacy would likely outweigh nearly any benefit of catching a few more cybercriminals. In this regard, public health is a more benevolent model than law enforcement or straight economics. A tool like network monitoring, for instance, can gather information in an anonymous, minimized, and decentralized way which protects individual privacy (as in the public health context), or it can be used as a mechanism for espionage and crushing political dissent. When the motivation for improving cybersecurity is merely economic or strategic, privacy and personal freedom often end up sacrificed at the altar of security.

9.5 Conclusion

In this chapter I argued that rather than treating cybersecurity as the default way of thinking about network robustness, we must recognize that it represents a specific worldview – heavily influenced by the domains of military intelligence and criminal justice – which must be critically examined and compared to alternate frames that may better protect our interests. While the CWG achieved an unprecedented level of private sector collaboration and was largely successful in preventing the creators of Conficker from gaining control of the botnet, its lack of accountability and reliance on volunteer labor make it a poor model on which to base future global containment and remediation efforts. I have suggested an alternative framework based on a public health worldview, which focuses on populations (rather than individuals), on the shared nature of risks like Conficker, and on the need to balance effective solutions with individual rights. Coupled with public health's overarching goal of promoting human wellbeing, these principles provide a normative justification for governmental interventions in matters of cyberhealth and a model for assessing the proportionality and ethical cost of various interventions.

Notes

1 "Conficker Working Group: Lessons Learned," The Rendon Group, 2010, 10, http://www.confickerworkinggroup.org/wiki/uploads/Conficker_Working_Group_Lessons_Learned_17_June_2010_final.pdf; Mark Bowden, *Worm: The First Digital World War* (New York: Atlantic Monthly Press, 2011), 264. For those interested in a more technical breakdown of Conficker I would suggest Felix Leder and Tillman Werner's paper on the subject ("Know Your Enemy: Containing Conficker"), the Lessons Learned report, or ICANN's postmortem.
2 "Conficker Working Group: Lessons Learned," ii.
3 Bowden, *Worm*, 143.
4 Brent Rowe, Michael Halpern, and Tony Lentz, "Is a Public Health Framework the Cure for Cyber Security?" *Cross-Talk* 25, no. 6 (2012): 30–38.
5 Alun Lloyd and Robert May, "How Viruses Spread Among Computers and People," *Science* 292 (2001): 1316–1317.
6 "Conficker Working Group: Lessons Learned."
7 Dave Piscitello, "Conficker Summary and Review," ICANN, 2010, https://www.icann.org/en/system/files/files/conficker-summary-review-07may10-en.pdf.

8 Ibid., 5.
9 "Conficker Working Group: Lessons Learned," 16.
10 Ibid., 10.
11 Ibid., 16.
12 Ibid., 4.
13 Ibid.
14 Ibid.
15 Bowden, *Worm*, 232.
16 "Conficker Working Group: Lessons Learned."
17 Ibid., 34–36.
18 Ibid., 23.
19 Piscitello, "Conficker Summary and Review," 14.
20 Bowden, *Worm*, 230.
21 One notable systematic change was the development of ICANN's formal process for waiving fees for malware control efforts.
22 Piscitello, "Conficker Summary and Review," 12.
23 "Conficker Working Group: Lessons Learned," 41–42.
24 James Lewis, "Sovereignty and the Role of Government in Cyberspace," *The Brown Journal of World Affairs* 16, no. 2 (2010): 55–65.
25 Fred Kaplan, *Dark Territory: The Secret History of Cyber War* (New York: Simon & Schuster Paperbacks, 2016), 36–37, 247–252.
26 Elaine Sedenberg and Deirdre Mulligan, "Public Health as a Model for Cybersecurity Information Sharing," *Berkeley Technology Law Journal* 30, no. 3 (2015): 1687–1739.
27 P.W. Singer and Allan Friedman, *Cybersecurity and Cyberwar: What Everyone Needs to Know* (Oxford: Oxford University Press, 2014), 15.
28 Jeffrey O. Kephart, Steve R. White, and David M. Chess, "Computers and Epidemiology," *Spectrum IEEE* 30, no. 5 (1993): 20–26; Scott Charney, "Collective Defense: Applying the Public-Health Model to the Internet," *Security & Privacy IEEE* 10, no. 2 (2012): 54–59.
29 Angus Dawson, "Resetting the Parameters: Public Health as the Foundation for Public Health Ethics," in *Public Health Ethics*, ed. Angus Dawson (Cambridge: Cambridge University Press, 2011), 1–19; Bengt Brülde, "Health, Disease and the Goal of Public Health," in *Public Health Ethics*, ed. Angus Dawson (Cambridge: Cambridge University Press, 2011), 20–47.
30 John Coggon, *What Makes Health Public? A Critical Evaluation of Moral, Legal, and Political Claims in Public Health* (Cambridge: Cambridge University Press, 2012), 25; Bruce Jennings, "Public Health and Civic Republicanism," in *Ethics, Prevention, and Public Health*, ed. Angus Dawson and Marcel Verweij (New York: Oxford University Press, 2007), 30–58.
31 Nuffield Council on Bioethics, *Public Health: Ethical Issues* (London: Nuffield Council on Bioethics, 2007).
32 Jack Adler and David Rose, "Transmission and Patheogenesis of Tuberculosis," in *Tuberculosis*, ed. William N. Rom and Stuart M. Garay (Boston: Little Brown, 1996), 129–140.

33 Singer and Friedman, *Cybersecurity and Cyberwar: What Everyone Needs to Know*, 34.

34 Coggon, "What Makes Health Public," 266.

35 Jennings, "Public Health and Civic Republicanism," 30–58.

36 Coggon, "What Makes Health Public," 25.

37 Youfa Wang, May A. Beydoun, Lan Liang, Benjamin Caballero, and Shiriki K. Kumanyika, "Will All Americans Become Overweight or Obese? Estimating the Progression and Cost of the US Obesity Epidemic," *Obesity* 16, no. 10 (2008): 2323–2330.

38 Deborah Spar, "The Public Face of Cyberspace," in *Global Public Goods*, ed. Inge Kaul, Isabelle Grunberg, and Marc Stern (New York: Oxford University Press, 1999), 344–363.

39 In the case of public goods, market failure can be understood as unrealized social benefit due to inadequate private market incentives.

40 John G. Head, *Public Goods and Public Welfare* (Durham, NC: Duke University Press, 1975), 69.

41 John Rawls, *A Theory of Justice*, rev. ed. (Oxford: Oxford University Press, 1999), 235.

42 Inge Kaul, Isabelle Grunberg, and Marc A. Stern, "Defining Global Public Goods," in *Global Public Goods: International Cooperation in the Twenty-first Century*, ed. Inge Kaul, Isabelle Grunberg, and Marc A. Stern (New York; Oxford: Oxford University Press, 1999), 2–19..

43 Norimitsu Onishi, "Clashes Erupt as Liberia Sets an Ebola Quarantine," *New York Times*, August 20, 2014, accessed May 15, 2017, https://www.nytimes.com/2014/08/21/world/africa/ebola-outbreak-liberia-quarantine.html.

44 *Weekend Edition Sunday*, "Stephen Hawking Gets A Voice Upgrade," NPR, December 7, 2014, accessed May 30, 2017, http://www.npr.org/2014/12/07/369108538/stephen-hawking-gets-a-voice-tech-upgrade.

45 Numbers added. Nuffield Council on Bioethics, *Public Health: Ethical Issues*, XIX.

46 World Health Organization, "Research Ethics Review Committee," World Health Organization, accessed May 16, 2017, http://www.who.int/ethics/review-committee/en.

47 Centers for Disease Control and Prevention, "Public Health Ethics," Centers for Disease Control and Prevention, May 10, 2015, accessed May 16, 2017, https://www.cdc.gov/od/science/integrity/phethics.

48 Judith Summers, *Soho: A History of London's Most Colorful Neighborhood* (London: Bloomsbury, 1989), 113–117.

49 Lorenzo Franceschi-Bicchierai, "How 1.5 Million Connected Cameras Were Hijacked to Make an Unprecedented Botnet," Motherboard, September 29, 2016, accessed October 2, 2017, https://motherboard.vice.com/en_us/article/8q8dab/15-million-connected-cameras-ddos-botnet-brian-krebs.

10

Bug Bounty Programs

Institutional Variation and the Different Meanings of Security

Andreas Kuehn[1] and Ryan Ellis[2]

[1] *Global Cooperation in Cyberspace, EastWest Institute, New York, NY, USA*
[2] *Communication Studies, Northeastern University, Boston, MA, USA*

10.1 Introduction: Conspicuously Absent

On 13 February 2015, President Obama appeared at the Cybersecurity and Consumer Protection Summit at Stanford University. The White House organized the gathering to bring together industry and government to discuss and confront the stubborn challenges of cybersecurity. Cyber threats, President Obama remarked, threaten to undermine America's leadership in the digital economy. As he noted, cyber "attacks are hurting American companies and costing American jobs…[they are] a threat to America's economic security."[1] President Obama struck a familiar – if important – note, reiterating that cybersecurity is "a shared mission." Ensuring security and prosperity in the digital world requires public–private cooperation; neither the private sector nor the government alone can confront the maladies of the information age. As President Obama remarked, the proliferation of botnets, malware, phishing attempts, and ransomware – clever intrusions that maliciously encrypt a user's data and hold it hostage until a victim pays extortion – require the combined ingenuity and resources of both industry and government.[2]

The crowning moment of the summit was the signing of Executive Order 13691, "Promoting Private Sector Cybersecurity Information Sharing."[3] The Presidential Executive Order sought to encourage greater information sharing between industry and government. It outlined a new effort assisting in the creation of standards that would facilitate the easy exchange of information about cyber threats (including classified intelligence) between the public and private sectors. The order also encouraged the voluntary creation of new information sharing and analysis organizations (ISAOs) that would work to broker the exchange of data between government and industry organizations.[4]

Rewired: Cybersecurity Governance, First Edition. Edited by Ryan Ellis and Vivek Mohan.
© 2019 John Wiley & Sons, Inc. Published 2019 by John Wiley & Sons, Inc.

The order is the latest in a string of information-sharing efforts that stretch back to the mid-1990s.

Stanford was a natural venue for the summit. Nestled in the heart of Silicon Valley, Stanford famously has had a unique connection to the tech world for generations. Surrounded by the global headquarters of Google, Apple, Facebook, Yahoo!, Hewlett-Packard, and others, the University is rightly celebrated as a hub of innovation and an incubator of talent. What better place to underline the importance of public–private cooperation and launch a set of new initiatives designed to bring together industry and government?

Yet, despite the rosy rhetoric of cooperation, a number of senior tech executives were conspicuously absent from the proceedings. The CEOs of Google, Yahoo!, and Facebook all declined invitations to attend.[5] Their absence was interpreted as the latest sign of a growing wedge between the federal government and the tech world.[6] Increasingly, industry and government are sharply divided over questions regarding security and privacy. The detailed revelations of widespread spying and digital sabotage leaked by Edward Snowden, a former National Security Agency (NSA) contractor, sent shockwaves through Silicon Valley. Reports that the NSA had hacked into the servers of Google and Yahoo!, routinely inserted backdoors into a range of commercial software and hardware products, and undertaken a secret campaign to deliberately weaken encryption standards outraged the tech community.[7] Brad Smith, General Counsel & Executive Vice President at Microsoft, characterized NSA activity as an "advanced persistent threat" – a term more commonly used to describe insidious, sophisticated, network attacks emanating from hostile nations, rather than the activities of the US government.[8] Google engineer Brandon Downey offered a more colorful response to reports that the NSA had secretly breached internal data links connecting Google's trove of data centers: "Fuck these guys." In Downey's view, the NSA was undermining the real protections that he, and others in the tech sector, had spent their careers crafting.[9] The absence of Mark Zuckerberg (Facebook), Marissa Mayer (Yahoo!), and Larry Page and Eric Schmidt (Google) at the summit underlined the growing divide between the government and industry.

10.2 Scope and Aims

The tech world is not taking the continued growth of malicious behavior online lying down. This chapter explores the different ways in which three major tech companies – Google, Microsoft, and Facebook – are using market-based programs, often known as "bug bounty" programs or vulnerability purchase programs, to enhance the security of software and online services.[10] In the past decade, these and many other vendors have adopted programs that pay researchers for newly discovered bugs. Vulnerability disclosure – making public previously unknown flaws in software – is a key to cybersecurity. If flaws remain unpatched, they can become an effective entryway for exploits and attacks. Disclosure is vital. Once a vendor becomes aware of a flaw, it can develop and issue an update or patch to close the hole and protect users from exploitation by that particular security flaw. Vendors are not the only ones purchasing flaws. While vendors purchase flaws in order to patch or fix these bugs, a parallel market exists. Offensive players—intelligence agencies, militaries, government contractors, criminals, and others—purchase flaws not to fix, but to exploit them. These groups often pay staggering prices—six figures or more in some instances—to acquire previously unknown and undisclosed flaws. They are not interested in fixing these flaws, but rather exploiting them for intelligence collection, sabotage, or criminal purposes. Exploring the efforts of vendor-run bounty programs is revealing in three ways: (i) It demonstrates the institutional variation that exists within the market for flaws. Different companies are approaching the market in different sorts of ways. Indeed, Google, Microsoft, and Facebook are each experimenting with different ways of implementing and designing their bounty programs. (ii) It highlights the diverse aims that animate vendors to launch bounty programs. At their core, these efforts attempt to improve cybersecurity; yet each is driven by a different understanding of threats and risk. (iii) It highlights a key tension between the state and vendors over definitions of security.

10.3 A Market for Flaws: Bug Bounty Programs

Over the past several years, Facebook, Google, and Microsoft have begun purchasing vulnerabilities from the public. They offer independent researchers cash for new flaws through their bug bounty programs. They have collectively paid millions of dollars to independent researchers for thousands of newly discovered bugs. They are not alone. Over 100 different companies, ranging from Yahoo! to United Airlines, now offer "bug bounty" programs. A new start-up launched in 2013, HackerOne, hosts bounty programs for dozens of different companies. By 2015, HackerOne has coordinated payouts totaling over $4 million, reaching 1 800 different contributors and touching over 12 000 different flaws.[11] Bug bounties complement the usual panoply of security efforts – pen testing, security audits, and countless hours spent working to make sure that new code is sound – that companies routinely undertake. These new programs offer an opportunity to strengthen security in the lifecycle of software and services early on and, in some cases, subvert the offensive market for vulnerabilities. The design, operation, and rationale of these programs differ from company to company. Facebook, Google, and Microsoft each approach the market in unique ways. Generally speaking, these bug bounty programs were designed with two objectives in mind: (i) to harness the talent of security researchers to find vulnerabilities in software and services; and (ii) to frustrate malicious hackers, criminals, and states – and subsequently influence policy.

10.3.1 Case I, Microsoft: Rethinking the Market for Flaws

Microsoft was reluctant to adopt a bug bounty program, as the software giant had undertaken earlier outreach efforts to the security researcher community. In the BlueHat Prize contest, researchers competed for the $250000 prize by developing defensive security technologies that deal with entire exploit classes.[12] Compared to Google, Facebook, and others, they were late to the game. For years, Microsoft resisted paying researchers for submitted bugs.[13] In 2013, however, Microsoft reversed course and began offering bounties. In its announcement, Microsoft referred to the new program as "direct investments in the research community, calling upon the clever hackers of the world to work with us on strengthening our platform-wide defenses."[14] It saw this development as a decisive moment not only for the company but also for the entire industry. Importantly, Microsoft's program was explicitly designed to target the black market around illegal exploitation of security flaws. The company stated that it was "cutting down the time that exploits and vulnerabilities purchased on the black market remain useful, especially for targeted attacks that rely on stealthy exploitation without discovery."[15] Finally, Microsoft's structure of the bug bounty program was novel: they decided to offer limited, short-term programs, and to focus significant resources on purchasing new techniques – previously unknown methods for bypassing security controls – rather than seeking to purchase each newly discovered flaw. Microsoft's approach reflects recognition of some of the potential problems that traditional bug bounty programs encounter and a concerted effort to disrupt the black market for vulnerabilities.

Since 2013, Microsoft has run a number of limited, short-run, bounty programs. In 2013, it announced that it would, for the first time, pay researchers for qualifying reported bugs in Internet Explorer 11 (IE 11). The program offered rewards up to $11000 and was only open for 30 days, running from June to July. Unlike Facebook and Google, which had open-ended bounty programs, Microsoft decided to offer rewards during a fairly narrow window: rewards were only offered during the preview phase of IE 11, before the browser was rolled out to the general public. Subsequently, Microsoft repeated this approach and offered short-term bounty programs during the previews of Edge (Microsoft's new browser) and CoreCLR and ASP.NET 5.[16]

Offering bounties for programs in development (e.g. a beta version of soon-to-be-released software) is one strategy to depress the market for vulnerabilities. Competing directly with the offensive market is very difficult. The prices simply do not compare. Offering cash rewards during previews, however, is a smart way to undermine the offensive market. While a new version of a program is still being tested and is not yet widely deployed, the value of a newly discovered vulnerability is limited. For an offensive player, an exploit targeting a program that has very few users is likely of little use. By offering rewards at this point – when a program's user base is still small and testing is ongoing – the defensive market *can* compete with the offensive market. In this fashion, preview, or early-stage, bounties seek to drive down the price of a zero-day. They encourage the disclosure of bugs before the impacted program has grown large enough to support comparatively high prices.

In 2013, Microsoft also announced a new type of bounty program, a project to reward the discovery and disclosure of what are known as mitigation bypass techniques.[17] The focus on techniques – novel methods and ways of conducting exploitation – rather than individual vulnerabilities is significant. In Microsoft's view, techniques are far more valuable than any single vulnerability. In terms of supply, vulnerabilities may be large in number, but new techniques are presumed to be quite scarce. Discovering a new technique would allow Microsoft to protect against not just a single point of vulnerability, but rather an entire class of vulnerabilities. Here, Microsoft offered serious money: up to $100000 for a new technique that could compromise platform-wide protections. In the first two years of its "Mitigation Bypass Bounty," Microsoft has paid $480000 to eight different submitting teams (three submissions received awards of $100000 or more, while others received partial awards).[18] As of mid-2017, Microsoft's paid-out bounties totaled over $1.5 million.[19]

The prioritization of techniques over individual vulnerabilities recognizes some of the potential shortcomings and challenges associated with bug bounty programs. Programs with clear guidelines and rules reduce the transaction costs that researchers face when attempting to disclose a discovered vulnerability.[20] Indeed, this is one of their key benefits. Accepting submissions from anyone, however, is not without its costs and drawbacks. Simple, open submission windows invite a flood of reports, including a significant amount of junk. For firms running these programs sorting the wheat from the chaff, distinguishing between the real vulnerabilities that need to be addressed and irrelevant submissions, can be a significant burden. Google and Facebook both report that they receive an overwhelming amount of invalid reports to their bounty programs: 95% of all submissions to Facebook and 93% of all submissions to Google are simply noise.[21] Microsoft's focus on techniques moves away from treating vulnerability discovery and mitigation as an endless game of whack-a-mole. Rather than trying to encourage large numbers of vulnerability submissions, some of which will be valid problems, but many of which will likely turn out to be nonissues, encouraging the submission of new techniques is far more manageable. Here, the number of total submissions will likely be relatively small, easing the burden on staff to continually test and respond to new reports.

At the same time, limited-duration preview bounties introduce uncertainty into the market and pressure researchers to disclose quickly. Microsoft hopes to use its bounty programs to draw out more bugs early in the test-and-release cycle. Vulnerabilities are re-discoverable and, importantly, perishable.[22] For a researcher that has found a zero-day and hopes to sell it, the clock is always ticking. A third party may, at any moment, independently discover the same vulnerability that you have found. If they release their discovery to the public or vendor before you have had a chance to close a sale or claim a reward, the vulnerability that you were sitting on immediately becomes worthless. Preview bounties push researchers to disclose, rather than horde.

10.3.2 Case II, Google: Matching the Wisdom of Crowds and the Wisdom of Experts

Google has taken a slightly different approach to bug bounties. It operates a handful of different rewards programs, complementing these efforts with specialized grants for researchers and a unique program, "Project Zero," that brings together a team of talented researchers to hunt for new flaws across the digital ecosystem.[23] While Google's efforts replicate the benefits that Facebook and other defensive programs offer in harnessing and encouraging the wisdom of a large community of knowledgeable users, the company also incentivizes highly skilled researchers by offering individual, open-ended grants and by collecting significant talent in-house through Project Zero.

Google launched its first rewards program as an experiment in January 2010. The program offered to pay researchers who contributed qualifying bugs to Google's open-source Chromium project (which supports the development of the Google Chrome browser and the Google Chrome Operating System). The experiment sought to reward those who already provided bugs free-of-charge and, importantly, to entice new researchers to join the effort.[24]

The bug bounty experiment, in the eyes of Google engineers, worked.[25] Over the next several years, Google launched an expanded portfolio of rewards programs, steadily increasing the maximum payments offered and extending bounties to include additional corners of Google's vast offerings. Google now operates four different rewards programs (see Table 10.1), covering vulnerabilities found in Google's web properties (flaws impacting sites that Google operates, such as Google.com, YouTube.com, and others), vulnerabilities discovered in open-source software that are vital to the health of the larger internet and digital ecosystem, and flaws impacting Android, Google's mobile operating system.[26]

Google's security rewards programs have paid out over $4 million to researchers since 2010. In 2014, Google paid over $1.5 million to more than 200 different researchers (totaling over 500 bugs).[27] In 2016, Google's paid-out bounty rewards rose to over $3 million in the form of over 1 000 individual rewards to more than 350 researchers; the largest single bounty totaled $100 000.[28] For a company as large as Google, this may seem like a paltry sum. But the program, like Facebook's effort, offers a useful way to entice new contributions from outside of the company.[29] Within the first few months of launching both Chrome Rewards and the web-focused "Vulnerability Reward Program," Google engineers were pleased to see that the majority of participants were new: they had never previously submitted a bug report to Google.[30] Like Facebook's, Google's rewards programs attract a geographically diverse set of researchers. In 2014, the top three contributors to the Vulnerability Reward Program were from Romania, Poland, and Ukraine.[31] During the same year, the program received more valid bug submissions from Africa than it did from the United States.[32]

Google's programs, like Facebook's, are not intended to replace in-house testing and development. Rather, they offer another layer of security. Like

Table 10.1 Google's reward programs: an overview.

Program	Scope	Offered rewards (Min–Max)	Start date
Chrome Rewards[a]	Chrome or Chrome OS	$500–$50 000	January 2010
Vulnerability Rewards Program[b]	Google-owned web properties, such as *.google.com; *.youtube.com; *.blogger.com	$100–$20 000	November 2010
Path Rewards Program[c]	Open-source projects, libraries, and frameworks including OpenSSL, Angular, and OpenVPN	$500–$10 000	October 2013
Android Security Rewards[d]	Latest version of Android	$333–$30 000	June 2015

[a] Google, "Chrome Rewards Program," https://www.google.com/about/appsecurity/chrome-rewards.
[b] Google, "Vulnerability Rewards Program," https://www.google.com/about/appsecurity/reward-program.
[c] Google, "Patch Rewards Program," https://www.google.com/about/appsecurity/patch-rewards.
[d] Google, "Android Security Rewards Program," https://www.google.com/about/appsecurity/android-rewards.

Facebook and others offering bug bounty programs, Google has demonstrated a serious commitment to recognizing and encouraging the contributions of a vast and knowledgeable public. Google's programs, like many others, encourage those outside of the organization to contribute insights on how to improve security. Google, however, departs from other bug bounty programs in a significant way: rather than simply trying to harness knowledge and wisdom distributed across the large public, it also offers targeted support to highly skilled researchers. Google recently launched two new efforts, Project Zero and individual "Vulnerability Research Grants," that attempt to identify and support particularly skilled and talented researchers.

Project Zero was launched with a flourish in 2014. It was explicitly framed as a response to the growing tide of sophisticated criminal and state-sponsored attacks and exploits. In announcing the launch of Project Zero, Google noted that:

> [Users] should be able to use the web without fear that a criminal or state-sponsored actor is exploiting software bugs to infect your computer, steal secrets or monitor your communications. Yet in sophisticated attacks, we see the use of "zero-day" vulnerabilities to target, for example, human rights activists or to conduct industrial espionage. This needs to stop. We think more can be done to tackle this problem.[33]

With Project Zero, Google sought to hire the most talented security researchers it could find and turn them loose to look for flaws in widely used software – *any* software, not just software that fell under Google's ambit.[34] Project Zero attempted to beat criminals and nation-states to the punch: its team sought to uncover and help fix flaws before they could be exploited by even the most sophisticated state-backed hackers and criminals.[35] Project Zero recognizes that while more conventional bug bounty programs, including the various reward programs Google supports, are useful in attracting contributions from a large pool of smart users, highly skilled researchers are a particularly scarce commodity. Project Zero enlisted a number of extremely talented hackers – including Ben Hawkes, a researcher who previously uncovered a number of serious flaws in Adobe Flash and Microsoft Office, and Tavis Ormandy, a well-known researcher who had discovered vulnerabilities in antivirus software.[36] An examination of various bug bounty programs suggests that most programs are highly stratified: they are populated by a small core of highly skilled and productive researchers who find a large share of all reported bugs, and a much larger pool of participants who report a small number of bugs (often only participating in a program once) of varying quality. The skilled core discovers a disproportionate share of total vulnerabilities and accounts for the majority of total paid rewards.[37] Project Zero seeks to support this skilled core with financial support and few strings attached.[38] As Google remarks in its pitch to researchers, "we offer [what] we think is a new place to do what you love – but in the open and without distraction."[39]

More recently, Google began offering Vulnerability Research Grants to complement the work of Project Zero and its rewards programs. These small grants (the maximum amount offered is $3133.70) seek to support the most frequent and successful researchers participating in Google's rewards programs, as well as invited experts, to search for flaws in Google-owned properties. Unlike traditional rewards programs, however, researchers receive financial support (in the form of a grant) regardless of whether they uncover a new flaw or not.[40] Particularly talented researchers appear to be flexible and catholic in their work: they can find flaws in different pieces of software.[41] Grants offer a small nudge, encouraging talented researchers to look at Google's services rather than at competitors – an attempt to retain and commit these security researchers to Google.

Google's broad portfolio of rewards programs, along with Project Zero and the Vulnerability Research Grant program, represent a departure from traditional bug bounty programs. If bug bounty programs offer a hedge against the failings of traditional security practices – catching the bugs that slip through internal testing – by seizing on the wisdom of the crowd, Project Zero and Google's grant program are attempts to nurture and support the cream of the crop with few strings attached. While the pool of potential undiscovered vulnerabilities may indeed be large, exceptionally skilled and prolific researchers remain a scarce and precious resource. Google seeks to entice not only the odd user who has uncovered a potentially troubling bug but also to support elite hackers and researchers.

10.3.3 Case III, Facebook: Transaction Costs and Reputational Benefits

Facebook launched its bug bounty program in 2011. By 2016, it had paid over $5 million for newly discovered flaws.[42] Most payouts are fairly modest: the average award is $1810 and the minimum payout is $500.[43] Some participants, however, are earning real money. Facebook has occasionally paid over $30000 for a report. The top 10 most successful researchers have each netted over $100000 in to-date career earnings (the most lucrative walking away with $183000). In the first half of 2016, researchers submitted more than 9000 reports that resulted in $611741 worth of rewards spread across 149 recipients.

The program attracts a diverse group of sellers. 900 different researchers have participated in Facebook's bug bounty program during its first few years. Participants are drawn from across the globe. Researchers from India, Turkey, Pakistan, Egypt, and Russia make up a growing share of the program. Since 2011, Facebook has made awards to individuals from over 51 different countries, with the overwhelming majority of participants coming from outside of the United States. India, USA, and Mexico were the top three countries based on the number of payouts. The program attracts an eclectic mix: the youngest seller on record was just 13 years old.[44]

Facebook's program is straightforward: the company publishes a clear set of rules, describing what is eligible and what is not eligible, and lists helpful examples of what defines a good qualifying report.[45] Qualifying submissions are paid based on severity. Facebook offers rewards for bugs that compromise "the integrity of user data, circumvent the privacy protections of user data, or enable access" to a Facebook-internal system.[46] This includes a range of bugs, such as flaws that allow privilege escalation (allowing a user to acquire privileges beyond what they are allowed) and bugs that enable remote code execution (allowing an unauthorized third party to launch code or alter data on a user's device). The program complements Facebook's in-house testing and capitalizes on the talent of interested and engaged users. As Facebook notes:

> no matter how much we invest in security – and we invest a lot – we'll never have all the world's smartest people on our team and we'll never be able to think of all the different ways a system as complex as ours might be vulnerable. Our [program] allows us to harness the talent and perspective of people from all kinds of backgrounds, from all around the world.[47]

Facebook's program demonstrates two of the key benefits that defensive bug bounty programs have over the offensive market: (i) low transaction costs and

(ii) reputational benefits. Vendors and others operating defensive bug bounty programs cannot hope to compete with the offensive market on price. In 2012, *Forbes* examined the shadowy market for offensive exploits and compiled a price list for zero-days.[48] They found that newly discovered vulnerabilities targeting operating systems and browsers could fetch between $60 000 and $250 000.[49] More recently, Hacking Team, an Italian company that sold spyware and other forms of malicious code to governments across the globe, was, ironically, hacked by unknown parties. Leaked Hacking Team documents provide a window into the offensive market and suggest that the prices *Forbes* quoted in 2012 remain roughly accurate.[50] Offensive prices far outpace what Facebook, or others in the defensive market, offer. Yet, what Facebook and others *can* offer – which the offensive market largely cannot – are relatively simple transactions and public recognition. Facebook's program is straightforward: the terms of the program are clearly stated and sample prices are available. For someone looking to disclose a newly discovered flaw, the process is accessible. The steps one needs to follow to report a flaw and receive a reward are decidedly not mysterious. Additionally, disclosure to Facebook and other defensive programs can result in significant recognition for a researcher. Researcher contributions are acknowledged publicly and published, offering researchers a way to signal and promote their skills to peers and potential employers.[51]

Selling to the offensive market is cumbersome and typically lacks any broad reputational benefit, as it requires a degree of secrecy that limits reputational benefits. In other terms, in a secret, one-to-one transaction, reputational benefits are offered, but only to that particular seller-buyer relation; thus, these benefits are narrow (i.e. as opposed to open bug bounty programs, where the discoverers are publicly recognized and the reputational benefits transcend a particular bug bounty program). Charlie Miller, a well-known security researcher, noted the multiple hazards that researchers face when selling to offensive players: since most offensive purchases are conducted out-of-view by secretive agencies or criminals, actually identifying a buyer is a serious challenge. The lack of transparency in sales makes it difficult for a seller to effectively negotiate price: without a baseline of previous sales against which to compare prices, it is difficult to know if an offered price is reasonable or represents a below-market, low-ball, offer. Finally, sellers face the prospect of being burned by a buyer: in order to demonstrate that a zero-day vulnerability or an exploit exists, a seller must essentially turn over the product for inspection and risk that the buyer might walk away with the product without paying.[52] These information asymmetries place significant burdens on sellers and make transactions with offensive players difficult. Additionally, sellers participating in the offensive market will likely never have their contributions publicly acknowledged. The offensive market rests on keeping information about a newly discovered vulnerability secret (and hence, useful as a means of conducting exploits and attacks). Researchers selling vulnerabilities on the offensive market sacrifice reputational benefits. While bug bounty programs offer rewards in the defensive market that are significantly lower than those in the offensive market, they significantly reduce transaction cost. They also enable security researchers to build their reputations among ICT software and service firms, as well as among peers in the white hat security research community.[53]

Facebook's program, like many other bug bounty programs, cannot hope to compete with the offensive market in terms of price. But its other benefits should not be overlooked: providing a simple model of disclosure reduces the high transaction costs associated with offensive sales. At the same time, disclosing vulnerabilities to the defensive market carries broad reputational benefits – an opportunity to advertise skill and competency – that do not exist in the offensive market.

10.4 Conclusion

Vulnerabilities are not likely to disappear anytime soon. The complexities of creating new software and hardware ensure that we will continue to produce and rely on flawed code. At the same time, the development of offensive cyber capabilities shows no sign of abetting. Exploit code used for attacks is simply too valuable: criminals, intelligence agencies, and militaries will continue to seek out new ways to collect intelligence from adversaries, pilfer intellectual property and valuable data from targets, and develop tools that can be used to attack and damage critical systems. As more and more data are created, stored, and shared on digital devices and platforms, and as embedded devices wind their way into every corner of daily life, the number of targets for crime, sabotage, and espionage multiple. Software vulnerabilities – zero-days and n-days – will continue to be a prized commodity. Exploits and attacks relying on known vulnerabilities are, of course, also useful (and also widely used). For example, the 2017 WannaCry ransomware attack made use of a stolen and leaked NSA exploit referred to as EternalBlue, which was based on a security flaw for which Microsoft had issued a patch a couple of months earlier.[54] But for groups that want to be sure that their attacks and exploits can penetrate even well-protected computers and systems, zero-days are and will remain attractive. Yet, software vendors and security researchers have been working tirelessly to strengthen defensive cybersecurity to protect against the exploitation of security flaws for offensive purposes.[55] Spearheaded by Microsoft, Google, and Facebook, bug bounty programs developed and were widely adopted amidst growing tensions about different notions of security used by states, ICT companies, and security researchers. First, concerned with national security, states have been struggling to strike a balance between the need for defensive means to protect critical information infrastructure under an assurance paradigm and the need for offensive capabilities to conduct military, intelligence, and law-enforcement missions in cyberspace – leaving ICT and the public depending on it potentially vulnerable. The US government, for instance, reported that it disclosed (rather than kept secret) about 91% of discovered zero-days vulnerabilities.[56] Second, ICT and internet companies have at times been found to neglect the security of their products and services, as security to them is an externality, favoring reduced time-to-market cycles instead. Third, security researchers dedicated to finding and reporting software vulnerabilities have experienced resistance – including legal threats and repercussions – from software vendors attempting to prevent the disclosure of security flaws.

The tensions between different notions of security, particularly between offense and defense, are not going to go away. Bug bounty programs are one attempt by the tech community to fix exploitable flaws, but they are also an attempt to shape norms around security research and reframe disclosure. In addition, some of the high-profile programs should be viewed as attempts to critique and shape US and international policy regarding the acquisition and stockpiling of vulnerabilities for offensive purposes. *Some* of these programs seek to reduce the use of software vulnerabilities for offensive purposes. Bug bounty program have been critical in devising disclosure norms for security researchers and shaping their interactions with software vendors. Not only do these programs encourage research by a global pool of talent through monetary incentives but also they limit non-disclosure and full-disclosure, establishing a clear preference for coordination with software vendors. This development is an extension of earlier efforts by software vendors to steer away from full-disclosure toward responsible and coordinate disclosure mechanisms long favored by software vendors. Often overlooked, these novel programs can in some cases also practically offset limitations by the US Computer Fraud and Abuse Act (CFAA) that stifle security research, providing security researchers clear guidance and scope for their testing and reporting within a particular bug bounty program.

It is an interesting strategy: rewarding researchers who uncover and disclose new flaws in software, applications, and services. Indeed, it borrows some of the logic of open-source development – taking advantage of a large and talented public to spot and fix flaws to improve cybersecurity for business and users – while attempting to subvert the development of malicious tools by states and criminals. Bug bounty programs are becoming increasingly common and widely adopted; their structure is beginning to develop in novel directions. Bug bounty platforms such as HackerOne and Bugcrowd have helped spread the model to small and midsized technology firms, as well as to other industry sectors. For instance, Samsung offers a bug bounty program that covers its mobile devices; Fiat Chrysler and Tesla, among others in the automotive industry, have turned to bug bounty programs for testing automotive software; and the US government has already conducted several iterations of "Hack the Pentagon" and "Hack the Army," which found hundreds of security flaws.[57]

A prominent but late addition to the game was Apple, which long withstood this development; in 2016, however, it embraced a private bug bounty program with a small circle of selected security researchers and five narrow categories of eligible vulnerabilities.[58] In terms of bounty size, the high-end of bug bounty programs has increased the top payouts: Apple and Samsung offer up to $200000, while Microsoft offers up to $250000 in their respective bug bounty programs.[59]

Paying researchers for discovered flaws is, to be clear, not without risks. Creating ongoing programs that offer rewards for new flaws can lead to a flood of reports – both valuable flaws that were missed during testing and irrelevant submissions that are invalid – and tax the ability of development teams to respond in a timely manner. The bug bounty platform Bugcrowd reports that 45.38% of all submissions are invalid, while another 36.23% are duplicates.[60] At the same time, as bounty programs become standard, global competition for the most talented researchers might become more intense, leading to an increase in prices for high-severity, high-impact vulnerabilities – and thereby making the high end of bug bounty programs a relatively more interesting alternative to selling to the black market. Yet, bug bounty programs do offer real benefits: they can encourage the discovery and report of flaws that would have otherwise gone unreported; they draw on the talents and expertise of a large and diverse set of users; they provide an added layer of security (another line of defense beyond internal testing, third-party penetration testing, or security audits);[61] they can engender goodwill among the researcher community; and they can create uncertainty in the offensive market, possibly invalidating working exploit code through disclosure and patching, as well as driving down prices on black markets as an increasing numbers of bug hunters may codiscover the same or related vulnerabilities in a shorter time period.

Starting from ICT companies, bug bounty programs have been widely adopted in a relative short time, becoming a term of art in other industry sectors as well as in the government. As outlined in this chapter, these programs have had significant effects on cybersecurity at multiple levels and have helped identify and report hundreds of thousands of security flaws. Yet, one critical question about the effectiveness of these programs to improve cybersecurity has not been definitively answered. The effectiveness of fixing a vulnerability – through bug bounty programs or other means – depends largely on the distribution of security flaws in a particular piece of software. If flaws are "sparse," closing a security hole provides a critical improvement in security. If vulnerabilities are "dense," however, fixing a bug is essentially irrelevant, as plenty of other security flaws in the same code can be found and exploited.[62]

In the years since the Snowden revelations, Washington and Silicon Valley have in some ways become increasingly estranged. Issues related to security and privacy have driven a wedge between the two sides. This might have been inevitable: in cyberspace, the exigencies of intelligence collection and military readiness bump headlong into the efforts of large companies to create new software and services that are reliable and secure. Infrastructures are, at their core, a shared resource. New digital tools – messaging apps, web browsers, social networks, standards used for encryption – are all equally available to both the good and the bad. For years, it was taken as gospel that the only ones paying for flaws were on the offensive side of the field. That is no longer true. As companies ramp up efforts to purchase flaws to strengthen the cybersecurity of their software and services, the tension between offense and defense simply becomes harder to ignore. Bug bounty programs are not a cure-all: they are unlikely to put criminals and spies out of work, and they will certainly never lead to a world of perfect, error-free code. But, at their best, they offer a meaningful yet imperfect hedge against the growing tide of nasty exploits and attacks.

Notes

1 President Barack Obama, "Remarks by the President at the Cybersecurity and Consumer Protection Summit." Transcript. White House Press Office, February 13, 2015, https://www.whitehouse.gov/the-press-office/2015/02/13/remarks-president-cybersecurity-and-consumer-protection-summit.
2 Ibid. See also, Microsoft Malware Protection Center, "Ransomware," August 16, 2018, http://www.microsoft.com/security/portal/mmpc/shared/ransomware.aspx.
3 Executive Office of the President. Executive Order 13691 (February 13, 2015). "Promoting Private Sector Cybersecurity Information Sharing." https://www.whitehouse.gov/the-press-office/2015/02/13/executive-order-promoting-private-sector-cybersecurity-information-shari.
4 See Executive Office of President, "Promoting Private Sector Cybersecurity Information Sharing"; Executive Office of the President, Office of the Press Secretary, "Fact Sheet: Executive Order Promoting Private Sector Cybersecurity Information Sharing," February 12, 2015, https://www.whitehouse.gov/the-press-office/2015/02/12/fact-sheet-executive-order-promoting-private-sector-cybersecurity-inform.
5 Kate Vinton, "Obama Signs Executive Action, Calls for Collaboration to Fight Cyber Attacks at Stanford Summit," Forbes, February 13, 2015.
6 See Nicole Perlroth and David E. Sanger, "Obama Calls for New Cooperation to Wrangle the 'Wild West' Internet," The New York Times, February 13, 2015.
7 See Barton Gellman and Ashkan Soltani, "NSA Infiltrates Links to Yahoo, Google, Data Centers Worldwide, Snowden Documents Say," Washington Post, October 30, 2013; Jeff Larson, Nicole Perlroth ProPublica, and Scott Shane, "Revealed: The NSA's Secret Campaign to Crack, Undermine Internet Security," ProPublica, September 5, 2013; Spiegel Staff, "Inside TAO: Documents Reveal Top NSA Hacking Unit," Der Spiegel, December 29, 2013; David Sanger and Nicole Perlroth, "Obama Heads to Tech Security Talks Amid Tensions," New York Times, February 12, 2015.

8 Brad Smith, "Protecting Consumer Data from Government Snooping," December 4, 2013, http://blogs.microsoft.com/blog/2013/12/04/protecting-customer-data-from-government-snooping.

9 John Leyden, "Furious Google Techie on NSA Snooping: 'F*CK THESE GUYS," *The Register*, November 7, 2013, www.theregister.co.uk/2013/11/07/google_engineers_slam_nsa.

10 In addition to market-based programs to improve cybersecurity, global ICT firms have increasingly engaged in establishing and supporting cyber norms for states and the global ICT industry to curtail state behavior that has negative effects on the ICT industry, including their products and services, and undermines cybersecurity and trust. See, e.g. Scott Charney, "Cybersecurity Norms for Nation-States and the Global ICT Industry," *Microsoft on the Issues*, June 23, 2016, https://blogs.microsoft.com/on-the-issues/2016/06/23/cybersecurity-norms-nation-states-global-ict-industry.

11 Data collected from HackerOne website. HackerOne, https://hackerone.com, accessed September 21, 2015.

12 See Gregg Keizer, "Microsoft Kicks Off $250,000 Security Contest," *Computerworld*, August 3, 2011, http://www.computerworld.com/s/article/9218845/Microsoft_kicks_off_250_000_security_contest.

13 See Dennis Fisher, "Microsoft Says No to Paying Bug Bounties," *Threat Post*, July 22, 2010, https://threatpost.com/microsoft-says-no-paying-bug-bounties-072210/74249.

14 See, Microsoft, "Heart of Blue Gold – Announcing New Bounty Programs," *BlueHat Blog*, June 19, 2013, http://blogs.technet.com/b/bluehat/archive/2013/06/19/heart-of-blue-gold-announcing-new-bounty-programs.aspx.

15 See Microsoft, "Bounty Evolution: $100,000 for New Mitigation Bypass Techniques Wanted Dead or Alive," *BlueHat Blog*, November 1, 2013, http://blogs.technet.com/b/bluehat/archive/2013/11/01/bounty-evolution-100-000-for-new-mitigation-bypass-techniques-wanted-dead-or-alive.aspx.

16 Microsoft, "Microsoft Edge Technical Preview (Formerly Known as Project Spartan) Bug Bounty Program Terms," https://web.archive.org/web/20170325011129/https://technet.microsoft.com/en-us/security/dn972323; Microsoft, "Microsoft CoreCLR and ASP.NET 5 Beta Bug Bounty Program Terms," https://technet.microsoft.com/en-us/security/mt574248.

17 Microsoft, "Mitigation Bypass and Bounty for Defense Terms," October 1, 2018, https://technet.microsoft.com/en-us/security/dn425049.

18 Microsoft, "Honor Roll," June 19, 2017, https://web.archive.org/web/20170619124334/https://technet.microsoft.com/en-us/security/dn469163.

19 Microsoft, "Honor Roll," June 19, 2017, https://web.archive.org/web/20170619124334/https://technet.microsoft.com/en-us/security/dn469163.

20 See also, Andreas Kuehn and Milton Mueller, "Analyzing Bug Bounty Programs: An Institutional Perspective on the Economics of Software Vulnerabilities," 42nd Research Conference on Communication, Information

and Internet Policy (TPRC), 2014, https://papers.ssrn.com/sol3/papers.
cfm?abstract_id=2418812.

21 See HackerOne, "Improving Signal Over 10,000 Bugs," July 2015, https://
hackerone.com/blog/improving-signal-over-10000-bugs. To drill further
down in the Facebook example, in 2015, the social network giant received
13 233 total submissions from 5 543 researchers in 127 countries, which gives
an indication of the effort needed to screen and assess the large number of
submissions and researchers. Of those, 210 researchers were paid $936 000 for
a total of 526 valid reports (average payout: $1 780). See Facebook,
"Highlights: Less Low-Hanging Fruit," *Facebook Bug Bounty*, February 9, 2016,
https://www.facebook.com/notes/facebook-bug-bounty/2015-highlights-
less-low-hanging-fruit/1225168744164016/

22 See Trey Herr, Bruce Schneier, and Christopher Morris, "Taking Stock:
Estimating Vulnerability Rediscovery," *Belfer Cyber Security Project White
Paper Series*, 2017, https://papers.ssrn.com/sol3/papers.cfm?abstract_
id=2928758; Lillian Ablon, and Timothy Bogart, "Zero Days, Thousands of
Nights The Life and Times of Zero-Day Vulnerabilities and Their Exploits,"
RAND, 2017, https://www.rand.org/pubs/research_reports/RR1751.html.

23 For Google's Project Zero, see https://googleprojectzero.blogspot.com.

24 Google, "Encouraging More Chromium Security Research," *Google Online
Security Blog*, January 28, 2010, http://blog.chromium.org/2010/01/
encouraging-more-chromium-security.html.

25 Chris Evans, Neel Mehta, Adam Mein, Matt Moore, and Michael Zalewski,
"Rewarding Web Application Security Research," *Google Online Security Blog*,
November 1, 2010, https://googleonlinesecurity.blogspot.com/2010/11/
rewarding-web-application-security.html.

26 These programs operate somewhat differently. Google's "Patch Rewards
Program," for example, pays for contributions made by researchers to a
number of different open-source projects (projects that are community-
developed and not run by Google). Unlike the programs covering Google
Chrome or Google's web properties, the Patch Rewards Program only pays
researchers who submit both identified vulnerabilities and patches or other
ways to mitigate discovered flaws. Google's Android program will pay for
identified vulnerabilities, but pays significantly more for researchers who
submit both flaws and a corresponding fix.

27 Eduardo Vela Nava, "Security Reward Programs: Year in Review, Year in Preview,"
Google Online Security Blog, January 30, 2015, https://googleonlinesecurity.
blogspot.com/2015/01/security-reward-programs-year-in-review.html.

28 Google, "Vulnerability Rewards Program: 2016 Year in Review, 2017," *Google
Online Security Blog*, January 30, 2017, https://security.googleblog.
com/2017/01/vulnerability-rewards-program-2016-year.html.

29 Adam Mein, "Celebrating One Year of Web Vulnerability Research," *Google
Online Security Blog*, February 9, 2012, https://googleonlinesecurity.blogspot.
com/2012/02/celebrating-one-year-of-web.html.

30 See Mein, "Celebrating One Year of Web Vulnerability Research"; Adam Mein and Chris Evans, "Dosh4Vulns: Google's Vulnerability Reward Programs," AppSecUSA 2011, https://software-security.sans.org/downloads/appsec-2011-files/vrp-presentation.pdf.

31 Vela Nava, "Security Reward Programs: Year in Review, Year in Preview."

32 Google, "Charts and Graphs," Bughunter University, 2014–2016, https://sites.google.com/site/bughunteruniversity/behind-the-scenes/charts.

33 Chris Evans, "Announcing Project Zero," *Google Online Security Blog*, July 15, 2014, https://googleonlinesecurity.blogspot.com/2014/07/announcing-project-zero.html.

34 Ibid.

35 Andy Greenberg, "Meet Project Zero: Google's Secret Team of Bug-Hunting Hackers," *Wired*, July 15, 2014, http://www.wired.com/2014/07/google-project-zero.

36 Ibid.

37 Bugcrowd, "The State of Bug Bounty," June 2016, https://pages.bugcrowd.com/hubfs/PDFs/state-of-bug-bounty-2016.pdf.

38 Greenberg, "Meet Project Zero: Google's Secret Team of Bug-Hunting Hackers."

39 Evans, "Announcing Project Zero."

40 Google, "Vulnerability Research Grants," https://www.google.com/about/appsecurity/research-grants.

41 Ibid.

42 Data collected through June 2016.

43 For a detailed review and examination of the Facebook data, see Ellis, Ryan, Keman Huang, Michael Siegel, Katie Moussouris, and James Houghton. "Fixing a Hole: The Labor Market for Bugs." In *New Solutions for Cybersecurity*, edited by Howard Shrobe, David L. Shrier, and Alex Pentland, 129-159. Cambridge: MIT Press, 2018.

44 See Facebook Security Team, "An Update on our Bug Bounty Program," August 2, 2013, https://www.facebook.com/notes/facebook-security/an-update-on-our-bug-bounty-program/10151508163265766; Facebook Security Team, "White Hat Information," September 12, 2018, https://www.facebook.com/whitehat; Facebook Security Team, "An Update on our Bug Bounty Program," August 2, 2013, https://www.facebook.com/notes/facebook-security/an-update-on-our-bug-bounty-program/10151508163265766; Facebook, "Facebook Bug Bounty: $5 Million Paid in 5 Years," *Facebook Bug Bounty*, October 12, 2016, https://www.facebook.com/notes/facebook-bug-bounty/facebook-bug-bounty-5-million-paid-in-5-years/1419385021409053/.

45 Ibid.

46 Facebook Security Team, "White Hat Information."

47 Ibid.

48 Greenberg, "Shopping for Zero-Days: A Price List for Hackers' Secret Software Exploits." *Forbes*, March 23, 2012.

49 Ibid.

50 See Vlad Tsyrklevich, "Hacking Team: A Zero-Day Case Study," *Vlad Tsyrklevich's Blog*, August 1, 2015, https://tsyrklevich.net/2015/07/22/hacking-team-0day-market/.

51 See also, Andreas Kuehn, and Milton Mueller, "Analyzing Bug Bounty Programs: An Institutional Perspective on the Economics of Software Vulnerabilities," in 42nd Research Conference on Communication, Information and Internet Policy (TPRC), 2014, https://papers.ssrn.com/sol3/papers.cfm?abstract_id=2418812.

52 Charlie Miller, "The Legitimate Vulnerability Market: Inside the Secretive World of 0-Day Exploit Sales," Workshop on the Economics of Information Security, 2007, http://www.econinfosec.org/archive/weis2007/papers/29.pdf.

53 See Andreas Kuehn and Milton Mueller, "Analyzing Bug Bounty Programs: An Institutional Perspective on the Economics of Software Vulnerabilities," in 42nd Research Conference on Communication, Information and Internet Policy (TPRC), 2014, https://papers.ssrn.com/sol3/papers.cfm?abstract_id=2418812.

54 Dan Goodin, "Windows 7, not XP, was the Reason Last Week's WCry Worm Spread so Widely," *Ars Technica*, May 20, 2017, https://arstechnica.com/information-technology/2017/05/windows-7-not-xp-was-the-reason-last-weeks-wcry-worm-spread-so-widely.

55 Note that in addition to approaches that tackle technical aspects of cybersecurity, such as bug bounty programs, states and ICT firms including Microsoft have been working toward norms for state behavior in cyberspace that aim to codify measures of restraint and principles for the handling of software vulnerabilities. See, e.g. UN GGE, "Report of the Group of Governmental Experts on Developments in the Field of Information and Telecommunications in the Context of International Security, A/70/174," July 22, 2015, http://www.un.org/ga/search/view_doc.asp?symbol=A/70/174; Microsoft, "From Articulation to Implementation: Enabling Progress on Cybersecurity Norms," June 2016, https://query.prod.cms.rt.microsoft.com/cms/api/am/binary/REVmc8.

56 Sean Lyngaas, "NSA Chief Says Agency Discloses '91 percent' of Zero Day Bugs," *FCW*, November 9, 2015, https://fcw.com/articles/2015/11/09/rogers-zero-days-nsa-lyngaas.aspx.

57 Thuy Ong, "Samsung's Bug Bounty Program will Pay Rewards of up to $200,000," *The Verge*, September 7, 2017, https://www.theverge.com/2017/9/7/16265926/samsung-bug-bounty-program-rewards; Dan Lohrmann, "Auto Industry Bug Bounty Programs Point to Our Security Future," *Government Technology*, July 17, 2016, http://www.govtech.com/blogs/lohrmann-on-cybersecurity/auto-industry-bug-bounty-programs-point-to-our-security-future.html; Mark Rockwell, "Why Bug Bounty Programs are Worth the Risk," *FCW*, March 30, 2017, https://fcw.com/articles/2017/03/30/bug-bounties-gsa-dod.aspx.

58 Josephine Wolff, "Apple Has a New 'Bug Bounty' Program. It Could Be a Game-Changer," *Slate*, August 9, 2016, http://www.slate.com/blogs/future_ tense/2016/08/09/why_apple_s_bug_bounty_program_is_unlike_any_other.html.

59 Thuy Ong, "Samsung's Bug Bounty Program will Pay Rewards of up to $200,000," *The Verge*, September 7, 2017, https://www.theverge. com/2017/9/7/16265926/samsung-bug-bounty-program-rewards.

60 Bugcrowd, "The State of Bug Bounty," June 2016, https://pages.bugcrowd.com/ hubfs/PDFs/state-of-bug-bounty-2016.pdf.

61 According to Bug crowd's 2016 "The State of Bug Bounty" report, 63% of survey respondents considered bug bounty results to be better or on par with traditional security testing methods. See "The State of Bug Bounty," June 2016, https://pages.bugcrowd.com/hubfs/PDFs/state-of-bug-bounty-2016.pdf). Also, Bugcrowd (2017) reported that the average bug bounty findings (2014– 2016) were about three times as high as the average pen test findings (2011– 2013) for noncritical and high critical vulnerabilities; see Bugcrowd, "3 Reasons to Swap Your Next Pen Test With a Bug Bounty Program," Webcast, April 2017, https://www.slideshare.net/bugcrowd/3-reasons-to-swap-your- next-pen-test-with-a-bug-bounty-program.

62 Dan Geer, "For Good Measure: The Undiscovered. Login, 40(2)," 2015, http:// geer.tinho.net/fgm/fgm.geer.1504.pdf; Bruce Schneier, "Should U.S. Hackers Fix Cybersecurity Holes or Exploit Them?" *The Atlantic*, May 19, 2014, https://www.theatlantic.com/technology/archive/2014/05/should-hackers- fix-cybersecurity-holes-or-exploit-them/371197.

11

Rethinking Data, Geography, and Jurisdiction

A Common Framework for Harmonizing Global Data Flow Controls

Jonah Force Hill[1,2] *and Matthew Noyes*[1]

[1] *Cyber Policy, U.S. Secret Service, Washington, DC, USA*
[2] *New America, Washington, DC, USA*

> *Everyone has the right to freedom of opinion and expression; this right includes freedom to hold opinions without interference and to seek, receive and impart information and ideas through any media and regardless of frontiers.*
> –Article 19, Universal Declaration of Human Rights

11.1 Introduction

The internet has fundamentally upended the rules, norms, and mechanisms governing the flow of information around the world. From the first moment in time when governments kept written records of taxes levied and paid, and merchants kept records of buyers and sellers of goods, the information contained in those records occupied a known physical place (for example, at the business, or in the counting house). If one wanted to review those records, the task was simple: go to the physical place where the records were kept. Records may have been hidden, but they would generally be found near where they were made or used.

Today, however, with the advent of the internet (and other global digital networks), digitized information (hereafter, simply "data") is regularly stored by multinational companies on computer systems that may be physically located far away from the places in which the data originated or are used. Data are often copied and then stored and/or cached in multiple servers in disparate locations in several countries simultaneously. Through use of modern data-storage methods, data are increasingly being sliced into small portions (i.e. "sharded") and then distributed out across the world, shifting

Rewired: Cybersecurity Governance, First Edition. Edited by Ryan Ellis and Vivek Mohan.
© 2019 John Wiley & Sons, Inc. Published 2019 by John Wiley & Sons, Inc.

from one geography to another, on an automated basis, as more efficient storage space becomes available elsewhere in the world.[1]

This sea change in the way information moves and is stored around the world is challenging longstanding approaches to controlling information flows. The interrelated questions of who "owns" what data, which sovereign laws apply to which data overseas, and when and how governments should assist one another with law-enforcement investigations seeking to obtain data have quickly become some of the most vexing and persistent questions of law and policy in the Internet age. Governments, tech companies, and legal and policy experts across the globe are struggling to reconcile the internet's globalization of data with the often-competing demands of law enforcement, privacy, national sovereignty, and the desire to maintain longstanding notions of international comity and cooperation.

What is emerging is a set of highly complex and intertwined international disputes that are threatening the growth of the internet and the broader information economy, while simultaneously undermining international cooperation on other pressing global issues. Many nations are advancing new legal and policy regimes to address these challenges, regimes that are once again premised on the geographic location of data as a basis for asserting legal jurisdiction, thereby further exacerbating the underlying problem.[2] These disputes have become more frequent and more contentious over time, a trend that seems likely to increase. It is becoming clear that the current piecemeal response by the international community to these range of challenges needs to be radically rethought.

This chapter describes these various challenges as a means of illustrating the need for a new and comprehensive approach to data flow controls (we use the phrase "data flow controls" to refer to the broad set of state actions that affect the flow of data, including prohibitions on certain data, retention requirements, or production requirements). To harmonize the various approaches in use today, we propose a new common framework for data flow controls, derived from Control Points Analysis (CPA)[3] and the Contextual Integrity Model (CIM),[4] two established analytic methodologies designed to allow for technical policy discussions in computer science and digital privacy theory, respectively. Both methodologies avoid using geography as a primary factor in their analytical approach. This chapter also offers some potential avenues for advancing international cooperation on several of the more troublesome international data flow conflicts through new or expanded international cooperation mechanisms, such as treaties and voluntary agreements between states.

This advocacy and proposed common framework for data flow controls should not be interpreted as an endorsement of any new omnibus international legal instrument, such as a global treaty on cybercrime. On the contrary, given the complexity of the problems and the diverse set of interests and stakeholders involved, we suspect that any solution will require multiple arrangements, some legal, some normative, and some procedural. Nevertheless, we maintain that in the absence of a harmonized approach to data flow controls, the escalating fragmentation of the internet[5] will further split the global internet into separate, semi-sovereign networks. This fragmentation, we argue, would fundamentally degrade the internet's future potential for innovation, economic growth, and other social, scientific, and democratic advancements we have come to expect from today's globally accessible and interoperable network.[6] The status quo of conflicting data flow controls is no longer sustainable; a fundamentally different approach to data and jurisdiction is required.

11.2   The Challenge of Extraterritorial Data

Government efforts to regulate data flows and investigate and enforce their laws are substantially challenged by transnational data flows. This challenge has motivated government actions that present substantial risks to the open and interoperable nature of the internet, and the potential of the internet to fuel the information economy and realize the human right to send and receive information regardless of frontiers. Accordingly, understanding and addressing the challenges that transnational data flows present to legitimate government activities is essential for realizing the full potential of the internet.

11.2.1   The Challenge to Law Enforcement

A core function of any government is the enforcement of law, particularly criminal law.[7] However, this function is challenged by modern transnational data flows and the resulting inability of governments to access, or control, the information necessary to effectively investigate and enforce their laws. In the pre-internet era, there were comparatively few and limited circumstances in which law-enforcement officials needed to exert their legal authorities overseas.[8] Police might have needed to track a murder suspect escaping to a neighboring country or to investigate an organized crime group laundering money through an overseas bank. However, with the rise of globalized information flows and commercial storage practices, data necessary to investigations and prosecutions are now located all over the world and entirely under the control of private companies; even routine investigations of an entirely domestic nature often now require law-enforcement officials to seek out critical evidence stored beyond their borders.

Cross-border law-enforcement information sharing has historically been provided through negotiated assistance among national governments, most importantly through the mutual legal assistance treaty (MLAT) system. MLATs are broadly worded bilateral and multilateral treaties designed to allow for cooperation on a specified range of law-enforcement issues, such as locating and extraditing individuals, freezing assets, requesting searches and seizures, and taking testimony.[9] In recent years, the MLAT system has struggled to keep pace with the growth of globalized data and the expansion of cloud-based services and data storage.[10] The total number of MLAT requests has skyrocketed as data critical to domestic investigations have moved overseas. The United States Department of Justice (DOJ), which both processes MLAT requests from other governments and issues MLAT requests for overseas assistance with its own investigations, estimated in 2014 that over the past decade the "number of MLAT requests for assistance from foreign authorities has increased by nearly 60 percent, and the number of requests for computer records has increased ten-fold."[11]

Additionally, the digital issues falling under MLAT provisions have grown vastly more complex in recent years, exceeding the scope of the treaty language. Most of today's MLATs were drafted prior to the internet's widespread global adoption and therefore few of the treaties address core questions of data jurisdiction, such as how to treat data held overseas by a subsidiary of a domestic parent company. Perhaps, most significantly, MLATs frequently do not specify what constitutes "protected data" or under what conditions "content" differs from "metadata" for the purposes of information sharing.[12] This lack of clarity and agreement on terminology hinders cooperation between states with differing domestic legal regimes and understanding of these terms.

The increase in MLAT requests and the accompanying legal uncertainty surrounding how and when privacy and data protection regulations apply in investigations have caused significant delays in responding to requests for legal assistance. The President's Review Group on Intelligence and Communication Technologies (the independent review board tasked with assessing US intelligence collection practices following Edward Snowden's disclosures) estimated in 2013 that it takes an average of 10 months for the DOJ to process MLAT requests, and can take years.[13] Foreign countries' processing of MLAT requests is similarly drawn out, and can take far longer.[14]

Further adding to the MLAT backlog, various so-called "blocking features" in domestic privacy law often prohibit or constrain online hosts and providers from responding to data requests by foreign authorities directly. These blocking features, such those as contained in the Electronic Communications Privacy Act (ECPA)[15] in the United States, are intended to provide privacy protections to domestic citizens by preventing companies operating domestically from being compelled to transfer data to foreign law enforcement without a preliminary government review to ensure that the overseas request is valid.[16] But as more and more of the world's data is stored outside of national jurisdictions, most critically in the United States where the blocking provisions of ECPA are in force, governments around the world are finding that legal provisions designed to protect privacy are today forcing law-enforcement agencies to operate exclusively through the MLAT system, thus significantly delaying, or even preventing, otherwise lawful government access to data critical to domestic criminal matters.

Expectedly, such delays are simply unacceptable to law-enforcement officials who urgently need information for their cases. As the UK Independent Reviewer of Terrorism Legislation, David Anderson QC, summarized in his 2014 Report, "There is little dispute that the MLAT route is currently ineffective. Principally this is because it is too slow to meet the needs of an investigation, particularly in relation to a dynamic conspiracy; a request to the United States, for instance, might typically take nine months to produce what is sought."[17] For example, the Brazilian government has been frustrated by extended delays in the MLAT system, especially pertaining to its request for information from Google's US-based servers for several cases pending before the Brazilian Supreme Court.[18] India too has found the MLAT process with the United States to be ineffective. It has often invoked the US–India MLAT to request that America serve summonses on Google, Facebook, Twitter, and others for failing to prevent the dissemination of online speech prohibited under Indian law, but these requests have been repeatedly rejected due to US civil liberties requirements and privacy protections enshrined in ECPA.[19] The United Kingdom, France, China, and many others have faced similar obstacles to receiving data or enforcing domestic laws.

US law enforcement has likewise found that the MLAT system can be an ineffective means of acquiring data stored overseas, despite the United States' unique position as the home of the lion's share of stored electronics communications data maintained by United States-headquartered technology companies. Rather than waiting months for an MLAT request to be fulfilled, the US has regularly relied upon court orders to compel providers to produce data directly, regardless of where that data might be stored. Yet, even with court orders in hand, US law-enforcement officials are experiencing challenges. Most famously, in the *Microsoft Ireland* case,[20] the DOJ is seeking data from a Microsoft Outlook account based in Ireland for a criminal investigation in the Southern District of New York. Prosecutors obtained a Stored Communications Act (SCA) warrant instructing Microsoft to produce information from the Ireland-based account directly. Microsoft challenged the warrant, however, based on the legal assertion that the SCA does not permit extraterritorial application to data stored outside of the United States.[21] This argument persuaded the Second Circuit panel that heard the case,[22] but the US government sought review by the Supreme Court,[23] which on 16 October 2017 agreed to take up the case.[24] But one policy consideration was also central to Microsoft's position: the company argued that circumvention of the MLAT process sets a troubling precedent for future extraterritorial data requests. Meanwhile, the Irish government both noted that they would consider a MLAT request made by US authorities, and that under Irish law their courts have the authority to compel the production of documents stored abroad, but seek to avoid violating the law of a foreign sovereign. However, the Irish government was silent on the question of whether there would be a violation of their domestic laws if Microsoft was compelled to produce data stored in Ireland.[25]

The Microsoft case is hardly unique; other cases touching on similar transnational data access challenges have gained national attention, and at times involve exigent matters, which the MLAT process is particularly ill-suited to address in a timely matter. For example, in January 2017, a Mississippi investigator obtained a search warrant for an e-mail account of a suspected criminal involved in exchanging and viewing images of child exploitation, but as of June 2017, the contents of the account – which are stored outside of the United States – had not been provided to law enforcement.[26] In California, likewise, investigators have waited months to receive the contents of an overseas account pertaining to the disappearance and suspected murder of a young girl.[27]

Central to the argument of this chapter is the fact that MLATs and existing legal regimes have at times been ineffective not because they are slow or because their language fails to account for digitized information, but because the data required by law enforcement are not located in *any specific single geographic location*. This has been the situation in a number of prominent court cases involving Google, which as a regular practice stores data in a cloud architecture through a process called "sharding."[28] The sharding process splits data into small portions that are in turn spread out and stored in multiple Google servers, which are themselves often spread across several countries. In such a data storage model, it is impractical to identify what government has jurisdiction over the information when using a geographic basis for such issues. As of September 2017, at least 11 magistrate and district judges, outside of the Second Circuit, have rejected that court's analysis in *Microsoft Ireland*.[29] Instead, they have ruled that Google is required to reassemble the needed data and turn it over to law enforcement in the United States, irrespective of where those pieces of information are located.

While these rulings do little to resolve the underlying international policy questions surrounding jurisdiction over data, they do represent a pragmatic recognition by the US courts that the geographic location of data should not be a predominate question. Rather, these cases were decided, consistent with US law-governing subpoenas, on the grounds that the entity (here, Google) was lawfully subject to the government's subpoena process, and had the power to produce the information. The courts did not focus on the location in which the data were stored as the particularly relevant factor.[30] Of course, while this pragmatic approach by many courts may be advantageous to US prosecutors and regulators, it provides no assistance to their foreign counterparts, whose governments have no such robust authority over Google and the other American internet giants.

11.2.2 Alternative Approaches to MLATs

It is clear that the MLAT system in its inefficiency has in many ways failed to address the challenges of transnational law-enforcement cooperation in the modern internet era. It can be argued, as the US entered into the majority of its existing MLATs prior to the advent of the cross-border data-flow phenomenon, that MLATs are further philosophically unsuited to answer the challenges presented by balancing operational efficiency in law-enforcement response with a considered decision on the merits of a particular form of process – to say nothing of a government's entire system for issuing process. Reform of the MLAT system (i.e. modernizing the mechanisms by which data requests are processed, increasing funding to speed up MLAT request processing, or renegotiating the treaties to account for modern digitized evidentiary requirements) has become the elementary fix and the topic *du jour* of academics and justice ministries around the world looking to address this problem.[31] But while discussions of MLAT reform have proliferated and raised a number of potentially fruitful improvements to the existing system,[32] the reality is that little actual substantive progress has been made to date. MLAT modernization efforts have been lethargic. In fact, the problem seems only to be getting worse, as governments are finding that the MLAT system simply does not allow – and indeed may not be structurally designed to allow – for the kind of rapid international cooperation that is required in today's globalized digital environment.

As a result of glacial progress on MLAT reform, and in recognition of the increasing demand for transnational access to evidence, governments are now looking for alternative approaches, or by-passes, to MLATs as a means of acquiring the data they need. One seemingly straightforward solution has been simply to enable domestic law-enforcement authorities to have expanded reach into overseas jurisdictions. For instance, lawmakers in the United States have been exploring whether or not to amend the SCA to clarify that court orders, issued pursuant the act, can compel the production of data stored outside of the United States, thus by statute effectively overturning the Second Circuit's ruling in *Microsoft Ireland*.[33]

Other governments are taking the expansion of their police power in a far more problematic direction by seeking to provide their law-enforcement agencies with the authority to forcefully infiltrate (i.e. to hack) the computer systems of companies overseas, with little regard for the laws of other countries or the privacy and property rights of foreign companies and individuals. State-authorized hacking allows law-enforcement agencies to access the data directly without having to use a MLAT, and without having to obtain the cooperation of the private company with access to the data.[34] Of the countries pursuing this approach, China appears to be acting most conspicuously. There, regulations issued in 2016 – by the Supreme People's Court, the Supreme People's Procuratorate

(China's prosecutor), and the Public Security Bureau – appear to authorize "the unilateral extraction of data concerning anyone (or any company) being investigated under Chinese criminal law from servers and hard drives located outside of China."[35] Others describe this regulation as merely restating what has been longstanding Chinese law-enforcement practice.[36] Either way, the 2016 regulation makes it clear that Chinese law-enforcement agencies are permitted, under Chinese law, to remotely access any computer system anywhere in the world.[37]

But the Chinese are not alone. Under recent revisions to Rule 41 of the Federal Rules of Criminal Procedure, the United States has clarified that magistrate judges have the jurisdiction to issue search warrants authorizing law enforcement to "lawfully hack" computer systems that are in unknown locations – which may lead to US authorities unwittingly searching computers located overseas. Specifically, under Rule 41, magistrate judges have the power to issue search warrants to US law enforcement in situations in which the location of the computer "has been concealed through technological means," or in the case of a botnet where computers "have been damaged without authorization and are located in five or more districts."[38]

It can be argued that these readings of Chinese and American approaches (or at least authorities) are vastly divergent in their scope, with the US powers much more narrowly tailored, and of course subject to review of judicial officers not subservient to law enforcement. But as many prominent computer security experts have noted, the "lawful hacking" approach (which has been discussed in other settings at length, often in the context of the "going dark" debate[39]) risks further undermining global cybersecurity by adding law-enforcement agencies to the already crowded cadre of militaries,[40] intelligence agencies, and cyber-criminals that are routinely hacking overseas computer systems and stockpiling software vulnerabilities and offensive exploits, rather than working with technology providers to correct those vulnerabilities.[41]

Some observers have proposed a kind of hybrid model that considers a number of factors to determine what process the governments should use to obtain data. For example, a July 2017 paper published by the Information Technology & Innovation Foundation (ITIF) proposed a model that focuses first on the location of the stored data, with the location of the business itself as a second factor.[42] However, such a model fails to consider the location of the crime, the nature of the offense, or situations in which a business intentionally obscures its location. Like the other alternatives to MLATs, this approach seems to reinforce the anachronistic notion that the geographic location where data are stored is a particularly relevant consideration, ignoring the reality that the geographic location of data is often unknown.[43]

More promising efforts have focused on creating new diplomatic arrangements, separate from, but complementary to, MLATs, which would allow law-enforcement agencies to directly request data from overseas firms in the participating countries.[44] Most notably, the US and UK governments have been exploring a new diplomatic and legal instrument, the UK–US Bilateral Agreement on Data Access,[45] as a potential path forward. If accepted by both nations, the Agreement would provide law-enforcement agencies of the two countries with an effective alternative to the MLAT system (under certain specified conditions and subject to new oversight mechanisms) and permit them to make requests for data to the providers holding the data directly. Adoption of the proposed agreement, however, would require that the United States amend ECPA to allow American companies to fulfill UK requests for data without violating ECPA's "blocking features" that now prevent American companies from complying with foreign law-enforcement requests that have not gone through the US justice system.[46] Negotiators on both sides of the Atlantic are hoping to extend this system to additional countries as well, but it is currently unclear how this kind of arrangement[47] might expand beyond the United States and United Kingdom to countries with less similar or less well-developed legal systems that have fewer comparable oversight mechanisms.[48]

11.2.3 The Challenge to Regulators

Law enforcement's inability to access data stored overseas may be the primary driver of the debate surrounding data jurisdiction, but other unresolved questions of extraterritoriality present similar challenges and place additional pressure on existing systems of international cooperation. These questions span sectors, and include financial regulator issues and divergent notions of intellectual property protection. But, perhaps most importantly, the regulation of online speech, content, and privacy has emerged as the most contentious and impactful challenge in matters of public policy and international cooperation.

11.2.3.1 Content and Speech

From the earliest days of the internet, governments have encountered significant difficulties in curtailing the production and distribution of illegal, illicit, and/or harmful content online. However, as an increasing percentage of the world's content becomes digitized and made available globally, allowing internet users in one country to view or host content that is illegal in another, the challenges surrounding the control of content and speech have greatly proliferated and intensified.

This is primarily due to the fact that rules covering control of and access to information vary widely from country to country. In the United States, for instance, while the First Amendment protects most forms of speech online, certain forms of information and content – such as child pornography or defamatory speech – are still prohibited or actionable under US law. For democracies without American-style First Amendment protections, such as in western and central Europe, the range of restricted speech and content is generally broader and more fluid. Domestic laws and regulations in these countries may prohibit such content as hate speech or radicalizing propaganda (categories of speech generally protected in the United States). Limitations are often even more expansive in authoritarian countries or in countries with strict religious laws, where broad categories of content that challenge the state or insult religious figures or symbols are strictly prohibited. In all these countries, democratic or otherwise, there are unique intellectual property rules limiting what movies, music, and other protected material internet users may access, rules that are often rendered toothless when the proscribed material is hosted overseas.

These disparate national approaches to speech and content are substantially challenging anachronistic notions of national sovereignty based primarily on geography. Regulators are finding that they are often unable to force providers and hosts to take down content that is prohibited under their nation's domestic laws. Content providers and internet intermediaries are all being caught in the middle of intersecting legal systems and contradictory demands from regulators, forced to decide between two sets of government rules, or to judge the legal merits or human rights implications of a particular request.[49] Often, providers are unable to remove content in response to the demands of one country without potentially violating the laws of another. They are frequently left with no option but to take no action at all, which is, needless to say, entirely unacceptable to government agencies looking to fulfill their regulatory missions.

The recent Canadian case of *Google v. Equustek* provides an instructive example of how the enforcement of domestic content rules can have significant extraterritorial impacts. The case stems from a dispute between Equustek, a Canadian company, and Datalink, an American company, over Data link's alleged unlawful acquisition of Equustek's confidential information and trade secrets and subsequent sale of counterfeit Equustek products. Equustek obtained an injunction from a British Columbia court that ordered Google (which, while not a party to the underlying litigation, provided search results linking to Datalink websites) to remove the infringing websites from its search index. This was an order to remove links to the infringing websites not just for searches initiated by persons located in Canada, but by all searchers everywhere, amounting to a global takedown order. Google challenged the court order, but its appeal was ultimately denied by the Court of Appeal for British Columbia, a ruling which was then upheld by the Canadian Supreme Court.[50] Google has subsequently filed a complaint[51] in the Northern District of California, challenging the enforceability of the Canadian ruling; it argues, among other things,[52] that enforcement in the United States would violate the First Amendment.

Google and others[53] have noted that the Equustek cases present a potentially calamitous precedent. As Andrew Woods notes, "[t]he parties [did] not dispute Canada's authority to settle the underlying lawsuit between Equustek and Datalink, nor do they dispute Canada's authority to enjoin Google from displaying content that violates Canadian law. Rather, the parties dispute the *territorial reach* of that authority."[54] By requiring Google to delist Datalink websites worldwide, the Canadian Equustek ruling has set a precedent that, if adopted in other jurisdictions, could result in forcing internet intermediaries like Google to remove any offending material globally at the order of any court in any country. As Daphne Keller writes, "[t]he [Equustek case] was closely watched in part because of the message that it sends to other courts and governments, which are increasingly asserting their own appetites for global enforcement of national laws."[55]

The issues raised by court rulings that purport to have a global reach are similar to those seen in the so-called "right to be forgotten" debate, which concerned the question of whether internet users have a right to "de-index" certain information about themselves from internet search results. This debate goes back to 2013, when the European Court of Justice ruled[56] that European Council Directive 95/46[57] empowers Europeans who feel they are being misrepresented by search results that are no longer accurate or relevant (for instance, information about crimes committed as a minor) to force search engines, like Google or Bing, to "de-index" that information from search results. The information in question would remain online at the original website, but would no longer come up under certain search engine queries.

De-indexing in this context presents search engines with a significant challenge, one similarly raised in the Equustek case: Can a search engine remove or de-index a particular web page in one country without deleting that information globally? In response to this challenge, Google and others have tried to limit de-indexing measures to those searches made within the jurisdiction of a particular request by using geolocation techniques[58] and by only de-indexing searches made within specific country-code top-level domains (such as www.google.fr for de-indexing requests made in France). According to Google, regulators (especially in Europe) have found this limited approach unacceptable.[59] They have noted that internet users can easily circumvent these measures by visiting www.google.com, and thus have insisted that results be removed on a global scale. In light of the push by countries in Latin America,[60] Asia,[61] and elsewhere for their own de-indexing requirements, the growth of the "right to be forgotten" trend seems likely to continue, and the conflicts surrounding the extraterritorial application of domestic law and incompatibility of national approach likely to intensify.

11.2.3.2 Privacy and Data Protection

We are witnessing a similar conflict between divergent national approaches with respect to online privacy. Lawmakers around the world have been working to modernize national privacy and personal data-protection rules to keep pace with developments in the collection, control, and sharing of personal information. Often contained within these modernization efforts are regulatory provisions that, as a prerequisite for the cross-border transfer of personal information to another country, require a third country receiving personal data to have its domestic privacy protections deemed "adequate."[62] Most notably, the European Union has taken this approach[63]; however, it is also being adopted as a generalized model in other large markets, such as Brazil.[64] China[65] and Russia[66] have imposed even more onerous requirements on personal data transfers.

Yet, while these kinds of arrangements might be well-intentioned efforts to protect personal data (some question if such policies are actually disguised attempts at trade protectionism or backhanded efforts to enable law-enforcement access to data), the incompatibility of the various national approaches risks fracturing the internet by preventing data flows to countries with perceived "inadequate" data-protection rules or oversight. Indeed, this risk of a catastrophic fissure in the internet nearly became a reality in 2015, when the European Court of Justice invalidated the longstanding EU–US Safe Harbor Agreement,[67] which had previously provided protections for European personal data to travel to the United States.[68]

11.3   The Threat of Data Localization

In response to all these various interrelated challenges – law-enforcement access to evidence, conflicts over intellectual property protection, content regulation, online privacy, etc. – a number of governments have implemented, are implementing, or are considering implementing so-called "data localization" requirements. These are rules that seek to limit the storage, movement, and/or processing of data to specific geographies and jurisdictions, or that limit the companies that are legally permitted to manage data based on the company's nation of incorporation or principal site of operations and management.[69] To date, more than 20 countries have implemented or are considering implementing such restrictions.[70]

Through these data localization measures, governments are seeking to address in one fell swoop their difficulties in obtaining what they believe is appropriate relief in foreign jurisdictions (principally in the United States), as well as the inability of their law enforcement and regulatory agencies to control data or access the data they want. But once again, while efforts to put in place such measures might in many cases be well-meaning (although, it must also be noted that there is a protectionist incentive at play here as well, with some governments offering security and privacy concerns as a pretext for erecting trade barriers through these policies), data-localization rules are problematic on a number of fronts. By restricting data flows and competition between firms, data-localization policies raise costs for internet users and businesses and reduce technological innovation. In countries with underdeveloped oversight mechanisms, they may enable domestic surveillance and abuses of power. Perhaps, most worryingly, data localization policies, if implemented on a wide international scale, risk profoundly fragmenting the internet, turning back the clock on the integration of global communication and commerce, and putting into jeopardy the myriad of societal benefits that a globally integrated internet has engendered.

Moreover, data-localization policies actually do little to improve security or to protect privacy. The global nature of internet communications has made data security or privacy almost entirely independent of location. Data breaches can and do occur anywhere, and privacy violations happen in every country. Security and privacy are primarily functions of the quality and effectiveness of the mechanisms and controls maintained to protect the data in question, not where the data physically resides. What matters is not *where* data are stored, but *how* they are stored. Even with respect to law-enforcement access, data-localization policies are generally not an effective means of providing access to data, as recent criminal cases involving encryption have demonstrated.[71]

Ultimately, data-localization policies should be viewed as an understandable – however, deeply flawed and problematic – reaction by governments unable to cope with the diverse set of challenges presented by the globalization of data described above (as well as other challenges that were not discussed).[72] But, data localization policies are not a viable solution to the range of problems governments are facing, and are likely to do far more harm than good. They present a host of unintended consequences, and only serve to further institutionalize, and thus perpetuate, outdated notions of geography and jurisdiction that, as we have shown, do not comport with the realities of data in the twenty-first century.[73] An alternative to data localization – and, relatedly, to data transfers predicated on the notional protection of privacy – is desperately needed.

11.4 A New Approach to Data Flow Controls

The diversity and complexity of the legal and policy challenges described above, and the requisite international policy coordination required to address these challenges, are unquestionably daunting. Efforts to resolve one conflict only seem to create or exacerbate another. It has become clear that an entirely new framework for thinking about data and jurisdiction is needed, as well a renewed global effort to harmonize the rules, norms, and mechanisms of international cooperation.

Considering the inherent contradictions of geography-based controls described above,[74] we propose a common framework for data flow controls that uses a limited set of relevant *premises for data flow controls*, applied based on a state's relationship with certain *control points*, rather than on the physical location of data. This proposed policy framework does not itself harmonize data flow controls among nations; rather, it provides policymakers with a common lexicon and ontology to discuss and formulate agreed-upon standards for data flow controls. It is a framework that could be leveraged as the basis for new or expanded international agreements, regulations, and/or statutes, and even could help facilitate the automation of data flow processes, such as MLAT requests.

11.4.1 Control Points Analysis

Governments have consistently demonstrated that they have robust means of exerting sovereign control over communications,[75] irrespective of the location of that data. This sovereign control is exerted through control points,[76] the levers of control over a particular information system. These include such entities as search engines, internet service providers, hosting companies, and payment service providers, as well as technical infrastructure over which those entities have control. CPA, as described by MIT's David Clark, is a methodology for identifying the elements of a system necessary for its functioning, and the actors that have power and control over those various functions.[77]

Thus, CPA provides a practical methodology for identifying the full set of entities involved in a data flow and the options for impacting that data flow. By focusing on the full set of control points, rather than the physical location of data storage or hosting, governments can identify opportunities to exert appropriate sovereign influence over a data flow. They can do this through the actors that have control of key component mechanisms of a data flow, independent of the geographic location of the data in question. Accordingly, any effort to establish a data flow control should begin with an analysis of the available control points as a means of identifying the full range of actors and options available to achieve the desired effect. Based upon that analysis, policymakers can then determine the most appropriate action in a particular circumstance. In this approach, geography is no longer the primary analytical consideration.

However, adopting a non-geographic jurisdiction model based upon CPA does not render geography irrelevant to policy considerations. Many geographic factors remain critical, including the physical location of companies, their infrastructure and customers, and their employees' workplaces and residences. Moreover, CPA does not resolve the critical normative and policy question of which legal obligations should be imposed on the various control points; rather it provides policymakers the full range of options by focusing on their relationship with, and influence over, the various control points. Policymakers must still identify which control point(s) are the most appropriate to leverage, how and when to restrict actions taken toward specific actors that maintain influence over specific control points, and what enforcement and appeal mechanisms should be available for achieving the desired impact. Throughout this entire process – from control point identification to selected government action – it is necessary to ensure that such determinations are grounded in sound legal, ethical, and normative principles, rather than nationalist or populist political considerations (here, using a multistakeholder process can help to ensure a fulsome consideration of the merits of a particular control).

As an example of this process in action, and the kinds of constraints governments need to weigh, consider the challenge of the "right to be forgotten" highlighted in section 11.2.3.1. In addition to identifying which control points are available to enforce de-indexing orders, governments need to decide on the most appropriate control point to leverage: search engines (which have the ability to de-index certain search results), the platforms that supply the data, the domain registrars that host the data, or the internet service providers (ISPs) that serve the data to a particular audience. In certain cases, perhaps all four control points – search engines, platforms, domain hosts, and ISPs – should be leveraged in tandem. CPA alone does not determine which actions should be taken against which control point(s). Instead, it aids in identifying the full set of control points and associated entities involved in the data flow, thus enabling policymakers to identify the most appropriate control point for achieving a particular effect.

11.4.2 A Common Framework for Data Flow Controls

In order to help governments decide when and how to utilize the control points available to them, we suggest employing a policy framework derived and abstracted from Helen Nissenbaum's popular CIM.[78] CIM provides a common set of factors for determining privacy-appropriate data flow controls based upon both the normative and legal privacy standards of a particular "context," such as healthcare or finance. It "ties adequate protection for privacy to norms of [those specific contexts], demanding that information gathering and dissemination be appropriate to that context and obey the governing norms of distribution within it."[79] Importantly, it does not include a reference to the location of information, thus providing a framework for protecting privacy, without instituting geographic-based controls.

Nissenbaum describes the fundamentals of CIM norms based on five independent parameters or criteria. These five factors help policymakers identify whether or not data flows or data flow controls are appropriate from a privacy perspective based upon contextual information norms. They include:

1) The *data subject* (such as a hospital patient, a customer, or a viewer of a movie)
2) The *sender of the data* (such as a bank, the police, an online retailer, or a friend)
3) The *recipient of the data* (such as a bank, the police, an online retailer, or a friend)
4) The *information type* (such as e-mail contents, metadata, or social security numbers)
5) The *transmission principle* (such as consent, coercion, theft, or sale)

While the CIM was designed specifically to address privacy of digital communications, by generalizing Nissenbaum's model, we seek to address the full range of data flow issues through a single ontology that is interoperable and consistent with the existing CIM framework (which is already widely used and recognized by privacy practitioners and theorists). Accordingly, we propose a three-factor model for instituting data flow controls, which is premised on: (1) *An entity's role in the data flow*, (2) *the nature of the data*, and (3) *the ownership, access, or other rights to the data*.

1) *An entity's role in the data flow*[80]

An entity's role in the data flow includes not just the sender and recipient but also the creator, transmitter, storage provider, transporter, software system provider, platform owner, and domain name registry, among others. Essentially, this factor encompasses any entity, identifiable through CPA, that has a role – and therefore ability – to directly affect the data flow from creation to reception, rather than simply the sender and recipient specified in the CIM. States have a variety of means to exert sovereign control or influence upon such entities, often independent of their physical location, and often seek the assistance of foreign states to do so.

2) *The nature of the data*[81]

The nature of the data refers to a wide variety of specified categories of data. For example, this could be health information of a patient, sensitive personally identifiable information, hate speech, child pornography, or evidence of a crime. Data may fit in within multiple categories, and nations will certainly disagree over the categories of data and the associated controls they should leverage over such categories.

3) *Ownership, access, or other rights to the data*[82]

Ownership or access rights to the data refers to who has lawful authority over or right to the data. For example, the copyright holder possesses certain rights to the data, law-enforcement authorities have legal authority to access to data in particular circumstances, and the person who is the subject of the data may have some rights related to the data flow.

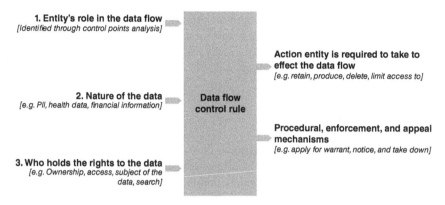

These three factors could serve as the legal or policy basis by which a government authority may compel an entity involved in the data-flow process to take a particular action. For example, a government may require a bank to: (i) preserve information about a customer's account, (ii) keep records of who created or sent particular funds relevant to that account, (iii) provide account data to a third party (for example, a law-enforcement agency), (iv) implement particular security protections to safeguard that account data, or (v) ensure the integrity of the data in question. All such requirements are applied to an entity involved in the data flow (e.g. bank) to a specific nature of data (e.g. account records), and based upon their rights to the data (e.g. information already in the bank's possession). The geographic location of the entities being compelled still matters, but the location of the data itself is irrelevant.

Again, this policy framework does not itself harmonize data flow controls across countries. Rather, it can provide policymakers with a common vocabulary and ontology to discuss and formulate agreed-upon standards. The legal and normative particulars of the various types of controls (for instance, requirements that a request go through independent judicial review or receive the consent of the owner or subject of the data) will, in each country, generally be based upon the laws and norms of that country's particular legal system. Nations are certain to differ regarding the categories of data upon which they impose these controls, the entities upon which they exert those controls, and the types of controls that they implement. These differences present their own risks. Less democratic countries will likely maintain a far more flexible interpretation of governmental powers than those countries in which the rule of law is robust. There will be opportunities for authoritarian governments to abuse a control point framework, such as we have described, toward undemocratic ends.

Nevertheless, it is not clear that a control point framework would be any worse in that respect than the existing geographic-based system, and it could potentially be significantly better. After all, the process of harmonization would necessarily embed less democratic countries into global diplomatic arrangements that would promote and reward domestic reforms. In any case, it is difficult to imagine that working toward harmonization, based upon our three-factor model, would not substantially improve the effectiveness of today's deeply flawed efforts at controlling data flows.

11.5 Recommendations

Fostering a harmonized international system that supports appropriate transnational data flows, under a common framework for data flow controls, will require engagement on numerous contentious issues, including international law-enforcement cooperation, privacy, intellectual property, and even cybersecurity. Many, if not most, of the negotiations on these matters will need input and buy-in from lawmakers, various government ministries, and industry and civil society stakeholders. Accordingly, we recognize that there is unlikely to be broad international consensus on the key normative obligations and constraints that determine the appropriateness of data flows, or the suitable set of state controls to enforce new normative or legal agreements. Nevertheless, progress can be made in incremental steps, using the framework we have described as a basis for additional harmonization efforts.

11.5.1 Recommendation One: Establish a Common Framework for Data Flow Controls Through the Development of International Standards, Norms, and Principles

As a first step toward harmonization, states will need to arrive at a baseline agreement on *terminology, norms,* and the *scope* of data flow policy issues, for both control points (CPA) and the policy considerations that determine the appropriateness of particular government actions. One potentially useful example of such a baseline agreement is the "Asia-Pacific Economic Cooperation (APEC) Privacy Framework" ("Privacy Framework"),[83] which has been used by the APEC member economies since 2004 to fashion comprehensive privacy legislation, and by industry groups and individual companies to implement self-regulatory standards.[84]

The APEC Privacy Framework is comprised of nine guiding principles, and accompanying guidance on implementation to assist APEC Economies in developing consistent domestic approaches to personal information privacy protections. Unlike the EU Data Protection Directive, referenced above, the Privacy Framework is not binding and explicitly notes that APEC member economies will vary their implementation of the principles contained in the framework based upon "differences in [their] social, cultural, economic, and legal backgrounds."[85] By providing this kind of flexibility, the Privacy Framework seeks to reconcile digital privacy with business and societal needs, and, at the same time, accords due recognition to cultural, legal, and other diversities among member economies. The APEC Privacy Framework was modeled on the OECD "Guidelines Governing the Protection of Privacy and Transborder Data Flows of Personal Data" ("OECD Guidelines"), which at that time represented the most widely shared international consensus on "what constitutes fair and trustworthy treatment of personal information,"[86] and has since been updated to take into account additional business and consumer input.

A similar approach to the APEC Privacy Framework could be developed to address other thorny jurisdictional issues, such as cross-border law-enforcement cooperation, using a control point methodology. Government officials, companies, and civil society groups could come together and create a list of principles, implementation guidelines, and enforcement and arbitration mechanisms to govern law-enforcement requests for data outside of a MLAT context, for instance, or for best practices for hate speech and intellectual property violations. The United Nations Group of Governmental Experts on Developments in the Field of Information and Telecommunications in the Context of International Security (UNGGE), which has since 2004 has sought to develop international norms for responsible State behavior for offensive cyber activities, could also provide some lessons for how to, or how not to as the case may be, reach broad international agreement on baseline standards for cyberspace issues.[87]

Some of the largest internet companies have already endorsed and sought to substantively advance this kind of standards-based approach to data flow controls.[88] For instance, Google, focusing specifically on the question of law enforcement's extraterritorial access to data, has proposed that "countries that honor baseline principles of privacy, human rights, and due process should be able to make direct requests to service providers for user data that pertains to serious crimes that happen within their borders and users who are within their jurisdiction." Google goes on to recommend that "[the] United States and foreign governments ... sign new agreements that could provide an alternative to the MLAT process," based upon adherence to those principles, and identifies categories of standards for the US government to promote, pertaining to such criteria as notice, redress, and reciprocity. Most importantly, Google notes that "[l]aw enforcement requests for digital evidence should be based on the location and nationality of users, *not the location of data*" (emphasis added).[89]

In its proposal, Google does not attempt to offer its own set of standards. It instead relies on those standards identified by the DOJ in its effort to develop the UK–US data access agreement. Yet, while DOJ's set of baseline standards might serve as a starting point for further discussions, a far broader range of stakeholders beyond government officials ought to be included in the discussion and decision-making process for a standard or group of standards to be viewed as broadly legitimate. Such stakeholders should consider how the UK–US data access agreement could be modified to accommodate participation from a broader set of countries.

Fortunately, a number of groups are already taking on the task. One in particular, the Internet and Jurisdiction Policy Network (I&J),[90] based in Paris, has been seeking to bring in such a broader coalition. Since 2012, the I&J has been convening multistakeholder dialogs to advance collaboration on a number of the jurisdictional challenges highlighted above.[91] It has established three working groups (one addressing questions of *data and jurisdiction,* one focused on *content and jurisdiction,* and another on *internet domains and jurisdiction*) to develop standards for user notification, authentication of requesters, and the establishment of single points of contact for various data flow issues. Notably, among the preliminary policy recommendations of the process is an acknowledgement of "the strong benefit in moving away from [geographic-based] criteria and replacing it by the notion of control."[92] The work of the I&J is still in its early stages, but the initiative and others like it have the potential to help facilitate the kind of baseline agreement needed to harmonize national approaches.

11.5.2 Recommendation Two: Formalize Agreed-upon Standards, Norms, and Principles Through the Adoption of Voluntary and Treaty-Based International Agreements

Reaching agreement on standards and principles based on a common framework, such as the one we have proposed, is just one piece of the harmonization puzzle. Those agreed-upon standards and principles must in turn be inserted into domestic law and policy and formalized through international agreements. Implementation can take place in a number of venues, both internationally and domestically; it can be carried out through voluntary and involuntary agreements between states.

Here again the APEC Privacy Framework provides an instructive example of a voluntary, principles-based approach. Since 2011, the Privacy Framework has served not just as a baseline agreement on principles and guidelines for data privacy, as described above, but also as the basis for the APEC Cross Border Privacy Rules (CBPR) arrangement,[93] a voluntary, accountability-based system designed to facilitate privacy-respecting data flows among APEC economies. The CBPR system creates baseline standards that companies and governments can follow and reference, as well as mechanisms for enforcement and dispute resolution. It has allowed for interoperability on personal data-protection regulations across vastly different national environments. Under the CBPR system, companies and organizations that have a presence in the member countries – and that have adopted the system, and chosen to implement privacy policies and practices consistent with the APEC Framework – gain certain regulatory protections when transferring certain private information to and from member countries. Once an organization has been certified for participation in the CBPR System by an APEC-recognized "Accountability Agent," these privacy policies and practices become legally binding and enforceable by a domestic government authority, such as a regulator, to ensure compliance (for instance, in the case of the United States, the Federal Trade Commission can levy penalties against companies for failing to meet their CBPR obligations). Similar voluntary, yet domestically enforceable, arrangements could be developed in other areas as well, and in such venues as the G7 and G20 forums.

In certain cases, even more formalized approaches to harmonization may be necessary. For instance, international trade agreements such as the attempted Trans-Pacific Partnership (TPP),[94] the proposed Transatlantic Trade and Investment Partnership (T-TIP), or the Trade in Services Agreement,[95] might provide a constructive avenue to cement standards and principles, based on a common frame for data flow controls into law. A number of these agreements already contain draft language addressing questions of data localization. But, trade agreements could also enable countries to agree on broader issues of data flow governance. By linking data flow questions to matters of trade, harmonization could substantially improve the global digital economy, similar to the way that the 1958 "Convention on the Recognition and Enforcement of Foreign Arbitral Awards" (also known as the "New York Convention") impacted international business. The New York Convention provided common legislative standards for the recognition of arbitration agreements, as well as court recognition and enforcement of foreign and non-domestic arbitral awards.[96] However, trade negotiations often take decades to complete,[97] if they are completed at all, and thus may not be the most appropriate means of reaching agreements on quickly moving and geopolitically complex technology policy issues.

11.5.3 Recommendation Three: Reform Domestic Law and Policy Frameworks Consistent with Agreed-upon Standards, Norms, and Principles

To ensure that new data control agreements and mechanisms are consistent with a common framework, a wide range of domestic laws will also need to be reexamined. For example, in the United States, the recently enacted CLOUD Act amended ECPA to reduce the general prohibition on US companies responding to requests from foreign law enforcement, and clarified that the SCA, one of ECPA's three titles, can be used to compel providers to produce data regardless of where the data are stored.

Of course, the United States is not the only country with blocking provisions preventing foreign law-enforcement officials from accessing broad categories of data, absent an MLAT request. A recent survey of the European Commission revealed that the majority of EU Member States' laws "do not cover/allow that service providers established in a Member State respond to direct requests from law enforcement authorities from another EU Member State or third country."[98] In fact, it appears that "only two Member States" allow for such cooperation. The United States could use its own privacy law-update process to coax European governments to follow suit, perhaps by imposing some form of federal legislation that would address baseline protections for privacy sufficient to mollify other countries that perceive inadequacy, while simultaneously establishing a workable framework for access to data under legitimate circumstances. Irrespective of the specific laws in question, as domestic rules are reformed, governments should look for opportunities to leverage the reform process to incentivize other states to take similar and reciprocal actions.

11.5.4 Recommendation Four: Focus First on Specific Policy Matters of Broad International Consensus, Then Move on to the more Contentious Issues

An issue-specific approach could also provide significant opportunities for incremental progress, and provide an example that could spread laterally to other issue areas. For example, the importance of countering child exploitation is already a matter of broad international agreement.[99] Swift progress on combatting it may be possible by working to ensure that law enforcement can rapidly obtain the digital evidence necessary to conduct child exploitation investigations, including identifying and rescuing children who are being abused. Other issues subject to broad international rapprochement and interest, such as the use of the internet by international terrorist organizations, or domain-specific matters like the Anti-Money Laundering (AML), are also potential areas for establishing an issue-specific harmonized international data flow-control framework. Starting with issues of broad consensus such as these can provide an initial basis for subsequent bilateral or multilateral efforts to expand a harmonized framework to other forms of criminal activity, or to other places where there is a shared interest in establishing harmonized data-flow mechanisms.

Critical to all these efforts will be sequencing. Most likely, agreement between like-minded countries with similar legal regimes (as is the case with negotiations on a UK–US Bilateral Agreement on Data Access) will need to precede agreements between countries with more divergent worldviews. For instance, the United States, United Kingdom, Canada, Australia, and New Zealand, given their similar legal regimes and history of close partnership, could reach agreement on a common framework for data flow controls, and then expand the set of countries committed to this common framework.

At the same time, there may also be opportunities to start bilaterally, even between countries that often do not see eye to eye. For instance, consider the 2013 agreement between US President Obama and Chinese Premier Xi Jinping, which limited government-enabled theft of intellectual property and appears to have had some success.[100] It could provide a useful example of how agreement between the largest and most powerful actors can establish norms that can be expanded to other countries. In all cases, issue selection and sequencing will necessarily depend upon the specific political and policy environments in question.

11.6   Additional Challenges

This chapter identified the central challenge to transnational data flow controls – the lack of a harmonized international framework – and provided recommendations for how the international community might work toward a more harmonized system. However, additional issues remain; chief among them, the question of cooperation between major technology providers and law enforcement and regulators.

In order to ensure that governments can effectively enforce their laws and regulations, a reasonable level of cooperation between government agencies and companies is essential. The reality is that absent robust, effective cooperation, governments are far more likely to implement laws and regulations that risk greatly impeding the growth and potential of the information economy. This risk is most substantial in nations where domestic commercial interests align with the imposition of strict rules and requirements on large, often foreign, providers. Accordingly, governments and providers alike must cooperate on a range of issues impacting global data flows, including such matters as encryption, provider compliance with court orders, and the question of retention and provision of data to law enforcement. Multinational providers will undoubtedly face challenges in doing this, as their services are used by highly diverse communities and cultures, requiring them to understand the societal and legal norms in the jurisdictions they operate and to make appropriate accommodations. However, providers that do not make reasonable accommodations are more likely to be impacted by laws or regulations that seek to compel them to take actions to abide by local norms. This is particularly the case when providers are unable to propose reasonable compliance alternatives to local authorities in places they do business.

Further, while harmonizing data flow controls is clearly important to the future of the internet and the information economy, it remains unclear precisely just how important this issue is within the intersecting policy matters of trade, cybersecurity, and differing notions of appropriate state control of activities occurring in cyberspace ("cyber sovereignty"). It is thus critical that governments, companies, and concerned citizens work to identify where and how data jurisdiction questions might be most effectively raised within multilateral or bilateral negotiations, and within debates about broader matters of international cooperation. Finding the right venues, the right cultural and diplomatic approaches to politically sensitive questions, and the most suitable timing for these discussions will be essential, as the international community seeks to make progress on these most pressing policy questions.

11.7 Conclusion

We hope this chapter has demonstrated that current approaches to international data flow controls and the geographic-based framework for data jurisdiction are failing and need dramatic reworking. The solution to the problem lies in the harmonization of international data flow controls based upon flexible modes of cooperation between states and companies, without using geography as the primary consideration. Governments, technology companies, civil society groups, and academia need to foster shared global norms for appropriate data flow controls and to inject those shared principles into domestic law and policy, as well as international agreements. Absent such an effort, the situation will only become more intractable, jeopardizing the internet's continued potential as a platform for communication, innovation, and commerce.

We recognize the many challenges at hand, yet we believe the international community has a tremendous opportunity to begin the process of harmonizing data flow controls around a common set of standards. By doing so, the world can help preserve an open, interoperable, and global internet that spurs innovation and grows the economy; an internet that allows the world to freely communicate across borders, thus advancing the fundamental human right, enshrined in Universal Declaration of Human Rights, "to seek, receive and impart information and ideas through any media and regardless of frontiers."

Acknowledgments

The authors studied together at Harvard's John F. Kennedy School of Government and developed this paper through discussions in the Transatlantic Digital Debates, a leadership program organized by New America in Washington D.C. and the Global Policy Institute in Berlin. The views expressed here are their own and should not be interpreted as official US government policy.

Notes

1 For more background on how information is stored and distributed on the internet, see The Harvard Law National Security Research Group (Ivana Deyrup, Shane Matthews, Aatif Iqbal, Benjamin Black, Catherine Fisher, John Cella, Jonathan Abrams, Miranda Dugi, and Rebecca Leventhal), "Cloud Computing and National Law," 2010, https://lawfare.s3-us-west-2.amazonaws.com/staging/s3fs-public/uploads/2010/10/Cloud-Final.pdf; and Dillion Reisman, "Where Is Your Data, Really?: The Technical Case Against Data Localization," *Lawfare*, May 22, 2017, https://www.lawfareblog.com/where-your-data-really-technical-case-against-data-localization.

2 Deven R. Desai, "Beyond Location: Data Security in the 21st Century," *Communications of the ACM* 56 (January 2013), https://ssrn.com/abstract=2237712.

3 David D. Clark, "Control Point Analysis," 2012 TRPC, September 10, 2012, or https://papers.ssrn.com/sol3/papers.cfm?abstract_id=2032124.

4 Helen Nissenbaum, *Privacy In Context: Technology, Policy, And The Integrity Of Social Life* (Stanford: Stanford University Press, 2009).

5 William J. Drake, Vinton G. Cerf, and Wolfgang Kleinwächter, "Internet Fragmentation: An Overview," *World Economic Forum*, January 2016, http://www3.weforum.org/docs/WEF_FII_Internet_Fragmentation_An_Overview_2016.pdf; Jonah Force Hill, "Internet Fragmentation: Highlighting the Major Technical, Governance and Diplomatic Challenges for U.S. Policy Makers," Paper, Science, Technology, and Public Policy Program, Belfer Center, Harvard Kennedy School of Government, May 2012, http://www.belfercenter.org/sites/default/files/legacy/files/internet_fragmentation_jonah_hill.pdf.

6 Manyika, et al., "Global Flows in a Digital Age: How Trade, Finance, People, and Data Connect the World Economy," McKinsey Global Institute, April 2014, http://www.mckinsey.com/business-functions/strategy-and-corporate-finance/our-insights/global-flows-in-a-digital-age.

7 Alexander Hamilton, Federalist Paper No. 15, "The Insufficiency of the Present Confederation to Preserve the Union." *The Independent Journal*, December 1, 1787.

8 For example, the European Police Office's "2016 Internet Organized Crime Threat Assessment (IOCTA)," https://www.europol.europa.eu/activities-services/main-reports/internet-organised-crime-threat-assessment-iocta-2016.

9 For example, see the Mutual Legal Assist Treaty Between the United States of America and the United Kingdom of Great Britain and Northern Ireland, signed January 6, 1994, https://www.state.gov/documents/organization/176269.pdf

10 Vivek Krishnamurthy, "Cloudy with a Conflict of Laws," February 16, 2016, Berkman Center Research Publication No. 2016-3, https://ssrn.com/abstract=2733350.

11 U.S. Department of Justice, "FY 2015 Budget Request: Mutual Legal Assistance Treaty Process Reform," July 2014, https://www.justice.gov/sites/default/files/jmd/legacy/2014/07/13/mut-legal-assist.pdf.

12 Access Now, "Mutual Legal Assistance Treaties," accessed December 18, 2018, https://www.mlat.info/.

13 President's Review Group on Intelligence and Communications Technologies, "Liberty and Security in a Changing World," December 12, 2013, https://obamawhitehouse.archives.gov/sites/default/files/docs/2013-12-12_rg_final_report.pdf.

14 Vivek Krishnamurthy, "Cloudy with a Conflict of Laws," February 16, 2016, Berkman Center Research Publication No. 2016-3, https://ssrn.com/abstract=2733350.

15 For more on the challenges posed by the block-features of ECPA, see Andrew Woods, "The Simplest Cross-Border Fix: Removing ECPA's Blocking Features," *Lawfare*, June 15, 2017, https://www.lawfareblog.com/simplest-cross-border-fix-removing-ecpas-blocking-features.

16 Other provisions of ECPA prohibit companies from voluntarily disclosing "stored communications" to governments (US and ex-US) absent specified exceptions (18 U.S.C. 2702).

17 David Anderson Q.C., "A Question of Trust: Report of the Investigatory Powers Review," June 2015, https://terrorismlegislationreviewer.independent.gov.uk/wp-content/uploads/2015/06/IPR-Report-Print-Version.pdf.

18 Paulo Marcos Rodriguez Brancher and Douglas Cohen Moreira, "Brazilian Superior Court of Justice Decision and the Disclosure of Gmail Data for Investigation," *Lexology*, April 29, 2013, accessed June 12, 2014, http://www.lexology.com/library/detail.aspx?g=793d848f-5877-4675-9336-aa28eec3d971; Rebecca Blumenstein and Loretta Chao, "Brazil's Rousseff Pressures U.S. on Data Collection," *The Wall Street Journal*, January 25, 2014, https://www.wsj.com/articles/brazil8217s-rousseff-pressures-us-on-data-collection-1390604047?tesla=y.

19 "MLATS and International Cooperation for Law Enforcement Purposes," presentation at the Centre for Internet and Society, https://cis-india.org/internet-governance/blog/presentation-on-mlats.pdf.

20 Matter of Warrant to Search a Certain E-Mail Account Controlled & Maintained by Microsoft Corp., 829 F.3d 197 (2d Cir. 2016).

21 For more on Microsoft's perspective, see the blog post by Brad Smith, "A Legislative Path to Create New Laws is Better than Arguing Over Old Laws," *Microsoft Blog*, June 23, 2017, https://blogs.microsoft.com/on-the-issues/2017/06/23/legislative-path-create-new-laws-better-arguing-old-laws.

22 The Second Circuit ruled that a warrant issued under Section 2703 of the Stored Communications Act could not compel American companies to produce data stored in servers outside the United States. *Supra* 829 F.3d 197 (2d Cir. 2016).

23 On 14 July 2016, a panel of the Second Circuit Court of Appeals ruled in favor of Microsoft, finding that the Stored Communications Act could not be used to obtain data stored outside of the United States. On 28 June 2017, the Department of Justice petitioned the US Supreme Court to hear this case. US Department of Justice, "In The Matter Of A Warrant To Search A Certain E-mail Account Controlled And Maintained By Microsoft Corporation," June 28, 2017, https://www.justice.gov/sites/default/files/briefs/2017/06/28/17-2_microsoft_corp_petiton.pdf.

24 United States v. Microsoft Corporation, 584 U. S. (2018): "Whether a United States provider of email services must comply with a probable-cause-based warrant issued under 18 U.S.C. § 2703 by making disclosure in the United States of electronic communications within that provider's control, even if the provider has decided to store that material abroad," https://www.supremecourt.gov/docket/docketfiles/html/public/17-2.html.

25 Counsel for Amicus Curiae Ireland, "Brief Of Amicus Curiae Ireland in 14-2985-CV," December 23, 2014, https://www.eff.org/files/2015/01/12/ireland_microsoft_second_circuit_amicus_brief.pdf.

26 Richard Littlehale, Testimony before the U.S. House of Representatives Committee on the Judiciary, hearing on "Data Stored Abroad: Ensuring Lawful Access and Privacy Protection in the Digital Era," June 15, 2017, https://judiciary.house.gov/hearing/data-stored-abroad-ensuring-lawful-access-privacy-protection-digital-era.

27 Ibid.

28 For a brief introduction to data sharing see Microsoft, "Sharding Pattern," June 23, 2017, https://docs.microsoft.com/en-us/azure/architecture/patterns/sharding.

29 Jeffrey Wall, "Reply Brief for the United States. In the Matter of a Warrant to Search a Certain E-Mail Account Controlled and Maintained By Microsoft Corporation," September 2017, https://arstechnica.com/wp-content/uploads/2017/09/scotusmsftgoogyahoo.pdf. Additionally, see In re Search Warrant No. 16-960-M-1 to Google (E.D. Pen. Aug. 17, 2017); In re Search of Content that Is Stored at Premises Controlled by Google Inc. and as Further Described in Attachment A, No. 16-mc-80263 (N.D. Cal. Aug. 14, 2017), aff'g 2017 WL 1487625 (N.D. Cal. Apr. 25, 2017); In re Search of Info. Associated with [Redacted]@http://gmail.com that Is Stored at Premises Controlled by Google, Inc., No. 16-mj-757, 2017 WL 3445634 (D.D.C. July 31, 2017), aff'g 2017 WL 2480752 (D.D.C. June 2, 2017); In re Search of Info. Associated with Accounts Identified as Redacted]@http://gmail.com and Others Identified in Attachment A that Are Stored at Premises Controlled by Google Inc., No. 16-mj-2197, 2017 WL 3263351 (C.D. Cal. July 13, 2017); In re Search Warrant to Google, Inc., Mag. No. 16-4116, 2017 WL 2985391 (D.N.J. July 10, 2017) (objections filed); In re Two Email Accounts Stored at Google, Inc., No. 17-M-1235, 2017 WL 2838156 (E.D. Wisc. June 30, 2017) (objections filed);

In re Search of Premises Located at Redacted]@http://yahoo.com, No. 17-mj-1238 (M.D. Fla. Apr. 7, 2017); In re Search Warrant No. 16-960-M-01 to Google, 232 F. Supp. 3d 708 (E.D. Pa. Feb. 3, 2017).

30 In contrast, search warrants usually require specifying the location to be searched, which is a significant legal constraint on the scope of US law enforcement's power.

31 See, e.g. CCIPS-CSIS (The Center for Strategic and International Studies [CSIS] and the U.S. Department of Justice Computer Crime and Intellectual Property Section [CCIPS]), CCIPS-CSIS Cybercrime Symposium 2016: Cooperation and Electronic Evidence Gathering Across Borders, U.S. Dep't of Just., Comput. Crime & Intell. Prop. Section, June 6, 2016, https://www.csis.org/events/ccips-csis-cybercrime-symposium-2016. As an additional example, see the "Cross-Border Requests for Data Project" at the Institute for Information Security and Privacy at Georgia Tech, http://www.iisp.gatech.edu/cross-border-data-project. The Dutch Presidency of the European Union convened the "Crossing Borders: Jurisdiction in Cyberspace" conference in Amsterdam on March 6–7, 2016.

32 For instance, Peter Swire and Justin Hemmings of Georgia Tech have suggested that a streamlined MLAT system could be possible through statutory changes akin to the current Visa Waiver Program. They argue that eligible countries with high-quality procedures for seeking evidence would be eligible for a streamlined process for obtaining evidence in the United States, in much the same way that certain countries are exempted from background checks for visas. See Peter Swire and Justin D. Hemmings, "Mutual Legal Assistance in an Era of Globalized Communications: The Analogy to the Visa Waiver Program," January 11, 2016 71 NYU Annual Survey of American Law 687 (2017); Georgia Tech Scheller College of Business Research Paper No. WP 38, SSRN, https://ssrn.com/abstract=2728478 or http://dx.doi.org/10.2139/ssrn.2728478.

33 Two notable examples are the "Law Enforcement Access to Data Stored Abroad Act" (LEADS Act), https://www.congress.gov/114/bills/hr1174/BILLS-114hr1174ih.xml, and the "International Communications Privacy Act" (ICPA), available at https://www.congress.gov/114/bills/s2986/BILLS-114s2986is.xml.

34 In the United Kingdom, the Parliament has passed the Investigatory Powers Act, which greatly expands the extraterritorial reach of British law enforcement, allowing for expansive "equipment interference," or hacking of computers, outside of UK territory. Home Office of the United Kingdom, "Equipment Interference, DRAFT Code of Practice," Fall 2016, https://www.gov.uk/government/uploads/system/uploads/attachment_data/file/557861/IP_Bill_-_Draft_EI_code_of_practice.pdf. Additionally, the government of Ethiopia was alleged, in a US civil case, to have used FinSpy to gather information from a US citizen's electronic devices located in the United States.

Interestingly, the US Court of Appeals for the District of Columbia Circuit ruled that the Foreign Sovereign Immunities Act (FSIA) provided the government of Ethiopia immunity from such a lawsuit. See *Doe v. Fed. Democratic Republic of Ethiopia*, No. 16-7081, 2017 U.S. Appl. LEXIS 4414.

35 Susan Hennessey and Chris Mirasola, "Did China Quietly Authorize Law Enforcement to Access Data Anywhere in the World?" *Lawfare*, March 27, 2017, https://www.lawfareblog.com/ did-china-quietly-authorize-law-enforcement-access-data-anywhere-world.

36 Jeremy Daum, "Sometimes a Rule of Evidence is Just a Rule of Evidence," *China Law Translate*, March 29, 2017), http://www.chinalawtranslate.com/ sometimes-a-rule-of-evidence-is-just-a-rule-of-evidence/?lang=en.

37 In the fall of 2017, it was alleged that China hacked the law firm representing a Chinese dissident located in and seeking asylum from the United States. See Bill Gertz, "FBI Eyes China in Posting Hacked Documents on Chinese Dissident," *The Washington Free Beacon*, September 29, 2017, http:// freebeacon.com/national-security/ fbi-eyes-china-posting-hacked-documents-chinese-dissident.

38 Federal Rules of Criminal Procedure, 41(b)(6), June 20, 2016. For further discussion, see: https://www.justice.gov/archives/opa/blog/rule-41-changes-ensure-judge-may-consider-warrants-certain-remote-searches.

39 For example, see Ben Buchanan, "Cryptography and Sovereignty," *Survival* 58, no. 5 (September 20, 2016): 95–122, http://www.tandfonline.com/doi/full/ 10.1080/00396338.2016.1231534;Steven M. Bellovin, Matt Blaze, Sandy Clark, and Susan Landau, "Lawful Hacking: Using Existing Vulnerabilities for Wiretapping on the Internet," *Northwestern Journal of Technology and Intellectual Property* 12, no. 1 (April 2014), http://scholarlycommons.law. northwestern.edu/cgi/viewcontent.cgi?article=1209&context=njtip; Jonathan Mayer, "Constitutional Malware," November 14, 2016, SSRN, https://papers. ssrn.com/sol3/papers.cfm?abstract_id=2633247.

40 According to joint testimony of the Honorable Clapper, the Honorable Lettre, and Admiral Rogers, more than 30 countries are developing offensive cyberattack capabilities. See James R. Clapper, Marcel Lettre, and Michael S. Rogers. "Joint Statement for the Record to the Senate Armed Services Committee: Foreign Cyber Threats to the United States," January 5, 2017, https://www.armed-services.senate.gov/imo/media/doc/Clapper-Lettre-Rogers_01-05-16.pdf.

41 For more on the potential risks related to "lawful hacking," we recommend this paper by Orin Kerr and Sean Murphy: "Government Hacking to Light the Dark Web," July 2017, https://www.stanfordlawreview.org/online/ government-hacking-to-light-the-dark-web.

42 Alan McQuinn and Daniel Castro, "How Law Enforcement Should Access Data Across Borders," Information Technology & Innovation Foundation, July 2017, http://www2.itif.org/2017-law-enforcement-data-borders.pdf.

43 For example, consider the recent US criminal case involving the Bitcoin Exchange BTC-e. In this case, a web service with obscured ownership and unknown data storage location was used by criminals throughout the world for a wide range of crimes. For more on the BTC-E case, see: Department of Justice, U.S. Attorney's Office, Northern District of California, "Russian National and Bitcoin Exchange Charged in 21-Count Indictment for Operating Alleged International Money Laundering Scheme and Allegedly Laundering Funds from Hack of Mt. Gox," July 26, 2017, https://www.justice. gov/usao-ndca/pr/russian-national-and-bitcoin-exchange-charged-21- count-indictment-operating-alleged.

44 Paul Rosenzweig, "The US-UK Deal Is Actually Quite Good," *Lawfare*, July 19, 2017, https://lawfareblog.com/us-uk-deal-actually-quite-good.

45 Paddy McGuinness, "Written Testimony of Mr Paddy McGuinness, United Kingdom Deputy National Security Adviser, Before the Judiciary Sub- Committee on Crime and Terrorism United States Senate," May 10, 2017, https://www.judiciary.senate.gov/imo/media/doc/05-24-17%20 McGuinness%20Testimony.pdf.

46 ECPA was enacted to provide additional protections for electronic communications, beyond those provided by the Fourth Amendment to the US Constitution; its provisions (18 U.S.C. §§ 2510-2522, 2701-2712, 3121-3127) impose broad prohibitions on electronic communications providers disclosing communications information, except in specified circumstances. For more on the blocking aspects of ECPA, see the "Written Testimony of Andrew Keane Woods before the House Judiciary Committee," June 15, 2017, https:// judiciary.house.gov/wp-content/uploads/2017/06/Woods-Testimony.pdf.

47 For more on the framework for allowing for cross-border data requests, see the various works of Jennifer Daskal and Andrew Keane Woods; for example, "Cross-Border Data Requests: A Proposed Framework," *Lawfare*, November 24, 2015, https://lawfareblog.com/ cross-border-data-requests-proposed-framework.

48 Also of note is the International Communications Privacy Act (ICPA), proposed by Senators Hatch, Coons, and Heller on August 1, 2017. ICPA primarily focuses on the citizenship and location of the suspects, rather than the location in which data may be stored or even who controls that data. The text of ICPA is available at: https://www.congress.gov/bill/ 115th-congress/senate-bill/1671/cosponsors. It bears note that any comparison of national legal orders to determine "compatibility" in this context is an exceptionally complex undertaking, and attempts to do so have almost universally been subject to reasonable critique regarding the politicization of their conclusions.

49 For example, see Matthew Prince, "Why We Terminated Daily Stormer," *Cloudflare*, August 16, 2017, https://blog.cloudflare.com/ why-we-terminated-daily-stormer.

50 Court of Appeal for British Columbia, *Equustek Solutions Inc. v. Google Inc.*, 2015 BCCA 265, https://www.canlii.org/en/bc/bcca/doc/2015/2015bcca265/ 2015bcca265.pdf.

51 *Google v. Equustek Solutions Inc.*, U.S. District Court of Northern District of California San Jose Division, 2017, https://assets.documentcloud.org/ documents/3900043/Google-v-Equustek-Complaint.pdf.

52 Andrew Keane Woods, "Google Takes the Global Delisting Debate to a U.S. Court," *Lawfare*, July 27, 2017, https://www.lawfareblog.com/ google-takes-global-delisting-debate-us-court.

53 For example, see Daphne Keller, "Ominous: Canadian Court Orders Google to Remove Search Results Globally, Center for Internet and Society, June 28, 2017, http://cyberlaw.stanford.edu/blog/2017/06/ominous-canadian-court-orders-google-remove-search-results-globally; Electronic Frontier Foundation (EFF), "Google v. Equustek," https://www.eff.org/cases/google-v-equustek;Jacob Rogers, "Wikimedia Foundation Advises Canadian Supreme Court to Support Freedom of Expression Worldwide in Intervention Filing for Google v. Equustek," *Wikimedia Foundation Blog*, October 14, 2016, https:// blog.wikimedia.org/2016/10/14/intervention-google-v-equustek;Eugene Volokh, "Canadian Court Orders Google to Remove Search Results Globally," *The Washington Post*, June 29, 2017, https://www.washingtonpost.com/news/ volokh-conspiracy/wp/2017/06/29/ canadian-court-orders-google-to-remove-search-results-globally.

54 Andrew Keane Woods, "No, the Canadian Supreme Court Did Not Ruin the Internet," *Lawfare*, July 6, 2017, https://www.lawfareblog.com/ no-canadian-supreme-court-did-not-ruin-internet.

55 Daphne Keller, "Ominous: Canadian Court Orders Google to Remove Search Results Globally," Center for Internet and Society, June 28, 2017, http:// cyberlaw.stanford.edu/blog/2017/06/ ominous-canadian-court-orders-google-remove-search-results-globally.

56 For a summary, see "Google Spain SL v. Agencia Española de Protección de Datos," *Harvard Law Review*, May 13, 2014, https://harvardlawreview. org/2014/12/google-spain-sl-v-agencia-espanola-de-proteccion-de-datos.

57 Council Directive 95/46, 1995 O.J. (L 281) 31 (EC).

58 Peter Fleischer, "Adapting Our Approach to the European Right to be Forgotten," *Google Blog*, March 4, 2016, https://www.blog.google/topics/ google-europe/adapting-our-approach-to-european-rig.

59 Kent Walker, "A Principle that Should not be Forgotten," *Google Blog*, May 19, 2016, https://www.blog.google/topics/ google-europe/a-principle-that-should-not-be-forgotten.

60 For example, see Laurence Iliff, "Google Wages Free-Speech Fight in Mexico," *The Wall Street Journal*, May 27, 2015, https://www.wsj.com/articles/google-wages-free-speech-fight-in-mexico-1432723483; Global Voices Advox, "Right to Be Forgotten: A Win for Argentina's Lawsuit-Happy Celebrities?"

September 18, 2014, https://advox.globalvoices.org/2014/09/18/
right-to-be-forgotten-a-win-for-argentinas-lawsuit-happy-celebrities.

61 James Lim, "South Korea Releases Right to Be Forgotten Guidance," *Bloomberg
BNA*, May 9, 2016, https://www.bna.com/
south-korea-releases-n57982070847.

62 See Sidley Austin LLP, "Essentially Equivalent: A Comparison of the Legal
Orders for Privacy and Data Protection in the European Union and United
States," January 25, 2016, https://www.sidley.com/en/insights/
publications/2016/01/essentially-equivalent.

63 Paul Rosenzweig, "Europe Is Deeply Unserious," *Lawfare*, July 27, 2017,
https://www.lawfareblog.com/europe-deeply-unserious.

64 Personal Data Protection Law Draft Bill – Brazil. As published for public
comment by the Executive Branch on January 28, 2015, https://iapp.org/
media/pdf/resource_center/Brazil_PDPL_Draft_Bill-final.pdf; https://
uk.practicallaw.thomsonreuters.com/4-520-1732.

65 Chinese National People's Congress, "People's Republic of China Internet
Security Law," November 7, 2016, www.npc.gov.cn/npc/xinwen/2016-11/07/
content_2001605.htm.

66 Russian Federal Law No. 242-FZ, "On making amendments to certain laws of
the Russian Federation regarding clarification of the order of processing of
personal data in information and telecommunication networks."

67 See "Judgment in Case C-362/14 Maximillian Schrems v Data Protection
Commissioner, Luxembourg," October 6, 2015, https://curia.europa.eu/jcms/
upload/docs/application/pdf/2015-10/cp150117en.pdf.

68 The invalidation of the EU–US Safe Harbor Agreement did not lead to a major
fracturing of the internet because governments, companies, and individual
internet users understood that a total stoppage of data flows to the United
States would cripple the digital economy on both sides of the Atlantic. The US
and the EU were able to (i) ensure that European Data Protection Authorities
provided a grace period for transition to the use of other instruments to
permit data transfers, such as the execution of contracts based on the
European Commission's approved Standard Contractual Clauses, and perhaps
more impactfully (ii) successfully negotiate and implement a new agreement,
the EU–US Privacy Shield Arrangement, which when paired with the Judicial
Redress Act, a law passed in 2016 by the US Congress and signed into law by
President Obama, provided additional safeguards and redress mechanisms for
EU citizens concerned about the privacy of their data transferred to the
United States. Interestingly, despite the close attention to "data protection" in
the United States and critical commentary as compared to the European
Union's own regime, there has been comparatively little attention to the
"adequacy" of other countries to which the European Union regularly transfers
data, including notably the People's Republic of China. Indeed, the
Directorate-General for Internal Policies recognizes this tension in a report to

the LIBE Committee, acknowledging: "one cannot talk of a proper data protection regime in China ... even if one chooses to disregard the human rights parameter for sake of analysis ... the basics of international data protection are not unequivocally in place in China today." See European Parliament Directorate-General for Internal Policies, "The data protection regime in China: In-depth Analysis for the LIBE Committee," October 2015, http://www.europarl.europa.eu/RegData/etudes/IDAN/2015/536472/IPOL_IDA(2015)536472_EN.pdf.

69 Jonah Force Hill, "The Growth of Data Localization Post-Snowden," Lawfare Research Paper Series, July 21, 2014, https://www.lawfareblog.com/jonah-force-hill-growth-data-localization-post-snowden-lawfare-research-paper-series.

70 For a comprehensive list of restrictions, see Nigel Cory, "Cross-Border Data Flows: Where Are the Barriers, and What Do They Cost?" Information Technology and Innovation Foundation (ITIF), May 2017, http://www2.itif.org/2017-cross-border-data-flows.pdf?_ga=2.244607109.1624330899.1511348753-1808609825.1511348753.

71 The New York County District Attorney's Office, "Ensuring Lawful Access to Smartphones," June 13, 2017, http://manhattanda.org/smartphone-encryption.

72 Importantly, data localization requirements are also often viewed by lawmakers – incorrectly – as a kind of panacea for cybersecurity challenges. But as with privacy, the physical location of data has little to no impact on security.

73 Other countries, most notably Estonia, are considering anti-localization strategies, seeking to ensure that their data are stored abroad and under the protection of foreign partners. Estonia Ministry of Economic Affairs and Communications and Microsoft, "Implementation of the Virtual Data Embassy Solution," https://www.mkm.ee/sites/default/files/implementation_of_the_virtual_data_embassy_solution_summary_report.pdf.

74 Again, our advocacy for this approach should not imply that what is needed is a new all-encompassing international treaty or another single international legal mechanism. The chances of success of such a treaty are low in light of the number of governments and other actors that would be impacted and thus need to be involved in the process. Rather, we suggest rethinking prior notions of geography as a basis for jurisdiction as a means of beginning to develop new mechanisms of cooperation.

75 Jack Goldsmith and Tim Wu, *Who Controls the Internet? Illusions of a Borderless World* (New York: Oxford University Press, 2006).

76 David D. Clark, "Control Point Analysis," 2012 TRPC, September 10, 2012, SSRN, https://ssrn.com/abstract=2032124 or http://dx.doi.org/10.2139/ssrn.2032124.

77 Similarly, the Electronic Frontier Foundation (EFF) applies a control point analysis to illustrate potential constraints to speech on the internet. The EFF's

depiction of the control points involved in web communication is available at: https://www.eff.org/free-speech-weak-link.

78 Helen Nissenbaum, *Privacy In Context: Technology, Policy, And The Integrity Of Social Life* (Stanford: Stanford University Press, 2009).

79 Helen Nissenbaum, "Privacy as Contextual Integrity," *Washington Law Review*, 2004, https://crypto.stanford.edu/portia/papers/RevnissenbaumDTP31.pdf.

80 This factor encompasses the "sender" and "recipient" factors of CIM, while also including various entities involved in content distribution: hosters, domain registrars, ISPs, etc.

81 This factor encompasses the "information type" factor of CIM, while recognizing that there is a potentially far greater set of defined types of data in the broad context of data controls compared to privacy controls.

82 This factor encompasses both the "transmission principles" and "subject" factors of CIM. We agree that subjects are a particularly relevant factor in considering privacy protections; however, in the broad set of data flow controls, we consider them one among many with various rights to the data (for example, the creator or copyright holder).

83 APEC Secretariat, "APEC Privacy Framework 2015," http://www.cbprs.org.

84 Ibid.

85 Ibid.

86 Ibid.

87 The United Nations Group of Governmental Experts on Developments in the Field of Information and Telecommunications in the Context of International Security (UNGGE), which has since 2004 has sought to develop international norms for responsible state behavior for offensive cyber activities, could also provide some lessons for how to (or how not to, as the case may be) reach broad international agreement on baseline standards for cyberspace issues. More information available at: https://www.un.org/disarmament/topics/informationsecurity.

88 Google, "Digital Security & Due Process: Modernizing Cross-Border Government Access Standards for the Cloud Era," *Google Blog*, June 22, 2017, https://www.blog.google/documents/2/CrossBorderLawEnforcement RequestsWhitePaper_2.pdf

89 Ibid.

90 For more on the Internet and Jurisdiction Policy Network, see: https://www.internetjurisdiction.net.

91 The goal of the I&J is to "catalyze the development of shared cooperation frameworks and policy standards that are as transnational as the Internet itself in order to promote legal interoperability and establish due process across borders."

92 Data and Jurisdiction Program, Cross Border Access to User Data, Problem Framing, May 2017. https://www.internetjurisdiction.net/uploads/pdfs/Papers/Data-Jurisdiction-Program-Paper.pdf

93 See the APEC CBPR system, available at: http://www.cbprs.org.

94 The eCommerce Chapter of TPP provides a useful example of how data flow standards can be incorporated into a trade agreement. See the 2016 negotiated language at: https://ustr.gov/sites/default/files/TPP-Final-Text-Electronic-Commerce.pdf

95 For a discussion of counter-data localization provisions in trade agreements, see William J. Drake, "Background Paper for the workshop on Data Localization and Barriers to Transborder Data Flows," The World Economic Forum, Geneva, September 14–15, 2016, http://www3.weforum.org/docs/Background_Paper_Forum_workshop%2009.2016.pdf.

96 Convention on the Recognition and Enforcement of Foreign Arbitral Awards, New York, 1958 (the "New York Convention"), http://www.uncitral.org/uncitral/en/uncitral_texts/arbitration/NYConvention.html.

97 For instance, the Doha Development Round, the latest trade negotiation round of the World Trade Organization, has been ongoing since 2011 and has not yet been completed.

98 European Commission, "Questionnaire on Improving Criminal Justice in Cyberspace: Summary of Response," https://ec.europa.eu/home-affairs/sites/homeaffairs/files/e-library/documents/policies/organized-crime-and-human-trafficking/e-evidence/docs/summary_of_replies_to_e-evidence_questionnaire_en.pdf.

99 WePROTECT, "The WePROTECT Global Alliance," July 12, 2016, http://www.weprotect.org/strategylaunch.

100 Council on Foreign Relations, "The U.S.-China Cyber Espionage Deal One Year Later," September 2016. https://www.cfr.org/blog/us-china-cyber-espionage-deal-one-year-later

12

Private Ordering Shaping Cybersecurity Policy

The Case of Bug Bounties

Amit Elazari Bar On

School of Information, University of California, Berkeley, CA, USA

12.1   Introduction

Society is producing more lines of code than ever before,[1] and everything – from cars to sex toys – is becoming connected.[2] This means that more vulnerabilities and exploits are produced daily, inviting breaches that can impose astronomic costs, whether legal, reputational, or even personal.[3] As the risks and costs of cybersecurity risks are growing,[4] a legitimate market for vulnerabilities thrives. Governments and companies enact vulnerability rewards programs in which they pay individual security experts for performing adversarial research and exposing critical vulnerabilities, previously uncovered by organizations' internal checks and quality-assurance processes.[5]

Bug bounty programs fuel security research on a multitude of platforms, paying millions,[6] influencing the income of tens of thousands of friendly hackers, and keeping the data of billions of users (more) secure.[7] From Silicon Valley giants and Dark Web sites[8] to the Department of Homeland Security[9] and US army, bug bounties are gradually expanding their reach into traditional industries as well as governmental organizations, while still maintaining their dominance in the area of web and mobile applications.[10]

While recently rising to prominence, bug bounties are not a recent invention. The first bug bounty was initiated in 1995 by Netscape, which offered to pay $1000 for vulnerabilities found in its Navigator 2.0 Internet Browser.[11] In 2004, Mozilla followed, offering researchers rewards for vulnerabilities found in Firefox; this bug bounty program is still running, paying millions. The logic of bug bounties also rests upon a piece of old "tech" wisdom that originated with the open software culture, according to which "given enough eyeballs, all bugs are shallow."[12] This means that if we can invite every security researcher in the world to join the "co-developer base," security bugs will be discovered and fixed faster.[13]

Rewired: Cybersecurity Governance, First Edition. Edited by Ryan Ellis and Vivek Mohan.
© 2019 John Wiley & Sons, Inc. Published 2019 by John Wiley & Sons, Inc.

Bug bounties harvest this logic, which proved especially potent in the cybersecurity context, by expanding the circle of researchers (and skillsets) engaged in penetration testing and the search for security bugs.[14] Empirical research supports this logic, finding that bug bounties are a cost-effective mechanism for conducting security research, compared to the alternative of hiring full-time employees.[15]

Although bug bounties play a dominant role in the cybersecurity landscape and the evolving market for vulnerabilities, there is still little discussion in the legal literature relating to bug bounties' use of form-contracts to create an alternative legal regime for vulnerabilities' transactions. Much of the academic debate concerning these programs evolved within the computer science and economics disciplines.[16] This is surprising, considering that the operation and effectiveness of a bug bounty program highly depend on how its legal terms are drafted and on the set of legal incentives and guarantees provided to hackers. Such guarantees include clear communication of the program's scope and the type of reward allocated for each vulnerability,[17] as well as the type of legal risk assumed by the researcher and scope of authorization given to her to operate under the law. Clear program terms are critical to ensure bug bounties continue to operate as a "legal" marketplace for vulnerabilities – an alternative to the black market. If the terms are crafted poorly, hackers might be breaching the law merely by participating in the program.[18]

In the currently murky landscape of anti-hacking laws, bug bounties present an interesting case study for how contracts could foster security research instead of stifling it – an alternative legal regime for facilitating ethical hacking. Currently, the law is still not well tailored to accommodate "white-hat" security research.[19] This is somewhat paradoxical, considering that cybersecurity is becoming an increasingly regulated field, and that more regulations (and regulators) are requiring companies to engage in penetration testing and to enact procedures for receiving vulnerabilities.[20] Bug bounty legal terms operate in this landscape as a contract between the hacker and the sponsoring company, and are the focal point of determining the legal liability and risks of hackers engaged in bug hunting.[21]

As will be explained, anti-hacking laws, mainly the Digital Millennium Copyright Act (DMCA) and Computer Fraud and Abuse Act (CFAA), partially facilitate security testing. However, they also require that the contract language "authorizes" testing. Therefore, the program terms should establish genuine "safe harbors" for hackers,[22] by authorizing access, waiving liability in case the hacker follows the program guidelines, and specifically allowing the employment of research techniques such as reverse engineering, which are often prohibited under general end-user-license agreements (EULAs). By employing this boilerplate language for safe harbor, bug bounties offer a unique opportunity to affect the legal landscape of white-hat hacking at scale as a form of private regulation.

This paper offers the first comprehensive account of bug bounty *legal* terms. It claims that while programs usually clearly disclose the "technical scope" of authorization given to the researcher, the legal scope of "authorization" and "access" is often ignored, nonexistent, or lacking. Hacker platforms also contribute to this reality, by emphasizing the importance of defining the technical and economic (rewards) scope, while conferring less attention to the importance of crafting adequate legal terms.[23] Indeed, in some cases, the legal terms stand in direct tension with the purpose of the program, putting hackers who use basic research techniques in direct violation of terms, and exposing them to legal liability. In other cases, the terms create a reality in which hackers infringe the terms almost by default, if they do what the program wants them to do: find vulnerabilities.

Lack of safe harbor language has already resulted in at least one publicized case of a security researcher participating in bug bounty being allegedly threatened by the sponsoring company with CFAA legal action.[24] On the positive side, more and more companies are adopting a direct commitment not to pursue legal actions against hackers, and some have even adopted legal language that specifically authorizes access under the relevant anti-hacking laws. Unfortunately, this is still the exception, not the standard.

This paper presents key findings from a survey of legal terms for both public and private bug bounty programs: (i) "public," popular, and smaller bug bounties programs,[25] and (ii) the various terms of two leading hacker platforms, HackerOne and Bugcrowd. Hacker platforms, or "crowdsourcing platform vendors," serve as intermediaries between individual hackers and the vendor of the product or service that is being tested. Platforms operate both "public" bug bounties, which are generally open to all individual researchers, and are offered directly by the company sponsoring the program, and "private" programs, which are administrated by the hacker platform. The private programs offer "submission vetting and program management," as well as bigger rewards, and are limited to a number of elite researchers chosen by the platform or program (professional "bug hunters").[26]

Section 12.2 of this paper discusses the key findings of the legal terms survey and the legal landscape of bug bounties. It exposes the bug hunting "catch 22": the most rewarding vulnerabilities, the ones that require hackers to provide "proof of concepts" showing how they gained "unauthorized access,"[27] also require that hackers comply with "all laws," while not explicitly granting them access or exempting them from liability. The discussion will briefly present how the cyberlaw landscape, and specifically the DMCA and CFAA federal anti-hacking laws, coupled with poorly drafted terms, create a reality wherein "bug hunting" could be legally dangerous. As background, Section 12.2 will also introduce the structure of bug bounty program terms.

Section 12.3 recommends some changes to the legal terms, in the interest of creating genuine "safe harbors" for bug hunting; it also provides policy recommendations to improve this emerging area of private law, which governs hundreds of thousands of researchers and vulnerabilities. Once safe harbor language is standardized, the bug bounty economy will become an alternate private legal regime in which white-hat hacking is celebrated through regulatory incentives.

12.2 Are Bug Bounties Operating as a "Private" Safe Harbor? Key Findings of the Legal Terms Survey

This section reviews the key findings of the bug bounty legal terms survey. While bug bounty programs share some commonalities and terminology, there is also a striking disparity among them (as well as notable exceptions). Most importantly, this section focuses on the paradoxical reality often created by the combination of a program's terms, drafted by private entities, and US anti-hacking laws. To set the stage, I provide a brief description of the relevant anti-hacking law provisions, as well as some background on the structure of bug bounty legal terms.

12.2.1 The Bug Bounty Economy Anti-Hacking Legal Landscape

The United States has a variety of "anti-hacking" laws, at both the federal and state level, that aim to curb harmful computer hacking practices, imposing both criminal and civil liabilities on certain forms of computer hacking. Yet, these laws often fail to legitimize necessary security research, creating barriers for bug hunters.[28] Prominent among these laws are the CFAA[29] and the DMCA.[30] These laws have an exterritorial nature and might affect hackers engaged in a bug bounty program regardless of where they are situated.[31]

12.2.1.1 The CFAA
The CFAA criminalizes, among other things, intentionally accessing "protected" computers and "obtaining information" "without authorization," or in a manner that exceeds authorization.[32] The definition of a "protected computer" is incredibly broad,[33] and includes "essentially any computer connected to the internet."[34] "Obtaining information" is defined as merely being able to read or observe the data,[35] which is often exactly what hackers need to do to demonstrate a proof of concept of vulnerability. Scholarship commonly refers to two categories of exceeding authorization: (i) "code-based" (circumventing technical barriers) and (ii) "contract-based" (accessing in violation of the contract terms). Leading scholar Orin Kerr also suggests a "norms-based" exceeding of authorization, which occurs once access violates "accepted social practices."[36] While a comprehensive review of these categories is beyond the scope of this chapter, it is clear that effective security research might involve any of the

above; therefore, it is necessary that the researcher be granted authorization and that the program terms clarify the scope of such authorization.

Moreover, while the recent decision by the Court of Appeals for the Ninth Circuit in *Facebook, Inc. v. Power Ventures* supports the proposition that a mere violation of terms does not constitute CFAA violation,[37] we should not rely on that decision in this case for a few reasons. First, effective security research often requires something *more* than the mere violation of written terms, meaning an actual circumvention of technical barriers. Second, that is the decision of one circuit, not the law of the land.[38] Third and most importantly, why should researchers even risk legal violation, pending courts' interpretation of the law, when drafters can easily clarify they are granted authorization to engage in research, if they follow the guidelines of the program (in terms of targeting the defined products, minimization, disclosure, etc.). As will be elaborated, some programs include this type of language, while others "force" hackers to exceed the "contract-based" authorization by imposing contracts that prohibit hackers from reverse engineering or tinkering, or even attempting to gain unauthorized access.

12.2.1.2   The DMCA

Section 1201(a)(1) of the Copyright Act (codified under the DMCA) prohibits circumvention of technological measures that effectively control access to software code (as copyright-protected work). This includes avoiding or bypassing measures, without authorization of the copyright owner.[39] Again, authorization is key. The Librarian of Congress exempted in the sixth triennial rulemaking proceeding, under certain conditions, "good-faith security research" of software for consumer-oriented products, motorized land vehicles, and implemented medical devices from the DMCA prohibitions on circumvention of copyrighted systems,[40] yet, such temporary exemption, recently extended and expanded in 2018, simultaneously requires that the security research, among others, will not violate any *applicable law* including the CFAA (or contract law),[41] meaning that it cannot violate the terms of use. Paradoxically, contractual language often continues to ban researchers from "circumvention" such as reverse engineering or de-complying,[42] rendering this important exception less effective.

To summarize, even after the relatively new DMCA exception, it is vital that bug bounty terms authorize access to researchers and allow them to perform circumvention. The contractual language is key to establishing authorized access under both the DMCA and CFAA, and is often what determines whether the hacker is liable.

12.2.1.3   The Department of Justice Framework for a Vulnerability Disclosure Program for Online Systems

In July 2017, the Department of Justice (DOJ) Cybersecurity Unit – the agency entrusted with shaping the national strategy concerning CFAA enforcement – released a memo proposing a framework for a vulnerability disclosure program in order to provide "a rubric of considerations that may inform the content of vulnerability disclosure policies."[43] The importance of this document for each platform and company engaged in designing or employing a bug bounty cannot be stressed enough. Most importantly, the framework supports this chapter's view that a clause *explicitly* authorizing access and conduct under the CFAA would help to mitigate the legal risks associated with noncompliance with the CFAA.

The framework "outlines a process for designing a vulnerability disclosure program that will *clearly describe authorized vulnerability disclosure* and discovery conduct, thereby *substantially reducing* the likelihood that such described activities will result in a civil or criminal violation of law under the Computer Fraud and Abuse Act (18 U.S.C. § 1030)."[44] The framework, however, does not discuss contract law or the DMCA (although by ensuring compliance with the CFAA, the language partially supports the DMCA exemption). Therefore, I suggest that similar wording be included for the purpose of these laws, and most importantly, that platforms and programs refrain from subjecting hackers to conflicting contractual terms that stand in tension with the purpose of the DOJ's framework.

Part III of the framework specifically addresses the drafting of the bug bounty policy, which should be one that "accurately and unambiguously captures the organization's intent."[45] In a nutshell, the framework suggests, among other things, that bug bounty terms should "describe authorized and unauthorized conduct in plain, easily understood terms," "[a]void using vague jargon or ambiguous technical language to describe critical aspects of the policy, such as acceptable and unacceptable conduct, specifically identify the network components or data which are within and outside the scope of the program in the policy," and "explain the consequences of complying – and not complying – with the policy." The DOJ framework suggests, for example, that the policy state that:

1) The organization *will not to pursue* civil action for accidental, good faith violations of its policy or initiate a complaint to law enforcement for unintentional violations.
2) The organization considers activities conducted consistent with the policy to *constitute "authorized" conduct* under the CFAA.
3) If legal action is initiated by a third party against a party who complied with the vulnerability disclosure policy, the organization will take steps to make it known, either to the public or to the court, that the individual's actions were conducted in compliance with the policy.[46]

Section 12.4 builds on this proposed language and addresses some additional recommendations.

12.2.2 Bug Bounty Legal Terms: General Structure

As previously mentioned, bug bounty legal terms operate as a contract between the hacker and the sponsoring company and set the expectations between the parties.[47] Indeed, this is another manifestation of the use of boilerplate contract language to regulate a highly technological field – one that the law on the books sometimes struggles to govern effectively.[48]

Bug bounty terms usually follow a simple structure,[49] a combination of the following: (i) Introduction; (ii) Technical Scope and guidelines (accepted and non-eligible vulnerabilities, list of targeted products/servers/systems, commitment to maintain system integrity and to minimize harm and risk to users' privacy)[50]; (iii) Eligibility guidelines which pertain to originality, novelty (first to file a bug/report), nonacceptance of employees' report, ineligibility of social engineering and automatic tools, etc.; (iv) Reward guidelines, including explanations of how the company decides the amount rewarded, tables illustrating how much the company will pay for each bug (according to its criticality), guidance on how to claim a bounty, and on exclusion of hackers from countries sanctioned by the United States; (v) Disclosure guidelines, including proof of concept requirements, (in some cases) a template report,[51] and information on whether the hacker is allowed to disclose the report; and finally, usually at the end (vi) general legal terms.

While the majority of programs surveyed in the sample did specifically include legal terms, there are programs – such as Mozilla and FitBit – that do not. It is also noteworthy that some programs do not refer to the legal terms as binding legal contracts, and avoid presenting the legal terms jointly with the technical guidelines. Moreover, some platforms choose to draft the terms in combination with explanations and a "softer" language.[52] For example, Uber separates the legal and technical terms of the program published on the HackerOne platform, and only provides a hyperlink to the legal terms.[53] Microsoft includes the detailed legal terms and notice of the bug bounty separately under the "Frequently Asked Questions" page, although they clearly are expected to operate as a binding agreement.[54] Obviously, this practice could confuse hackers participating in the program, who should not be expected to perform in-depth searches just to receive adequate disclosure of the terms with which they are required to comply. The separation of the legal terms from all the other general and technical guidelines invites unnecessary confusion.

If a program is operated through a hackers' platform, the various legal terms of the platform will apply *in addition* to the specific terms of the program (each of the platforms include four to five separate guidelines or terms, which apply to all programs initiated under the platform – in other words, hundreds of programs). This creates potential conflicts between terms that might lead to confusion, and discrepancies between the general platform terms and the specific program terms may arise. The terms of the program supersede the general terms only with respect to disclosure.[55] While the default under HackerOne is to disclose vulnerabilities reported after 30 days (pending no objection of the parties), the Bugcrowd default is not to disclose reported vulnerabilities.[56] The platforms do not elaborate on how conflicts in nondisclosure-related areas or other discrepancies between their terms and the companies' terms should be resolved. This means that hackers are expected to master (and read) around 20–30 pages before submitting a bug, and also debate how to address potential conflicts: a considerable informational burden.

Aside from legal language related to anti-hacking laws (addressed in the following section), the survey identifies few standard legal clauses. Programs often prohibit public disclosure of vulnerabilities or refuse to reward vulnerabilities disclosed to the public, prior to the resolution of the bug.[57] One program, Net Gear, specifically alerts hackers that they will be subject to liability, and will breach contract, if they disclose information without prior consent.[58] Other programs use more "relaxed" phrasing, stating that researchers should allow sufficient time for the company to patch the vulnerability prior to releasing the report.[59] Of course, disclosure with respect to resolved vulnerabilities operates as a reputational market mechanism for companies to improve security. In this regard, standardized language that supports responsible disclosure is more desirable. Nondisclosure of reported, fixed and mitigated bugs undermines consumers' ability to assess the security level of the products and services they use and buy.[60]

In addition, platforms and companies often grant themselves copyright license in the report written and submitted by the hacker, clarifying that the hacker is the report owner. Some companies reserve the right to share the report with third-party vendors that might be affected by its findings. More generally, platforms' and companies' terms often exclude from the program researchers originating from countries sanctioned by the United States, and emphasize the hacker's tax liability. All of these issues are important and do not pose any substantial difficulty in the context of creating safe harbors.

12.2.3 The Bug Bounty Catch 22

Although claiming to operate as safe harbors, many programs include language that cannot be reconciled with the practice of security research, does not explicitly provide the contractual "authorization" that minimizes the hacker's risk, and generally undermines the purpose of the program. This is demonstrated in the terms of both platforms and companies.

Most commonly, the legal language requires that hackers comply with "all applicable laws," or forbids tests that "violate any law," instead of granting hackers clear authorization to construct a safe harbor under the DMCA and the CFAA. Similarly, hacker platform terms require hackers to represent that their actions do not violate third-party intellectual property rights,[61] and that their conduct generally complies with all applicable laws, domestically and internationally.[62]

This practice shifts the legal risk to the hacker.[63] Other programs do not include any reference to compliance with laws, thereby creating uncertainty.[64]

To this general finding, there are some exceptions: a minority of programs specifically include language that exempts hackers from liability, noting in the contract that they will not take legal action against hackers who comply with the guidelines.[65] An interesting example is General Motors, which specifically states that hackers should not violate any civil law "other than those that would result only in claims by GM." This language could be clearer and only addresses civil law (although both the DMCA and the CFAA could potentially give rise to criminal liability), but GM at least recognizes that effective security research, almost by definition, will result in claims under the law. While a contractual commitment not to pursue legal action is a positive step forward, specific authorization to access the system negates the legal basis for a possible criminal and civil complaint, as long as the hacker is within scope, of course, and therefore is more desirable.

In some cases hackers might get mixed signals with respect to the "authorized access." For example, Google defines the "scope" of its program as "virtually all the content in the following domains: *.http://google.com, *.http://youtube.com, *.http://blogger.com." Moreover, the combination of the sponsoring company general bug bounty policy and specific platform terms could result in discrepancies. For example, Bugcrowd limitations on program participation are rather broad, denying participation from all citizens of a country or region that is subject to US or any other "sovereign country sanctions or embargoes."[66] Yet, many programs operating on the platform only prohibit individuals from US trade sanctions' lists.

As mentioned, under some program terms hackers might be forced into contractual breach and civil and criminal liability. These programs specifically refer in their bug bounty terms to the general EULA terms, which prohibit reverse engineering and other tinkering and researching tools fundamental to security research – and sometimes even prohibit the mere attempt to gain unauthorized access. Instead of granting researchers permission to take such actions, the bug bounty terms prohibit them from doing so under contract, thereby undermining the DMCA exemption for security research discussed above. Notable examples of this practice include AVG terms stating that the submission of a bug "constitutes acceptance of the AVG End User License Agreement." The AVG End User License Agreement further stipulates that users "may not… (iii) except as expressly authorized by law,[67] (A) reverse engineer, disassemble, decompile, translate, reconstruct, transform or extract any [software] or any portion of the [software]…, or (B) change, modify or otherwise alter any [software]."

Facebook's bug bounty terms include a commitment not to sue hackers who follow the program guidelines, but also stipulate that "[the] use of Facebook services…, including for purposes of this [bug bounty] program, is subject to Facebook's Terms and Policies and the terms and policies of any member of the

Facebook family of companies whose services you use."[68] Meanwhile, WhatsApp's terms state that the users:

> must not (or assist others to) access, use, copy, adapt, modify, prepare... or otherwise exploit our Services...directly or through automated means: (a) reverse engineer, alter, modify, create derivative works from, decompile, or extract code from our Services; (b) send, store, or transmit viruses or other harmful computer code through or onto [their] Services; (c) gain or *attempt to gain* unauthorized access to [their] Services or systems...[69]

More problematic are bug bounty terms that explicitly deny authorization to access. For example, Alibaba's bug bounty terms specifically note: "No license or permission is given to any penetration or attack against any of Alibaba systems."[70]

12.2.4 Safe Harbor Language Matters

To understand the current legal risks imposed on hackers when companies and platforms *merely refrain* from including clear exempting safe harbor language, one must learn the story of security researcher Kevin Finisterre. On 28 August 2017, the well-known drone manufacturing company DJI announced its launch of a public bug bounty program.[71] At the time, DJI did not publish detailed guidelines, technical scope, or legal terms concerning the bug bounty. It did, however, state that "[s]tarting today [August 28, 2017], bug reports can be sent...for review by technical experts," that "[r]ewards for qualifying bugs will range from $100 to $30,000, depending on the potential impact of the threat," and that DJI was "developing a website with full program terms and a standardized form for reporting potential threats related to DJI's servers, apps or hardware."[72] In the days that followed, Finisterre discovered a vulnerability relating to DJI's servers, one that allegedly leaked identifiable information about DJI customers according to reports. He started to communicate with the DJI bug bounty team and began preparing his bug report.

Since DJI had yet to provide a clearer scope of authorization and technical boundaries, Finisterre, according to reports, communicated in e-mail with DJI's bug bounty team and received additional confirmation that servers (the subject of his security research) were within the scope of the bug bounty. Later, according to reports, an additional e-mail confirmed that his bug submission was rewarded with the top reward of $30 000.[73]

It could be claimed that DJI's announcement of its bug bounty implied the scope of the program: the company stated that the bug bounty would start *as of that day*, and that the "potential threats" were "related to DJI's servers, apps or hardware."[74] According to reports, DJI issued a draft legal letter to

Finisterre during the negotiations over the "bounty agreement" that finalized the terms of payment. In the letter, DJI allegedly threatened him with legal action under the CFAA, claiming that he accessed servers without authorized access,[75] and asking him to sign a one-sided agreement, according to Finisterre, that left him legally exposed. Finisterre ended up withdrawing from the bug bounty, foregoing the reward, and publishing his report along with his experience.[76]

Although DJI has its own version of the story,[77] much of this misunderstanding could have been prevented if DJI had launched a bug bounty with clear guidelines on disclosure and technical scope. More importantly, if the guidelines had included clear authorization to access the system and a commitment not to pursue legal action (instead of what seems like implied consent from the announcement, and the confirmation allegedly given to Finisterre by e-mail, according to reports), the company would have found it harder to send "draft" legal letters and employ them as a questionable negotiation technique. This case illustrates the potentially risky position in which hackers might find themselves, and the disparity in bargaining powers between the parties. Interestingly, a day after Finisterre published his story, DJI published a policy for its bug bounty including clear safe harbor language.[78] Indeed, clear bug bounty legal terms (and technical scope) work to a company's benefit, by creating a concrete legal basis for complaint if a hacker intentionally violates the terms of the program regarding scope or disclosure.

This case signals to the bug bounty industry not only that safe harbor legal language matters, but also that the magnitude of legal risk that is shifted toward hackers if such language is not adopted *ex ante*. Lack of safe harbor leaves hackers exposed to legal threats *ex post*, as it creates ambiguity regarding the boundaries of the hacker operation, both technically and legally. These threats could later be used in negotiations to stifle disclosure or even, in other cases, to silence law violations or cover data breaches. Conversely, if hackers avoid participating in programs with insufficient terms, they could increase the legal terms' *salience* – thereby creating a market incentive for platforms and companies to improve the quality of the provided safe harbor, and further attract the best talent. With time, this will create a "race to the top" over the quality of bug bounty terms, and help mitigate the bargaining disparity between hackers, platforms, and companies.

As previous sections illustrated, the legal bug bounty landscape is controlled by boilerplate language offered on a "take it or leave it" basis. Generally, as in other standard-form contracts and forms of private ordering, that transactional structure creates market failures if the quality of terms is not controlled in the market (i.e. terms are *non*-salient).[79] Interestingly, the bug bounty economy has strong reputation and network mechanisms that enable it to express concerns over low-quality terms – a gateway to improving individual hackers' bargaining power and pushing toward standardization. For example, hackers use Twitter and inner circles to share their negative or positive experiences with a specific bug bounty; and platforms, which control a significant volume of the bug bounty market, have the ability to serve as collective bargainers. The following sections illustrate additional recommendations for how the power of contracts could be harvested to foster safe harbors.

12.3 Policy Recommendations: Toward a Private Safe Harbor

Hackers participating in bug bounties want to play by the rules – but as we learned, the rules often do not let them. Therefore, the rules should change. While platforms and companies have an understandable and legitimate interest in minimizing their risk, drafters of bug bounty terms should not include terms that stand in direct tension with the purpose of the program: incentivizing and enabling effective testing and security research. Each of the main players in the bug bounty industry can do their part to change this reality. The following recommendations are informed by the latest framework suggested by the US DOJ Cybersecurity Unit, in July 2017.

12.3.1 Increase of Terms Salience

The bug bounty economy exhibits the same agency problems and market failures as other markets regulated by unilaterally drafted boilerplate language that operates as private law.[80] Since individual hackers have a limited ability to evaluate the legal implications of bug bounty terms, and there is a disparity in information and negotiation power between individual researchers, platforms, and sponsoring companies, it is possible that the terms might shift the legal risk to the researcher. If the bug bounty market does not police the quality of the terms, meaning that terms are *non*-salient (i.e. they do not affect consumers' decisions – in this case, a hacker's decision to participate in a specific program),[81] there is no incentive for the sponsoring companies or programs to provide better terms. Once individual researchers attach reputational or economic value to the quality of legal terms, drafters will have a strong incentive to increase their quality in order to attract the best talent.

Individual hackers could take steps to increase the salience of bug bounty terms by refusing to engage in programs that put them in legal risk. Indeed, sometimes it "takes a crowd" to create change. The research community should make sure that program quality is evaluated on how well it minimizes hackers' legal risks, not solely according to the monetary or reputational rewards – thereby increasing the *salience* of the legal terms. In this respect, hackers' platforms and companies must provide hackers simplified disclosures and promote competition over the contractual terms of the program, creating a "race to the top" mentality. Platforms could also consider implementing a reputational system for the contractual terms of bug bounty programs, similar to the one used to evaluate the reputations of individual researchers.[82]

12.3.2 Clear Safe Harbor Language

The most urgent takeaway from this survey is the crucial need to eliminate the paradoxical examples of bug bounty legal terms that include limitations on tinkering, de-complying, reverse engineering, and the like. Security researchers who perform bug hunting should be exempted from the general EULA terms, and programs should include exempting language from any legal liability, as well as an obligation not to prosecute and sue hackers who follow the guidelines.[83] These guidelines should not state generally that hackers are not allowed to breach any law, if they do not clearly create a "safe harbor" for bug hunting by authorizing access to the targeted systems.[84] Hackers are unable to conform with anti-hacking laws if such authorization is not granted, making it pointless to simply include vague statements that hackers should not be violating laws. As noted, some of the companies do not include any legal language in their terms. This practice is also not ideal: not only do the terms neglect to grant specific authorization to access systems but also they might suggest to the researcher that there are no legal limitations to his ability to test the systems.

The terms should also include specific authorization (with clear scope) for the purpose of the CFAA, the DMCA, and other anti-hacking laws. The proposed (example) language under the DOJ framework could be used to that effect, but it would be useful to broaden it to encompass the DMCA and other relevant laws (e.g. "the organization considers activities conducted consistent with the policy to constitute 'authorized' conduct under the Computer Fraud and Abuse Act, [*the DMCA, and any applicable law*]."[85] This commitment should be binding under the contractual terms.[86] In addition, companies that hire hacker platforms should undertake this commitment to not prosecute "the crowd" also toward the platforms, allowing platforms to enforce such contractual commitment in the name of hackers.

Simultaneously, and as mentioned above, companies should make sure that any additional contractual terms imposed on hackers (such as "community guidelines" or EULAs) do not undermine such exempting language by prohibiting the use of various research techniques.[87] Platforms could also review clients' terms to ensure the legal interests of participating hackers are safeguarded. Platforms should enable hackers to comply with their representations and the law, and mitigate their legal risk by negotiating the legal terms of the programs directly with the companies. In addition, I suggest that platforms redraft their default general guidelines to include language exempting hackers from liability if they follow the guidelines of the program, in line with the DOJ framework and the above recommendations. Platforms could also consider including language facilitating third-party vulnerability disclosure (as well authorization and appropriate copyright sub-license). Since the platforms' terms operate as an additional layer of agreements, and they can encourage (or even require) their clients to adhere to the DOJ framework, platforms have a key role in ensuring that hackers operate under a safe harbor. At minimum, platforms should commit to review all terms and inform hackers when terms are not aligned with the DOJ framework and proposed recommendations, as a reputational mechanism.

12.3.3 Standardization of Bug Bounty Legal Terms Across Platforms, Industries, and Sponsors

Standardization of bug bounty legal terms across industries and sponsors, in line with the DOJ framework, and akin to the licenses employed by Creative Commons and the open-source industry,[88] could reduce the informational burden and increase hackers' awareness of terms (salience). It could also signal whether a particular platform or company conforms with the standard terms that are considered best practice. Finally, it could reduce the drafting costs of the platform or sponsoring program, as well as the transactional costs. While some organizations (such as governmental or financial organizations) might require adjustments, generally the legal concerns of bug bounties' sponsors and platforms are similar and could be addressed in standardized language.

Moreover, standardization should be used to ensure that hackers have authorized access to any third-parties' data or components[89] implemented in the bug bounty administrator product/network, and to facilitate coordinated disclosure of third-party vulnerabilities found (and ethically disclosed).[90] Companies and platforms should coordinate to ensure that such clauses are included in all terms, facilitating a best practice mentality in the industry.

The rise of Internet of Things (IoT) devices, which include hundreds of libraries each, all with different terms dictating the limits of the research, further mandates clearly defined exemptions for friendly hackers. Platforms and companies should ensure that no third-party components or data are within the scope of the program – and, if they are, that the administrator of the bug bounty obtains sufficient authorization so as to not to subject the hacker (and the sponsoring company) to liability.

The DOJ's framework specifically states that bug bounty administrators should "[c]onsider whether any of the network components or data within the scope of the vulnerability disclosure program implicates third-party interests and, therefore, whether they should be excluded from the program entirely or require the organization to obtain additional authorization before including them in the program."[91] Given the complexity of identifying third-parties' interests in multilayered products and technologies, the industry can consider introducing an identical standard language among the bug bounty administrators that will enable authorization as well as coordinate disclosure in case a third-party vulnerability is identified. As the DOJ framework suggests, "[a]bsent an agreement with the [third party], the organization implementing the vulnerability disclosure program may lack the authority to authorize others to access the provider's servers as part of the vulnerability disclosure program."[92]

Utilizing agreed-upon standard language in all agreements with third-party vendors and bug bounty administrators could be helpful. Third parties will also benefit from crowd assistance in identifying vulnerabilities. Therefore, language that enables bug bounty administrators to share reports with relevant third parties (with the applicable copyright sub-license) is also important, and could be mutually agreed upon by different administrators. For example, platforms can require such language in their client contracts and policies, thereby creating, fairly easily, mutual agreement between their clients. Platforms and companies could consider how to cross-subsidize rewards in such cases, or create a separate mutual fund akin to the open-software/internet bug bounty,[93] so hackers will be compensated for third-parties' vulnerabilities as well.

With the release of the DOJ framework, it is more important than ever to review all terms and aspire to facilitate one contractual language that will operate as the best practice benchmark and model for the industry. Companies that do not operate under this model will have a market-based incentive to adopt better terms to attract hackers.[94]

12.3.4 Improved Disclosures and Educational Efforts

Lack of proper disclosure might confuse individual researchers and reduce terms salience. Companies should disclose key legal prohibitions alongside the technical definitions of the scope of the program, instead of sending hackers to terms buried in (multiple) hyperlinked contracts. In this respect, the DOJ framework notes that bug bounty administrators should "[m]ake the vulnerability disclosure policy easily accessible and widely available."[95] The legal scope of the program should be disclosed by companies and platforms in as much as the technical scope, in order to ensure compliance.

Companies and platforms could further simplify the legal language of the terms: disclosure should be made in clear language, accompanied with "you can do" and "you can't do" illustrations, and guidance should be provided.[96] This is aligned with the DOJ framework suggestions that the "authorized and unauthorized conduct [will be described] in plain, easily understood terms," that the program will be drafted "accurately and unambiguously," and that companies avoid "vague jargon or ambiguous technical language to describe critical aspects of the policy, such as acceptable and unacceptable conduct."[97] Furthermore, platforms should educate hackers on recent developments in the anti-hacking legal landscape, including recommendations for what to focus on when reviewing bug bounties' terms.

12.3.5 Individual Hackers as Collective Bargainers

The security industry has been in dialog with regulators to facilitate white-hat hacking,[98] yet the voice of the individual hacker is still often unheard. As this chapter illustrates, cyberlaw is changing, and it is shaped not only by regulators, but also by "private law" via the boilerplate, "take it or leave it" language of companies' EULA and programs' contractual terms, which often do not attend to hackers' "legal" needs. In addition, the terms place an informational burden on hackers (especially if the hacker is participating in a platform, and thus must read an additional set of terms), sometimes requiring them to be legal experts who know "all applicable laws" in order to comply and can resolve discrepancies between terms.[99]

As in all organizations, there is a risk of an agency problem when the legal incentives of the hacker platforms, the hackers, and the sponsoring companies are not aligned: one manifestation of this problem is terms drafted in a manner that shields the organization and platform, shifting the risk to hackers. Conflicts of interest will inevitably arise. For years, individuals in other industries facing similar realities (in other arenas) have united. Creators and authors stood against record companies, publishers, and even regulators that sought to delineate their rights and impose on them legal risks that prevented them from being (legally) free to do what they do best. With the help of others, they formed organizations such as the Authors' Alliance, to advocate for their rights.

This research demonstrates how hackers can improve their position by negotiating simple changes in contractual language and increasing terms salience. Such efforts can potentially affect the legal risks of tens of thousands of hackers engaged daily in bug hunting. It is just one example of how hackers can advocate as a united front for mitigating their risks and ensuring their rights. The hacker community should not depend on the fact that companies often neglect to enforce contractual language, but rather demand that the terms exempt friendly researchers. This will reduce the barriers to bug bounties and provide hackers with additional incentive to engage in friendly hacking.

12.4 Conclusion

As the practice of sharing vulnerabilities and cybersecurity information is looming in both private and governmental realms,[100] it has become more important than ever before to shield hackers seeking to participate in legitimate vulnerabilities trading from legal risks, and to incentivize participation in bug bounties. Yet, currently, the terms often do not facilitate safe harbors for hackers to engage in bug hunting. Companies and hacker platforms require hackers to comply with "any applicable laws," without allowing them to do so: not authorizing access to targeted systems, subjecting them to EULAs that prevent reverse engineering and tinkering, expecting hackers to become legal experts and resolve discrepancies between conflicting terms. Hackers want to play by the rules,[101] and avoid black markets,[102] but the rules would not let them: therefore, the rules should change.

I have proposed simple changes that could be easily implemented: terms should exempt hackers who follow the program guidelines, and clearly authorize access; simple disclosures should be implemented and paradoxical terms that subject hackers to EULAs should be amended. Hacker platforms should implement these steps in their general guidelines, ensure that participating programs do the same, and provide further guidance to the participating hackers on terms they should expect to see. Terms could be standardized, and platforms could enforce the companies' commitments not to prosecute or seek damages when hackers comply with the program terms. Once standardization of bug bounty legal language is achieved, the bug bounty economy will become an alternate private legal regime in which white-hat hacking is celebrated through regulatory incentives.

Indeed, this paper is just one manifestation of a general narrative in the cyberlaw landscape: the law continues to struggle to facilitate white-hat hacking security research practice, resulting in various anomalies, and often leaving hackers who seek to do good legally exposed. It is crucial that a least on their parts, entities seeking to facilitate security research – and that are engaged in private "cyber" ordering through boilerplate contracting – craft terms that support such research, instead of undermining it.

Acknowledgments

The author would like to thank the Center for Long-Term Cybersecurity at the University of Berkeley, California for supporting this project and future related projects it entails, and professor Chris Jay Hoofnagle for his valuable advice. Following this paper, both bug bounty platforms Bugcrowd and Hackerone introduced initiatives to support the efforts underlined in this paper. I would like to especially thank Dropbox for their pioneering efforts in this field and Bugcrowd for collaborating on the Disclose.io project.

Notes

1 For an explanation of why costs of data breaches may rise as the number of code lines grow exponentially, see "Why Everything is Hackable: Computer Security is Broken from Top to Bottom," *The Economist*, April 8, 2017, http://www.economist.com/news/science-and-technology/21720268-consequences-pile-up-things-are-starting-improve-computer-security.

2 This disruptive technological revolution is commonly referred to as the "Internet of Things" (IoT), where the "[i]nternet [is able] to reach out into the real world of physical objects."Mohamed Ali Feki et al., "The Internet of Things: The Next Technological Revolution," *Computer* 46, no. 2 (2013): 24–25. See also Sathish Alampalayam Kumar et al., "Security in Internet of Things: Challenges, Solutions and Future Directions," 49th Hawaii International Conference on System Sciences (HICSS), 2016, 5772, which discusses the challenges that IoT presents to security and suggests a new framework for IoT security.

3 A report issued by IBM estimates the costs of an individual breach at an average of $4 million. IBM, "Cost of Data Breach Study Data Breaches," http://www-03. ibm.com/security/data-breach/. A report done by Cybersecurity Ventures predicts that cybercrime's overall cost will reach a total of $6 trillion by 2021, while Juniper Research predicts a total of $2.1 trillion by 2019, a four-time increase since 2015, and estimates that cybercrime will cost businesses over $2 trillion by 2019. See, respectively, Steve Morgan, "2016 Cybercrime Report," Cybersecurity Ventures, 2017, http://cybersecurityventures.com/ hackerpocalypse-cybercrime-report-2016E; and Juniper Research, "Cybercrime Will Cost Businesses Over $2 Trillion By 2019," https://www.juniperresearch. com/press/press-releases/cybercrime-cost-businesses-over-2trillion.

4 The legal and business risks associated with data breaches are complex, and range from the FTC and other regulators' investigations to M&A complications and consumer-class actions. See Federal Trade Commission, "Privacy & Data Security Update: 2016," January 2016–December 2016, https://www.ftc.gov/ system/files/documents/reports/privacy-data-security-update-2016/privacy_ and_data_security_update_2016_web.pdf, which reports that as of the end of 2016, the FTC brought over 60 cases related to information security against companies engaged in "unfair or deceptive" practices. See also Steven Davidoff Solomon, "How Yahoo's Data Breach Could Affect Its Deal With Verizon," *The New York Times*, September 23, 2016, https://www.nytimes.com/2016/09/24/ business/dealbook/how-yahoos-data-breach-could-affect-its-deal-with-verizon.html, which discusses the relationship between data breaches and "material adverse change" (MAC) clauses in M&A agreements, in light of the recent Verizon-Yahoo! merger deal. Eventually, the massive data breach Yahoo suffered resulted in price reductions and renegotiations. See, e.g.James Fontanella-Khan and Hannah Kuchler, "Yahoo Agrees to $350m Price Cut in Verizon Deal," *Financial Times*, February 21, 2017, https://www.ft.com/ content/7541c82a-f843-11e6-9516-2d969e0d3b65. For a brief introduction to the corporate liability risks associated with data breaches and how bug bounties could arguably assist in limiting them, see Amit Elazari Bar On, "Bug Bounty Programs as a Corporate Governance 'Best Practice' Mechanism," *Berkeley Technology Law Journal Blog*, March 22, 2017, http://btlj.org/2017/03/ bug-bounty-programs-as-a-corporate-governance-best-practice-mechanism.

5 Berkeley Center for Law & Technology, the UC Berkeley School of Information and the International Computer Science Institute, "Cybersecurity Research: Addressing the Legal Barriers and Disincentives," workshop convened by the Berkeley Center for Law & Technology, UC Berkeley School of Information, and the International Computer Science Institute, September 28, 2015, https://www.ischool.berkeley.edu/sites/default/files/cybersec-research-nsf-workshop.pdf, 5. See also Bugcrowd, "2017 State of Bug Bounty Report – Bug crowd's third annual analysis of the global bug bounty economy," 2017, https://pages.bugcrowd.com/hubfs/Bugcrowd-2017-State-of-Bug-Bounty-Report.pdf. A comprehensive list of bug bounty programs, enacted by leading companies such as Google and Facebook, is available here: HackerOne, "Bug Bounty Programs," https://hackerone.com/bug-bounty-programs.

6 Bugcrowd reported an increase in 2017 in the all-time average payout per bug (on its platform): from $295 to $451. There are, of course, larger bounties. Bugcrowd occasionally distributes bounties in the amount of $10 000–$15 000. See Bugcrowd, "2017 State of Bug Bounty Report." Other programs, such as Apple's program, suggest rewards reaching up to $200 000 for highly critical bugs. See Nicole Perlroth, "Apple Will Pay a 'Bug Bounty' to Hackers Who Report Flaws," *New York Times*, August 4, 2016, https://www.nytimes.com/2016/08/05/technology/apple-will-pay-a-bug-bounty-to-hackers-who-report-flaws.html. For an in-depth analysis of how three tech giants – Facebook, Google, and Microsoft – specifically utilize bug bounties to improve the security of their products and the institutional variations between those programs, see Andreas Kuehn and Ryan Ellis, "Bug Bounty Programs: Institutional Variation and the Different Meanings of Security," in this volume.

7 See Bugcrowd, "2017 State of Bug Bounty Report," which reports that 53 332 hackers shared vulnerabilities via the platform as of March 2017; and HackerOne, "The 2016 Bug Bounty Hacker Report," September 13, 2016, https://www.hackerone.com/blog/hacker-surey-report-2016, which notes that over 70 000 hackers submitted reports via the HackerOne platform. Bugcrowd has paid out $6 392 992 for 52 000 valid vulnerability submissions. HackerOne reported over $17M in royalties. Google VRP reported $9M paid out since 2010, and Facebook reported over $5M paid out since 2013; Mozilla and Firefox reported approximately $3M since 2010, and Microsoft over $1.5M. See also Mozilla, "Bug Bounty Program," https://www.mozilla.org/en-US/security/bug-bounty.

8 For a description of the new bug bounty launched by Hansa, a dark net marketplace, see Catalin Cimpanu, "Dark Web Marketplace Launches Bug Bounty Program with $10,000 Rewards," *BleepingComputer*, February 6, 2017, https://www.bleepingcomputer.com/news/security/dark-web-marketplace-launches-bug-bounty-program-with-10-000-rewards.

9 Recently, Senators Maggie Hassan and Rob Portman introduced a bill titled the "Hack Department of Homeland Security (DHS) Act." The bill aims to establish

a federal framework for conducting bug bounties in the Department of Homeland Defense, which is in charge of securing all "gov" domains. It contains a specific provision about ensuring researchers a safe harbor under the CFAA and "similar provisions of law." See S. 1281, 115th Cong. §2(b)(2) (D) (2017): "consult with the Attorney General on how to ensure that computer security specialists and security researchers who participate in the pilot program are protected from prosecution under section 1030 of title 18, United States Code, and similar provisions of law for specific activities authorized under the pilot program." See also Maggie Hassan, "Senators Hassan, Portman Introduce Bipartisan Bill to Strengthen Cyber Defenses at Department of Homeland Security," May 26, 2017, https://www.hassan. senate.gov/news/press-releases/senators-hassan-portman-introduce-bipartisan-bill-to-strengthen-cyber-defenses-at-department-of-homeland-security.

10 See Bugcrowd, "2017 State of Bug Bounty Report," 6, reporting both the expansion and diversification of programs launched on the Bugcrowd platform and all other known programs. According to the report, "Industry diversification continued this year with 140% combined growth in the top 5 fastest growing industries: automotive (400% growth), leisure/travel (300% growth), computer networking (143% growth), healthcare (133% growth), and financial services (94% growth) industries."

11 See Netscape, "Netscape Announces 'Netscape Bugs Bounty' with Release of Netscape Navigator 2.0 Beta," October 10, 1995, https://web.archive.org/ web/19970501041756/http://www101.netscape.com/newsref/pr/ newsrelease48.html; and Andreas Kuehn and Milton Mueller, "Analyzing Bug Bounty Programs: An Institutional Perspective on the Economics of Software Vulnerabilities," 2014 TPRC/42nd Research Conference on Communication, Information and Internet Policy, George Mason University School of Law, Arlington, Virginia, September 12–14, 2014, 4, https://papers.ssrn.com/sol3/ papers.cfm?abstract_id=2418812.

12 This is Eric Raymond's famous "Linus Law," one of open-source culture's cornerstones, coined in Eric S. Raymond, "The Cathedral and the Bazaar: Musings on Linux and Open Source by an Accidental Revolutionary," Sebastopol: O'Reilly Media, 1999.

13 Ibid., 30.

14 As Maillart et al. put it, "bug bounty programs offer a way to capitalize on these diverse environments provided by the involvement of many security researchers." Thomas Maillart et al., "Given Enough Eyeballs, all Bugs are Shallow? Revisiting Eric Raymond with Bug Bounty Programs," *Journal of Cybersecurity* 3, no. 2 (2017): 81, 88.

15 See Matthew Finifter, Devdatta Akhawe, and David Wagner, "An Empirical Study of Vulnerability Rewards Programs," in 22nd USENIX Security Symposium, Washington, DC, August 14–16, 2013, 13, which presents data from two leading programs (Mozilla and Google) for the period 2010–2013, and reports that the

overall cost of bug bounty, per day, is on average $485 (on Chrome) or $658 (on Firefox), compared to the cost of highly skilled security engineer estimated at $500 per day. As the authors note, while the cost of the entire program resembles the cost of hiring one engineer, "the benefit of a VRP far outweighs that of a single security researcher because each of these VRPs finds many more vulnerabilities than any one researcher is likely to be able to find" (8).

16 For example, one of the most comprehensive studies done in the field of bug bounties is the dissertation of Mingyi Zhao, *Discovering and Mitigating Software Vulnerabilities Through Large-scale Collaboration* (The Pennsylvania State University, 2016), https://etda.libraries.psu.edu/files/final_submissions/13128. Zhao analyzed the effectiveness of "large-scale collaborations" for security research, and proposed new allocation mechanisms to reduce duplicated and invalid reports (which according to Zhao's findings, account for the majority of the submissions) (iii, 116). See also, in other research areas, Finifter et al.; Kuehn and Mueller; and Keman Huang et al., "Diversity or Concentration? Hackers' Strategy for Working Across Multiple Bug Bounty Programs," 2016, 1–2, http://www.ieee-security.org/TC/SP2016/poster-abstracts/13-poster_abstract.pdf. Huang et al. show how hackers strategize their participation in bug bounties, and find that "most hackers concentrate on few programs, empirically less than 5." As they point out, "It is important for hackers to balance between diversity and concentration [...], initially focus on few programs and then diversify to multiprograms to build reputation in the community." More recently, Maillart et al. performed an empirical investigation of the strategic interactions among program sponsors, platforms, and hackers; they found that there are inherent incentives for mobility across programs, and recommended that bug bounties "capture a larger market share by reducing transaction costs and thus offering an alternative to uncertainties associated with the black market." Indeed, this paper suggests a pathway toward decreasing the legal uncertainness currently associated with bug bounties.

17 See, e.g. Mingyi, 103, comparing the percentage of invalid reports, spam, or "noise" received in four major bug bounty programs: the Bugcrowd platform, the HackerOne platform, Facebook, and Google. In future novel research, that involved Mingyi as well, Laszka et al. further found that "that rules with more content (e.g. more detailed list of included/excluded areas and issues) and explicit statements on duplication, disclosure, etc. are associated with more bugs resolved." See Laszka, A., Zhao, M., Malbari, A. and Grossklags, J. "The Rules of Engagement for Bug Bounty Programs." Proceedings of the Twenty-Second International Conference on Financial Cryptography and Data Security (FC) (forthcoming), manuscript at 15. That finding could be associated with the maturity of the program as well, as there is a learning effect whereby companies amend and extend policies as their interaction with the hunters' community expands.

18 As Kirsch notes, "[w]hat's most troubling for the grey hat hacking community about these bug bounty programs is that nearly all hacking under bug bounty programs remains illegal if the contractual language of the program is not properly crafted."Cassandra Kirsch, "The Gray Hat Hacker: Reconciling Cyberspace Reality and the Law," *Northern Kentucky Law Review* 41 (2014): 383, 397.

19 See EFF, "A 'Grey Hat' Guide," https://www.eff.org/pages/grey-hat-guide; Trevor A. Thompson, "Terrorizing the Technological Neighborhood Watch: The Alienation and Deterrence of the White Hats Under the CFAA," *Florida State University Law Review* 36, no. 3 (2009): 537; and Kirsch. In the context of private ordering, see "Cybersecurity Research: Addressing the Legal Barriers and Disincentives," 6. This paper explains how private ordering could affect essential research efforts, by limiting tinkering and testing, and notes that while "the urgency of the cybersecurity threat has grown to affect more types of products and services ... contractual prohibitions on reverse engineering have proliferated." For example, contractual terms sought to limit most of the testing required for research that exposed critical vulnerabilities in voting machines (1, 23). For a general proposal for a legislated safe harbor for security research that is based on responsible disclosure, see Daniel Etcovitch and Thyla van der Merwe, "Coming in from the Cold: A Safe Harbor from the CFAA and the DMCA §1201 for Security Researchers," 2018. https://papers.ssrn.com/sol3/papers.cfm?abstract_id=3055814. In this paper (specifically, ch. VI), the authors aim to employ this general solution in cases in which there is no available bug bounty. See also the specific language proposed for a safe harbor and exemption from liability under the DMCA and CFAA (by way of amendment) for IoT security researchers, in the Senate bill "Internet of Things (IoT) Cybersecurity Improvement Act of 2017," S. 1691, 115th Cong. §3(c) (2017).

20 FTC, "Start With Security," https://www.ftc.gov/system/files/documents/plain-language/pdf0205-startwithsecurity.pdf, 12. For example, a newly adopted comprehensive cyber regulation for financial services companies regulated under the New York State Department of Financial Services, effective as of March 1, 2017, requires covered entities to conduct periodic penetration testing and vulnerability assessments. See New York State Department of Financial Services, 23 NYCRR 500, "Cybersecurity Requirements for Financial Services Companies," 2017, http://www.dfs.ny.gov/legal/regulations/adoptions/dfsrf500txt.pdf, § 500.05, 5–6. See also National Institute of Standards and Technology, "Framework for Improving Critical Infrastructure Cybersecurity," December 5, 2017, 43, https://www.nist.gov/sites/default/files/documents/2017/12/05/draft-2_framework-v1-1_without-markup.pdf.

21 While beyond the scope of the paper, it is noteworthy that browse-wrap contracts are generally enforceable in the United States, if sufficient notice is given (as generally seems to be case with bug bounties, and considering that hackers actively take affirmative action to manifest assent in the form of submitting their report). See, e.g. *Nguyen v. Barnes & Noble Inc.*, 763 F.3d 1171 (9th Cir. 2014). At least in the case of bug bounties operated on platforms, specific click-through consent is given by hackers, who also agree to comply with the general public bug bounty terms.

22 Bugcrowd claimed that it indeed provides "safe harbors" for hackers to operate. See Bugcrowd, "Webinar: Bug Hunting and The Law," https://pages. bugcrowd.com/bug-bounty-logistics-legalities, min. 9, 31. Yet, this survey suggests that at least some of the companies sponsoring programs through Bugcrowd employ paradoxical terms that prevent hackers from reverse engineering. See also HackerOne, "Vulnerability Disclosure Guidelines," https://www.hackerone.com/disclosure-guidelines ("Safe Harbor ... We are committed to protecting the interests of Finders [...]"). Following this paper, Bugcrowd introduced a comprehensive initiative to support safe harbor called disclose.io. Hackerone changed their template policy to support safe harbor as well.

23 See, e.g. the HackerOne and Bugcrowd general guides to designing bug bounties, which do not address legal aspects: HackerOne, "Bug Bounty Program Basics for Companies," https://www.hackerone.com/resources/ bug-bounty-basics, and Payton O'Neal, "Illustrated Guide to Bug Bounties," *Bugcrowd Blog*, April 12, 2017, https://blog.bugcrowd.com/illustrated-guide- to-bug-bounties-step-1-planning?utm_campaign=1704%20Top%204% 20Reasons%20to%20Build%20a%20Bug%20Bounty%20into%20Your% 20AppSec%20Strategy&utm_content=54427294&utm_medium= social&utm_source=twitter.

24 *See infra* Section 2.2.4 in this chapter.

25 Among the public programs surveyed in this paper are Pinterest, Hack the Army (Department of Defense), Yahoo!, Facebook, Microsoft, Mozilla, Google, Tesla, Alibaba, AVG, Fitbit, General Motors, Kaspersky Lab, NetGear, Avast, Twilio, Twitter, and Uber. All the information was gathered at the beginning of 2017. Contract terms often change, and this paper seeks to survey the landscape as of that date. The author encourages the reader to inquire if updates have been introduced since then.

26 Bugcrowd, "The State of Bug Bounty – Bug crowd's second annual report on the current state of the bug bounty economy," June 2016, 13, https://pages. bugcrowd.com/hubfs/PDFs/state-of-bug-bounty-2016.pdf. According to Bugcrowd, in 2017, 77% of all programs launched on its platform were "private." Elite researchers are chosen by their "bugcrowd" measurements for priority rate, acceptance rate, trust, and overall submission quality. Bugcrowd, "2017 State of Bug Bounty Report," 10.

27 For example, according to NetGear bug bounty terms, NetGear rewards hackers $10 000–$15 000 for vulnerabilities that lead to "unauthorized access" to NetGear cloud storage and customers' live video feeds. Simultaneously, the terms also require that the testing will not "violate any law, or disrupt or

254 Private Ordering Shaping Cybersecurity Policy

compromise any data or access data that is not yours." See Bugcrowd, "About NETGEAR Cash Reward Program," https://bugcrowd.com/netgear.

28 See Kirsch, "The Grey Hat Hacker." See also Jeff Kosseff, *Cybersecurity Law* (Hoboken: Wiley, 2017), 159–160.

29 18 U.S.C. 1030.

30 Pub. L. No. 105-304, 112 Stat. 2860 (1998) (codified in scattered sections of 5, 17, 28, and 35 U.S.C.).

31 On the CFAA, see Charles Doyle, "Cybercrime: An Overview of the Federal Computer Fraud and Abuse Statute and Related Federal Criminal Laws 6–7,"2008, https://fas.org/sgp/crs/misc/97-1025.pdf; and 18 U.S.C. 1030(e)(2)(B). On the DMCA, see, e.g. *United States v. Elcom Ltd.*, 203 F. Supp. 2d 1111 (N.D. Cal. May 8, 2002). This case addressed the matter of Elcomsoft, the employer of Skylarov, a Russian programmer arrested after presenting at Defcon 9, for creating a program that circumvented Adobe software encryption. For further discussion see Michael Geist, "Cyberlaw 2.0," *Boston College Law Review* 44 (2003): 323, 335–337. See also U.S. Department of Justice, Cybersecurity Unit, Computer Crime & Intellectual Property Section, Criminal Division, "A Framework for a Vulnerability Disclosure Program for Online Systems," July 2017, 2, https://www.justice.gov/criminal-ccips/page/file/983996/download: "The CFAA's scope is not limited to purely domestic conduct. For instance, it would apply if an Internet-connected computer in the United States were accessed or damaged by an actor from abroad or if an Internet-connected computer in a foreign country were accessed or damaged by an actor located in the United States."

32 § 1030(a)(2). See Daniel J. Solove and Paul M. Schwartz, *Information Privacy Law*, 5th edition (Blue Springs: Aspen Publishing Company, 2015), ch. 16; Doyle, "Cybercrime," 14–24; and Kosseff, *Cybersecurity Law*, ch. 5. The term "exceeds authorized access" is a defined term under the CFAA, which means "to access a computer with authorization and to use such access to obtain or alter information in the computer that the accesser is not entitled so to obtain or alter." The CFAA imposes civil liability where a person "suffers damage or loss by reason of a violation" of the applicable provisions. See 18 U.S.C. § 1030(g).

33 See Kosseff, *Cybersecurity Law*, 173, noting that the definition of "protected computer" is incredibly broad and that it is "difficult to imagine any U.S. companies whose computers do not qualify as 'protected computers.'"

34 See "Cybersecurity Research: Addressing the Legal Barriers and Disincentives," 7. See also Doyle, "Cybercrime," 18, explaining how The Identity Theft Enforcement and Restitution Act of 2008 broadened the application of 1030(a)(2) and redefined the term "protected computer" "to include computers 'affecting' interstate or foreign commerce," as well as how case law evolved to reach the conclusion that a computer with internet access is a computer used in commerce. See also *United States v. MacEwan*, 445 F.3d 237, 245 (3d Cir. Pa. Apr. 5, 2006). Cf. *United States v. Drew*, 259 F.R.D. 449, 457 (C.D. Cal. 2009) (the "MySpace case"), where the court noted that the commerce element "is satisfied whenever a person using a computer contacts an Internet website and reads any response from that site."

35 Kosseff, *Cybersecurity Law*, 173, quoting S. Rep. No. 99-432, 6 (1986), reprinted at 1986 U.S.C.C.A.N. 2479, 2484. See also Doyle, "Cybercrime," 17.

36 See Orin S. Kerr, "Cybercrime's Scope: Interpreting 'Access' and 'Authorization' in Computer Misuse Statutes," *New York University Law Review* 78 (2003): 1596; and Orin S. Kerr, "Norms of Computer Trespass," *Columbia Law Review* 116 (2016): 1143. See also Orin Kerr, "Obama's Proposed Changes to the Computer Hacking Statute: A Deep Dive," *The Washington Post*, January 14, 2015, https://www.washingtonpost.com/news/volokh-conspiracy/wp/2015/01/14/obamas-proposed-changes-to-the-computer-hacking-statute-a-deep-dive/?utm_term=.e87baf6cb938; Kosseff, *Cybersecurity Law*, 163; Doyle, "Cybercrime," 17; and Orin S. Kerr, *Computer Crime Law* (Eagan: West, 2006), ch. 2.

37 See *Facebook, Inc. v. Power Ventures, Inc.*, 828 F.3d 1068, 1077 (9th Cir. Cal. July 12, 2016), which states that a violation of the terms of use of a website – without more – cannot be the basis for liability under the CFAA. See also Doyle, "Cybercrime," 16, discussing the MySpace case (see endnote 33), where the court suggests that finding the violation of terms is sufficient to constitute intentionally accessing a computer without authorization under the CFAA, would be unconstitutionally vague. Cf. *United States v. Nosal*, 676 F.3d 854, 862 (9th Cir. 2012) and *WEC Carolina Energy Solutions LLC v. Miller*, 687 F.3d 199, 207 (4th Cir. 2012) (adopting a narrow interpretation of the CFAA), and more recently *hiQ Labs, Inc. v. LinkedIn Corp.*, 2017 U.S. Dist. LEXIS 129088 (finding that scraping a public website, in violation of the website terms of use, is not a violation of the CFAA since the defendants did not bypass a password authentication system) and Oracle USA, Inc. v. Rimini St., Inc., 879 F.3d 948, 961–3 (9th Cir. 2018) (finding that "taking data using a method prohibited by the applicable terms of use, when the taking itself generally is permitted, does not violate the California Comprehensive Data Access and Fraud Act" and concluding the same with respect to the interpretation of "without authorization" under Nevada Computer Crimes Law [California and Nevada anti-hacking law]).

38 Evidence for this Circuit split and the vagueness surrounding CFAA contract-based restrictions could be found in the DOJ manual for prosecuting computer crime, noting that "[i]t is relatively easy to prove that a defendant had only limited authority to access a computer in cases where the defendant's access was limited by restrictions that were memorialized in writing, such as terms of service, a computer access policy, a website notice, or an employment agreement or similar contract." See U.S. Department of Justice, "Prosecuting

Computer Crimes: Computer Crime and Intellectual Property Section Criminal Division," Office of Legal Education, Executive Office for United States Attorneys, 2010, 8–9, https://www.justice.gov/sites/default/files/criminal-ccips/legacy/2015/01/14/ccmanual.pdf. That language, among others, is currently the subject of a lawsuit led by the ACLU and a number of respected algorithmic auditors concerning the constitutionality of the CFAA. See ACLU, "Sandvig v. Sessions – Challenge to CFAA Prohibition on Uncovering Racial Discrimination Online," September 12, 2017, https://www.aclu.org/cases/sandvig-v-sessions-challenge-cfaa-prohibition-uncovering-racial-discrimination-online.

39 See "Cybersecurity Research: Addressing the Legal Barriers and Disincentives," 7; and Kosseff, *Cybersecurity Law*, 204 (which explain the various elements of this provision, and what constitutes effective "control" under case law and the language of the statute).

40 17 U.S.C. § 1201(1)(A),(C) and Exemption to Prohibition on Circumvention of Copyright Protection Systems for Access Control Technologies, 80 Fed. Reg. 69544 (October 28, 2015) (to be codified at 37 C.F.R. pt. 201).

41 *See* ibid., 65956 exempting "omputer programs, where the circumvention is undertaken on a lawfully acquired device or machine on which the computer program operates solely for the purpose of good-faith security research and does not violate any applicable law, including without limitation the Computer Fraud and Abuse Act of 1986, as amended and codified in title 18, United States Code." This exemption from is pending renewal, under a much-debated rule-making procedure with multiple comments submitted by opponents and supporters. See The Copyright Office. "Rulemaking Proceedings Under Section 1201 of Title 17," https://www.copyright.gov/1201.

42 *See* "Cybersecurity Research: Addressing the Legal Barriers and Disincentives," workshop convened by the Berkeley Center for Law & Technology, UC Berkeley School of Information, and the International Computer Science Institute, September 28, 2015, 5, https://www.ischool.berkeley.edu/sites/default/files/cybersec-research-nsf-workshop.pdf.

43 U.S. Department of Justice, "A Framework for a Vulnerability Disclosure Program for Online Systems." Although the DOJ framework is nonbinding and has no legal authority (see ibid., 1, n. 1 and *United States v. Caceres*, 440 U.S. 741 (1979)), it provides valuable insight as to how the legal risks associated with implementing and participating in bug bounties might be addressed through adequate procedures. Another valuable resource relating to CFAA enforcement more generally is the DOJ's "Prosecuting Computer Crimes" manual, intended to be "used by Federal prosecutors for training and law enforcement purposes." See also Office of the Attorney General, "Intake and Charging Policy for Computer Crime Matters" (2014), a document outlining the policy and providing guidance to federal prosecutors determining whether to bring charges or open an investigation under the CFAA.

44 Ibid., my emphasis.

45 Ibid., 6–8.

46 Ibid., 7, my emphasis. These suggestions are similar to the language employed by the DOD (see endnote 83).

47 See endnote 20.

48 On the operation of boilerplate as a form of private law, see Margaret Jane Radin, *Boilerplate: The Fine Print, Vanishing Rights, and the Rule of Law* (Princeton: Princeton University Press, 2012). On the use of private ordering in the context of copyright and intellectual property see, e.g.niva Elkin-Koren, "A Public Regarding Approach to Contracting Copyrights," in *Expanding the Boundaries of Intellectual Property: Innovation Policy for the Knowledge Society*, ed. Rochelle Dreyfuss, et al. (Oxford: Oxford University Press, 2001), 191–221.

49 For a discussion and useful taxonomy of bug bounties policies structure more generally, see Laszka, A., Zhao, M., Malbari, A. & Grossklags, J. "The Rules of Engagement for Bug Bounty Programs." Proceedings of the Twenty-Second International Conference on Financial Cryptography and Data Security (FC) (forthcoming) (Laszka et al. analyzed 111 policies on HackerOne platform, updated as of January 2016, and suggest the following statements categories: In-Scope areas (definition of program scope); Out-of-Scope areas; Eligible vulnerabilities; Non-eligible vulnerabilities; Deepening engagement with organizations (instructions as to how and where the hacker should focus their efforts, beyond the general in-scope description, such as Uber Treasure map); Prohibited or unwanted actions; Legal clauses (the focus of this chapter); Participation restrictions; Submission guidelines; Disclosure guidelines; Reward evaluation and Company statements).

50 Programs often include a term emphasizing that the privacy of their users (or their sensitive information) should not be comprised and requiring hunters must to use test accounts. See, e.g. Twitter's terms (HackerOne, "Twitter: Policy," (*Twitter*, Policy, https://hackerone.com/twitter): ("[w]hen researching security issues, especially those which may compromise the privacy of others, you must use test accounts in order to respect our users' privacy. Accessing private information of other users, performing actions that may negatively affect Twitter users... will immediately disqualify the report, and may result in additional steps being taken."). Indeed, this is an important aspect of the policy that is also emphasized in the DOJ framework (U.S. Department of Justice, "A Framework for a Vulnerability Disclosure Program for Online Systems," 2), and was central to the recent Senate Testimony involving bug bounties. See U.S. Senate Committee on Commerce, Science, & Transportation, Hearing on Data Security and Bug Bounty Programs: Lessons Learned from the Uber Breach and Security Researchers (February 6, 2018), https://www.commerce.senate.gov/public/index.cfm/2018/2/

data-security-and-bug-bounty-programs-lessons-learned-from-the-uber-breach-and-security-researchers. One of the advantages of creating clear safe harbors is explicitly conveying that violation of such guidelines may result in liability under CFAA and applicable laws.

51 Such a template report is included, for example, in Yahoo's bug bounty program terms. See HackerOne, "Yahoo Bug Bounty Program Rules," https://hackerone.com/yahoo.

52 For example, Google's bug bounty terms, titled "legal points" state that "[o]f course, your testing must not violate any law...." See Google, "Google Vulnerability Reward Program (VRP) Rules," https://www.google.com/about/appsecurity/reward-program.

53 See Uber's terms, which state, in the last sentence: "[y]our participation in the Bug Bounty Program is voluntary and subject to the Bug Bounty Program Terms, with a hyperlink to Uber's site." HackerOne, "Uber," https://hackerone.com/uber.

54 Microsoft Security TechCenter, "Frequently Asked Questions about Microsoft Bug Bounty Programs," https://technet.microsoft.com/en-us/security/dn425055.aspx. The company does prompt the hunter to visit that page, noting, for example, under the Microsoft Cloud Bug Bounty: "o get additional information on the Microsoft legal guidelines please go to the FAQ and scroll to 'Legal Notice.'"

55 See Bugcrowd, "Standard Disclosure Terms," 1, https://bugcrowd.com/resources/standard-disclosure-terms: "Terms specified in the Program Brief supersede these terms." See also Bugcrowd, "Researcher Code of Conduct," https://www.bugcrowd.com/resource/code-of-conduct; HackerOne, "Finder Terms and Conditions," February 16, 2017, 2 https://www.hackerone.com/terms/finder; and HackerOne, "Vulnerability Disclosure Guidelines," 3. Both platforms employ a separate set of terms for disclosure, allowing companies to choose among different schemes (no-disclosure, full public disclosure after vulnerability is patched, etc.). See HackerOne, "Vulnerability Disclosure Guidelines" (quotation in endnote 21); and Kymberlee Price, "Bugcrowd's Disclosure Policy," *Bugcrowd Blog*, February 23, 2016, https://blog.bugcrowd.com/public-disclosure-policy-2016.

56 Kymberlee Price, "Bugcrowd's Disclosure Policy," *Bugcrowd Blog*, February 23, 2016, https://blog.bugcrowd.com/public-disclosure-policy-2016 and Bugcrowd, "Public Disclosure Policy," https://researcherdocs.bugcrowd.com/docs/disclosure.

57 See, e.g. Twitter terms (HackerOne, "Twitter," https://hackerone.com/twitter), Avast terms (Avast, "The Avast bug bounty program," https://www.avast.com/bug-bounty), Pinterest terms (Bugcrowd, "Pinterest," https://bugcrowd.com/pinterest), and Microsoft terms (Microsoft Security Tech Center, "Frequently Asked Questions about Microsoft Bug Bounty Programs," https://technet.microsoft.com/en-us/security/dn425055.aspx).

58 The program states that: "by submitting the security bug, you affirm that you have not disclosed and agree that you will not disclose the security bug to anyone other than NETGEAR. Absent NETGEAR's prior written consent, any disclosure outside of this process would violate this Agreement. You agree that money damages may not be a sufficient remedy for a breach of this paragraph by you and that NETGEAR will be entitled to specific performance as a remedy for any such breach. Such remedy will not be deemed to be the exclusive remedy for any such breach but will be in addition to all other remedies *available at* law or equity to NETGEAR." See Bugcrowd, "About NETGEAR Cash Reward Program," https://bugcrowd.com/netgear. While it could be claimed that this provision simply states the obvious: if you disclose the report you are not following the terms, the "extra" legal language caused antagonism among the hackers community. One well-respected hacker, "Tony" noted in a tweet: "@NETGEAR @ Bugcrowd Multi Vuls to report, I refuse to accept these terms. Makes me liable? I'm trying to help." See @0xTony, TWITTER (March 31, 2017, 7:19 AM), https://twitter.com/0xTony/status/847815720020922370. See also United Airlines, "United Airlines bug bounty program," https://www.united.com/ual/en/us/fly/contact/bugbounty.html ("Bugs or potential Bugs you discover may not at any time be disclosed publicly or to a third-party. Doing so will disqualify you from receiving award miles.").

59 See, e.g. Tesla's terms (Bugcrowd, "Tesla," https://bugcrowd.com/tesla), which note that researchers should "ive Tesla a reasonable time to correct the issue before making any information public."

60 Similarly, under the new Trade Secret Defend Act whistleblower immunity provision, nondisclosure agreements should include a clause notifying the signee that under certain conditions he may report suspected violations of the law to an attorney or government official, while enjoying immunity from federal and state trade secret law. See the Defend Trade Secrets Act of 2016, § 7 (codified at 18 U.S.C. § 1833(b)). See also Peter S. Menell, "Misconstruing Whistleblower Immunity Under the Defend Trade Secrets Act," *Nevada Law Review Forum* 1 (2017): 92–97.

Yet, such provision does not explicitly provide immunity under the CFAA (18 U.S.C. § 1833(b)(5)), and therefore may present difficulties for whistleblowers engaged in security research – even if such research is key for uncovering potential privacy law violations. See Peter S. Menell, "The Defend Trade Secrets Act Whistleblower Immunity Provision: A Legislative History," *University of Missouri School of Law Business, Entrepreneurship & Tax Law Review* 1 (2018): 397–424, 426. I explore this interaction between the CFAA and the Defend Trade Secrets Act of 2016 immunity provision elsewhere (see Amit Elazari Bar On and Peter S. Menell, *Distinguishing Whistleblowers from Hackers: The Case for CFAA Whistleblower Immunity* (working draft).

61 HackerOne, "HackerOne Finder Terms and Conditions 2," February 16, 2017, https://www.hackerone.com/terms/finder; HackerOne, "HackerOne General Terms and Conditions 3," February 16, 2017, https://www.hackerone.com/terms/general.

62 Bugcrowd, "Terms of Service," December 1, 2014, 2, https://bugcrowd.com/terms.

63 See, e.g. Twitter's terms, Yahoo's terms, AVG's terms (HackerOne, "AVG Technologies." n.d. https://hackerone.com/avg), Google's terms, and Net Gear's terms.

64 *See*, e.g. Avast terms, Twilio terms (Bugcrowd, Twilio, https://bugcrowd.com/twilio), Tesla terms, Pinterest terms, Kaspersky terms (Hackerone, *Kaspersky Lab*, https://hackerone.com/kaspersky) and FitBit terms (Bugcrowd, Fitbit, https://bugcrowd.com/fitbit).

65 *See infra* endnotes 82, 83. My findings are supported also by Laszka et al. research, finding that only 17 out of 77 policies on HackerOne platform, as of 2016, had a clause stating they will not take legal action against researchers. See Laszka, A., Zhao, M., Malbari, A. and Grossklags, J. "The Rules of Engagement for Bug Bounty Programs." Proceedings of the Twenty-Second International Conference on Financial Cryptography and Data Security (FC) (forthcoming). However, as discussed in this chapter, that type of contractual commitment is desirable but only provides a partial safe harbor. Clear authorization under the relevant anti-hacking laws and consent to test the system negates the legal foundation for the complaint as opposed to a contractual commitment not to pursue legal action (that the company can choose to adhere to, and risk a contractual law suit). Both elements are recommended under the DOJ framework. For further discussion see Section 12.4.

66 *See* Bugcrowd, "Terms of Service," December 1, 2014, 5, https://bugcrowd.com/terms.

67 Hackers are not authorized under the law, if the EULA prohibits them from doing so.

68 Facebook Whitehat, "Information," May 23, 2017, https://www.facebook.com/whitehat.

69 WhatsApp, "WhatsApp Terms of Service," August 25, 2016, https://www.whatsapp.com/legal/#terms-of-service; and Facebook Whitehat, "Information."

70 ASRC, "Vulnerability Rewards Program," https://security.alibaba.com/en/reward.htm?spm=a219k.8075133.0.0.B5nMkA.

71 See DJI, "DJI To Offer 'Bug Bounty' Rewards for Reporting Software Issues," August 28, 2017, https://www.dji.com/newsroom/news/dji-to-offer-bug-bounty-rewards-for-reporting-software-issues.

72 Ibid., my emphasis.

73 Sean Gallagher, "Man Gets Threats – Not Bug Bounty – After Finding DJI Customer Data in Public View," *Ars Technica*, November 17, 2017, https://arstechnica.com/information-technology/2017/11/dji-left-private-keys-for-ssl-cloud-storage-in-public-view-and-exposed-customers.

74 DJI, "DJI To Offer Bug Bounty Rewards."

75 Ibid.

76 Ibid.

77 For DJI's response see DJI, "DJI To Offer Bug Bounty Rewards," and "Statement About DJI's Cyber Security and Privacy Practices," https://www.dji.com/newsroom/news/statement-about-dji-cyber-security-and-privacy-practices. See also Ben Popper, "DJI's Bug Bounty Program Starts with a Stumble: Legal Threats and Angry Researchers are Bad Outcomes for All," *The Verge*, November 20, 2017, https://www.theverge.com/2017/11/20/16669724/dji-bug-bounty-program-conflict-researcher.

78 See further discussion in Section 12.3.3.

79 See generally, Section 12.3.1.

80 For a discussion of the challenges that boilerplate language presents in the context of intellectual property rights more generally, see Amit Elazari Bar On, *Unconscionability 2.0 and the IP Boilerplate: A Revised Doctrine of Unconscionability for the Information Age* (working draft).

81 See Russell Korobkin, "Bounded Rationality, Standard Form Contracts, and Unconscionability," *University of Chicago Law Review* 70, no. 4 (2003): 1203. Moreover, the emergence of "super-hunters" reported by Bugcrowd and additional empirical research suggest that hackers tend to focus on few programs (less than five). This means that hackers do not have the privilege of switching between programs based on the legal terms, and it is vital to ensure that the terms of all platforms support their legal needs. See Bugcrowd, "2017 State of Bug Bounty Report," 19; and Huang et al., "Diversity or Concentration?"

82 See, e.g. HackerOne, "Introducing Reputation," https://www.hackerone.com/blog/introducing-reputation.

83 See, e.g. Tesla's terms, which note that: "o encourage responsible reporting, we will not take legal action against you nor ask law enforcement to investigate you providing you comply with the following Responsible Disclosure Guidelines." See also Facebook's terms, which note that: "[i]f you comply with the policies below when reporting a security issue to Facebook, we will not initiate a lawsuit or law enforcement investigation against you in response to your report."

84 For example, General Motors' terms state that "GM agrees to not pursue claims against researchers related to the disclosures submitted through this website who: [...] do not violate any criminal law; and do not violate any other law (other than those that would result only in claims by GM)." See HackerOne, "General Motors," https://hackerone.com/gm. Considering the CFAA, it makes sense to include the latter exception also under the criminal

law violation condition. See also the Department of Defense, "bugbounty terms," noting that if the hacker conducts his "security research and vulnerability disclosure activities in accordance with the restrictions and guidelines set forth in [their] policy, (1) DoD will not initiate or recommend any law enforcement or civil lawsuits related to such activities, and (2) in the event of any law enforcement or civil action brought by anyone other than DoD, DoD will take steps to make known that your activities were conducted pursuant to and in compliance with this policy." HackerOne, "DoD Vulnerability Disclosure Policy," https://hackerone.com/deptofdefense.

85 Prior to the release of the DOJ framework, I suggested this language: "[the company/platform] agrees to not pursue claims against researchers that follow these guidelines; it is hereby clarified that researchers that follow these guidelines are granted authorized access, for the purposes of the CFAA, DMCA and any applicable law, to test the targeted systems, solely in a manner and scope defined herein." For an example of a company that adopted similar language, see DJI, "DJI Bug Bounty Program Policy," last updated November 26, 2017, https://security.dji.com/policy?lang=en_US ("Waiver").

86 For a similar suggestion in a different context, see the "W3C DRM Circumvention Nonaggression Covenant" proposed by EFF, which only relates to the DMCA restriction discussed above. EFF suggested that W3C Members, W3C Team members, invited experts, and members of the public participating in a working group for the development of a specification that provides a DRM system undertake a covenant that states that "ach participant irrevocably covenants that it will not bring or join suit against any person under 17 U.S.C. § 1203, or under under [sic] any other law of any jurisdiction that regulates the circumvention of technological measures that effectively control access to a work protected by copyright, where the act complained of relates to:
(a) the circumvention of any implementation of the specification;
(b) the publication of any noncompliant implementation of the specification; or
(c) the publication or disclosure of any vulnerability in the specification or in any implementation of the specification. ..."
See Electronic Frontier Foundation, "Objection to the rechartering of the W3C EME group," https://www.eff.org/pages/objection-rechartering-w3c-eme-group#covenant.

87 PayPal, for example, clarify that the terms of the bug bounty policy will prevail in case of a conflict between the general user agreements that apply and the bug bounty. See PayPal, "PayPal Bug Bounty Program," https://www.paypal.com/us/webapps/mpp/security-tools/reporting-security-issues#indemnification ("These Program Terms supplement the terms of PayPal User Agreement, the PayPal Acceptable Use Policy, and any other agreement in which you have entered with PayPal (collectively 'PayPal Agreements'). The terms of those PayPal Agreements will apply to your use of, and participation in, the Bug Bounty Program as if fully set forth herein. If there is any inconsistency between the

Notes 263

terms of the PayPal Agreements and these Program Terms, these Program Terms will control, but only with regard to the Bug Bounty Program."

88 See Creative Commons, https://creativecommons.org.

89 This standard among companies and platforms should also address questions raised by the DOJ framework, such as: "[m]ay restricted information [under the bug bounty] only be disclosed to the organization from which it was obtained or may it also be shared with others for the purpose of validating the vulnerability?" US Department of Justice, "A Framework for a Vulnerability Disclosure Program for Online Systems," 7.

90 In this respect, the DOJ framework suggests that "an organization should consider including in its vulnerability disclosure program a process for contacting a coordination center in case a vulnerability also affects others organizations' services or systems, such as a technology or software vendor's. A coordination center such as United States Computer Emergency Readiness Team or CERT Coordination Center for information technology vulnerabilities or the Industrial Control System-CERT for operational technology vulnerabilities can make additional notifications to affected parties, if necessary." U.S. Department of Justice, "A Framework for a Vulnerability Disclosure Program for Online Systems," 7–8.

91 U.S. Department of Justice, "A Framework for a Vulnerability Disclosure Program for Online Systems," 4.

92 Ibid.

93 Internet Bug Bounty, https://internetbugbounty.org.

94 The drone-manufacturing company DJI is one company that adopted broad safe harbor language, following a highly publicized incident in which a hacker participating in the program, according to reports, was allegedly threatened with legal action under the CFAA. See Section 12.2.4. As of November 16, 2017, DJI bug bounty policy states the following waiver: "by participating in this program and abiding by these terms, DJI grants you [the hunter] limited authorized access to its systems under the Computer Fraud and Abuse Act in accordance with the terms of the program and will waive any claims under the Digital Millennium Copyright Act (DCMA) and other relevant laws. Furthermore, if you conduct your security research and vulnerability disclosure activities in accordance with the terms set forth in this policy, DJI will take steps to make known that your activities were conducted pursuant to and in compliance with this policy in the event of any law enforcement or civil action brought by anyone other than DJI." DJI is the first program (known to the author) to follow this paper's recommendations. See DJI, "DJI Bug Bounty Program Policy."

95 Ibid., 8.

96 To illustrate, Laszka et al. analyzed the readability of bug bounties policies more generally of 77 policies (utilizing established metrics from readability studies) and found that the average level of the Flesch Reading-Ease index of those policies is 39.6, meaning it required some *college education* (on average) to understand the policy (Law reviews, as the authors indicate, require a score

of 30). The authors found that 18 policies score *below* 30, meaning are less readable than a law review or academic paper. See Laszka, A., Zhao, M., Malbari, A. and Grossklags, J. "The Rules of Engagement for Bug Bounty Programs." Proceedings of the Twenty-Second International Conference on Financial Cryptography and Data Security (FC) (forthcoming). More specifically, I find that some of the legal language included in policies could only be understood by someone with legal education. PayPal, for example, has a comprehensive legal part in its bug bounty policy that includes an Indemnification clause and a copyright sublicense with the following texts: "you hereby waive all other claims of any nature, including express contract, implied-in-fact contract, or quasi-contract, arising out of any disclosure of the Submission to PayPal." See PayPal, "PayPal Bug Bounty Program," https://www.paypal.com/us/webapps/mpp/security-tools/reporting-security-issues#indemnification.

For the purpose of simplifying disclosures, lessons can be learned from privacy and consumer law in this respect; see Aaron Perzanowski and Chris Jay Hoofnagle, "What We Buy When We 'Buy Now'," *University of Pennsylvania Law Review* 165 (2017): 317.

97 U.S. Department of Justice, "A Framework for a Vulnerability Disclosure Program for Online Systems," 6.

98 For example, see *The Joint Comments to US Copyright Office Notice of Inquiry* (Docket No. 2015-8) report prepared by HackerOne, Bugcrowd, Rapid7, and Luta Security, October 27, 2016. This report calls for expansion of the DMCA security research exemption, and is available at https://www.rapid7.com/globalassets/_pdfs/rapid7-comments/rapid7-bugcrowd-hackerone-luta-security-joint-comments-to-copyright-office-request-for-additional-comments-docket-no.-2015-8-102716.pdf.

99 See text accompanying endnote 54.

100 In addition to the expansion of bug bounties, there are additional examples for this trend: the enactment of the Cybersecurity Information Sharing Act of 2015, aimed to facilitate, among other things, the sharing of cyberthreats between the government and the private sector. The emergence of schemes like TAXII, STIX, and CybOX to facilitate sharing of threat intelligence, ISAC organizations for sharing information among members, and even the proliferation of MSSPs, as well as newly founded programs such as Facebook's ThreatExchange and the CTA.

101 See Bugcrowd, "Webinar: Bug Hunting and The Law," wherein Bugcrowd Founder and CEO Casey Ellis mentions that the hackers engaged in the platform "want to play by the rules."

102 Research reports that an exploit or bug is likely to yield higher returns on black markets. See Abdullah M. Algarni and Yashwant K. Malaiya, "Software Vulnerability Markets: Discoverers and Buyers," *International Journal of Computer and Information Science & Engineering* 8, no. 3 (2014): 71. This is yet another reason why the legitimate market for vulnerabilities should not create additional barriers by shifting legal risks toward hackers, if it seeks to truly compete with the bounties offered on black markets.

Bibliography

"2011 ITRC Breach Report Key Findings." Identity Theft Resource Center, 2015. http://www.idtheftcenter.org/ITRC-Surveys-Studies/2011-data-breaches.html.

Ablon, Lillian and Timothy, Bogart. "Zero Days, Thousands of Nights: The Life and Times of Zero-Day Vulnerabilities and Their Exploits." *RAND*, 2017. https://www.rand.org/pubs/research_reports/RR1751.html.

AbuSaad, Belal, Fahad A. Saeed, Khaled, Alghathbar, and Bilal, Khan. "Implementation of ISO 27001 in Saudi Arabia – Obstacles, Motivations, Outcomes, and Lessons Learned." *Australian Information Security Management Conference*, January 1, 2011.

Access Now. "Mutual Legal Assistance Treaties," December 18, 2018. https://www.mlat.info/.

Ackerman, Elise. "Will A Secretive Summit In Dubai Mark The End Of The Open Internet?" *Forbes*, December 10, 2012. https://perma.cc/2TY7-DLKL.

ACLU. "Sandvig v. Sessions – Challenge to CFAA Prohibition on Uncovering Racial Discrimination Online," September 12, 2017. https://www.aclu.org/cases/sandvig-v-sessions-challenge-cfaa-prohibition-uncovering-racial-discrimination-online.

Adams, Samantha A., Marlou Brokx, Lorenzo Della Corte, Masa Galic, Kasper Kala, Bert-Jaap Koops, Ronald Leenes, Maurice Schellekens, Karine e Silva, and Ivan Skorvanek. "*The Governance of Cybersecurity. A Comparative Quick Scan of Approaches in Canada, Estonia, Germany, the Netherlands and the UK.*" Tilburg/The Hague: TILT/WODC, 2015. https://www.wodc.nl/binaries/2484-volledige-tekst_tcm28-73672.pdf.

Adler, Jack and David Rose. "Transmission and Pathogenesis of Tuberculosis." In *Tuberculosis*, edited by William N. Rom and Stuart M. Garay, 129–140. Boston: Little Brown, 1996.

Advanced Cyber Security Center (ACSC). "ACSC Membership." n.d. https://www.acscenter.org/membership/.

Advisen. "Cyber Liability Insurance Market Trends: Survey." Advisen, October 2014. http://www.partnerre.com/assets/uploads/docs/cyber-survey-results.pdf.

Rewired: Cybersecurity Governance, First Edition. Edited by Ryan Ellis and Vivek Mohan.
© 2019 John Wiley & Sons, Inc. Published 2019 by John Wiley & Sons, Inc.

Agrafiotis, Ioannis, Maria Bada, Paul Cornish, Sadie Creese, Michael Goldsmith, Eva Ignatuschtschenko, Taylor Roberts, and David M. Upton. "Cyber Harm: Concepts, Taxonomy and Measurement." *Saïd Business School WP 2016–23*, August 1, 2016. SSRN. https://ssrn.com/abstract=2828646 or http://dx.doi.org/10.2139/ssrn.2828646.

AIOTI WG03. *"High Level Architecture (HLA; Release 3.0)."* Brussels: Alliance for Internet of Things Innovation, 2017. https://aioti.eu/wp-content/uploads/2017/06/AIOTI-HLA-R3-June-2017.pdf.

AIOTI WG04. *"AIOTI Working Group 4 – Policy."* Brussels: Alliance for Internet of Things Innovation, October 15, 2015. https://aioti.eu/wp-content/uploads/2017/03/AIOTIWG04Report2015-Policy-Issues.pdf.

AIOTI WG04. *"AIOTI Digitisation of Industry Policy Recommendations."* Brussels: The Alliance for the Internet of Things Innovation, 2016. https://aioti.eu/wp-content/uploads/2017/03/AIOTI-Digitisation-of-Ind-policy-doc-Nov-2016.pdf.

Air Traffic Control Association. n.d. https://www.atca.org/cyber-home.

Air Traffic Transport Group. "Aviation Benefits Beyond Borders," April 2014. https://aviationbenefits.org/media/26786/ATAG__AviationBenefits2014_FULL_LowRes.pdf.

Airport World. "Top 10 Airports: Passenger Traffic in 2013." *Airport World*, February 14, 2014. http://www.airport-world.com/news/general-news/3674-top-10-airports-passenger-traffic-in-2013.

Aittokallio, Auri. "Virgin Mobile Launches in Saudi Arabia." Text, *Telecoms.Com*, September 30, 2014. https://perma.cc/N29W-QBCY.

Algarni, Abdullah M., and Yashwant K. Malaiya. "Software Vulnerability Markets: Discoverers and Buyers." *International Journal of Computer and Information Science & Engineering* 8, no. 3 (2014): 71–81.

Ali, Rouda Alamir. *"Cloud Computing in Arab States: Legal Aspect, Facts and Horizons."* ITU Arab Regional Office, July 2016.

Alkhouri, Laith, Alex Kassirer, and Allison Nixon. *"Hacking for ISIS: The Emergent Cyber Threat Landscape."* Flashpoint, 2016.

Allagui, Ilhem. "Internet in the Middle East: An Asymmetrical Model of Development." *Internet Histories* 1, no. 1–2 (January 2, 2017): 97–105.

Al-Rasheed, Madawi. *A History of Saudi Arabia.* Cambridge: Cambridge University Press, 2010.

Al-Rasheed, Madawi. "Saudi-Qatar Tensions Divide GCC." *Al-Monitor*, March 6, 2014. https://perma.cc/Y597-CYZJ.

Al-Saud, Naef bin Ahmed. "A Saudi Outlook for Cybersecurity Strategies: Extrapolated from Western Experience." *Joint Forces Quarterly*, no. 64 (2012): 75–81.

Alshitri, Khalid I., and Abdulmohsen N. Abanumy. "Exploring the Reasons Behind the Low ISO 27001 Adoption in Public Organizations in Saudi Arabia." In *2014 International Conference on Information Science Applications*, 2014.

Altayar, Mohammed Saleh. "A Comparative Study of Anti-Cybercrime Laws in the Gulf Cooperation Council Countries." *IEEEExplore*, 2017.

American Institute of Aeronautics and Astronautics. "AIAA's Framework on Cyber Security Now Available." August 13, 2013a. https://www.aiaa.org/SecondaryTwoColumn.aspx?id=19262.

American Institute of Aeronautics and Astronautics. "Cybersecurity of Global Aviation a Major Focus of AIAA AVIATION 2013." July 9, 2013b. https://www.aiaa.org/SecondaryTwoColumn.aspx?id=18754.

American Institute of Aeronautics and Astronautics. "The Connectivity Challenge: Protecting Critical Assets in a Networked World; A Framework for Aviation Cybersecurity." August 2013c. https://www.aiaa.org/uploadedFiles/Issues_and_Advocacy/AIAA-Cyber-Framework-Final.pdf.

Amnesty International. "Operation Kingphish: Uncovering a Campaign of Cyber Attacks against Civil Society in Qatar and Nepal." *Amnesty International*, February 14, 2017.

Anderson, Jon W. "Is Informationalization Good for the Middle East?" *Arab Media & Society* Summer, no. 18 (June 12, 2013): 1–14.

Anderson, Colin. "Considerations on Wassenaar Arrangement Control List Additions for Surveillance Technologies." Access, 2015.

Andress, Jason. "Working with Indicators of Compromise." *ISSA Journal* (May 2015). https://c.ymcdn.com/sites/www.issa.org/resource/resmgr/journalpdfs/feature0515.pdf.

APEC Secretariat. "APEC Privacy Framework 2015." n.d. http://www.cbprs.org/.

Article 29 Data Protection Working Party. "*Opinion 8/2014 on the on Recent Developments on the Internet of Things.*" Brussels: Article 29 Data Protection Working Party, 2014. https://www.dataprotection.ro/servlet/ViewDocument?id=1088.

Asghari, Hadi, Michael Ciere, and Michel J.G. van Eeten. "Post-Mortem of a Zombie: Conficker Cleanup After Six Years." In *Proceedings of the 24th USENIX Security Symposium*: Washington, DC, August 12–14, 2015. Accessed November 9, 2017. https://www.usenix.org/system/files/conference/usenixsecurity15/sec15-paper-asghari.pdf.

ASRC. "Vulnerability Rewards Program." n.d. https://security.alibaba.com/en/reward.htm?spm=a219k.8075133.0.0.B5nMkA.

Asselt, Marjolein van, and Ortwin Renn. "Risk Governance." *Journal of Risk Research* 14 (2011): 431–449.

Avast. "The Avast Bug Bounty Program." n.d. https://www.avast.com/bug-bounty.

Aviation Information Sharing and Analysis Center. "FAQs." n.d. https://www.a-isac.com/faqs.

Aviation Safety Network. "Fatal Airliner (14+ Passengers) Hull-loss Accidents". n.d. https://aviation-safety.net/statistics/period/stats.php?cat=A1.

Baer, Greg, and Rob Hunter. "A Tower of Babel: Cyber Regulation for Financial Services." *The Clearing House*, June 9, 2017. https://www.theclearinghouse.org/banking-perspectives/2017/2017-q2-banking-perspectives/articles/cyber-regulation-for-financial-services.

Bahrain Watch. "The IP Spy Files: How Bahrain's Government Silences Anonymous Online Dissent." 2013. https://bahrainwatch.org/ipspy/viewreport.php.

Baldini, Gianmarco, Antonio Skarmeta, Elizabeta Fourneret, Ricardo Neisse, Bruno Legeard, Franck Le Gall. "Security Certification and Labelling in Internet of Things." In *2016 IEEE 3rd World Forum on Internet of Things (WF-IoT)*, 627–632. Reston, VA, USA: IEEE, 2016. https://doi.org/10.1109/WF-IoT.2016.7845514.

Bange, Vinod, Graham Hann, Chris Jeffery, and Sally Annereau. *"An Overview of UK Data Protection Law."* London: Taylor Wessing, 2012. https://united-kingdom.taylorwessing.com/uploads/tx_siruplawyermanagement/NB_000168_Overview_UK_data_protection_law_WEB.pdf.

Barlow, John Perry. "A Declaration of the Independence of Cyberspace." February 8, 1996. https://www.eff.org/cyberspace-independence.

Barnett, Michael, and F. Gregory Gause. "Caravans in Opposite Directions: Society, State and the Development of a Community in the GCC." In *Security Communities*, edited by Emmanuel Adler and Michael Barnett, 161–197. New York: Cambridge University Press, 2008.

Bassiouni, Mahmoud Cherif. "Report of the Bahrain Independent Commission of Inquiry." *BICI*, December 10, 2011.

Bassiouni, Mahmoud Cherif. "Sex, Honour, Shame and Blackmail in an Online World." *BBC News*, October 26, 2016. https://perma.cc/Y3JT-6FY8.

BBC. "Four Jailed in Bahrain for Duping British Boys into Sex Acts." *BBC News*, April 25, 2014. https://perma.cc/V6YX-5PVN.

Beblawi, Hazem, and Giacomo Luciani, eds. *The Rentier State*. Routledge, 2016.

Bellamy III, Woodrow. "CANSO Chief Outlines Plan to Address Aviation Cyber Security." *Aviation Today*, October 27, 2015. http://www.aviationtoday.com/2015/10/27/canso-chief-outlines-plan-to-address-aviation-cyber-security/.

Bellovin, Steven M., Matt Blaze, Sandy Clark, and Susan Landau. "Lawful Hacking: Using Existing Vulnerabilities for Wiretapping on the Internet." *Northwestern Journal of Technology and Intellectual Property* 12, no. 1 (April 2014). http://scholarlycommons.law.northwestern.edu/cgi/viewcontent.cgi?article=1209&context=njtip.

Berg, Jan van den, Jacqueline van Zoggel, Mireille Snels, Mark van Leeuwen, Sergei Boeke, Leo van de Koppen, Jan van der Lubbe, Bibi van den Berg, and Tony de Bos. "On (the Emergence of) Cyber Security Science and its Challenges for Cyber Security Education." In *NATO STO/IST-122 Symposium*: Tallinn, October 13–14, 2014, 12-1–12-10.

Berkeley Center for Law & Technology, the UC Berkeley School of Information and the International Computer Science Institute. "Cybersecurity Research: Addressing the Legal Barriers and Disincentives." Workshop convened by the Berkeley Center for Law & Technology, UC Berkeley School of Information, and the International Computer Science Institute. September 28, 2015.

https://www.ischool.berkeley.edu/sites/default/files/cybersec-research-nsf-workshop.pdf.

Berry, Alex, Josh Homan, and Randi Eitzman. "WannaCry Malware Profile." *FireEye*, 2017. https://www.fireeye.com/blog/threat-research/2017/05/wannacry-malware-profile.html.

Better Regulation Task Force. *"Principles of Good Regulation."* London: Cabinet Office, 2003. http://webarchive.nationalarchives.gov.uk/20100407173247/http://archive.cabinetoffice.gov.uk/brc/upload/assets/www.brc.gov.uk/principlesleaflet.pdf.

Betz, David J., and Tim Stevens. *Cyberspace and the State: Toward a Strategy for Cyber-Power.* Routledge, 2011.

BI-ME. "Cisco and GBM Unveil Latest UAE Security Research at GITEX 2014." October 14, 2014. https://perma.cc/EU3X-Z9W3.

Bindiya, Thomas. "UAE Military To Set Up Cyber Command." *Defense World,* n.d. https://perma.cc/VP7F-EEXF.

Blank, Robert H., and Viola Burau. *Comparative Health Policy.* 3rd ed. Houndmills: Palgrave Macmillan, 2010.

Blumenstein, Rebecca, and Loretta Chao. "Brazil's Rousseff Pressures U.S. on Data Collection." *The Wall Street Journal,* January 25, 2014. https://www.wsj.com/articles/brazil8217s-rousseff-pressures-us-on-data-collection-1390604047?tesla=y.

Blythe, John M., Susan Michie, Jeremy Watson, Carmen E. Lefevre. *"Internet of Things in Healthcare: Identifying Key Malicious Threats, End-User Protective and Problematic Behaviours."* London: PETRAS IoT Research Hub, 2017.

Böhme, Rainer. "Cyber-Insurance Revisited." In *Workshop on the Economics of Information Security (WEIS),* 2005. http://infosecon.net/workshop/slides/weis_5_1.pdf.

Böhme, Rainer, and Galina Schwartz. "Modeling Cyber-Insurance: Towards a Unifying Framework." In *Proceedings of the 9th Annual Workshop on the Economics of Information Security,* 2010. http://www.icsi.berkeley.edu/pubs/networking/modelingcyber10.pdf.

Boland, Rita. "Countries Collaborate To Counter Cybercrime." *SIGNAL Magazine,* July 28, 2008. https://perma.cc/WUY2-TCT2.

Boon, Kristen, Aziz Z. Huq, and Douglas Lovelace. *U.S. Preparedness for Catastrophic Attacks.* New York, NY: Oxford University Press, 2012.

Bowcott, Owen. "UK and Saudi Arabia 'in Secret Deal' over Human Rights Council Place." *The Guardian,* September 29, 2015. https://perma.cc/9CAT-J66L.

Bowden, Mark. *Worm: The First Digital World War.* New York: Atlantic Monthly Press, 2011.

Brancher Rodriguez, Paulo Marcos, and Douglas Cohen Moreira. "Brazilian Superior Court of Justice Decision and the Disclosure of Gmail Data for

Investigation." *Lexology*, April 29, 2013. Accessed June 12, 2014. http://www. lexology.com/library/detail.aspx?g=793d848f-5877-4675-9336-aa28eec3d971.

Brandsen, Taco, Wim van de Donk, and Kim Putters. "Griffins or Chameleons? Hybridity as a Permanent and Inevitable Characteristic of the Third Sector." *International Journal of Public Administration* 28 (2005): 749–765.

Brass, Irina, Madeline Carr, Leonie Tanczer, Carsten Maple, and Jason Blackstock. "Unbundling the Emerging Cyber-Physical Risks in Connected and Autonomous Vehicles." In *Connected and Autonomous Vehicles: The Emerging Legal Challenges*, edited by Stephan Appt and Nicole Livesey. London: Pinsent Masons, May 2017. https://www.pinsentmasons.com/PDF/2017/Freedom-to-Succeed-AMT/Connected-autonomous-vehicles-report-2017.pdf.

Brass, Irina, Leonie Tanczer, Madeline Carr, Miles Elsden, and Jason Blackstock. "Standardising a Moving Target: The Development and Evolution of IoT Security Standards." In *Living in the Internet of Things: Cybersecurity of the IoT - 2018*. London, UK: IET, 2018. https://ieeexplore.ieee.org/document/8379711

"British Airways says computer outage causing global delays, cancels all London flights." CNBC, May 27, 2017. http://www.cnbc.com/2017/05/27/britishairways-says-computer-outage-causing-global-delays.html

Broeders, Dennis. *Investigating the Place and Role of the Armed Forces in Dutch Cyber Security Governance*. The Hague/Rotterdam: Netherlands Ministerie van Defensie/Erasmus Universiteit Rotterdam, 2014.

Broitman, Elana. "Smart Cyber Legislation." *New America Cybersecurity Initiative*, October 15, 2015. https://www.newamerica.org/cybersecurity-initiative/smart-cyber-legislation/.

Bronk, Christopher, and Eneken Tikk-Ringas. "The Cyber Attack on Saudi Aramco." *Survival* 55, no. 2 (May 1, 2013): 81–96.

Brown, Brian D. "The Ever-Evolving Nature of Cyber Coverage." *The Insurance Journal*, September 22, 2014. http://www.insurancejournal.com/magazines/features/2014/09/22/340633.htm.

Brülde, Bengt. "Health, Disease and the Goal of Public Health." In *Public Health Ethics*, edited by Angus Dawson, 20–47. Cambridge: Cambridge University Press, 2011.

Bryan, Victoria. "Airlines Step Up Efforts to Tackle Cyber Security Risks." *Reuters*, October 26, 2015. http://www.reuters.com/article/us-airlines-cybersecurity/airlines-step-up-efforts-to-tackle-cyber-security-risks-idUSKCN0SK24020151026.

Bubandt, N. "Vernacular Security: The Politics of Feeling Safe in Global, National and Local Worlds." *Security Dialogue* 36 (2005): 275–296.

Buchanan, Ben. "Cryptography and Sovereignty." *Survival* 58, no. 5 (September 20, 2016): 95–122. http://www.tandfonline.com/doi/full/10.1080/00396338.2016.1231534.

Bugcrowd. "Terms of Service." December 1, 2014. https://bugcrowd.com/terms.

Bugcrowd. "The State of Bug Bounty – Bugcrowd's Second Annual Report on the Current State of the Bug Bounty Economy." June 2016. https://pages.bugcrowd. com/hubfs/PDFs/state-of-bug-bounty-2016.pdf.

Bugcrowd. "3 Reasons to Swap Your Next Pen Test With a Bug Bounty Program." Webcast. April 2017a. https://www.slideshare.net/ bugcrowd/3-reasons-to-swap-your-next-pen-test-with-a-bug-bounty-program.

Bugcrowd. "2017 State of Bug Bounty Report – Bugcrowd's Third Annual Analysis of the Global Bug Bounty Economy." 2017b. https://pages.bugcrowd. com/hubfs/Bugcrowd-2017-State-of-Bug-Bounty-Report.pdf.

Bugcrowd. "About NETGEAR Cash Reward Program." n.d.-a https://bugcrowd. com/netgear.

Bugcrowd. "Fitbit." n.d.-b https://bugcrowd.com/fitbit.

Bugcrowd. "Pinterest." n.d.-c https://bugcrowd.com/pinterest.

Bugcrowd. "Public Disclosure Policy." n.d.-d https://researcherdocs.bugcrowd. com/docs/disclosure

Bugcrowd. "Researcher Code of Conduct." n.d.-e https://www.bugcrowd.com/ resource/code-of-conduct/.

Bugcrowd. "Standard Disclosure Terms." n.d.-f https://bugcrowd.com/resources/ standard-disclosure-terms.

Bugcrowd. "Tesla." n.d.-g https://bugcrowd.com/tesla.

Bugcrowd. "Twilio." n.d.-h https://bugcrowd.com/twilio.

Bugcrowd. "Webinar: Bug Hunting and The Law." n.d.-i https://pages.bugcrowd. com/bug-bounty-logistics-legalities.

Burton, Kelly. "The Conficker Worm." 2009. https://www.sans.org/security- resources/malwarefaq/conficker-worm.

Büthe, Tim. "Private Regulation in the Global Economy: Guest Editor's Note." *Business and Politics* 12, no. 3 (January 28, 2010). doi:https://doi. org/10.2202/1469-3569.1349.

Buzan, Barry, Ole Waever, and Jaap de Wilde. *Security: A New Framework for Analysis.* London: Lynne Riener, 1998.

Cabinet Office. "*The UK Cyber Security Strategy. Protecting and Promoting the UK in a Digital World.*" London: HM Government, November 2011. https:// www.gov.uk/government/uploads/system/uploads/attachment_data/ file/60961/uk-cyber-security-strategy-final.pdf.

Cabinet Office. "*National Cyber Security Strategy 2016–2021.*" London: HM Government, November 1, 2016a. https://www.ncsc.gov.uk/content/files/ protected_files/document_files/National%20Cyber%20Security%20Strategy% 20v20.pdf.

Cabinet Office. "*Summary of the 2016 Sector Security and Resilience Plans.*" London: Cabinet Office, November 2016b. https://www.gov.uk/government/ uploads/system/uploads/attachment_data/file/568546/sector_security_ resilience_plans_14_11_2016.pdf.

Campbell, Duncan. "Revealed: GCHQ's Beyond Top Secret Middle Eastern Internet Spy Base." *The Register*, June 3, 2014. https://perma.cc/K3YU-66XZ.

Cam-Winget, N., A.R. Sadeghi, and Y. Jin. "Invited: Can IoT Be Secured: Emerging Challenges in Connecting the Unconnected." In *2016 53nd ACM/EDAC/IEEE Design Automation Conference (DAC)*, 2016, 1–6. https://doi.org/10.1145/2897937.2905004.

Cardenes, Alvaro A., Svetalana Radosavac, Jens Grossklags, John Chuang, and Chris Hoofnagle. "An Economic Map of Cybercrime." Working Paper 2009. Accessed November 9, 2017. http://chess.eecs.berkeley.edu/pubs/772/cardenas_2009.pdf.

Carr, Madeline. "Public–private Partnerships in National Cyber-Security Strategies." *International Affairs* 92, no. 1 (January 1, 2016).

Carr, Madeline, and Leonie Tanczer. "UK Cybersecurity Industrial Policy: An Analysis of Drivers, Market Failures and Interventions. *Journal of Cyber Policy* 3.3 (2018): 430–444.

Castillo, Andrea, and Adam D. Thierer. *"Projecting the Growth and Economic Impact of the Internet of Things."* SSRN Scholarly Paper. Rochester, NY: Social Science Research Network, June 15, 2015. https://papers.ssrn.com/abstract=2618794.

CCIPS-CSIS (The Center for Strategic and International Studies [CSIS] and the U.S. Department of Justice Computer Crime and Intellectual Property Section [CCIPS]). *CCIPS-CSIS Cybercrime Symposium 2016: Cooperation and Electronic Evidence Gathering Across Borders*, U.S. Department of Justice, Computer Crime & Intellectual Property Section, June 6, 2016. https://www.csis.org/events/ccips-csis-cybercrime-symposium-2016.

Cellan-Jones, Rory. "Divisions over Internet Governance Intensify in Dubai." *BBC News*, December 10, 2012. https://perma.cc/9TUB-BS7D.

Centers for Disease Control and Prevention. "Public Health Ethics." Centers for Disease Control and Prevention, May 10, 2015. Accessed May 16, 2017. https://www.cdc.gov/od/science/integrity/phethics/.

Charney, Scott. "Collective Defense: Applying the Public-Health Model to the Internet." *Security & Privacy IEEE* 10, no. 2 (2012): 54–59.

Charney, Scott. "Cybersecurity Norms for Nation-states and the Global ICT Industry." *Microsoft on the Issues*, June 23, 2016. https://blogs.microsoft.com/on-the-issues/2016/06/23/cybersecurity-norms-nation-states-global-ict-industry.

Chatterjee, Pratap. "Turkmenistan and Oman Negotiated to Buy Spy Software: Wikileaks in Spy Files." *WikiLeaks Supporters Forum*, September 4, 2013. https://perma.cc/J264-JW5U.

Chaudhuri, Saabira. "Cost of Replacing Credit Cards After Target Breach Estimated at $200 Million." *The Wall Street Journal*, February 18, 2014. https://www.wsj.com/articles/cost-of-replacing-credit-cards-after-target-breach-estimated-at-200-million-1392746456?mg=prod/accounts-wsj.

Chertoff, Michael, and Frank Cilluffo. "Trump Administration Can Help Finance Sector Shift Cybersecurity Paradigm." *Forbes*, January 18, 2017. https://www.forbes.com/sites/realspin/2017/01/18/trump-administration-can-help-finance-sector-shift-cybersecurity-paradigm/#3b7561db645d.

China Academy of Information and Communication Technology and European Commission – DG CONNECT. "*EU-China Joint White Paper on the Internet of Things.*" Brussels: EU-China IoT Advisory Group, January 2016. https://ec.europa.eu/digital-single-market/en/news/eu-china-joint-white-paper-internet-things.

Chinese National People's Congress. "People's Republic of China Internet Security Law." November 7, 2016. http://www.npc.gov.cn/npc/xinwen/2016-11/07/content_2001605.htm.

Chivers, C.J., and Eric Schmitt. "In Shift, Saudis Are Said to Arm Rebels in Syria." *The New York Times*, February 25, 2013. https://www.nytimes.com/2013/02/26/world/middleeast/in-shift-saudis-are-said-to-arm-rebels-in-syria.html.

Choucri, Nazli, Gihan Daw Elbait, and Stuart E. Madnick. "What Is Cybersecurity? Explorations in Automated Knowledge Generation." *SSRN Electronic Journal* (2012): 1–27. https://doi.org/10.2139/ssrn.2178616.

Chris Preimesberger. "Router Crashes Trigger Major Southwest IT System Failure." *eWeek*, July 21, 2016. http://www.eweek.com/enterprise-apps/router-crashes-trigger-major-southwest-it-system-failure.

Chris Roberts Application for Search Warrant. April 17, 2015. Case No: 5:15-MJ-00154 (ATB). https://www.wired.com/wp-content/uploads/2015/05/Chris-Roberts-Application-for-Search-Warrant.pdf.

Cimpanu, Catalin. "Dark Web Marketplace Launches Bug Bounty Program with $10,000 Rewards." *BleepingComputer*, February 6, 2017. https://www.bleepingcomputer.com/news/security/dark-web-marketplace-launches-bug-bounty-program-with-10-000-rewards/.

CISCO. "Cisco and GBM Outline Key Steps for Digitization to Help Middle East Organizations Become IoT Ready." October 19, 2015. https://perma.cc/UZA5-5ACM.

Cisco. "SNORT." 2017. Accessed July 1, 2017. https://www.snort.org.

CityVerve. "CityVerve Manchester: Manchester's Smart City Demonstrator." *CityVerve*, 2017. http://www.cityverve.org.uk/.

Civil Aviation Cybersecurity Action Plan. December 5, 2014. https://www.icao.int/cybersecurity/SiteAssets/ICAO/Civil%20Aviation%20Cybersecurity%20Action%20Plan%20-%20SIGNED.pdf.

Clapper, James R., Marcel Lettre, and Michael S. Rogers. "Joint Statement for the Record to the Senate Armed Services Committee: Foreign Cyber Threats to the United States." January 5, 2017. https://www.armed-services.senate.gov/imo/media/doc/Clapper-Lettre-Rogers_01-05-16.pdf.

Clark, David D. "Control Point Analysis." 2012 TRPC, September 10, 2012.
  https://papers.ssrn.com/sol3/papers.cfm?abstract_id=2032124.
Clarke, Richard A., and Robert K. Knake. *Cyber War: The Next Threat to National
  Security and What To Do About It. Terrorism and Political Violence.* New York:
  HarperCollins, 2012.
Coggon, John. *What Makes Health Public?: A Critical Evaluation of Moral, Legal, and
  Political Claims in Public Health.* Cambridge: Cambridge University Press, 2012.
Coglianese, Cary, and Evan Mendelson. "Meta-Regulation and Self-Regulation." In
  The Oxford Handbook of Regulation, edited by Robert Baldwin, Martin Cave,
  and Martin Lodge. Oxford: Oxford University Press, 2010.
Consolidated Appropriations Act. 2016, Pub. L. 114-113 (December 18, 2015).
  https://www.congress.gov/114/plaws/publ113/PLAW-114publ113.pdf.
Convention on Cybercrime. Budapest, 2001. CETS 185.
Convention on Offences and Certain Other Acts Committed on Board Aircraft.
  Tokyo, September 14, 1963. *United Nations Treaty Series.* https://treaties.
  un.org/doc/db/terrorism/conv1-english.pdf.
Convention on the Recognition and Enforcement of Foreign Arbitral Awards.
  New York, 1958. http://www.uncitral.org/uncitral/en/uncitral_texts/
  arbitration/NYConvention.html.
Corbridge, Stuart, Glyn Williams, Manoj Srivastava, and Rene Veron. *Seeing the
  State: Governance and Governmentality in India.* Cambridge: Cambridge
  University Press, 2005.
Cornish, Paul. "Governing Cyberspace through Constructive Ambiguity," *Survival*
  57, no. 3 (May 4, 2015): 153–176.
Cory, Nigel. *"Cross-Border Data Flows: Where Are the Barriers, and What Do
  They Cost?"* Information Technology and Innovation Foundation (ITIF), May
  2017. http://www2.itif.org/2017-cross-border-data-flows.pdf?_ga=2.244607109.
  1624330899.1511348753-1808609825.1511348753.
Council on Foreign Relations. "Cyber Security & the Governance Gap:
  Complexity, Contention, Cooperation." 2014. https://ecir.mit.edu/sites/default/
  files/documents/2014%20ECIR%20Conference%20Agenda.pdf.
Counsel for Amicus Curiae Ireland. "Brief of Amicus Curiae Ireland in 14-2985-
  CV." December 23, 2014. https://www.eff.org/files/2015/01/12/ireland_
  microsoft_second_circuit_amicus_brief.pdf.
Court of Appeal for British Columbia, *Equustek Solutions Inc. v. Google Inc.,* 2015
  BCCA 265. https://www.canlii.org/en/bc/bcca/doc/2015/2015bcca265/
  2015bcca265.pdf.
Court of Justice of the European Union. "Judgment in Case C-362/14 Maximillian
  Schrems v Data Protection Commissioner, Luxembourg." October 6, 2015.
  https://curia.europa.eu/jcms/upload/docs/application/pdf/2015-10/
  cp150117en.pdf.
Crawford, Shaun, and David Piesse. *"Mitigating Cyber Risk for Insurers."* Ernst and
  Young, 2014. https://www.ey.com/Publication/vwLUAssets/

EY_-_Insights_into_cybersecurity_and_risk_(Part_2)/$FILE/ey-mitigating-cyber-risk-for-insurers.pdf.

Creative Commons. n.d. https://creativecommons.org/.

Crosman, Penny. "A Glimmer of Hope for Cyberthreat Data Sharing." *American Banker*, August 16, 2016. https://www.americanbanker.com/news/a-glimmer-of-hope-for-cyberthreat-data-sharing.

Cross-Border Privacy Rules (CBPR) System. n.d. http://www.cbprs.org/.

Cutler, A. Claire, Virginia Haufler, and Tony Porter. *Private Authority and International Affairs*. Suny Press, 1999. https://books.google.com/books/about/Private_Authority_and_International_Affa.html?id=M8O2b6oCaBoC.

Cyber Threat Alliance. "A New Way To Share Threat Intelligence." 2017a. Accessed May 25, 2017. https://web.archive.org/web/20150813022557/http://cyberconsortium.org/papers/Cyber_Threat_Alliance_White_Paper_9_5_2014.pdf.

Cyber Threat Alliance. "Cyber Threat Alliance Expands Mission through Appointment of President, Formal Incorporation as Not-for-Profit and New Founding Members." 2017b. https://web.archive.org/web/20170301141408/http://www.cyberthreatalliance.org/pr/pr-021317.html.

Dalek, Jakub, Jakub Dalek, Ron Deibert, Bill Marczak, Sarah McKune, Helmi Noman, Irene Poetranto, and Adam Senft. "Tender Confirmed, Rights at Risk: Verifying Netsweeper in Bahrain." *Citizen Lab*, September 21, 2016.

Dark Reading. "New Financial System Analysis & Resilience Center Formed." *Dark Reading*, October 24, 2016. http://www.darkreading.com/threat-intelligence/new-financial-system-analysis-and-resilience-center-formed-/d/d-id/1327276

Daskal, Jennifer, and Andrew Keane Woods. "Cross-Border Data Requests: A Proposed Framework." *Lawfare*, November 24, 2015. https://lawfareblog.com/cross-border-data-requests-proposed-framework.

Daum, Jeremy. "Sometimes a rule of evidence is just a rule of evidence." *China Law Translate*, March 29, 2017. http://www.chinalawtranslate.com/sometimes-a-rule-of-evidence-is-just-a-rule-of-evidence/?lang=en.

David Anderson Q.C. "A Question of Trust: Report of the Investigatory Powers Review." June 2015. https://terrorismlegislationreviewer.independent.gov.uk/wp-content/uploads/2015/06/IPR-Report-Print-Version.pdf.

Davidson, Christopher M. *The United Arab Emirates: A Study in Survival*. Lynne Rienner Publishers, 2005.

Dawson, Angus. "Resetting the Parameters: Public Health as the Foundation for Public Health Ethics." In *Public Health Ethics*, edited by Angus Dawson, 1–19. Cambridge: Cambridge University Press, 2011.

Deacon, Roger. "Strategies of Governance: Michel Foucault on Power." *Theoria: A Journal of Social and Political Theory*, no. 92 (1998): 113–148.

Defaiya, Al. "Saudi Arabia to Host Electronic Warfare Symposium." October 18, 2013. https://perma.cc/5E6S-4HEZ.

Defense Industrial Base Information Sharing and Analysis Center. n.d. http://
www.dibisac.net/.

Deibert, Ronald J., and Rafal Rohozinski, "The New Cyber Military-Industrial
Complex." *The Globe and Mail*, March 28, 2011. https://perma.cc/
PJL9-AKGU.

Deloitte. "Cyber Insurance: One Element of Risk Management – Deloitte Risk &
Compliance – WSJ." *Risk and Compliance – Wall Street Journal*, March 18,
2015. http://deloitte.wsj.com/riskandcompliance/2015/03/18/
cyber-insurance-one-element-of-a-cyber-risk-management-strategy/.

Demarest, Joseph. "Taking Down Botnets." Testimony Before the United States
Senate Judiciary Committee, Subcommittee on Crime and Terrorism, July 15,
2014. http://www.fbi.gov/news/testimony/taking-down-botnets.

Demchak, Chris C., and Peter Dombrowski. "Rise of a Cybered Westphalian Age."
Strategic Studies Quarterly (Spring 2011). http://www.au.af.mil/au/ssq/2011/
spring/demchak-dombrowski.pdf.

DeNardis, Laura. *The Global War for Internet Governance*. New Haven: Yale UP,
2014.

Department for Culture, Media and Sport. "UK Digital Strategy 2017." London:
Department for Culture, Media and Sport. March 1, 2017. https://www.gov.uk/
government/publications/uk-digital-strategy/uk-digital-strategy.

Department for Digital, Culture, Media and Sport. "Security of Network and
Information Systems. Government Response to Public Consultation." London:
Department for Digital, Culture, Media and Sport. January 29, 2018. https://
www.gov.uk/government/consultations/consultation-on-the-security-of-network-and-
information-systems-directive.

Department for Digital, Culture, Media and Sport. *Secure by Design: Improving
the Cyber Security of Consumer Internet of Things Report*, 1–37. London:
Department for Digital, Culture, Media & Sport, 2018a. https://www.gov.uk/
government/uploads/system/uploads/attachment_data/file/686089/Secure_by_
Design_Report_.pdf

Department of Digital, Culture, Media and Sport. *Code of Practice for Consumer
IoT Security*, 1–24. London: Department for Digital, Culture, Media and Sport,
2018b. https://assets.publishing.service.gov.uk/government/uploads/system/
uploads/attachment_data/file/747413/Code_of_Practice_for_Consumer_IoT_
Security_October_2018.pdf

Department of Homeland Security. "Cyberspace Policy Review: Assuring a
Trusted and Resilient Information and Communications Infrastructure," 2009.
https://fas.org/irp/eprint/cyber-review.pdf.

Department of Homeland Security. "Cyber Information Sharing and
Collaboration Program (CISCP)." n.d.-a https://www.dhs.gov/ciscp.

Department of Homeland Security. "Homeland Open Security Technology
(HOST)." n.d.-b https://www.dhs.gov/science-and-technology/csd-host.

Department of Homeland Security. "Information Sharing." n.d.-c https://www.dhs.gov/topic/cybersecurity-information-sharing.

Department of Homeland Security. "United States Secret Service Electronic Crimes Taskforce," n.d.-d https://www.dhs.gov/sites/default/files/publications/USSS_Electronic-Crimes-TaskForces.pdf.

Department of Justice, U.S. Attorney's Office, Northern District of California. "Russian National and Bitcoin Exchange Charged in 21-Count Indictment for Operating Alleged International Money Laundering Scheme and Allegedly Laundering Funds from Hack of Mt. Gox," July 26, 2017. https://www.justice.gov/usao-ndca/pr/russian-national-and-bitcoin-exchange-charged-21-count-indictment-operating-alleged

Department of State, University of America. "Mutual Legal Assist Treaty Between the United States of America and the United Kingdom of Great Britain and Northern Ireland." Signed January 6, 1994. https://www.state.gov/documents/organization/176269.pdf.

Department of Transport and Centre for the Protection of National Infrastructure. "*The Key Principles of Cyber Security for Connected and Automated Vehicles*." London: HM Government, August 2017. https://www.gov.uk/government/uploads/system/uploads/attachment_data/file/624302/cyber-security-connected-automated-vehicles-key-principles.pdf.

Desai, Deven R. "Beyond Location: Data Security in the 21st Century." (December 3, 2012). *Communications of the ACM* 56 (January 2013). https://ssrn.com/abstract=2237712

Dijk, Jan van, and Anneleen Winters-van Beek. "The Perspective of Network Government: The Struggle between Hierarchies, Markets and Networks as Modes of Governance in Contemporary Government." In *ICTs, Citizens and Governance: After the Hype!*, edited by Albert Meijer, Kees Boersma, Pieter Wagenaar, 235–255. Lancaster: Gavelle Books, 2009.

Dillon, Michael, and Andrew Neal. "Introduction." In *Foucault on Politics, Security and War*, edited by Michael Dillon and Andrew Neal, 1–20. Springer, 2015.

Division of Corporation Finance. "CF Disclosure Guidance: Topic No. 2." *Securities and Exchange Commission*, October 13, 2011. https://www.sec.gov/divisions/corpfin/guidance/cfguidance-topic2.htm.

DJI. "DJI Bug Bounty Program Policy." Last updated November 26, 2017a. https://security.dji.com/policy?lang=en_US.

DJI. "DJI To Offer 'Bug Bounty' Rewards for Reporting Software Issues." August 28,2017b.https://www.dji.com/newsroom/news/dji-to-offer-bug-bounty-rewards-for-reporting-software-issues.

DJI. "Statement About DJI's Cyber Security and Privacy Practices." November 25, 2017c.https://www.dji.com/newsroom/news/statement-about-dji-cyber-security-and-privacy-practices.

Dodge, Martin, and Rob Kitchin. *Mapping Cyberspace*. London: Routledge, 2000.

Doe v. Fed. Democratic Republic of Ethiopia, No. 16-7081, 2017 U.S. Appl. LEXIS 4414.

Donaghy, Rori. "Falcon Eye: The Israeli-Installed Mass Civil Surveillance System of Abu Dhabi." *Middle East Eye*, February 28, 2015. https://perma.cc/3WX8-XMM5.

Dourado, Eli. "Behind Closed Doors at the UN's Attempted 'Takeover of the Internet." *Ars Technica*, December 20, 2012. https://perma.cc/TCG3-2LST.

Dourado, Eli. "Protecting the Open Internet May Require Defunding the ITU." *Washington Post*, September 18, 2013. https://perma.cc/H2WS-2CFP.

Dowle, Chad, and Corey Judson. "Data Protection in United Arab Emirates." *Thomson Reuters Practical Law*, May 10, 2016. https://perma.cc/35XY-M5QF.

Doyle, Charles. "Cybercrime: An Overview of the Federal Computer Fraud and Abuse Statute and Related Federal Criminal Laws 6–7." 2008. https://fas.org/sgp/crs/misc/97-1025.pdf.

Drake, William J. "Background Paper for the Workshop on Data Localization and Barriers to Transborder Data Flows." *The World Economic Forum*, Geneva, September 14–15, 2016. http://www3.weforum.org/docs/Background_Paper_Forum_workshop%2009.2016.pdf

Drake, William J., Cerf, Vinton G., and Kleinwächter, Wolfgang. "Internet Fragmentation: An Overview." *World Economic Forum*, January 2016. http://www3.weforum.org/docs/WEF_FII_Internet_Fragmentation_An_Overview_2016.pdf.

Duffy, Matt. "Arab Media Regulations: Identifying Restraints on Freedom of the Press in the Laws of Six Arabian Peninsula Countries." *Berkeley Journal of Middle Eastern & Islamic Law* 6, no. 1 (April 1, 2014): 1–31.

Dunn Cavelty Myriam. "The Militarisation Of Cyber Security as A Source Of Global Tension." In *Strategic Trends and Analysis: Key Developments in Global Affairs*, edited by Daniel Möckli, 103–124. Zurich: Center for Security Studies, 2012. http://www.css.ethz.ch/publications/pdfs/Strategic-Trends-2012-Cyber.pdf.

Dunn Cavelty Myriam, and Manuel Suter, "Public-private Partnerships are no Silver Bullet: An Expanded Governance Model for Critical Infrastructure Protection." *International Journal of Critical Infrastructure Protection* 2 (2009): 179–187.

Dutton, William H. "Multistakeholder Internet Governance?" *World Bank*, 2016. https://papers.ssrn.com/sol3/papers.cfm?abstract_id=2615596.

Dutton, William H, and Malcolm Peltu. "The Emerging Internet Governance Mosaic: Connecting the Pieces." *Information Polity* 12, no. 1–2 (2007): 63–81.

Eckert, Sue. *"Protecting Critical Infrastructure: The Role of the Private Sector."* University of Pittsburgh Center for International Securities Studies, 2005. http://www.ridgway.pitt.edu/Portals/1/pdfs/Publications/Eckert.pdf.

Economidis, Nicholas, Richard Betterley, Leigh McMullan, David Navetta, Robert A. Parisi. "Cyber Liability on Main Street: What Coverages Do You Need?"

November 9, 2012. http://plusweb.org/Portals/0/Conference%20Material%
202012/Cyber%20Liability%20on%20Main%20Street.pdf.

Edwards, Don. United States House of Representatives Committee on the
Judiciary, United States Subcommittee on Civil and Constitutional Rights,
House of Representatives. "Federal Computer Systems Protection Act of 1981."
September 23, 1982.

Eelco van, Hout, Kim Putters, and Mirjan Oude Vrielink. "Governance of Local
Care and Public Service Provision." Paper presented at the EGPA Conference,
Madrid, September 19–22, 2007. Accessed November 9, 2017. https://www.
researchgate.net/profile/Mirjan_Oude_Vrielink/publication/254795863_
Governance_of_local_care_and_public_service_provision/
links/00b495369ded73014c000000/Governance-of-local-care-and-public-
service-provision.pdf.

eGov innovation. "ITU-IMPACT to Hold Arab Cross-Border Cyber Drill."
Enterprise Innovation, July 3, 2012. https://perma.cc/BAY6-YHAX.

Elazari Bar On, Amit. "Bug Bounty Programs as a Corporate Governance 'Best
Practice' Mechanism." *Berkeley Technology Law Journal Blog*, March 22, 2017.
http://btlj.org/2017/03/
bug-bounty-programs-as-a-corporate-governance-best-practice-mechanism/.

Elazari Bar On, Amit. *Unconscionability 2.0 and the IP Boilerplate: A Revised
Doctrine of Unconscionability for the Information Age* (working draft). n.d.

Elazari Bar On, Amit, and Peter S. Menell. *Distinguishing Whistleblowers from
Hackers: The Case for CFAA Whistleblower Immunity* (working draft). n.d.

Electronic Frontier Foundation (EFF). "Free Speech Weak Link." n.d.-a https://
www.eff.org/free-speech-weak-link.

Electronic Frontier Foundation (EFF). "Google v. Equustek." n.d.-b https://www.
eff.org/cases/google-v-equustek

Electronic Frontier Foundation (EFF). "A 'Grey Hat' Guide." n.d.-c https://www.
eff.org/pages/grey-hat-guide.

Electronic Frontier Foundation (EFF). "Objection to the rechartering of the W3C
EME group." n.d.-d https://www.eff.org/pages/
objection-rechartering-w3c-eme-group#covenant.

Elkin-Koren, Niva. "A Public Regarding Approach to Contracting Copyrights." In
*Expanding the Boundaries of Intellectual Property: Innovation Policy for the
Knowledge Society*, edited by Rochelle Dreyfuss, Diane L. Zimmerman, and
Harry First, 191–221. Oxford: Oxford University Press, 2001.

Ellis, Ryan, Keman Huang, Michael Siegel, Katie Moussouris, and James
Houghton. "Fixing a Hole: The Labor Market for Bugs." In *New Solutions for
Cybersecurity*, edited by Howard Shrobe, David L. Shrier, and Alex Pentland,
129–159. Cambridge: MIT Press, 2018.

ENISA. *Baseline Security Recommendations for IoT in the Context of Critical
Information Infrastructures*, 1–103. Heraklion, Greece: European Union
Agency For Network And Information Security, 2017. https://www.enisa.
europa.eu/publications/baseline-security-recommendations-for-iot.

ENISA. "National Cyber Security Strategy of Saudi Arabia." n.d. https://perma. cc/4RW3-WUH4.

Enoch, Nick. "Hamas Hails Hack Attack against Websites of Israel's Stock Exchange, El Al Airline and Three Banks." *Mail Online*, January 16, 2012. https://perma.cc/B4UK-G9Q3.

EPFL IRGC. "*Governing Cybersecurity Risks and Benefits of the Internet of Things: Connected Medical & Health Devices and Connected Vehicles.*" Lausanne: EPFL International Risk Governance Center, 2017. https://www. irgc.org/wp-content/uploads/2017/04/IRGC.-2017.-Cybersecurity-in-the-IoT.-Workshop-report.pdf.

Estonia Ministry of Economic Affairs and Communications and Microsoft. "Implementation of the Virtual Data Embassy Solution." n.d. https://www.mkm. ee/sites/default/files/implementation_of_the_virtual_data_embassy_solution_ summary_report.pdf

Etcovitch, Daniel, and Thyla van der Merwe. "Coming in from the Cold: A Safe Harbor from the CFAA and the DMCA §1201 for Security Researchers." 2018. https://papers.ssrn.com/sol3/papers.cfm?abstract_id=3055814.

European Commission. "*COM (2017) 477 Final/2: Proposal for a Regulation of the European Parliament and the Council on ENISA, the 'EU Cybersecurity Agency,' and Repealing Regulation (EU) 526/2013, and on Information and Communication Technology Cybersecurity Certification ("Cybersecurity Act").*" Brussels: European Commission, April 10, 2017. https://ec.europa.eu/transparency/regdoc/ rep/1/2017/EN/COM-2017-477-F1-EN-MAIN-PART-1.PDF.

European Commission. "Questionnaire on improving criminal justice in cyberspace: Summary of Response." n.d. https://ec.europa.eu/home-affairs/ sites/homeaffairs/files/e-library/documents/policies/organized-crime-and-human-trafficking/e-evidence/docs/summary_of_replies_to_e-evidence_ questionnaire_en.pdf.

European Parliament Directorate-General for Internal Policies. "The data protection regime in China: In-depth Analysis for the LIBE Committee (October 2015)." 2015. http://www.europarl.europa.eu/RegData/etudes/ IDAN/2015/536472/IPOL_IDA(2015)536472_EN.pdf.

European Police Office. "2016 Internet Organized Crime Threat Assessment (IOCTA)." 2016. https://www.europol.europa.eu/activities-services/main-reports/internet-organised-crime-threat-assessment-iocta-2016.

Europol. "International Action Against 'GameOver Zeus' Botnet and 'Cryptolocker' Ransomware." June 4, 2014. Accessed November 9, 2017. https:// www.europol.europa.eu/newsroom/news/international-action-against-gameover-zeus-botnet-and-cryptolocker-ransomware.

Evans, Chris. "Announcing Project Zero." *Google Online Security Blog*, July 15, 2014. https://googleonlinesecurity.blogspot.com/2014/07/announcing-project-zero.html.

Evans, Chris, Neel Mehta, Adam Mein, Matt Moore, and Michael Zalewski. "Rewarding Web Application Security Research." *Google Online Security Blog*, November 1, 2010. https://googleonlinesecurity.blogspot.com/2010/11/rewarding-web-application-security.html.

Executive Branch of the Federative Republic of Brazil. Personal Data Protection Law Draft Bill. January 28, 2015. https://iapp.org/media/pdf/resource_center/Brazil_PDPL_Draft_Bill-final.pdf; https://uk.practicallaw.thomsonreuters.com/4-520-1732.

Executive Office of the President. Executive Order 13010. "Critical Infrastructure Protection." July 15, 1996. https://www.gpo.gov/fdsys/pkg/FR-1996-07-17/pdf/96-18351.pdf.

Executive Office of the President. Executive Order 13231. "Critical Infrastructure Protection in the Information Age." October 16, 2001. https://www.gpo.gov/fdsys/pkg/FR-2001-10-18/pdf/01-26509.pdf.

Executive Office of the President. Executive Order 13691. "Promoting Private Sector Cybersecurity Information Sharing."February 13, 2015. https://www.whitehouse.gov/the-press-office/2015/02/13/executive-order-promoting-private-sector-cybersecurity-information-shari.

Executive Office of the President. Office of the Press Secretary. "Fact Sheet: Executive Order Promoting Private Sector Cybersecurity Information Sharing." February 12, 2015. https://www.whitehouse.gov/the-press-office/2015/02/12/fact-sheet-executive-order-promoting-private-sector-cybersecurity-inform.

Facebook. "Facebook Bug Bounty: $5 Million Paid in 5 Years." *Facebook Bug Bounty*, October 12, 2016a. https://www.facebook.com/notes/facebook-bug-bounty/facebook-bug-bounty-5-million-paid-in-5-years/1419385021409053/.

Facebook. "Highlights: Less Low-Hanging Fruit." *Facebook Bug Bounty*, February 9,2016b.https://www.facebook.com/notes/facebook-bug-bounty/2015-highlights-less-low-hanging-fruit/1225168744164016/.

Facebook Security Team. "An Update on our Bug Bounty Program." August 2, 2013. https://www.facebook.com/notes/facebook-security/an-update-on-our-bug-bounty-program/10151508163265766.

Facebook Security Team. "White Hat Information." September 12, 2018. https://www.facebook.com/whitehat/.

Facebook Whitehat. "Information." May 23, 2017. https://www.facebook.com/whitehat.

Fair, Lesley. "D-Link Case Alleges Inadequate Internet of Things Security Practices | Federal Trade Commission." *Federal Trade Commission*, January 5, 2017.https://www.ftc.gov/news-events/blogs/business-blog/2017/01/d-link-case-alleges-inadequate-internet-things-security.

FBI National Press Office. "*The FBI and the National Infrastructure Protection Center Publicly Introduce the National InfraGard Program.*" Washington, DC, 2001. https://archives.fbi.gov/archives/news/pressrel/press-releases/

the-fbi-and-the-national-infrastructure-protection-center-publically-introduce-the-national-infragard-program.

FBIIC. "FBIIC Members." n.d.-a https://www.fbiic.gov/fbiic-members.html.

FBIIC. "Mission and History." n.d.-b https://www.fbiic.gov/mission-history.html.

Federal Assembly of the Swiss Confederation. *Swiss Criminal Code.* 1937.

Federal Aviation Administration. "ADS-B Frequently Asked Questions (FAQs)." n.d.-a https://www.faa.gov/nextgen/programs/adsb/faq/.

Federal Aviation Administration. "Air Traffic By The Numbers." n.d.-b https://www.faa.gov/air_traffic/by_the_numbers/.

Federal Aviation Administration. "Regulations and Policies." n.d.-c https://www.faa.gov/aircraft/air_cert/design_approvals/air_software/software_regs/.

Federal Department of Defence, Civil Protection, and Sport. "Cyber-Spionage-Angriff Auf RUAG." 2016. http://www.vbs.admin.ch/de/aktuell/medienmitteilungen.detail.nsb.html/61618.html.

Federal Rules of Criminal Procedure, 41(b)(6). June 20, 2016. https://www.justice.gov/archives/opa/blog/rule-41-changes-ensure-judge-may-consider-warrants-certain-remote-searches.

Federal Trade Commission. "Privacy & Data Security Update: 2016." January 2016–December 2016. https://www.ftc.gov/system/files/documents/reports/privacy-data-security-update-2016/privacy_and_data_security_update_2016_web.pdf.

Feki, Mohamed Ali, Fahim Kawsar, Mathieu Boussard, and Lieven Trappeniers. "The Internet of Things: The Next Technological Revolution." *Computer* 46, no. 2 (2013): 24–25.

FFIEC. "Cybersecurity Assessment Tool." n.d.-a https://www.ffiec.gov/cyberassessmenttool.htm.

FFIEC. "Federal Financial Institutions Examination Council (FFIEC) About." n.d.-b https://www.ffiec.gov/about.htm.

Finifter, Matthew, Devdatta Akhawe, and David Wagner. "An Empirical Study of Vulnerability Rewards Programs." In *22nd USENIX Security Symposium*, Washington, DC, August 14–16, 2013.

Finkle, Jim. "Exclusive: SWIFT Discloses More Cyber Thefts Pressures Banks on Security." *Reuters*, August 31, 2018. http://www.reuters.com/article/us-cyber-heist-swift-idUSKCN11600C.

Finkle, Jim, and Dhanya Skariachan. "Target Cyber Breach Hits 40 Million Payment Cards at Holiday Peak." *Reuters*, December 18, 2013. https://www.reuters.com/article/us-target-breach/target-cyber-breach-hits-40-million-payment-cards-at-holiday-peak-idUSBRE9BH1GX20131219.

Fisher, Dennis. "Microsoft Says No to Paying Bug Bounties." *Threat Post*, July 22, 2010. https://threatpost.com/microsoft-says-no-paying-bug-bounties-072210/74249/.

Fleischer, Peter. "Adapting Our Approach to the European Right to be Forgotten." *Google.* March 4, 2016. https://www.blog.google/topics/google-europe/adapting-our-approach-to-european-rig/.

Foley, Sean. *The Arab Gulf States: Beyond Oil and Islam.* Boulder: Lynne Rienner Publishers, 2010.

Fontanella-Khan, James, and Hannah Kuchler. "Yahoo Agrees to $350m Price Cut in Verizon Deal." *Financial Times,* February 21, 2017. https://www.ft.com/content/7541c82a-f843-11e6-9516-2d969e0d3b65.

Fox-Brewster, Thomas. "Petya or NotPetya: Why The Latest Ransomware Is Deadlier Than WannaCry." *Forbes,* June 27, 2017. https://www.forbes.com/sites/thomasbrewster/2017/06/27/petya-notpetya-ransomware-is-more-powerful-than-wannacry/.

Franceschi-Bicchierai, Lorenzo. "How 1.5 Million Connected Cameras Were Hijacked to Make an Unprecedented Botnet." *Motherboard,* September 29, 2016. https://motherboard.vice.com/en_us/article/8q8dab/15-million-connected-cameras-ddos-botnet-brian-krebs.

Friis, Karsten, and Jens Ringsmose. *Conflict in Cyber Space: Theoretical, Strategic and Legal Pespectives.* Routledge Studies in Conflict, Security and Technology. London: Taylor & Francis, 2016.

FS-ISAC. "New Soltra Network Offering to Connect and Coordinate Cyber Threat Intelligence Sharing." October 12, 2014. https://www.fsisac.com/sites/default/files/news/Soltra%20Network%20Press%20Release%20101215%20%28final%29.pdf.

FS-ISAC. "Best Practices for Financial Institutions Reducing Risks Associated with Destructive Malware." November 23, 2015a.

FS-ISAC. "FS-ISAC to Offer Security Threat Information to Over 10,000 Federal Reserve Bank Financial Institution Customers." September 16, 2015b. https://www.fsisac.com/sites/default/files/news/FRB-FS-ISAC-Press_Release_Sept_2015FINAL.pdf.

FS-ISAC. "European Banking Federation and the Financial Services Information Sharing and Analysis Center (FS-ISAC) Partner on Trans-Atlantic Initiative to Fight Cyber Crime." September 30, 2016a. https://www.fsisac.com/sites/default/files/news/EBF%20and%20FS%20ISAC%20agree%20Trans-Atlantic%20cybercrime%20cooperation.pdf.

FS-ISAC. "FS-ISAC Announces the Formation of the Financial Systemic Analysis & Resilience Center (FSARC)." October 24, 2016b. https://www.fsisac.com/sites/default/files/news/FS-ISAC%20Announces%20the%20Formation%20of%20the%20Financial%20Systemic%20Analysis%20%28FSARC%29.pdf.

FS-ISAC. "Preliminary Findings from Latest DDoS Attacks." November 2016c. http://iiac.ca/wp-content/uploads/FS-ISAC-SIRG-Cybersecurity-Brief-for-North-America-November-2016.pdf.

FS-ISAC. "Sheltered Harbor." November 23, 2016d. https://www.fsisac.com/sites/
   default/files/news/SH_FACT_SHEET_2016_11_22_FINAL3.pdf.
FS-ISAC. "FS-ISAC Community Institution and Association Membership Grows
   3,800 Members. Heather McCalman Joins as Credit Union Council Manager."
   March 22, 2017. https://www.fsisac.com/sites/default/files/news/FS-ISAC_
   Press_Release_Community_Inst_3-22-2017_Final.pdf.
FS-ISAC. "About FS-ISAC." n.d.-a https://www.fsisac.com/about.
FS-ISAC. "Membership Benefits." n.d.-b https://www.fsisac.com/join.
FS-ISAC. "Mission." n.d.-c https://www.fsisac.com/about/mission.
FSSCC. "Financial Services Sector Coordinating Council for Critical Infrastructure
   Protection and Homeland Security Charter." March 20, 2015. https://www.dhs.
   gov/sites/default/files/publications/FSSCC-Charter-03-15-508.pdf.
FSSCC. "About FSSCC." n.d.-a https://www.fsscc.org/About-FSSCC.
FSSCC. "Financial Services Sector Coordinating Council for Critical
   Infrastructure Protection and Homeland Security Annual Report 2013–2014."
   n.d.-b https://www.aba.com/Tools/Function/Cyber/Documents/FSSCC
   AnnualReport2013-2014.pdf.
FTC. "Start With Security." n.d. https://www.ftc.gov/system/files/documents/
   plain-language/pdf0205-startwithsecurity.pdf.
Gallagher, Sean. "How One Rent-a-Botnet Army of Cameras and DVRs Caused
   Internet Chaos." *Ars Technica UK*, October 30, 2016. https://arstechnica.co.uk/
   information-technology/2016/10/inside-the-machine-uprising-how-cameras-dvrs-
   took-down-parts-of-the-internet/.
Gallagher, Sean. "Man gets threats – not bug bounty – after finding DJI customer
   data in public view." *Ars Technica*, November 17, 2017. https://arstechnica.
   com/information-technology/2017/11/dji-left-private-keys-for-ssl-cloud-
   storage-in-public-view-and-exposed-customers/.
Gartner. "Definition: Threat Intelligence." May 16, 2013. https://www.gartner.
   com/doc/2487216/definition-threat-intelligence.
Gartner. "Middle East & North Africa Information Security Spending to Reach
   US$1.3 Billion in 2016." October 31, 2016. https://perma.cc/3LWW-GUGP.
Gassen, Jan, Elmar Gerhards-Padilla, and Peter Martini. "Botnets: How to Fight
   the Ever-Growing Threat on a Technical Level." In *Botnets*, edited by Heli
   Tirmaa-Klaar, Jan Gassen, Elmar Gerhards-Padilla, and Peter Martini, 41–97.
   London: Springer, 2013.
Gause, F. Gregory. *Oil Monarchies*. New York: Council on Foreign Relations Press,
   1994.
Geer, Dan. "For Good Measure: The Undiscovered." *Login* 40, no. 2 (2015). http://
   geer.tinho.net/fgm/fgm.geer.1504.pdf
Geist, Michael. "Cyberlaw 2.0." *Boston College Law Review* 44 (2003): 323–358.
Gellman, Barton, and Ashkan Soltani. "NSA Infiltrates Links to Yahoo, Google,
   Data Centers Worldwide, Snowden Documents Say." *Washington Post*, October
   30, 2013.

Germano, Judith H. "*Cybersecurity Partnerships: A New Era of Public-Private Collaboration.*" New York: Center on Law and Security, New York University, 2014.

Gertz, Bill. "FBI Eyes China in Posting Hacked Documents on Chinese Dissident." *The Washington Free Beacon*, September 29, 2017. http://freebeacon.com/national-security/fbi-eyes-china-posting-hacked-documents-chinese-dissident/.

Gilbert, David. "Anonymous Knocks Saudi Government Websites Offline." *International Business Times*, September 28, 2015. https://perma.cc/6Q8Y-4DVN.

Global Semiconductor Alliance and McKinsey & Company. "*Security in the Internet of Things. How Semiconductor Companies Can Address the Major Obstacle to IoT Growth, and Benefit in the Process.*" Texas: Global Semiconductor Alliance & McKinsey & Company, April 2017. http://www.mckinsey.com/industries/semiconductors/our-insights/security-in-the-internet-of-things.

Global Voices Advox. "Right to Be Forgotten: A Win for Argentina's Lawsuit-Happy Celebrities?" September 18, 2014. https://advox.globalvoices.org/2014/09/18/right-to-be-forgotten-a-win-for-argentinas-lawsuit-happy-celebrities/.

Goldsmith, Jack L. "Against Cyberanarchy." *University of Chicago Law Review* 65, no. 4 (1998): 1199–1250.

Goldsmith, Jack and Tim Wu. *Who Controls the Internet?: Illusions of a Borderless World*. New York, NY: Oxford University Press, 2006.

Golesorkhi, Lara-Zuzan. "Cases of Contention: Activism, Social Media and Law in Saudi Arabia." *Arab Media & Society*, no. 20 (2015): 1–16.

Golson, Jordan. "Jeep Hackers at it Again, This Time Taking Control of Steering and Braking Systems." *The Verge*, August 2, 2016. https://www.theverge.com/2016/8/2/12353186/car-hack-jeep-cherokee-vulnerability-miller-valasek.

Goodin, Dan. "Creepy IoT Teddy Bear Leaks >2 Million Parents' and Kids' Voice Messages." *Ars Technica UK*, February 28, 2017a. https://arstechnica.co.uk/information-technology/2017/02/creepy-iot-teddy-bear-leaks-2-million-parents-and-kids-voice-messages/.

Goodin, Dan. "Windows 7, Not XP, was the Reason Last Week's WCry Worm Spread So Widely." *Ars Technica*, May 20, 2017b. https://arstechnica.com/information-technology/2017/05/windows-7-not-xp-was-the-reason-last-weeks-wcry-worm-spread-so-widely/.

Google. "Encouraging More Chromium Security Research." *Google Online Security Blog*, January 28, 2010. http://blog.chromium.org/2010/01/encouraging-more-chromium-security.html.

Google. "Charts and Graphs." Bughunter University. 2014–2016. https://sites.google.com/site/bughunteruniversity/behind-the-scenes/charts.

Google. "Digital Security & Due Process: Modernizing Cross-Border Government Access Standards for the Cloud Era." *Google Blog*, June 22, 2017a. https://www.blog.google/documents/2/CrossBorderLawEnforcementRequestsWhitePaper_2.pdf.

Google. "Vulnerability Rewards Program: 2016 Year in Review, 2017." *Google Online Security Blog*, January 30, 2017b. https://security.googleblog. com/2017/01/vulnerability-rewards-program-2016-year.html.

Google. "Android Security Rewards Program." n.d.-a https://www.google.com/ about/appsecurity/android-rewards/.

Google. "Chrome Rewards Program." n.d.-b https://www.google.com/about/ appsecurity/chrome-rewards/.

Google. "Google Vulnerability Reward Program (VRP) Rules." n.d.-c https://www. google.com/about/appsecurity/reward-program/.

Google. "Patch Rewards Program." n.d.-d https://www.google.com/about/ appsecurity/patch-rewards/.

Google. "Vulnerability Research Grants." n.d.-e https://www.google.com/about/ appsecurity/research-grants/.

"Google Spain SL v. Agencia Española de Protección de Datos." *Harvard Law Review*, May 13, 2014. https://harvardlawreview.org/2014/12/ google-spain-sl-v-agencia-espanola-de-proteccion-de-datos/.

Google v. Equustek Solutions Inc. U.S. District Court of Northern District of California San Jose Division. 2017. https://assets.documentcloud.org/ documents/3900043/Google-v-Equustek-Complaint.pdf.

Greenberg, Andy. "Shopping for Zero-Days: A Price List for Hackers' Secret Software Exploits." *Forbes*, March 23, 2012.

Greenberg, Andy. "Meet Project Zero: Google's Secret Team of Bug-Hunting Hackers." *Wired*, July 15, 2014. http://www.wired.com/2014/07/google-project-zero/.

GSMA. "*IoT Security Guidelines Overview Document. Version 1.1.*" Unknown: GSM Association, 2016. https://www.gsma.com/iot/wp-content/uploads/ 2016/02/CLP.11-v1.1.pdf.

H. M. Government. "*Cyber Security Regulation and Incentives Review.*" HM Government, 2016. https://www.gov.uk/government/uploads/system/uploads/ attachment_data/file/579442/Cyber_Security_Regulation_and_Incentives_ Review.pdf.

H. M. Government. "Cyber Essentials." *Cyber Aware*, June 17, 2017, https://www. cyberaware.gov.uk/cyberessentials/.

Haasnoot, Marjolijn, Jan H. Kwakkel, Warren E. Walker, and Judithter Maat. "Dynamic Adaptive Policy Pathways: A Method for Crafting Robust Decisions for a Deeply Uncertain World." *Global Environmental Change* 23, no. 2 (April 2013): 485–498. https://doi.org/10.1016/j.gloenvcha.2012.12.006.

HackerOne. "Introducing Reputation." October 28, 2014. https://www.hackerone. com/blog/introducing-reputation.

HackerOne. "Improving Signal Over 10,000 Bugs." July 2015. https://hackerone. com/blog/improving-signal-over-10000-bugs.

HackerOne. "The 2016 Bug Bounty Hacker Report." September 13, 2016. https:// www.hackerone.com/blog/hacker-surey-report-2016.

HackerOne. "Finder Terms and Conditions." February 16, 2017a. https://www. hackerone.com/terms/finder.

HackerOne. "HackerOne Finder Terms and Conditions 2." February 16, 2017b. https://www.hackerone.com/terms/finder.

HackerOne. "HackerOne General Terms and Conditions 3." February 16, 2017c. https://www.hackerone.com/terms/general.

HackerOne. "AVG Technologies." n.d.-a https://hackerone.com/avg.

HackerOne. n.d.-b https://hackerone.com/.

HackerOne. "Bug Bounty Program Basics for Companies." n.d.-c https://www. hackerone.com/resources/bug-bounty-basics.

HackerOne. "Bug Bounty Programs." n.d.-d https://hackerone.com/bug-bounty-programs.

HackerOne. "DoD Vulnerability Disclosure Policy." n.d.-e https://hackerone.com/ deptofdefense.

HackerOne. "General Motors." n.d.-f https://hackerone.com/gm.

HackerOne. "Kaspersky Lab." n.d.-g https://hackerone.com/kaspersky.

HackerOne. "Twitter: Policy." n.d.-h https://hackerone.com/twitter.

HackerOne. "Uber." n.d.-i https://hackerone.com/uber.

HackerOne. "Vulnerability Disclosure Guidelines." n.d.-j https://www.hackerone. com/disclosure-guidelines

HackerOne. "Yahoo Bug Bounty Program Rules." n.d.-k https://hackerone.com/ yahoo.

"Hail a TAXII." n.d. http://hailataxii.com/.

Halliday, Josh. "UAE to Tighten BlackBerry Restrictions." *The Guardian*, April 18, 2011. https://perma.cc/PH46-HF32.

Hamelink, Cees J. *The Ethics of Cyberspace.* Thousand Oaks, CA: Sage, 2001.

Hamilton, Alexander. Federalist Paper No. 15. "The Insufficiency of the Present Confederation to Preserve the Union." *The Independent Journal*, December 1, 1787. https://www.congress.gov/resources/display/content/The+Federalist+ Papers#TheFederalistPapers-15.

Hansen, Lene, and Helen Nissenbaum. "Digital Disaster, Cyber Security, and the Copenhagen School." *International Studies Quarterly* 53 (2009): 1155–1175.

Hansen, Mark, Carolyn McAndrews, and Emily Berkeley. "*History of Aviation Safety Oversight in the United States.*" U.S. Department of Transportation, Federal Aviation Administration, July 2008. http://www.tc.faa.gov/its/worldpac/ techrpt/ar0839.pdf.

Hartwig, Robert P., and Claire Wilkinson. "*Cyber Risks: The Growing Threat.*" Insurance Information Institute, June 2014. http://www.iii.org/sites/default/ files/docs/pdf/paper_cyberrisk_2014.pdf.

Harvard Law National Security Research Group (Ivana Deyrup, Shane Matthews, Aatif Iqbal, Benjamin Black, Catherine Fisher, John Cella, Jonathan Abrams, Miranda Dugi, & Rebecca Leventhal). "Cloud Computing and National Law."

2010. https://lawfare.s3-us-west-2.amazonaws.com/staging/s3fs-public/uploads/2010/10/Cloud-Final.pdf.

Harwood, Matthew. "Lack of Trust Thwarts Cybersecurity Information Sharing." *Security Management*, 2011.

Haselton, Bennett. "Smartfilter: Miscategorization and Filtering in Saudi Arabia and UAE." *Citizen Lab*, November 28, 2013.

Hassan, Maggie. "Senators Hassan, Portman Introduce Bipartisan Bill to Strengthen Cyber Defenses at Department of Homeland Security." May 26, 2017. https://www.hassan.senate.gov/news/press-releases/senators-hassan-portman-introduce-bipartisan-bill-to-strengthen-cyber-defenses-at-department-of-homeland-security.

Head, John G. *Public Goods and Public Welfare*. Durham, NC: Duke University Press, 1975.

Held, David, and Kristian Ulrichsen, eds. *The Transformation of the Gulf: Politics, Economics and the Global Order*. Routledge, 2011.

Helderman, Jan-Kees, Gwyn Bevan, and George France. "The Rise of the Regulatory State in Healthcare: A Comparative Analysis of the Netherlands, England and Italy." *Health Economics Policy and Law* 7 (2012): 103–124.

Hennessey, Susan, and Mirasola Chris. "Did China Quietly Authorize Law Enforcement to Access Data Anywhere in the World?" *Lawfare*, March 27, 2017. https://www.lawfareblog.com/did-china-quietly-authorize-law-enforcement-access-data-anywhere-world.

Herr, Trey, Bruce Schneier, and Christopher Morris. "Taking Stock: Estimating Vulnerability Rediscovery." *Belfer Cyber Security Project White Paper Series*, 2017. https://papers.ssrn.com/sol3/papers.cfm?abstract_id=2928758.

Hertog, Steffen. "The Private Sector and Reform in the Gulf Cooperation Council." Kuwait Programme on Development, Governance and Globalisation in the Gulf States. July 2013.

Hickens, Michael. "Insurer Warns Client of Possible Breach." *Wall Street Journal – CIO Journal*, March 11, 2014. http://blogs.wsj.com/cio/2014/03/11/insurer-warns-client-of-possible-breach/.

Hill, Jonah Force. "Internet Fragmentation: Highlighting the Major Technical, Governance and Diplomatic Challenges for U.S. Policy Makers." Paper, Science, Technology, and Public Policy Program, Belfer Center, Harvard Kennedy School of Government, May 2012. http://www.belfercenter.org/sites/default/files/legacy/files/internet_fragmentation_jonah_hill.pdf.

Hill, Jonah Force. "The Growth of Data Localization Post-Snowden." *Lawfare Research Paper Series*, July 21, 2014. https://www.lawfareblog.com/jonah-force-hill-growth-data-localization-post-snowden-lawfare-research-paper-series

Hiremath, S., G. Yang, and K. Mankodiya. "Wearable Internet of Things: Concept, Architectural Components and Promises for Person-Centered Healthcare." In

2014 4th International Conference on Wireless Mobile Communication and Healthcare – Transforming Healthcare Through Innovations in Mobile and Wireless Technologies (MOBIHEALTH), 2014, 304–307. https://ieeexplore.ieee.org/document/7015971.

Hofmann, Jeanette. "Internet Governance: A Regulative Idea in Flux." In *Internet Governance: An Introduction*, edited by Ravi Kumar and Jain Bandamutha, 74–108. Hyderabad: ICFAIUniversity Press, 2007.

Home Office of the United Kingdom. "Equipment Interference, DRAFT Code of Practice." Fall 2016. https://www.gov.uk/government/uploads/system/uploads/attachment_data/file/557861/IP_Bill_-_Draft_EI_code_of_practice.pdf.

Homeland Security Annual Report. "Letter to Senator Warren and Representative Cummings." December 9, 2014. https://www.fsscc.org/files/galleries/FSSCC_12-09-14_Letter_to_Sen_Warren-Rep_Cummings.pdf.

Homeland Security Annual Report. "Financial Services Sector Cybersecurity Recommendations." January 18, 2017. https://www.fsscc.org/files/galleries/FSSCC_Cybersecurity_Recommendations_for_Administration_and_Congress_2017.pdf.

Homeland Security Presidential Directive 7/HSPD-7, December 17, 2003. "Critical Infrastructure Identification, Prioritization, and Protection." https://www.dhs.gov/homeland-security-presidential-directive-7.

Howard, Philip N. *The Digital Origins of Dictatorship and Democracy: Information Technology and Political Islam*. Oxford: Oxford University Press, 2010.

Hoye, Matthew, and Rene Marsh. "GAO: Newer Aircraft Vulnerable to Hacking." *CNN*, April 14, 2015. http://www.cnn.com/2015/04/14/politics/gao-newer-aircraft-vulnerable-to-hacking/index.html.

Huang, Keman, et al. "Diversity or Concentration? Hackers' Strategy for Working Across Multiple Bug Bounty Programs." 2016. http://www.ieee-security.org/TC/SP2016/poster-abstracts/13-poster_abstract.pdf.

Human Rights Watch. "Saudi Arabia: 7 Convicted for Facebook Postings About Protests." *Human Rights Watch*, June 29, 2013a. https://perma.cc/39GS-52ED.

Human Rights Watch. "UAE: Concerns About Muslim Brotherhood Trial." *Human Rights Watch*, November 4, 2013b. https://perma.cc/DB8R-6HH3.

Human Rights Watch. "GCC: Joint Security Agreement Imperils Rights." *Human Rights Watch*, April 26, 2014. https://perma.cc/5LLC-BXEE.

Hypponen, Mikko, and Linus Nyman. "The Internet of (Vulnerable) Things: On Hypponen's Law, Security Engineering, and IoT Legislation." *Technology Innovation Management Review* 7, no. 4 (2017): 5–11.

IBM. "Cost of Data Breach." n.d. http://www-03.ibm.com/security/data-breach/.

ICANN. "Microsoft Collaborates With Industry to Disrupt Conficker Worm." February 2009. https://www.icann.org/news/announcement-2-2009-02-12-en.

ICANNWiki. "Multistakeholder Model." 2017. https://icannwiki.org/index.php/Multistakeholder_Model.

ictQatar. "Qatar National Cyber Security Strategy." Government of Qatar, May 2014.

Iliff, Laurence. "Google Wages Free-Speech Fight in Mexico." *The Wall Street Journal*, May 27, 2015. https://www.wsj.com/articles/google-wages-free-speech-fight-in-mexico-1432723483.

Infineon et al. *"Common Position on Cybersecurity."* Heraklion, Greece: European Union Agency for Network and Information Security, December 2016. https://www.enisa.europa.eu/publications/enisa-position-papers-and-opinions/infineon-nxp-st-enisa-position-on-cybersecurity.

Information Commissioner's Office. "Overview of the General Data Protection Regulation (GDPR)." ICO.org.uk. October 20, 2017. https://ico.org.uk/for-organisations/data-protection-reform/overview-of-the-gdpr/.

Infosecurity. "Saudi Aramco Cyber Attacks a 'Wake-up Call,' Says Former NSA Boss." May 8, 2014. https://perma.cc/NXT5-3J57.

International Air Transport Association. "Another Strong Year for Airline Profits in 2017." Press Release No. 76. December 8, 2016. http://www.iata.org/pressroom/pr/Pages/2016-12-08-01.aspx.

International Air Transport Association. "The Impact of September 11 2001 on Aviation." n.d. http://www.iata.org/pressroom/Documents/impact-9-11-aviation.pdf.

International Civil Aviation Organization. "ICAO Summit formalizes new Dubai Declaration to ensure global aviation remains united, proactive on cybersecurity preparedness." April 6, 2017. https://www.icao.int/Newsroom/Pages/ICAO-Summit-formalizes-new-Dubai-Declaration-ensures-global-aviation-remains-united-proactive-on-cybersecurity-preparedness.aspx.

International Civil Aviation Organization. "Convention on International Civil Aviation – Doc 7300." n.d. https://www.icao.int/publications/pages/doc7300.aspx.

"International Communications Privacy Act" (ICPA). S. 2986, 114th Congress (2016). https://www.congress.gov/114/bills/s2986/BILLS-114s2986is.xml.

International Organization for Standardization. "ISO/IEC 27001 – Information Security Management." 2013. http://www.iso.org/iso/home/standards/management-standards/iso27001.htm.

Internet and Jurisdiction Policy Network. n.d. https://www.internetjurisdiction.net/.

Internet Bug Bounty. n.d. https://internetbugbounty.org/.

"Internet of Things (IoT) Cybersecurity Improvement Act of 2017." S. 1691, 115th Congress (2017). https://www.congress.gov/115/bills/s1691/BILLS-115s1691is.pdf.

IoTUK. "IoTUK Launches to Support and Advance the UK's Internet of Things Capability." *IoTUK (blog)*, September 10, 2015. https://iotuk.org.uk/iotuk-launches-to-support-and-accelerate-the-uks-internet-of-things-capability/.

ISAO Standards Organization. "Information Sharing Groups About Us." 2017a. Accessed May 25, 2017. https://www.isao.org/about/.

ISAO Standards Organization. "Information Sharing Groups." 2017b. Accessed May 25, 2017. https://www.isao.org/information-sharing-groups/.

IT Governance Institute. *"COBiT 4.1 Framework."* IT Governance Institute, 2007. https://www.isaca.org/Knowledge-Center/cobit/Documents/COBIT4.pdf.

ITU. "ITU-IMPACT Establishes First Cybersecurity Innovation Centre for Arab Region." *Global Security Mag Online*, December 2012. https://perma.cc/ MF8F-GZ83.

ITU. "Regional Cybersecurity Centres." 2017. https://perma.cc/VB8H-6SF3.

Jaffee, Dwight M. "The Role of Government in the Coverage of Terrorism Risks." In *Terrorism Risk Insurance in OECD Countries*, Vol. 9. Policy Issues in Insurance. OECD Publishing, 2005. http://faculty.haas.berkeley.edu/jaffee/ papers/091DJOECD.pdf.

Jansen, Bart. "Delta Outage a Reminder of Fragility of Airline Computers." *USA Today*, January 30, 2017. https://www.usatoday.com/story/news/2017/01/30/ delta-outage-airline-technology-problems/97250834/.

Jennings, Bruce. "Public Health and Civic Republicanism." In *Ethics, Prevention, and Public Health*, edited by Angus Dawson and Marcel Verweij, 30–58. New York: Oxford University Press, 2007.

Johnson, Bobby. "Conficker Worm Explained: What Is a Botnet?" *The Guardian*, March 31, 2009. https://www.theguardian.com/technology/2009/mar/31/ botnets-explainer.

Joyce, Miriam. *Bahrain from the Twentieth Century to the Arab Spring*. London: Palgrave Macmillan, 2012.

JPMorgan Chase. *"Cybersecurity: Maintaining Strong Defenses."* Vol. 2 (Spring 2017).

JPMorgan Chase & Co. "Annual Report 2016." 2017. https://www.jpmorganchase. com/corporate/investor-relations/document/2016-annualreport.pdf.

Juniper Research. "Cybercrime Will Cost Businesses Over $2 Trillion By 2019." n.d. https://www.juniperresearch.com/press/press-releases/ cybercrime-cost-businesses-over-2trillion

Kamerstukken I [Dutch Parliamentary Proceedings First Chamber] 2016/17, 34372, no. E, 39-45 and no. F, 2-4 2016/17.

Kaplan, Fred. *Dark Territory: The Secret History of Cyber War*. New York: Simon & Schuster Paperbacks, 2016.

Karim, Ahmad, Rosli Bin Salleh, Muhammad Shiraz, Syed Adeel Ali Shah, Irfan Awan, and Nor Badrul Anuar. "Botnet Detection Techniques: Review, Future Trends, and Issues." *Journal of Zhejiang University-Science C (Computers & Electronics)* 15 (2014): 943–983.

Karp, Brad S. "Federal Guidance on the Cybersecurity Information Sharing Act of 2015." *Harvard Law School Forum on Corporate Governance and Financial Regulation*, 2016. https://corpgov.law.harvard.edu/2016/03/03/ federal-guidance-on-the-cybersecurity-information-sharing-act-of-2015/.

Kaspersky Lab. "Gauss: Abnormal Distribution." Kaspersky Lab, August 9, 2012.

Kaspersky Lab. "From Shamoon to Stonedrill: Wipers Attacking Saudi Organizations and Beyond." Kaspersky Lab, March 7, 2017.

Kaul, Inge, Isabelle Grunberg, and Marc A. Stern. "Defining Global Public Goods." In *Global Public Goods: International Cooperation in the 21st Century*, edited by Inge Kaul, Isabelle Grunberg, and Marc A. Stern, 2–19. New York: Oxford University Press, 1999.

Kean, Thomas, ed. *The 9/11 Commission Report: Final Report of the National Commission on Terrorist Attacks upon the United States*. Government Printing Office, 2011. https://books.google.com/books?hl=en&lr=&id=UabGPLhbGckC&oi=fnd&pg=PA1&dq=9-11+commission&ots=KEWrVMKEEU&sig=BOR06yIdF8Swt0hyTUSptg4R__o.

Keast, Robyn, Myrna P. Mandell, and Kerry Brown. "Mixing State, Market and Network Governance Modes: The Role of Government in "Crowded" Policy Domains." *International Journal of Organization Theory and Behavior* 9, no. 1 (2006): 27–50.

Keizer, Gregg. "Microsoft kicks off $250,000 security contest." *Computerworld*, August 3, 2011. http://www.computerworld.com/s/article/9218845/Microsoft_kicks_off_250_000_security_contest.

Keller, Daphne. "Ominous: Canadian Court Orders Google to Remove Search Results Globally." *Center for Internet and Society*, June 28, 2017. http://cyberlaw.stanford.edu/blog/2017/06/ominous-canadian-court-orders-google-remove-search-results-globally.

Kello, Lucas. "The Meaning of the Cyber Revolution: Perils to Theory and Statecraft." *International Security* 38, no. 2 (October 1, 2013): 7–40.

Kelly, Susan. "Data Breaches Spur Demand for Cyber Liability Coverage." *Treasury & Risk*, 2015. Accessed December 31, 2015. http://www.treasuryandrisk.com/2015/01/15/data-breaches-spur-demand-for-cyber-liability-cove".

Keohane, Robert O, and David G. Victor. "The Regime Complex for Climate Change." *Perspectives on Politics* 9, no. 1 (2011): 7–23. https://doi.org/10.1017/S1537592710004068.

Kephart, Jeffrey O., Steve R. White, and David M. Chess. "Computers and Epidemiology." *Spectrum IEEE* 30, no. 5 (1993): 20–26.

Kerr, Orin S. "Cybercrime's Scope: Interpreting 'Access' and 'Authorization' in Computer Misuse Statutes." *N.Y.U. Law Review* 78 (2003): 1596–1668.

Kerr, Orin S. *Computer Crime Law*. St. Paul: West Group, 2006.

Kerr, Orin S. "Obama's Proposed Changes to the Computer Hacking Statute: A Deep Dive." *The Washington Post*, January 14, 2015. https://www.washingtonpost.com/news/volokh-conspiracy/wp/2015/01/14/obamas-proposed-changes-to-the-computer-hacking-statute-a-deep-dive/?utm_term=.e87baf6cb938.

Kerr, Orin S. "Norms of Computer Trespass." *Columbia Law Review* 116 (2016): 1143–1184.

Kerr, Orin, and Murphy, Sean. "Government Hacking to Light the Dark Web." July 2017. https://www.stanfordlawreview.org/online/ government-hacking-to-light-the-dark-web/.

Kesan, Jay P., Ruperto P. Majuca, and William J. Yurcik. "*The Economic Case for Cyberinsurance*," 2005. http://papers.ssrn.com/sol3/papers.cfm?abstract_id=577862.

Khalaf, Roula, and Abigail Fielding Smith. "Qatar Bankrolls Syrian Revolt with Cash and Arms." *Financial Times*, May 16, 2013.

Khan, Taimur. "UAE Joins Airstrikes on ISIL Bases in Syria." *The National*, 2014. https://www.thenational.ae/world/mena/uae-joins-airstrikes-on-isil-bases-in-syria-1.238060.

Kirsch, Cassandra. "The Grey Hat Hacker: Reconciling Cyberspace Reality and the Law." *Northern Kentucky Law Review* 41 (2014): 383–404.

Klimburg, Alexander, ed. *National Cybersecurity Framework Manual*. Tallinn, Estonia: NATO, 2012. Accessed November 9, 2017. https://ccdcoe.org/ publications/books/NationalCyberSecurityFrameworkManual.pdf.

Knake, Robert K. "Internet Governance in an Age of Cyber Insecurity." *Council on Foreign Relations* (2010): 1–55.

Knockless, Trudy. "Demand for Cyber Risk Insurance Market on the Rise." *Property Casualty 360*, October 1, 2015. http://www.propertycasualty360. com/2015/10/01/demand-for-cyber-risk-insurance-market-on-the-rise.

Ko, Carol. "Fighting Cyber Terrorism." *Computerworld*, June 17, 2008. https:// perma.cc/6CZF-QG2J.

Kohnstamm, Jacob, and Drudeisha Madhub. "Mauritius Declaration on the Internet of Things." In *36th International Conference of Data Protection and Privacy Commissioners, Balaclava, Mauritius: International Conference of Data Protection and Privacy Commissioners*, 2014. https://icdppc.org/wp-content/ uploads/2015/02/Mauritius-Declaration.pdf.

Koops, Bert-Jaap. "Technology and the Crime Society: Rethinking Legal Protection." *Law, Innovation and Technology* 1 (2009): 93–124.

Koppel, Ted. *Lights Out: A Cyberattack, A Nation Unprepared, Surviving the Aftermath*. New York: Penguin, 2015.

Korobkin, Russell. "Bounded Rationality, Standard Form Contracts, and Unconscionability." *University of Chicago Law Review* 70, no. 4 (2003): 1203–1295.

Kosseff, Jeff. *Cybersecurity Law*. Hoboken: John Wiley & Sons, 2017.

Krahmann, Elke. "Conceptualizing Security Governance." *Cooperation and Conflict* 38, no. 1 (March 1, 2003): 5–26.

Krebs, Brian. "Who Makes the IoT Things Under Attack?" *Krebs on Security Blog*, October 3, 2016. Accessed November 9, 2017. https://krebsonsecurity.com/ 2016/10/who-makes-the-iot-things-under-attack/#more-36566.

Krishnamurthy, Vivek. "Cloudy with a Conflict of Laws." Berkman Center Research Publication No. 2016-3. February 16, 2016. https://ssrn.com/abstract=2733350.

Kshetri, Nir. *The Global Cybercrime Industry: Economic, Institutional and Strategic Perspectives*. London: Springer, 2010.

Kshetri, Nir. "Cybersecurity in the Gulf Cooperation Council Economies." In *The Quest to Cyber Superiority: Cybersecurity Regulations, Frameworks, and Strategies of Major Economies*, 183–194. New York: Springer, 2016.

Kuchler, Hannah. "Yahoo Says 2013 Cyber Breach Affected All 3bn Accounts." *Financial Times*, October 3, 2017. https://www.ft.com/content/9412c2b0-a87c-11e7-93c5-648314d2c72c.

Kuehn, Andreas, and Milton Mueller. "Analyzing Bug Bounty Programs: An Institutional Perspective on the Economics of Software Vulnerabilities." In *2014 TPRC/42nd Research Conference on Communication, Information and Internet Policy, George Mason University School of Law*, Arlington, Virginia, September 12–14, 2014. https://papers.ssrn.com/sol3/papers.cfm?abstract_id=2418812.

Kumar, Sheetal. "Cybersecurity: What's the ITU Got to Do with It?" July 9, 2015. https://perma.cc/BE4P-SBQ5.

Kumar, Sathish Alampalayam, Tyler Vealey, and Harshit Srivastava. "Security in Internet of Things: Challenges, Solutions and Future Directions." In *49th Hawaii International Conference on System Sciences (HICSS)*, 5772–5781, 2016.

Kunreuther, Howard, and Erwann Micheal-Kerjan. "Terrorism Insurance 2005." *Regulation* 28 (2005): 44.

Kurbalija, Jovan. "*Politorbis*," no. 57 (2014).

Kuypers, Marshall A., Thomas Maillart, and Elisabeth Paté-Cornell. "An Empirical Analysis of Cyber Security Incidents at a Large Organization," 1–22, 2016.

Lakdawalla, Darius, and George Zanjani. "Insurance, Self-Protection, and the Economics of Terrorism." *Journal of Public Economics* 89, no. 9 (2005): 1891–1905.

Larson, Jeff, ProPublica, Nicole Perlroth, and Scott Shane. "Revealed: The NSA's Secret Campaign to Crack, Undermine Internet Secuirty." *ProPublica*, September 5, 2013.

Laszka, A., Zhao, M., Malbari, A., and Grossklags, J. "The Rules of Engagement for Bug Bounty Programs." In *Proceedings of the Twenty-Second International Conference on Financial Cryptography and Data Security (FC)* (forthcoming).

"Law Enforcement Access to Data Stored Abroad Act" (LEADS Act). H.R. 1174, 114th Congress (2015). https://www.congress.gov/114/bills/hr1174/BILLS-114hr1174ih.xml.

Lawson, Sean. "*Cyber-Intifada Resource Guide: A Resource for Tracking the Intifada in Cyberspace*." The Arab Information Project, Georgetown University, 2001.

Leder, Felix, and Tillman Werner. "Know Your Enemy: Containing Conficker." *The Honeynet Project*, April 7, 2009. Accessed February 18, 2018. https://www.honeynet.org/files/KYE-Conficker.pdf.

Legrenzi, Matteo. *The GCC and the International Relations of the Gulf: Diplomacy, Security and Economic Coordination in a Changing Middle East*. I.B. Tauris, 2015.

Lelarge, M., and J. Bolot. "Economic Incentives to Increase Security in the Internet: The Case for Insurance." In *IEEE INFOCOM 2009* (*Proceedings of the Twenty-Eighth IEEE International Conference on Computer Communications*, Rio de Janeiro, 2009), 1494–1502. https://doi.org/10.1109/INFCOM.2009.5062066.

Lewis, James A. "Sovereignty and the Role of Government in Cyberspace." *The Brown Journal of World Affairs* 16, no. 2 (2010): 55–65.

Lewis, James A. "Internet Governance: Inevitable Transitions." *Internet Governance Papers*. 2013.

Lewis, James Andrew. "Cybersecurity and Stability in the Gulf." CSIS, January 2014. https://perma.cc/ST48-NVGX.

Leyden, John. "Furious Google Techie on NSA Snooping: 'F*CK THESE GUYS.'" *The Register*, November 7, 2013. http://www.theregister.co.uk/2013/11/07/google_engineers_slam_nsa/.

Libicki, Martin C. *Cyberdeterrence and Cyberwar*. RAND Corporation, 2009.

Lim, James. "South Korea Releases Right to Be Forgotten Guidance." *Bloomberg BNA*, May 9, 2016. https://www.bna.com/south-korea-releases-n57982070847/.

Lindsay, Jon R., Tai Ming Cheung, and Derek S. Reveron. *China and Cybersecurity: Espionage, Strategy, and Politics in the Digital Domain*. Oxford University Press, 2015.

Littlehale, Richard. "Data Stored Abroad: Ensuring Lawful Access and Privacy Protection in the Digital Era." Testimony before the U.S. House of Representatives Committee on the Judiciary, June 15, 2017. https://judiciary.house.gov/hearing/data-stored-abroad-ensuring-lawful-access-privacy-protection-digital-era/.

Lloyd, Alun and Robert May. "How Viruses Spread Among Computers and People." *Science* 292 (2001): 1316–1317.

Lohrmann, Dan. "Auto Industry Bug Bounty Programs Point to Our Security Future." *Government Technology*, July 17, 2016. http://www.govtech.com/blogs/lohrmann-on-cybersecurity/auto-industry-bug-bounty-programs-point-to-our-security-future.html.

Lyngaas, Sean. "*NSA Chief Says Agency Discloses '91 Percent' of Zero Day Bugs*." *FCW*, November 9, 2015. https://fcw.com/articles/2015/11/09/rogers-zero-days-nsa-lyngaas.aspx.

McAfee Labs. "Global Energy Cyberattacks: 'Night Dragon.'" *McAfee*, February 10, 2011.

Maier, Juergen. "*Made Smarter. Review 2017*." London: HM Government. 2017. https://assets.publishing.service.gov.uk/government/uploads/system/uploads/attachment_data/file/655570/20171027_MadeSmarter_FINAL_DIGITAL.pdf.

Maillart, Thomas, et al. "Given enough eyeballs, all bugs are shallow? Revisiting Eric Raymond with bug bounty programs." *Journal of Cybersecurity* 3, no. 2 (2017): 81–90.

Manyika, James, Jacques Bughin, Susan Lund, Olivia Nottebohm, David Poulter, Sebastian Jauch, and Sree Ramaswamy. *"Global Flows in a Digital Age: How Trade, Finance, People, and Data Connect the World Economy."* McKinsey Global Institute. April 2014. http://www.mckinsey.com/business-functions/strategy-and-corporate-finance/our-insights/global-flows-in-a-digital-age.

Maras, Marie-Helen. "Inside Darknet: The Takedown of Silk Road." *Criminal Justice Matters* 98 (2014): 22–23.

Marchau, V. A. W. J., W. E. Walker, and G. P. van Wee. "Dynamic Adaptive Transport Policies for Handling Deep Uncertainty." *Technological Forecasting and Social Change, Two Special Sections: Risk and Technology Addressing Deep Uncertainty Using Adaptive Policies* 77, no. 6 (July 1, 2010): 940–950. https://doi.org/10.1016/j.techfore.2010.04.006.

Marczak, Bill, and Morgan Marquis-Boire. "From Bahrain with Love: Finfisher's Spy Kit Exposed?" *Citizen Lab*, July 25, 2012.

Marczak, Bill, and John Scott-Railton. "The Million Dollar Dissident: NSO Group's IPhone Zero-Days Used against a UAE Human Rights Defender." *Citizen Lab*, August 24, 2016.

Marquis-Boire, Morgan. "Backdoors Are Forever: Hacking Team and the Targeting of Dissent?" *Citizen Lab*, October 10, 2012.

Marquis-Boire, Morgan, John Scott-Railton, Claudio Guarnieri, and Katie Kleemola "Some Devices Wander by Mistake: Planet Blue Coat Redux." *Citizen Lab*, July 9, 2013.

Marquis-Boire, Morgan, John Scott-Railton, Claudio Guarnieri, and Katie Kleemola. "Police Story: Hacking Team's Government Surveillance Malware." *Citizen Lab*, June 2014.

Marsh Company. "Benchmarking Trends: As Cyber Concerns Broaden, Insurance Purchases Rise." *Marsh & McLennan Companies*, March 2015. https://www.marsh.com/us/insights/benchmarking-trends-cyber-concerns-broaden-insurance-purchases-rise.html.

Mathew, Jerin. "British Airways Suffers Cyber-attack Affecting Thousands of Frequent Flyer Accounts." *International Business Times*, March 30, 2015. http://www.ibtimes.co.uk/british-airways-suffers-hacking-attack-thousands-frequent-flyer-accounts-affected-1494076.

Mathews, Lee. "Travel Giant Sabre Confirms Its Reservation System Was Hacked." *Forbes*, July 6, 2017. https://www.forbes.com/sites/leemathews/2017/07/06/travel-giant-sabre-confirms-its-reservation-system-was-hacked/#23755cb74b20.

"Matter of Warrant to Search a Certain E-Mail Account Controlled & Maintained by Microsoft Corp." 829 F.3d 197 (2d Cir. 2016).

Mattern, Friedemann, and Christian Flörkemeier. "Vom Internet der Computer zum Internet der Dinge." *Informatik-Spektrum* 33, no. 2 (April 1, 2010): 107. https://doi.org/10.1007/s00287-010-0417-7.

Matthews, Ron. "The UK Offset Model: From Participation to Engagement." *RUSI*, July 29, 2014.

Matthiesen, Toby. *Sectarian Gulf: Bahrain, Saudi Arabia and the Arab Spring That Wasn't*. Stanford: Stanford University Press, 2013.

Matthiesen, Toby. *The Other Saudis: Shiism, Dissent And Sectarianism*. New York: Cambridge University Press, 2014.

Mayer, Jonathan. "Constitutional Malware." November 14, 2016. SSRN. https://papers.ssrn.com/sol3/papers.cfm?abstract_id=2633247.

Maynard, Trevor, and Nick Beecroft. "Business Blackout – The Insurance Implications of a Cyber Attack on the US Power Grid." Lloyds of London, May 2015. https://www.lloyds.com/~/media/files/news-and-insight/risk-insight/2015/business-blackout/business-blackout20150708.pdf.

McBride, Stephen. "UAE Cyber-Security Authority Unveils Policies, Standards." *ITP.Net*, June 25, 2014. https://perma.cc/HF7X-VFH5.

McDermott, Evan, and David Inserra. "Why Cybersecurity Information Sharing Is a Positive Step for Online Security." *The Daily Signal*, 2016. http://dailysignal.com/2016/01/25/why-cybersecurity-information-sharing-is-a-positive-step-for-online-security/.

McGuinness, Paddy. "Written Testimony of Mr Paddy McGuinness, United Kingdom Deputy National Security Adviser, Before the Judiciary Sub-Committee on Crime and Terrorism United States Senate." May 10, 2017. https://www.judiciary.senate.gov/imo/media/doc/05-24-17%20McGuinness%20Testimony.pdf.

MCIT. "*National Information Security Strategy*." Saudi Arabia: Ministry of Communications and Information Technology, January 2011.

McQuinn, Alan and Castro, Daniel. "How Law Enforcement Should Access Data Across Borders." Information Technology & Innovation Foundation. July 2017. http://www2.itif.org/2017-law-enforcement-data-borders.pdf.

MEE. "Qatar National Bank Allegedly Hacked, Data of 1,200 Entities Leaked." *Middle East Eye*, April 27, 2016. https://perma.cc/6TMA-VCDC.

Mein, Adam. "Celebrating One Year of Web Vulnerability Research." *Google Online Security Blog*, February 9, 2012. https://googleonlinesecurity.blogspot.com/2012/02/celebrating-one-year-of-web.html.

Mein, Adam, and Chris Evans. "Dosh4Vulns: Google's Vulnerability Reward Programs." *AppSecUSA*, 2011. https://software-security.sans.org/downloads/appsec-2011-files/vrp-presentation.pdf.

Menell, Peter S. "Misconstruing Whistleblower Immunity Under the Defend Trade Secrets Act." *Nevada Law Review Forum* 1 (2017): 92–97.

Menell, Peter S. "The Defend Trade Secrets Act Whistleblower Immunity Provision: A Legislative History." *University of Missouri School of Law Business, Entrepreneurship & Tax Law Review* 1 (2018): 397–424.

Meuleman, Louis. *Public Management and the Metagovernance of Hierarchies, Networks and Markets*. Contributions to Management Science. Heidelberg: Physica-Verlag, 2008.

Micromarketmonitor. "Middle East and Africa Cyber Security Market Research Report." 2015. https://perma.cc/3EV9-PFDE.

Microsoft. "Bounty Evolution: $100,000 for New Mitigation Bypass Techniques Wanted Dead or Alive." *BlueHat Blog*, November 1, 2013a. http://blogs.technet.com/b/bluehat/archive/2013/11/01/bounty-evolution-100-000-for-new-mitigation-bypass-techniques-wanted-dead-or-alive.aspx.

Microsoft. "Heart of Blue Gold – Announcing New Bounty Programs." *BlueHat Blog*. June 19, 2013b. http://blogs.technet.com/b/bluehat/archive/2013/06/19/heart-of-blue-gold-announcing-new-bounty-programs.aspx.

Microsoft. "From Articulation to Implementation: Enabling progress on cybersecurity norms." June 2016. https://query.prod.cms.rt.microsoft.com/cms/api/am/binary/REVmc8.

Microsoft. "Honor Roll." June 19, 2017a https://web.archive.org/web/20170619124334/https://technet.microsoft.com/en-us/security/dn469163.

Microsoft. "Sharding Pattern." June 23, 2017b. https://docs.microsoft.com/en-us/azure/architecture/patterns/sharding.

Microsoft. "Mitigation Bypass and Bounty for Defense Terms." October 1, 2018 https://technet.microsoft.com/en-us/security/dn425049.

Microsoft. "Microsoft CoreCLR and ASP.NET 5 Beta Bug Bounty Program Terms." n.d.-a https://technet.microsoft.com/en-us/security/mt574248.

Microsoft. "Microsoft Edge Technical Preview (Formerly Known as Project Spartan) Bug Bounty Program Terms." n.d.-b https://web.archive.org/web/20170325011129/https://technet.microsoft.com/en-us/security/dn972323.

Microsoft Malware Protection Center. "Ransomware." August 16, 2018. http://www.microsoft.com/security/portal/mmpc/shared/ransomware.aspx.

Microsoft Security TechCenter. "Frequently Asked Questions about Microsoft Bug Bounty Programs." n.d. https://technet.microsoft.com/en-us/security/dn425055.aspx.

Miller, Charlie. "The Legitimate Vulnerability Market: Inside the Secretive World of 0-Day Exploit Sales." Workshop on the Economics of Information Security. 2007. http://www.econinfosec.org/archive/weis2007/papers/29.pdf.

Miorandi, Daniele, et al. "Internet of Things: Vision, Applications and Research Challenges." *Ad Hoc Networks* 10, no. 7 (September 2012): 1497–1516. https://doi.org/10.1016/j.adhoc.2012.02.016.

"Mission Operations Security Trust (or 'Ops-T')." 2017. Accessed July 1, 2017. https://portal.ops-trust.net/.

"MLATS and International Cooperation for Law Enforcement Purposes." Presentation at the Centre for Internet and Society. n.d. https://cis-india.org/internet-governance/blog/presentation-on-mlats.pdf

Monetary Authority of Singapore. "FS-ISAC and MAS Establish Asia Pacific (APAC) Intelligence Centre for Sharing and Analysing Cyber Threat Information." December 1, 2016. http://www.mas.gov.sg/News-and-Publications/Media-Releases/2016/FS-ISAC-and-MAS-Establish-APAC-Intelligence-Centre.aspx.

Morgan, Steve. "2016 Cybercrime Report." Cybersecurity Ventures. 2017. http://cybersecurityventures.com/hackerpocalypse-cybercrime-report-2016/.

Morris, Chris. "465,000 Pacemakers Recalled on Hacking Fears." *Fortune*, August 31, 2017. http://fortune.com/2017/08/31/pacemaker-recall-fda/.

Mozilla. "Bug Bounty Program." n.d. https://www.mozilla.org/en-US/security/bug-bounty/.

Mueller, Milton, Andreas Schmidt, and Brenden Kuerbis. "Internet Security and Networked Governance in International Relations." *International Studies Review* 15, no. 1 (March 1, 2013): 86–104.

Mulligan, Deirdre K., and Fred B. Schneider. "Doctrine for Cybersecurity." *Daedalus* 140, no. 4 (2011): 1–30. doi:https://doi.org/10.1162/DAED_a_00116.

Murdoch, Robin, and Paul Johnson. *"Digital Trust in the IoT Era."* Dublin: Accenture, 2015. https://www.accenture.com/t20160318T035041__w__/us-en/_acnmedia/Accenture/Conversion-Assets/LandingPage/Documents/3/Accenture-3-LT-3-Digital-Trust-IoT-Era.pdf.

Murphy, Emma C. "Theorizing ICTs in the Arab World: Informational Capitalism and the Public Sphere." *International Studies Quarterly* 53, no. 4 (December 1, 2009), 1131–1153.

Mustafa, Awad. "UAE To Double Security Budget, Focus on Cyber," February 25, 2014. https://perma.cc/8GYK-2FTL.

n.runs Professionals. "Aircraft Hacking Practical Aero Series." April 2013. https://conference.hitb.org/hitbsecconf2013ams/materials/D1T1%20-%20Hugo%20Teso%20-%20Aircraft%20Hacking%20-%20Practical%20Aero%20Series.pdf.

Nabi, Syed Irfan, Abdulrahman A. Mirza, and Khaled Alghathbar. "Information Assurance in Saudi Organizations – An Empirical Study." In *Security Technology, Disaster Recovery and Business Continuity*, edited by Wai-chi Fang, Muhammad Khurram Khan, Kirk P. Arnett, Heau-jo Kang, and Dominik Slezak, 18–28. Berlin, Heidelberg: Springer, 2010.

National Council of ISACs. "About NCI." n.d.-a https://www.nationalisacs.org/about-nci.

National Council of ISACs. "Member ISACs." n.d.-b https://www.nationalisacs.org/member-isacs.

National Council of ISACs. n.d.-c https://www.nationalisacs.org/.

National Health ISAC & Aviation ISAC. "2016 Spring Agenda." National Health ISAC & Aviation ISAC Spring Summit 2016. Lake Buena Vista, FL, May 11–13, 2016. https://www.eiseverywhere.com/ehome/150989/343519/.

National Institute of Standards and Technology. "Framework for Improving Critical Infrastructure Cybersecurity," December 5, 2017. https://www.nist.gov/sites/default/files/documents/2017/12/05/draft-2_framework-v1-1_without-markup.pdf.

NC4. "NC4 to buy cyber threat intelligence company, Soltra, from FS-ISAC, DTCC." November 23, 2016. https://www.fsisac.com/sites/default/files/news/PR-NC4_and_Soltra_Press_Release.pdf.

NCFTA. "Who We Are." n.d. https://www.ncfta.net/.

Nelson, Libby. "The US Once Had More Than 130 Hijackings in 4 years. Here's Why They Finally Stopped." *Vox*, March 29, 2016. https://www.vox.com/2016/3/29/11326472/hijacking-airplanes-egyptair.

Netscape. "Netscape Announces 'Netscape Bugs Bounty' with Release of Netscape Navigator 2.0 Beta," October 10, 1995. https://web.archive.org/web/19970501041756/http://www101.netscape.com/newsref/pr/newsrelease48.html.

New York State Department of Financial Services, 23 NYCRR 500, "Cybersecurity Requirements for Financial Services Companies," 2017. http://www.dfs.ny.gov/legal/regulations/adoptions/dfsrf500txt.pdf, § 500.05, 5–6.

Newman, Craig. "Target's Cyber Insurance: A $100 Million Policy vs. $300 Million (So Far) In Costs." *Data Security Law Blog*, April 7, 2016. https://datasecuritylaw.com/targets-cyber-insurance-a-100-million-policy-vs-300-million-so-far-in-costs/.

Newman, Lily Hay. "Equifax Officially Has No Excuse." *Wired*, September 14, 2017. https://www.wired.com/story/equifax-breach-no-excuse/.

Nissenbaum, Helen. "Privacy as Contextual Integrity." *Washington Law Review*, 2004. https://crypto.stanford.edu/portia/papers/RevnissenbaumDTP31.pdf.

Nissenbaum, Helen. *Privacy In Context: Technology, Policy, And The Integrity Of Social Life.* Stanford, CA: Stanford University Press, 2009.

Nuffield Council on Bioethics. *Public Health: Ethical Issues.* London: Nuffield Council on Bioethics, 2007.

Nye, Joseph S. "Nuclear Lessons for Cyber Security?" *Strategic Studies Quarterly* 5, no. 4 (2011): 18–38.

Nye, Joseph S. "The Regime Complex for Managing Global Cyber Activities." 2014. https://www.cigionline.org/sites/default/files/gcig_paper_no1.pdf.

O'Mahoney, Siobhan. "The governance of open source initiatives: what does it mean to be community managed?" *Journal of Management & Governance* 11, 2 (2007): 139–150. https://link.springer.com/article/10.1007/s10997-007-9024-7.

O'Neal, Payton. "Illustrated Guide to Bug Bounties." *Bugcrowd Blog*, April 12, 2017. https://blog.bugcrowd.com/illustrated-guide-to-bug-bounties-step-1-planning?utm_campaign=1704%20Top%204%20Reasons%20to%20Build%20a%20Bug%20Bounty%20into%20Your%20AppSec%20Strategy&utm_content=54427294&utm_medium=social&utm_source=twitter.

Obama, Barack. "Address Before a Joint Session of Congress on the State of the Union." February 12, 2013. Online by Gerhard Peters and John T. Woolley, *The American Presidency Project.* http://www.presidency.ucsb.edu/ws/index.php?pid=102826.

Obama, Barack. "Remarks by the President at the Cybersecurity and Consumer Protection Summit." Transcript. White House Press Office. February 13, 2015. https://www.whitehouse.gov/the-press-office/2015/02/13/remarks-president-cybersecurity-and-consumer-protection-summit.

OCERT. "OCERT Event Details." October 23, 2013. https://perma.cc/XY4F-7ZBN.

Odell, Laura A., J. Corbin Fauntleroy, and Ryan R. Wagner. "Cyber Insurance – Managing Cyber Risk." Institute for Defense Analyses, April 2015. https://www.ida.org/~/media/Corporate/Files/Publications/IDA_Documents/ITSD/2015/D-5481.ashx.

OECD. "Governance." Last modified July 23, 2007a. https://stats.oecd.org/glossary/detail.asp?ID=7236.

OECD. "The Development of Policies for the Protection of Critical Information Infrastructure." *OECD Ministerial Background Report*, 2007b.

Office of the Attorney General. "Intake and Charging Policy for Computer Crime Matters." 2014.

Ong, Thuy. "Samsung's bug bounty program will pay rewards of up to $200,000." *The Verge*, September 7, 2017. https://www.theverge.com/2017/9/7/16265926/samsung-bug-bounty-program-rewards.

Onishi, Norimitsu. "Clashes Erupt as Liberia Sets an Ebola Quarantine." *New York Times*, August 20, 2014. https://www.nytimes.com/2014/08/21/world/africa/ebola-outbreak-liberia-quarantine.html.

Osborne, Stephen P. *The New Public Governance?: Emerging Perspectives on the Theory and Practice of Public Governance.* Routledge, 2010.

Osborne, George. "Chancellor's Speech to GCHQ on Cyber Security." *GOV.UK*, November 17, 2015. https://www.gov.uk/government/speeches/chancellors-speech-to-gchq-on-cyber-security.

Owtram, Francis. *A Modern History of Oman: Formation of the State Since 1920.* London: I.B.Tauris, 2004.

Pal, Ranjan. "*Improving Network Security through Cyber-Insurance.*" University of Southern California, 2014. http://digitallibrary.usc.edu/cdm/ref/collection/p15799coll3/id/514919.

Paramount Pictures International. The Big Short | Clip: "Jenga" | Paramount Pictures International. n.d. https://www.youtube.com/watch?v=r7H6Go_shP8.

Patrikios, Antonis. "What Does EU Regulatory Guidance on the Internet of Things Mean in Practice? Part 1." *Blog, Fieldfisher*, October 31, 2014a. http://privacylawblog.fieldfisher.com/2014/what-does-eu-regulatory-guidance-on-the-internet-of-things-mean-in-practice-part-1/.

Patrikios, Antonis, "What Does EU Regulatory Guidance on the Internet of Things Mean in Practice? Part 2." *Blog, Fieldfisher*, November 1, 2014b. http://privacylawblog.fieldfisher.com/2014/what-does-eu-regulatory-guidance-on-the-nternet-of-things-mean-in-practice-part-2/.

PayPal, "PayPal Bug Bounty Program", n.d. https://www.paypal.com/us/webapps/mpp/security-tools/reporting-security-issues#indemnification.

Perlo-Freeman, Sam. "SIPRI Background Paper: Arms Transfers to the Middle East." *SIPRI*, July 2009.

Perlroth, Nicole. "Apple Will Pay a 'Bug Bounty' to Hackers Who Report Flaws." *New York Times*, August 4, 2016. https://www.nytimes.com/2016/08/05/technology/apple-will-pay-a-bug-bounty-to-hackers-who-report-flaws.html.

Perlroth, Nicole, and David E. Sanger. "Obama Calls for New Cooperation to Wrangle the 'Wild West' Internet." *The New York Times*, February 13, 2015.

Perrin, Chad. "The Danger of Complexity: More Code, More Bugs." *TechRepublic*, February 1, 2010. http://www.techrepublic.com/blog/it-security/the-danger-of-complexity-more-code-more-bugs/.

Perzanowski, Aaron, and Chris Jay Hoofnagle. "What We Buy When We 'Buy Now'." *University of Pennsylvania Law Review* 165 (2017): 315–378.

Peterson, Andrea. "The Sony Pictures Hack, Explained." *The Washington Post*, December 18, 2014. https://www.washingtonpost.com/news/the-switch/wp/2014/12/18/the-sony-pictures-hack-explained/?utm_term=.c6b95c35a27b.

Peterson, Andrea. "Senate Passes Cybersecurity Information Sharing Bill despite Privacy Fears." *The Washington Post*, October 27, 2015. https://www.washingtonpost.com/news/the-switch/wp/2015/10/27/senate-passes-controversial-cybersecurity-information-sharing-legislation/?utm_term=.d9b199957b9c.

PETRAS. "PETRAS IoT Research Hub." June 23, 2017. https://www.petrashub.org/.

Piscitello, Dave. "Conficker Summary and Review." *ICANN*, 2010. https://www.icann.org/en/system/files/files/conficker-summary-review-07may10-en.pdf. http://www.atlarge.icann.org/files/meetings/sydney2009/presentation-alac-piscitello-23jun09-en.pdf

Ponemon Institute. "*Managing Cyber Security as a Business Risk: Cyber Insurance in the Digital Age.*" Ponemon Institute, August 2013. http://www.ponemon.org/local/upload/file/Cyber%20Insurance%20white%20paper%20FINAL%207.pdf.

Popper, Ben. "DJI's Bug Bounty Program Starts with a Stumble: Legal Threats and Angry Researchers are Bad Outcomes for All." *The Verge*, November 20, 2017. https://www.theverge.com/2017/11/20/16669724/dji-bug-bounty-program-conflict-researcher.

Potter, Laurence, ed. *The Persian Gulf in Modern Times: People, Ports, and History.* London: Palgrave Macmillan, 2014.

Presidential Decision Directive/PDD-63 (May 22, 1998). "Critical Infrastructure Protection." https://fas.org/irp/offdocs/pdd/pdd-63.htm.

Presidential Policy Directive/PPD-21 (February 12, 2013). "Critical Infrastructure Security and Resilience." https://obamawhitehouse.archives.gov/the-press-office/2013/02/12/presidential-policy-directive-critical-infrastructure-security-and-resil.

President's Review Group on Intelligence and Communications Technologies. "Liberty and Security in a Changing World." December 12, 2013. https://obamawhitehouse.archives.gov/sites/default/files/docs/2013-12-12_rg_final_report.pdf.

Price, Kymberlee. "Bugcrowd's Disclosure Policy." *Bugcrowd Blog*, February 23, 2016. https://blog.bugcrowd.com/public-disclosure-policy-2016.

Prince, Matthew. "Why We Terminated Daily Stormer." *Cloudflare*, August 16, 2017. https://blog.cloudflare.com/why-we-terminated-daily-stormer/.

Project Zero. n.d. https://googleprojectzero.blogspot.com/.

Radin, Margaret Jane. *"Boilerplate: The Fine Print, Vanishing Rights, and the Rule of Law."* Princeton: Princeton University Press, 2012.

Rawls, John. *A Theory of Justice.* Rev. Ed. Oxford: Oxford University Press, 1999.

Raymond, Eric S. *The Cathedral and the Bazaar: Musings on Linux and Open Source by an Accidental Revolutionary.* Sebastopol: O'Reilly Media, 1999.

Raymond, Mark, and Laura DeNardis. "Multistakeholderism: Anatomy of an Inchoate Global Institution." *International Theory* 7, no. 3 (November 2015): 572–616. https://doi.org/10.1017/S1752971915000081.

Recon, Somerset. "Hello Barbie Security: Part 2 – Analysis." *Somerset Recon.* January 25, 2016. http://www.somersetrecon.com/blog/2016/1/21/hello-barbie-security-part-2-analysis.

Reisman, Dillion. "Where Is Your Data, Really?: The Technical Case Against Data Localization." *Lawfare,* May 22, 2017. https://www.lawfareblog.com/where-your-data-really-technical-case-against-data-localization.

Reporters without Borders. "Enemies of the Internet." 2014. https://rsf.org/sites/default/files/2014-rsf-rapport-enemies-of-the-internet.pdf.

Reporting and Analysis Centre for Information Assurance. "Technical Report about the Espionage Case at RUAG." 2016. https://www.melani.admin.ch/melani/en/home/dokumentation/reports/technical-reports/technical-report_apt_case_ruag.html.

Richtel, Matt. "Egypt Cuts Off Most Internet and Cellphone Service." *The New York Times,* January 28, 2011. https://perma.cc/RSH4-HYDR.

Rid, Thomas. "Highly Significant: Swiss Gov't Publishes Detailed APT Report, Links Ruag Cyber Attack to Turla, Ancestor: Agent.BTZ." May 23, 2016. https://twitter.com/ridt/status/734662844843741184.

Riley, Michael, Glen Carey, and John Fraher. "Saudi Arabia Has Just Suffered a Series of Major Cyber Hack Attacks." *Bloomberg.Com,* December 1, 2016. https://perma.cc/FRK8-AV2P.

Rockwell, Mark. "Why bug bounty programs are worth the risk." *FCW,* March 30, 2017. https://fcw.com/articles/2017/03/30/bug-bounties-gsa-dod.aspx.

Rodriguez-Gomez, Rafael A., Gabriel Macia-Fernandez, and Pedro Garcia-Teodoro. "Survey and Taxonomy of Botnet Research through Life-cycle." *ACM Computing Surveys* 45 (2013): 1–33.

Rogers, Jacob. "Wikimedia Foundation advises Canadian Supreme Court to support freedom of expression worldwide in intervention filing for Google v. Equustek." *Wikimedia Foundation Blog,* October 14, 2016. https://blog.wikimedia.org/2016/10/14/intervention-google-v-equustek/.

Romanosky, Sasha, Lillian Ablon, Andreas Kuehn, and Therese Jones. "Content Analysis of Cyber Insurance Policies: How Do Carriers Write Policies and Price Cyber Risk?" In *Proceedings of the 16th Annual Workshop on the Economics of Information Security.* La Jolla, CA, 2017. https://papers.ssrn.com/sol3/papers.cfm?abstract_id=2929137.

Romm, Joseph J. *Defining National Security: The Nonmilitary Aspects.* New York: Council on Foreign Relations Press, 1993.

Rosenzweig, Paul. "Europe Is Deeply Unserious." *Lawfare*, July 27, 2017a. https://www.lawfareblog.com/europe-deeply-unserious.

Rosenzweig, Paul. "The US-UK Deal Is Actually Quite Good." *Lawfare*, July 19, 2017b. https://lawfareblog.com/us-uk-deal-actually-quite-good.

Rowe, Brent, Michael Halpern, and Tony Lentz. "Is a Public Health Framework the Cure for Cyber Security?" *Cross-Talk 25/6* (2012): 30–38.

RUAG. "Cyber Attack on RUAG: Major Damage Averted." 2016. https://www.ruag.com/en/news/cyber-attack-ruag-major-damage-averted

RUAG. "About RUAG." 2017. https://www.ruag.com/en/ruag-home.

Rugh, Andrea B. *The Political Culture of Leadership in the United Arab Emirates.* Basingstoke: Palgrave Macmillan, 2010.

Rushe, Dominic. "Apple CEO Tim Cook Challenges Obama with Impassioned Stand on Privacy." *The Guardian*, February 13, 2015.

Russian Federal Law No. 242-FZ. "On Making Amendments to Certain Laws of the Russian Federation Regarding Clarification of the Order of Processing of Personal Data in Information and Telecommunication Networks." July 9, 2014. https://pd.rkn.gov.ru/authority/p146/p191/.

Saab, Bilal Y. "The Gulf Rising: Defense Industrialization in Saudi Arabia and the UAE." *The Atlantic Council*, May 2014.

Sabel, Charles F., and Jonathan Zeitlin. "Experimentalist Governance." In *The Oxford Handbook of Governance*, edited by David Levi-Faur, 169–186. Oxford: Oxford University Press, 2012.

Salgado, Richard. "Written Testimony of Richard Salgado, Director, Law Enforcement and Information Security, Google Inc." House Judiciary Committee Hearing on "Data Stored Abroad: Ensuring Lawful Access and Privacy Protection in the Digital Era." June 15, 2017. https://judiciary.house.gov/wp-content/uploads/2017/06/Salgado-Testimony.pdf.

Sambridge, Andy. "Dubai Sets up E-Security Centre to Fight Cyber Criminals." *ITP.Net.* June 13, 2014 https://perma.cc/F7LX-R2VZ.

Sanger, David, and Nicole Perlroth. "Obama Heads to Tech Security Talks Amid Tensions." *New York Times*, February 12, 2015.

Santora, Marc. "In Hours, Thieves Took $45 Million in A.T.M. Scheme." *The New York Times*, May 9, 2013. https://perma.cc/3A8A-5RG6.

Santus, Rex. "Facebook's ThreatExchange Is a Social Platform for Sharing Cybersecurity Threats." *Mashable*, 2015. http://mashable.com/2015/02/11/threatexchange-facebook/#jnGMpTqOlZqb.

Saracco, Robert. "Guess What Requires 150 Million Lines of Code..." *IEEE Future Directions*, January 13, 2016. http://sites.ieee.org/futuredirections/2016/01/13/guess-what-requires-150-million-lines-of-code/.

Savage, John E., and Bruce W. McConnell. *"Exploring Multi-Stakeholder Internet Governance."* EastWest Institute, January 2015.

Schmidt, Andreas. "Hierarchies in Networks: Emerging Hybrids of Networks and Hierarchies for Producing Internet Security." In *Cyberspace and International*

Relations: Theory, Prospects and Challenges, edited by Kremer JF, Müller B, 181–202. Berlin, Heidelberg: Springer, 2013. doi:https://doi.org/10.1007/978-3-642-37481-4_11.

Schmidt, Andreas. *Secrecy versus Openness.* Delft: Uitgeverij BOXPress, 2014.

Schneier, Bruce. "iPhone Encryption and the Return of the Crypto Wars." *Schneier on Security,* October 6, 2014a. https://www.schneier.com/blog/archives/2014/10/iphone_encrypti_1.html.

Schneier, Bruce. "Should U.S. Hackers Fix Cybersecurity Holes or Exploit Them?" *The Atlantic,* May 19, 2014b. https://www.theatlantic.com/technology/archive/2014/05/should-hackers-fix-cybersecurity-holes-or-exploit-them/371197/.

Schutzer, Dan. "CTO Corner: An Assessment of Cyber Insurance." *Financial Services Roundtable,* February 2015.

Schwartz, Mathew J. "Swiss Defense Firm Hack Tied to 'Turla' Malware." *BankInfoSecurity.* May 23, 2016. http://www.bankinfosecurity.com/swiss-government-ruag-hack-ties-to-turla-malware-a-9128.

Scott, Susan V., and Markos Zachariadis. *The Society for Worldwide Interbank Financial Telecommunication (SWIFT): Cooperative Governance for Network Innovation, Standards, and Community.* Routledge Global Institutions Series. London: Routledge, 2013.

Sedenberg, Elaine, and Deirdre Mulligan. "Public Health as a Model for Cybersecurity Information Sharing." *Berkeley Technology Law Journal* 30, no. 3 (2015): 1687–1739.

Senate Committee on the Judiciary, Subcommittee on Crime and Terrorism. "Law Enforcement Access to Data Stored Across Borders: Facilitating Cooperation and Protecting Rights." May 24, 2017. https://www.judiciary.senate.gov/meetings/law-enforcement-access-to-data-stored-across-borders-facilitating-cooperation-and-protecting-rights.

Sengupta, Somini. "United Nations Chief Exposes Limits to His Authority by Citing Saudi Threat." *The New York Times,* June 9, 2016. https://perma.cc/3XJ8-GNSK.

Shah, Sonali K. "Motivation, Governance, and the Viability of Hybrid Forms in Open Source Software Development." *Management Science* 52, no. 7 (July 2006): 1000–1014.

Sheidlower, Nate. "The Rise in the Demand for CISOs." *Security Current,* July 30, 2015. https://web.archive.org/web/20170606074326/http://www.securitycurrent.com/en/analysis/ac_analysis/the-rise-in-the-demand-for-cisos.

Sidel, Robin. "Big Banks Team Up to Fight Cyber Crime." *Wall Street Journal,* August 9, 2016. https://www.wsj.com/articles/big-banks-team-up-to-fight-cyber-crime-1470758719.

Sidley Austin LLP. "Essentially Equivalent: A Comparison of the Legal Orders for Privacy and Data Protection in the European Union and United States." January 25, 2016. https://www.sidley.com/en/insights/publications/2016/01/essentially-equivalent.

Sinclair, Timothy J. "Guarding the Gates of Capital: Credit Rating Processes and The Global Political Economy." PhD Dissertation, York University, 1995.

Sinclair, Timothy J. "Bond Rating Agencies and Coordination in the Global Political Economy." In *Private Authority and International Affairs*, edited by A. Claire Cutler, Virginia Haufler, and Tony Porter. Albany, NY: SUNY Press, 1999

Singer, Peter W., and Allan Friedman. *Cybersecurity and Cyberwar: What Everyone Needs to Know*. Oxford: Oxford University Press, 2014.

SITA. "Aviation Cybersecurity Symposium 2017." 2017. https://www.sita.aero/events/events-listing/2017-aviation-cybersecurity-symposium.

SITA. "Community Cyber Threat Center." n.d.-a https://www.sita.aero/about-us/working-for-the-community/industry-initiatives/cyber-threat-center.

SITA. "Solutions & Services." n.d.-b https://www.sita.aero/solutions-and-services.

Slaughter, Anne-Marie. "Everyday Global Governance." *Daedalus* 132, no. 1 (2003): 83–90.

Smith, Brad. "Protecting Consumer Data from Government Snooping." December 4, 2013. http://blogs.microsoft.com/blog/2013/12/04/protecting-customer-data-from-government-snooping/.

Smith, Brad. "A Legislative Path to Create New Laws is Better than Arguing Over Old Laws." *Microsoft Blog*, June 23, 2017. https://blogs.microsoft.com/on-the-issues/2017/06/23/legislative-path-create-new-laws-better-arguing-old-laws/.

Snell, Jim, and Christian Lee. "The Internet of Things Changes Everything, or Does It? –Your Handy Guide to Legal Issue-Spotting in a World Where Everything Is Connected." *The Computer and Internet Lawyer* 32, no. 11 (2015): 1–8.

Solomon, Steven Davidoff. "How Yahoo's Data Breach Could Affect Its Deal With Verizon." *The New York Times*, September 23, 2016. https://www.nytimes.com/2016/09/24/business/dealbook/how-yahoos-data-breach-could-affect-its-deal-with-verizon.html.

Solove, Daniel J., and Paul M. Schwartz. *Information Privacy Law*. 5th ed. Blue Springs: Aspen Publishing Co., 2015.

Soltra. "The Soltra Story." n.d. https://www.soltra.com/en/about/.

Souaiaia, A. *Anatomy of Dissent in Islamic Societies: Ibadism, Rebellion, and Legitimacy*. London: Palgrave Macmillan, 2013.

Spar, Deborah. "The Public Face of Cyberspace." In *Global Public Goods*, edited by Inge Kaul, Isabelle Grunberg, and Marc Stern, 344–363. New York: Oxford University Press, 1999.

Sparrow, Andrew. "WhatsApp Must Be Accessible to Authorities, Says Amber Rudd." *The Guardian*, March 26, 2017. https://www.theguardian.com/technology/2017/mar/26/intelligence-services-access-whatsapp-amber-rudd-westminster-attack-encrypted-messaging.

Spiegel Staff. "Inside TAO: Documents Reveal Top NSA Hacking Unit." *Der Spiegel*, December 29, 2013.

SSRN. "Georgia Tech Scheller College of Business Research Paper No. WP 38." SSRN. July 2017. https://ssrn.com/abstract=2728478 or http://dx.doi.org/10.2139/ssrn.2728478

Statement of David Bitkower. Principal Deputy Assistant Attorney General, Criminal Division, U.S. Department of Justice, before the Committee on the Judiciary, United States House of Representatives. February 25, 2016. https://www.justice.gov/opa/file/828686/download.

Stoker, Gerry. "Governance as Theory: Five Propositions." *International Social Science Journal* 155 (1998): 17–28.

Stone, Jeff, and Kate Fazzini. "U.S. Financial Sector Begins 'Sheltered Harbor' Rollout." *Wall Street Journal*, March 9, 2017. https://www.linkedin.com/pulse/us-financial-sector-begins-sheltered-harbor-rollout-jeff-stone.

Streeck, Wolfgang, and Philippe Schmitter. "Community, Market, State and Associations? The Prospective Contribution of Interest Governance to Social Order." *European Sociological Review* 1 (1985): 119–138.

Strobl, Günter, and Han Xia. "The Issuer-Pays Rating Model and Ratings Inflation: Evidence from Corporate Credit Ratings." Mimeo, University of North Carolina, 2011. https://papers.ssrn.com/sol3/papers.cfm?abstract_id=2002186

Summers, Judith. *Soho: A History of London's Most Colourful Neighborhood.* London: Bloomsbury, 1989.

Swanson, Darren, Stephan Barg, Stephen Tyler, Henry Venema, Sanjay Tomar, Suruchi Bhadwal, Sreeja Nair, Dimple Roy, and John Drexhage. "Seven Tools for Creating Adaptive Policies." *Technological Forecasting and Social Change, Two Special Sections: Risk and Technology Addressing Deep Uncertainty Using Adaptive Policies*, 77, no. 6 (July 1, 2010): 924–939. https://doi.org/10.1016/j.techfore.2010.04.005.

Swire, Peter, and Justin D. Hemmings. "Mutual Legal Assistance in an Era of Globalized Communications: The Analogy to the Visa Waiver Program." January 11, 2016. *71 NYU Annual Survey of American Law* 687 (2017).

swissinfo.ch, S. W. I. "Hackers Target Swiss Defence Ministry." May 4, 2016. https://www.swissinfo.ch/eng/politics/industrial-espionage_hackers-target-swiss-defence-ministry/42131890.

Symantec. "W32.Duqu: The Precursor to the next Stuxnet." Symantec, November 23, 2011.

Symantec. "Simple NjRAT Fuels Nascent Middle East Cybercrime Scene." Symantec Security Response. March 30, 2014. https://perma.cc/3CVF-QKGP.

Symantec. "Corporate Fact Sheet." 2016a. https://www.symantec.com/content/dam/symantec/docs/other-resources/symantec-corporate-fact-sheet-060517-en.pdf.

Symantec. *Dridex: Tidal Waves of Spam Pushing Dangerous Financial Trojan. Whitepaper.* Mountain View: Symantec, 2016b. http://www.symantec.com/content/en/us/enterprise/media/security_response/whitepapers/dridex-financial-trojan.pdf.

Symantec."Internet Security Threat Report." April 2017a. https://www.symantec.com/content/dam/symantec/docs/reports/istr-22-2017-en.pdf.

Symantec."Ransom.Wannacry Technical Details." May 2017b. https://www.symantec.com/security_response/writeup.jsp?docid=2017-051310-3522-99&tabid=2.

Symantec. "What You Need to Know about the WannaCry Ransomware." October 23, 2017c. https://www.symantec.com/connect/blogs/ what-you-need-know-about-wannacry-ransomware.

Symantec. *2018 Annual Report*. 2019. https://s1.q4cdn.com/585930769/files/ doc_financials/2018annual-report/532571_015_BMK_WEB1.pd[4].pdf.

Tadeo, Maria, and Christopher Jasper. "British Airways Owner Says Power Outag Cost 80 Million Pounds." *Bloomberg Markets*, June 15, 2017. https://www. bloomberg.com/news/articles/2017-06-15/ british-airways-owner-says-power-outage-cost-80-million-pounds.

Tanczer, Leonie. "The 'Snooper's Charter' Is a Threat to Academic Freedom." *The Guardian*, December 1, 2016. https://www.theguardian.com/higher-education-network/2016/dec/01/the-snoopers-charter-is-a-threat-to-academic-freedom.

Tanczer, Leonie, Madeline Carr, Irina Brass, Ine Steenmans, and Jason Blackstock. "IoT and Its Implications for Informed Consent." PETRAS IoT Hub, STEaPP: London, 2017. https://papers.ssrn.com/sol3/papers. cfm?abstract_id=3117293.

Tanczer, Leonie, John Blythe, Fareeha Yahya, Irina Brass, Miles Elsden, Jason Blackstock, and Madeline Carr. *Summary Literature Review of Industry Recommendations and International Developments on IoT Security*, 1–18. London: Department for Digital, Culture, Media & Sport; PETRAS IoT Hub, 2018a. https://www.gov.uk/government/uploads/system/uploads/attachment_ data/file/686090/PETRAS_Literature_Review_of_Industry_Recommendations_ and_International_Developments_on_IoT_Security.pdf

Tanczer, Leonie, Ine Steenmans, Miles Elsden, Jason Blackstock, and Madeline Carr. "Emerging Risks in the IoT Ecosystem: Who's Afraid of the Big Bad Smart Fridge? In *Living in the Internet of Things: Cybersecurity of the IoT* – 2018, 2018b. https://ieeexplore.ieee.org/document/8379720.

Tanczer, Leonie, Ine Steenmans, Irina Brass, and Madeline Carr. *Networked World: Risks and Opportunities in the Internet of Things*. London: Lloyds's of London, 2018c. https://www.lloyds.com/news-and-risk-insight/risk-reports/ library/technology/networked-world.

Taylor, Alan. "The Exxon Valdez Oil Spill: 25 Years Ago Today." *The Atlantic*, March 24, 2014. https://www.theatlantic.com/photo/2014/03/ the-exxon-valdez-oil-spill-25-years-ago-today/100703/.

Techopedia. "*What Is Active Directory (AD)?*" 2017a. https://www.techopedia. com/definition/25/active-directory.

Techopedia. "WannaCry Ransomware Has Links to North Korea, Cybersecurity Experts Say." May 15, 2017b. https://www.theguardian.com/technology/2017/ may/15/wannacry-ransomware-north-korea-lazarus-group.

Tenbensel, Tim. "Multiple Modes of Governance." *Public Management Review* 7 (2005): 267–288.

"Testimony of John W. Carlson on behalf of the Financial Services Information Sharing & Analysis Center (FS-ISAC) before the U.S. House of Representatives Committee on Financial Services (June 24, 2015)." https://www.fsisac.com/sites/default/files/news/JCarlson%20June%2024%20Testimony%20FINAL.pdf.

The Committee of Public Accounts. *"Protecting Information across Government. Thirty-Eighth Report of Session 2016–17."* London: House of Commons, February 3, 2017. https://www.publications.parliament.uk/pa/cm201617/cmselect/cmpubacc/769/769.pdf.

The Copyright Office. "Rulemaking Proceedings Under Section 1201 of Title 17," n.d. https://www.copyright.gov/1201/

The Global Political Economy." PhD Dissertation. "Passing Judgement: Credit Rating Processes as Regulatory Mechanisms of Governance in the Emerging World Order." *Review of International Political Economy* 1, no. 1 (March 1, 1994): 133–159. doi:https://doi.org/10.1080/09692299408434271.

The Institute for Information Security and Privacy at Georgia Tech."Cross-Border Requests for Data Project." The Institute for Information Security and Privacy at Georgia Tech. n.d. http://www.iisp.gatech.edu/cross-border-data-project.

"The Joint Comments to US Copyright Office Notice of Inquiry" (Docket No. 2015-8). Report prepared by HackerOne, Bugcrowd, Rapid7, and Luta Security. October 27, 2016. https://www.rapid7.com/globalassets/_pdfs/rapid7-comments/rapid7-bugcrowd-hackerone-luta-security-joint-comments-to-copyright-office-request-for-additional-comments-docket-no.-2015-8-102716.pdf.

The New York County District Attorney's Office. "Ensuring Lawful Access to Smartphones." June 13, 2017. http://manhattanda.org/smartphone-encryption.

The Rendon Group. *"Conficker Working Group: Lessons Learned."* The Rendon Group, 2010a. http://www.confickerworkinggroup.org/wiki/uploads/Conficker_Working_Group_Lessons_Learned_17_June_2010_final.pdf.

The Rendon Group. "Conficker Working Group: Lessons Learned." *Contract*, January 2010b.

"The SpamHaus Project." 2017. https://www.spamhaus.org/.

Thompson, Fred. United States Senate Committee on Governmental Affairs. "Weak Computer Security in Government: Is the Public at Risk?" May 19, 1998.

Thompson, Ben. "UAE Blackberry Update Was Spyware." *BBC News*, July 21, 2009. https://perma.cc/97UP-3APN.

Thompson, Trevor A. "Terrorizing the Technological Neighborhood Watch: The Alienation and Deterrence of the White Hats under the CFAA." *Florida State University Law Review* 36, no. 3 (2009): 537–584.

Thoyts, Rob. *Insurance Theory and Practice*. New York: Routledge, 2010. https://books.google.com/books?hl=en&lr=&id=gpdaBwAAQBAJ&oi=fnd&pg=PP1&dq=Thoyts,+Rob.+2010.+Insurance+Theory+and+Practice.+Routledge.&ots=ufzrDsV3Pw&sig=xWWiQ5f6x8FnBWoM8QTNrNCQruY.

Tishuk, Brian S. "Effectively Managing Partnership Evolution: A Case Study from Chicago." *Journal of Business Continuity & Emergency Planning* 6, no. 2 (2013): 111–121.

Toumi, Habib. "GCC Ministers Sign Major Security Agreement." *GulfNews*, November 12, 2012. https://perma.cc/5S7N-CBN5.

TRA. "TRA Heads Bahrain's Delegation to US-GCC Cyber Security Strategic Cooperation Forum." September 14, 2015. https://perma.cc/2JCT-55BA.

Transport Security Administration. "Mission." https://www.tsa.gov/about/tsa-mission.

Travis, Alan. "UK Mass Digital Surveillance Regime Ruled Unlawful." *The Guardian*, January 30, 2018. http://www.theguardian.com/uk-news/2018/jan/30/uk-mass-digital-surveillance-regime-ruled-unlawful-appeal-ruling-snoopers-charter.

Trendmicro. "BrickerBot Malware Emerges, Permanently Bricks IoT Devices." April 19, 2017. https://www.trendmicro.com/vinfo/us/security/news/internet-of-things/brickerbot-malware-permanently-bricks-iot-devices.

Tripputi, Christian. "New Reconnaissance Threat Trojan.Laziok Targets the Energy Sector." Symantec Security Response, March 30, 2015. https://perma.cc/Z6NW-M6U9.

Tropina, Tatiana, and Cormac Callanan. *Self- and Co-Regulation in Cybercrime, Cybersecurity and National Security. SpringerBriefs in Cybersecurity.* Cham: Springer International Publishing, 2015. https://doi.org/10.1007/978-3-319-16447-2.

Tsyrklevich, Vlad. "Hacking Team: A Zero-Day Case Study." *Vlad Tsyrklevich's Blog*, August 1, 2015. https://tsyrklevich.net/2015/07/22/hacking-team-0day-market/.

Tuohy, Carolyn H. "Agency, Contract and Governance: Shifting Shapes of Accountability in the Health Care Arena." *Journal of Health Politics, Policy and Law* 28 (2003): 195–215.

Tuttle, Brad, and Scott D. Vandervelde. "An Empirical Examination of CobiT as an Internal Control Framework for Information Technology." *International Journal of Accounting Information Systems* 8, no. 4 (2007): 240–263.

Tweak, Gulshan. "Snort – What Is Snort (Network Intrusion Detection System)." *YouTube*, 2014. https://www.youtube.com/watch?v=S9J4SpbeJJE.

U.S. Cyber Command. "Cyber Guard 15 Fact Sheet." n.d. https://dod.defense.gov/Portals/1/features/2015/0415_cyber-strategy/Cyber_Guard_15_Fact_Sheet_010715_f.pdf.

U.S. Department of Justice. "Prosecuting Computer Crimes: Computer Crime and Intellectual Property Section Criminal Division." Office of Legal Education, Executive Office for United States Attorneys. 2010. https://www.justice.gov/sites/default/files/criminal-ccips/legacy/2015/01/14/ccmanual.pdf.

U.S. Department of Justice. "FY 2015 Budget Request: Mutual Legal Assistance Treaty Process Reform." July 2014. https://www.justice.gov/sites/default/files/jmd/legacy/2014/07/13/mut-legal-assist.pdf.

U.S. Department of Justice. "In The Matter Of A Warrant To Search A Certain E-mail Account Controlled And Maintained By Microsoft Corporation." June 28, 2017a. https://www.justice.gov/sites/default/files/briefs/2017/06/28/17-2_microsoft_corp_petiton.pdf.

U.S. Department of Justice, Cybersecurity Unit, Computer Crime & Intellectual Property Section, Criminal Division. "A Framework for a Vulnerability Disclosure Program for Online Systems." July 2017b. https://www.justice.gov/criminal-ccips/page/file/983996/download.

U.S. Senate Committee on Commerce, Science, & Transportation. Hearing on Data Security and Bug Bounty Programs: Lessons Learned from the Uber Breach and Security Researchers. February 6, 2018. https://www.commerce.senate.gov/public/index.cfm/2018/2/data-security-and-bug-bounty-programs-lessons-learned-from-the-uber-breach-and-security-researchers.

U.S. Trade Representative. Trans-Pacific Partnership Agreement, Chapter 14. February 4, 2016. https://ustr.gov/sites/default/files/TPP-Final-Text-Electronic-Commerce.pdf.

UK Government Chief Scientific Adviser. "*The Internet of Things (Blackett Review): Making the Most of the Second Digital Revolution.*" London: Government Office for Science, December 18, 2014. https://www.gov.uk/government/uploads/system/uploads/attachment_data/file/409774/14-1230-internet-of-things-review.pdf.

UN GGE. Report of the Group of Governmental Experts on Developments in the Field of Information and Telecommunications in the Context of International Security, A/70/174, July 22, 2015. http://www.un.org/ga/search/view_doc.asp?symbol=A/70/174.

UN-ESCWA. "Cyberlaws and Regulations for Enhancing E-Commerce." *ESCWA Cyber Legislation Digest*, March 2015.

United Airlines. "United Airlines Bug Bounty Program." n.d.-a https://www.united.com/web/en-US/content/Contact/bugbounty.aspx.

United Airlines. "United Airlines Bug Bounty Program." n.d.-b https://www.united.com/ual/en/us/fly/contact/bugbounty.html.

United Nations General Assembly. "Universal Declaration of Human Rights" (217 [III] A), 1948. Paris. http://www.un.org/en/universal-declaration-human-rights/.

United Nations Office for Disarmament Affairs. n.d. https://www.un.org/disarmament/topics/informationsecurity/.

United States Computer Emergency Readiness Team. "Traffic Light Protocol (TLP) Definitions and Usage." 2017. Accessed May 25, 2017. https://www.us-cert.gov/tlp.

United States Federal Bureau of Investigation (FBI). "Bugat Botnet Administrator Arrested. "GameOver Zeus Botnet Disrupted Collaborative Effort Among International Partners." June 2, 2014. Accessed November 9, 2017. https://www.fbi.gov/news/stories/gameover-zeus-botnet-disrupted.

United States Federal Bureau of Investigation (FBI). "Bugat Botnet Administrator Arrested and Malware Disabled." October 13, 2015. Accessed November 9,

2017. https://www.fbi.gov/contact-us/field-offices/pittsburgh/news/press-releases/bugat-botnet-administrator-arrested-and-malware-disabled.

United States Government Accountability Office. "FAA Needs a More Comprehensive Approach to Address Cybersecurity As Agency Transitions to NextGen." April 2015a. http://www.gao.gov/assets/670/669627.pdf.

United States Government Accountability Office. "FAA Needs to Address Weaknesses in Air Traffic Control Systems." January 2015b. http://www.gao.gov/assets/670/668169.pdf.

United States of America vs. Evgeniy Mikhailovich Bogachev [2014] Civil Action No. 14-0685 (United States District Court for the Western District of Pennsylvania). 2014

United States v. Microsoft Corporation, 584 U. S. (2018).

Urrico, Roy. "Data Breaches on Record Pace for 2015." Credit Union Times, July 5, 2015. http://www.cutimes.com/2015/07/05/data-breaches-on-record-pace-for-2015.

US Department of Justice, "In The Matter Of A Warrant To Search A Certain E- mail Account Controlled And Maintained By Microsoft Corporation," June 28, 2017. https://www.justice.gov/sites/default/files/briefs/2017/06/28/172_microsoft_corp_petiton.pdf

US Secret Service. "The Investigation Mission." 2017. Accessed May 25, 2017. https://www.secretservice.gov/investigation/.

Vela Nava, Eduardo. "Security Reward Programs: Year in Review, Year in Preview." *Google Online Security Blog*, January 30, 2015. https://googleonlinesecurity.blogspot.com/2015/01/security-reward-programs-year-in-review.html.

Vigliarolo, Brandon. "WannaCry: The Smart Person's Guide." *TechRepublic*, June 20, 2017. http://www.techrepublic.com/article/wannacry-the-smart-persons-guide/.

Villeneuve, Nart, Thoufique Haq, and Ned Moran. "Operation Molerats: Middle East Cyber Attacks Using Poison Ivy," *FireEye*, August 23, 2013, https://perma.cc/6UJT-WKZ2.

Vinton, Kate. "Obama Signs Executive Action, Calls for Collaboration to Fight Cyber Attacks at Stanford Summit." *Forbes*, February 13, 2015.

Volokh, Eugene. "Canadian Court Orders Google to Remove Search Results Globally." *The Washington Post*, June 29, 2017. https://www.washingtonpost.com/news/volokh-conspiracy/wp/2017/06/29/canadian-court-orders-google-to-remove-search-results-globally/.

Walker, Kent. "A Principle that Should not Be Forgotten." *Google Blog*, May 19, 2016. https://www.blog.google/topics/google-europe/a-principle-that-should-not-be-forgotten/.

Walker, W. E., and VAWJ Marchau. "Dealing with Uncertainty in Policy Analysis and Policymaking." *Integrated Assessment* 4, no. 1 (2003): 1–4.

Wall, Jeffrey. "Reply Brief for the United States. In the Matter of a Warrant to Search a Certain E-Mail Account Controlled and Maintained By Microsoft Corporation." September 2017. https://arstechnica.com/wp-content/uploads/2017/09/scotusmsftgoogyahoo.pdf.

Wang, Youfa, May A. Beydoun, Lan Liang, Benjamin Caballero, and Shiriki K. Kumanyika. "Will All Americans Become Overweight or Obese? Estimating the Progression and Cost of the US Obesity Epidemic." *Obesity* 16, no. 10 (2008): 2323–2330.

Waqas. "Hackers Leak Confidential Data from Saudi Ministry of Foreign Affairs! It's Crazy." *HackRead*, May 22, 2015. https://perma.cc/R923-JR9H.

Webber, Mark. "The Regulatory Outlook for the Internet of Things – Privacy, Security and Information Law." *Blog, Fieldfisher*, October 22, 2014. http://privacylawblog.fieldfisher.com/2014/part-2-the-regulatory-outlook-for-the-internet-of-things/.

Webel, Baird. "Terrorism Risk Insurance: Issue Analysis and Overview of Current Program." *Congressional Research Service*, July 23, 2014. https://www.fas.org/sgp/crs/terror/R42716.pdf.

Weber, Rolf H. "Internet of Things – New Security and Privacy Challenges." *Computer Law & Security Review* 26, no. 1 (January 2010): 23–30. https://doi.org/10.1016/j.clsr.2009.11.008.

Weekend Edition Sunday. "Stephen Hawking Gets A Voice Upgrade." *NPR*, December 7, 2014. http://www.npr.org/2014/12/07/369108538/stephen-hawking-gets-a-voice-tech-upgrade.

Weizhen, Tan. "Public, Private Sectors Take Part in Annual Cyber Security Exercise," *Today Online*, July 18, 2017. http://www.todayonline.com/singapore/national-cyber-security-exercise-involves-all-11-critical-sectors-first-time.

WePROTECT. "The WePROTECT Global Alliance." July 12, 2016. http://www.weprotect.org/strategylaunch.

WhatsApp. "WhatsApp Terms of Service." August 25, 2016. https://www.whatsapp.com/legal/#terms-of-service.

White, Lawrence J. "Credit-Rating Agencies and the Financial Crisis: Less Regulation of CRAs Is a Better Response." *Journal of International Banking Law* 25, no. 4 (2010): 170.

"Why everything is hackable: Computer security is broken from top to bottom." *The Economist*, April 8, 2017. http://www.economist.com/news/science-andtechnology/21720268-consequences-pile-up-things-are-starting-improvecomputer-security.

Wikileaks Forum. "WikiLeaks Cable: Skype Crackdown in Oman." May 17, 2013. https://perma.cc/XFS9-2WE7.

Wikipedia. "Conficker." 2017. https://en.wikipedia.org/wiki/Conficker.

Winter, Tom, and Andrew Blankstein. "Feds Remind U.S. Airports, Airlines They Are Terror Targets." *NBC News*, March 22, 2017. https://www.nbcnews.com/news/us-news/feds-remind-u-s-airports-airlines-they-are-terror-targets-n737416.

Wintour, Patrick. "UN Accuses Saudi Arabia of Using Terror Laws to Suppress Free Speech." *The Guardian*, May 4, 2017. https://perma.cc/X9LP-YTCM.

Wolff, Josephine. "Apple Has a New 'Bug Bounty' Program. It Could Be a Game-Changer." *Slate*, August 9, 2016. http://www.slate.com/blogs/future_tense/2016/08/09/why_apple_s_bug_bounty_program_is_unlike_any_other.html.

Woo, Gordon. "Quantifying Insurance Terrorism Risk." Manuscript, Risk Management Solutions, Newark, CA, 2002. http://www.rit.edu/cos/math/cmmc/conferences/2007/literature/Woo_2002b.pdf.

Woods, Andrew Keane. "Google Takes the Global Delisting Debate to a U.S. Court." *Lawfare*, July 27, 2017a. https://www.lawfareblog.com/google-takes-global-delisting-debate-us-court.

Woods, Andrew Keane. "No, the Canadian Supreme Court Did Not Ruin the Internet." *Lawfare*, July 6, 2017b. https://www.lawfareblog.com/no-canadian-supreme-court-did-not-ruin-internet.

Woods, Andrew Keane. "The Simplest Cross-Border Fix: Removing ECPA's Blocking Features." *Lawfare*, June 15, 2017c. https://www.lawfareblog.com/simplest-cross-border-fix-removing-ecpas-blocking-features.

Woods, Andrew Keane. "Written Testimony of Andrew Keane Woods before the House Judiciary Committee." June 15, 2017d. https://judiciary.house.gov/wp-content/uploads/2017/06/Woods-Testimony.pdf.

World Economic Forum. "Why Cybersecurity Is Now Top of the Agenda for the World's Decision-Makers." 2017. https://medium.com/world-economic-forum/why-cybersecurity-is-now-top-of-the-agenda-for-the-worlds-decision-makers-fb74e17b09b5.

World Health Organization. "*Research Ethics Review Committee*." World Health Organization. 2017. Accessed May 16, 2017. http://www.who.int/ethics/review-committee/en/.

Wright, Alex. "Cyber Market Dramatically Increases." *Risk & Insurance*, December 1, 2015. http://www.riskandinsurance.com/cyber-market-dramatically-increases/.

Yanai, Shaul. *Political Transformation of Gulf Tribal States: Elitism & the Social Contract in Kuwait, Bahrain & Dubai, 1918-1970s*. Brighton: Sussex Academic Press, 2014.

Zahlan, Rosemary Said. *The Making of the Modern Gulf States: Kuwait, Bahrain, Qatar, the United Arab Emirates and Oman*. Ithaca: Ithaca Press, 1998.

Zetter, Kim. *Countdown to Zero Day*. New York: Penguin Random House, 2014.

Zetter, Kim. "Hackers Could Commandeer New Planes Through Passenger Wi-Fi." *Wired*, April 15, 2015a. https://www.wired.com/2015/04/hackers-commandeer-new-planes-passenger-wi-fi/.

Zetter, Kim. "Is It Possible For Passengers to Hack Commercial Aircraft?" *Wired*, May 26, 2015b. https://www.wired.com/2015/05/possible-passengers-hack-commercial-aircraft/.

Zetter, Kim. "That insane, $81M Bangladesh Bank heist? Here is what we know." *Wired*, May 17, 2018. https://www.wired.com/2016/05/insane-81m-bangladesh-bank-heist-heres-know/.

Zhao, Mingyi. *Discovering and Mitigating Software Vulnerabilities Through Large-scale Collaboration*. Dissertation, The Pennsylvania State University, 2016. https://etda.libraries.psu.edu/files/final_submissions/13128.

Index

Rewired: Cybersecurity Governance, First Edition. Edited by Ryan Ellis and Vivek Mohan.
© 2019 John Wiley & Sons, Inc. Published 2019 by John Wiley & Sons, Inc.